# www.wadsworth.com

*www.wadsworth.com* is the World Wide Web site for Thomson Wadsworth and is your direct source to dozens of online resources.

At *www.wadsworth.com* you can find out about supplements, demonstration software, and student resources. You can also send email to many of our authors and preview new publications and exciting new technologies.

**www.wadsworth.com**
Changing the way the world learns[®]

# FROM THE WADSWORTH SERIES IN COMMUNICATION STUDIES

# COMMUNICATING IN PROFESSIONAL CONTEXTS

## Skills, Ethics, and Technologies
### Second Edition

**H. L. Goodall, Jr.**
Director of the Hugh Downs
School of Human Communication
Arizona State University

**Sandra Goodall**

**THOMSON** ™

**WADSWORTH**

Australia • Canada • Mexico • Singapore
Spain • United Kingdom • United States

## THOMSON
## WADSWORTH

Communicating in Professional Contexts: Skills, Ethics,
and Technologies, Second Edition

*H. L. Goodall, Jr., Sandra Goodall*

*Publisher:* Holly J. Allen
*Editor:* Annie Mitchell
*Assistant Editor:* Aarti Jayaraman
*Editorial Assistant:* Trina Enriquez
*Senior Technology Project Manager:* Jeanette Wiseman
*Senior Marketing Manager:* Kimberly Russell
*Marketing Assistant:* Andrew Keay
*Marketing Communications Manager:* Shemika Britt
*Project Manager, Editorial Production:* Mary Noel
*Art Director:* Maria Epes

*Print Buyer:* Lisa Claudeanos
*Permissions Editor:* Sarah Harkrader
*Production Service:* Jamie Armstrong, G&S Book Services
*Text Designer:* Brad Greene
*Photo Researcher:* Linda Sykes
*Copy Editor:* Angela Buckley
*Cover Designer:* Cuttriss & Hambleton
*Cover Images:* Chad Baker/Ryan McVay/Getty Images
*Compositor:* G&S Book Services
*Printer:* Webcom, Ltd.

Printed in Canada
1 2 3 4 5 6 7 09 08 07 06 05

For more information about our products, contact us at:
**Thomson Learning Academic Resource Center**
**1-800-423-0563**

For permission to use material from this text or product,
submit a request online at **http://www.thomsonrights.com.**
Any additional questions about permissions can be
submitted by email to **thomsonrights@thomson.com.**

Library of Congress Control Number: 2004114631

ISBN 0-534-63229-7

**Thomson Higher Education**
**10 Davis Drive**
**Belmont, CA 94002-3098**
**USA**

**Asia (including India)**
Thomson Learning
5 Shenton Way
#01-01 UIC Building
Singapore 068808

**Australia/New Zealand**
Thomson Learning Australia
102 Dodds Street
Southbank, Victoria 3006
Australia

**Canada**
Thomson Nelson
1120 Birchmount Road
Toronto, Ontario M1K 5G4
Canada

**UK/Europe/Middle East/Africa**
Thomson Learning
High Holborn House
50–51 Bedford Row
London WC1R 4LR
United Kingdom

**Latin America**
Thomson Learning
Seneca, 53
Colonia Polanco
11560 Mexico
D.F. Mexico

**Spain (including Portugal)**
Thomson Paraninfo
Calle Magallanes, 25
28015 Madrid, Spain

# Contents in Brief

# Contents

## Chapter 3

## Chapter 4

## Chapter 5

## THE POWER OF VERBAL AND NONVERBAL COMMUNICATION IN THE WORKPLACE 121

## Chapter 8

## Chapter 9

# Chapter 10

# Chapter 11

## Chapter 12

### MAKING THE PERSUASIVE CASE AT WORK  314

# Preface

We are very excited about the second edition of *Communicating in Professional Contexts*. We would like to thank the adoptors of the first edition for their support. Thanks also to the reviewers of both the first and second editions for their generous gift of time and their valuable insights on how to improve the book for future audiences.

The reviewers of the first edition indicated that they would like to have more diverse examples, covering a larger range of occupations and professions. In the second edition, we have made these changes to appeal to a wider audience of students. In Chapter 1, we added a section on speaker anxiety. We increased the discussion of ethics throughout the book, placing *Focus on Ethics* discussion boxes in each chapter. These discussions pose an ethical dilemma tied to the material in that chapter and provide questions to guide class discussion. We also addressed requests for more information on communication and gender research by citing the research throughout the book and in concentrated form in Chapter 4, "Listening in the Workplace," Chapter 5, "The Power of Verbal and Nonverbal Communication in the Workplace," Chapter 7, "Exploring Interpersonal Communication," and the chapters on interviewing. These are just a few of the improvements we've made to the second edition.

The ancillaries that accompany the book have also been updated and improved. We would also like to acknowledge the contributions of Patricia Fairfield-Artman. She did a great job of updating the ancillaries and seamlessly joining the text and the ancillaries for the second edition.

Today, as we begin our journey through the twenty-first century, we again need a new vision for business and professional communication. This vision must be capable of responding to the rapid changes in communication understanding and skills created by a global economy, advances in information technologies, and an increasingly diverse workforce. *Communicating in Professional Contexts* provides this new vision.

The world of business is a messy place. It is rare when communication situations in the workplace conform to scripts learned in a college classroom. In the world of work, valid notions of fairness, political correctness, and gender and racial sensitivity are often at odds with generational, regional, and cultural understanding. The way we *should* treat one another in the workplace may not be the way we *do* treat one another. The narratives in this book are derived from the authors' actual consulting experiences. They were included not as examples of exemplary workplace communication, but as examples of how people actually communicate in the workplace. They are offered as rhetorical openings for classroom conversations and exercises. Best Practices boxes are interspersed in the text to reiterate the best ways to handle oneself in various business settings.

In Chapter 1, "Breakthrough Skills for the Global Workplace," we introduce our definition and model of the communication process and describe the functions of communication in business and professional contexts: organizing tasks and people, creating identities, and sensemaking and interpretation. We also lay out the CCCD system and explain how it can be used to develop understanding and skills. We discuss ways to reduce speaker anxiety, and we conclude this chapter with a self-test of communication strategies applied to various business and professional communication contexts.

Chapter 2, "The Evolution of Communication in the Workplace," is dedicated to explaining how organizational and communication theories have coalesced over the years into a distinct set of practical skills and understanding. We incorporate the best ideas from the classical, transactional, systems, and cultures approaches, and include new work on organizational narratives, dialogue, and learning organizations.

Chapter 3, "Preparing for Conscious Communication in the Workplace," develops our CCCD system within an organizational application. This approach is useful for teachers who assign a presentational speech early in the term. Of particular interest will be the presentational worksheets used to guide the development of a presentation, as well as the step-by-step guide to researching, organizing, practicing, and delivering the speech.

In Chapter 4, "Listening in the Workplace," we discuss the types of listening as well as how to become a more conscious listener. We also include new materials on self-reflexive listening, how to listen for cultural and gender differences, and how listening strategies differ for meetings, for conflict situations, or when asking a colleague for help.

In Chapter 5, "The Power of Verbal and Nonverbal Communication in the Workplace," we discuss the importance of effective verbal communication in achieving workplace equity and understanding individual differences. We discuss various message strategies, including ambiguity, inclusive and exclusive messages, and supportive and nonsupportive messages. In the nonverbal segments, we provide a comprehensive treatment of topics that includes new materials on the layout of personal workspace, choosing clothing, personal appearance, and voice. A major feature of this chapter is our section on recognizing and dealing with sexual harassment.

Chapter 6, "Information Technology and Conscious Communication," discusses communication strategies for networking, video conferencing, using voice and e-mail, and doing web-based research. We also provide a section called "How Much Technology Do I Need?" as a guide to thinking about the relationships between information technology and human communication in the workplace.

Chapter 7, "Exploring Interpersonal Communication," begins with a unique format for delivering information on this vital subject; the chapter is organized around an example human resources seminar. In this example, new employees are guided through theories and practices associated with scripts, expectations and boundaries, ethical behavior, equity, self-disclosure and risk-taking, dialectics and dialogue, and relational conflict, as well as theories and practices associated with asking for feedback, creating communities at work, and negotiating cultural and gender differences.

Chapters 8 and 9 are dedicated to interviewing. In Chapter 8, "Interviewing and Conscious Communication," we explore the organization's perspective on interviews; in Chapter 9, "The Job Search and Conscious Communication," we develop the potential employee's perspective on interviewing. Both chapters offer sound information on conducting a job search, writing resumes and cover letters, and developing scripts to guide communication choices in interviews. We also include information on electronic formats and electronic submission of employment materials, as well as a section on how to make arrangements for an interview.

Chapter 10, "Communicating in Groups and Teams," begins by distinguishing between group and team communication. We then focus on the uses of communication to develop teamwork, leadership, and team-based presentations. Throughout the chapter, we highlight the ethical and mindful choices teams must make.

Chapter 11, "Informative Presentations in the Workplace," builds on material presented in Chapter 3, and reinforced in every other chapter, on the importance of using the CCCD system to guide communication. The chapter offers a way to think about informative presentations in relation to speaker credibility. We also include comprehensive materials on using PowerPoint or other presentation software to develop supporting materials for an informative presentation.

In Chapter 12, "Making the Persuasive Case at Work," we develop our conscious communication model to include four types of persuasion in business and professional contexts. We then use the CCCD system to develop appropriate strategies for each type. Unlike other texts, we show how persuasion is used in interpersonal, group, and presentational contexts, and how differences in each context should inform and guide our choice of communication goals and strategies.

Our goal throughout this project has been to incorporate state-of-the-art academic approaches with the most up-to-date skill set on the market. For this reason, readers will find that our text builds, in an evolutionary sense, on time-tested practices common to the best books our field has produced. There is, after all, still a strong demand for basic instruction in researching, organizing, and delivering informative and persuasive presentations in business contexts. Likewise, there is still a need to provide materials on employment interviewing, small group and team work, and effective interpersonal communication at work. Of course, no book in this field would be complete without comprehensive discussions of listening, verbal and nonverbal communication, and the components of a communication process.

What makes our approach to these timeless topics unique is:

+ a consistent theoretical orientation to guide each chapter, derived from current research on *mindful* and *ethical* communication practices.

+ a consistent model for building competencies in each chapter, based on the same communication process—in our case, the CCCD system: *Choose* (a communication goal and strategy), *Create* (the message), *Coordinate* (with other people), and *Deliver* (the message).

+ a consistent use of *information technologies* to underscore how exchanges of e-mail, cross-company networking, using the Internet to find information and conduct research, using PowerPoint to develop presentations, and using the telephone to conduct initial employment interviews intersect with everyday interpersonal, group, team, and presentational business contexts.

+ integrated materials and examples of *cultural diversity* and *gender differences* in most chapters.

+ a consistent application of communication skills in each chapter, in the exercise "Practicing Communication in Professional Contexts," which is designed to build competencies through examples and exercises.

+ a *narrative approach*, telling the story of communication in a business context in each chapter as understanding and skills are systematically developed.

+ a *focus on ethics* that combines a posed dilemma and discussion questions for each chapter.

+ an emphasis on practical exercises that come from actual business consulting experience.

Each chapter includes a comprehensive introduction, summary, and Communicating in Professional Contexts Online section. Communicating in Professional Contexts Online appears at the end of each chapter and includes a list of key terms (which are defined in the text and in the book's glossary) and practical student activities, many of which make use of InfoTrac® College Edition and the Internet. In addition, a "What You Should Have Learned" section provides a review of the chapter material, and the "Practicing Communication in Professional Contexts" section enables students to apply a skill pertinent to the chapter. Select chapters feature a prompt for students to use their Communicating In Professional Contexts CD-ROM to link to the book's website and to watch, listen to, and analyze model presentations and the interview featured in Chapter 9. You will also find Skill Builder Workshop boxes in key chapters that are tied to the Speech Builder Express tool available through the CD. Furthermore, we provide a unique way to help students develop communication competencies by linking sample CCCD charts and worksheets to the material in each chapter.

Overall, we believe we have created a very useful text for anyone interested in providing students with current information and skill development for business and professional contexts in the twenty-first century.

# Chapter One

## Breakthrough Skills for the Global Workplace

*It takes a smart company to build a tough hog. Behind all the chrome and leather, behind the brawny bikers and burly bikes, is a company that competes on . . . brains. Harley [-Davidson] is one smart operation—and its top managers see to it that learning is the engine that continues to drive the business.*

*In addition to providing workers with 80 hours of training each year . . . the Harley Leadership Institute focuses on three competencies the company believes all employees should have, including communication, conflict resolution, and team skills.*

*— Gina Imperato, Harley Shifts Gears*

A s you read the excerpt about Harley-Davidson, three things should stand out. First, Harley-Davidson is a company committed to the idea of continuous learning. Second, their commitment to learning focuses on employees' communication skills. Third, developing effective communication skills is essential to success in a business or profession.

We begin with this example because it illustrates that the standards have been raised for business and professional communication competence in the workplace. Many view communication as a breakthrough skill for the twenty-first century (Arygris, 1999).

What is a "breakthrough skill"? It is a communication skill, or skill set, that allows people to act purposefully and competently on what they know. For example, in the field of accounting, it used to be enough to simply be a technically proficient accountant, but not anymore. In a recent article, a senior manager of Allen, Gibbs & Houlik, L.C., said, "Professional accountants need more than technical knowledge. They need communication and organizational skills. They need to be well-rounded" (Dove, 1998, p. 16). More and more, traditional professions—law, accounting, architecture, design, engineering, education, and business—seek graduates with communication as well as technical skills.

Which is why we have teamed together to write this book. As organizational communication professionals, we recognize that our students will spend most of their lives communicating in business and professional contexts. We know that students who learn about business and professional communication significantly improve their ability to use communication to obtain their personal and career goals. These students use the communication skills they learn in business and professional communication classes to break through the human and technological barriers to business effectiveness and professional success. And so can you.

What are those barriers? Consider the following examples:

+ You notice a supervisor at work staring at you in a suggestive manner. Is there a way to resolve this form of harassment without totally alienating the supervisor?

+ You have to make a business presentation and want to use colorful graphics and animation to illustrate your main points. What is the best way to ensure that the presentation benefits from the inclusion of these forms of support?

+ You are assigned to lead a team work effort. The members of the team come from different departments and none of them knows you very well. What is the best way to organize a meeting?

+ A Brazilian business counterpart speaks Portuguese, Spanish, and a little English. You speak only English and freshman-level Spanish. How do you conduct business with someone who doesn't share your native language?

- ✦ You receive an e-mail message from a colleague in another department about an upcoming meeting. From the tone of his message, you sense something is wrong. The e-mail was posted last night. You think it is very important to check out your impressions with him prior to that meeting. How do you address your concerns to your colleague?

- ✦ You and a coworker constantly struggle over the best way to complete a project. How would you use communication to effectively manage your differences?

Business and professional communication skills go beyond the ability to engage in casual talk with friends and family or the chitchat we use to pass the time in social settings. Trying to resolve any of the above scenarios with the communication values you learned at home, or skills you routinely use with your friends, may backfire. It is important at the outset to understand that business settings require specific communication skills and knowledge.

**Business and professional communication** is a shorthand term that refers to all forms of speaking, listening, relating, writing, and responding in the workplace, both human and electronically mediated. **Human communication** includes informal conversations, interviews, group and team meetings, informative briefings and speeches, sales pitches, and persuasive presentations. **Electronically mediated communication** includes telephone conversations and vocal messages on answering machines, satellite conferences, e-mail, and Internet communication, such as images and sounds represented on personal and company web pages, and the use of the Internet for business communication and e-commerce. As you will learn, business and professional contexts require communication skills that are both appropriate to and effective in the workplace.

We designed this course and this textbook to provide you with the breakthrough skills, knowledge, and experiences required for successful business and professional communication. Our goal is to help you understand the new professional standards for communication competency and help you develop the skills and confidence to move ahead in whatever business or profession you choose.

## Components of Business and Professional Communication

Early models of business communication posited the idea that communication was simply the instructions (messages) given by a boss or manager (sender) to employees (receivers). (See Figure 1.1.) This model assumed that most business communication was top-down.

As our understanding of business communication improved, new models

**Figure 1.1**
Top-Down Model
of Business
Communication

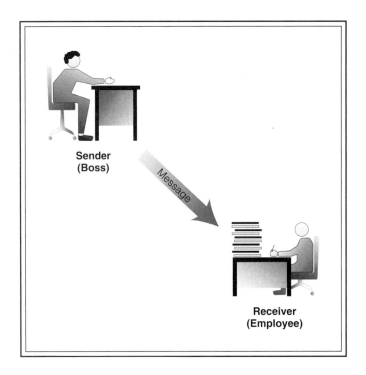

Sender
(Boss)

*Message*

Receiver
(Employee)

included the responses (feedback) employees give to bosses and to one another. (See Figure 1.2.) These newer models recognized the possibility for misunderstandings caused by disruptions (noise) in, or misinterpretations of, a message. They also introduced the idea that messages are conveyed in different ways (channels), via airwaves (sound) or lightwaves (sight). This idea of "channel" was expanded to include electronically mediated methods of message delivery, such as radio, television, computers, and satellites, as well as the full range of print media, such as office memos and letters, newspapers, magazines, advertising flyers and brochures, and books.

Later, communication theorists added the physical, historical, and cultural environments (**context**) that inform a communication situation or episode. Today, when we speak of the "components of a communication model," we include all of the terms: *sender, receiver, message, channel, noise, feedback,* and *context.* (See Figure 1.3.) Let's take a look at these components in more detail.

## Sender

The **sender** is the originator or source of a message. In the earliest organizational models, the sender was a boss. We now realize that messages originate from a variety of sources, at all levels, inside and outside an organiza-

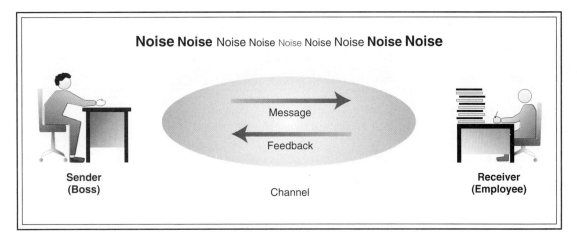

**Noise Noise** Noise Noise Noise Noise Noise **Noise Noise**

Message

Feedback

**Sender
(Boss)**

Channel

**Receiver
(Employee)**

**Figure 1.2**
Current Model
of Business
Communication

tion. For example, a customer entering a department store to make a complaint would be considered the originator of a message to the customer service representative.

## Receiver

The **receiver** is the person to whom a message is initially directed. In early organizational models, this person was an employee. Today we realize that anyone in an organization can receive messages. For example, the customer service representative is the receiver of the customer's complaint. However, the customer service representative may report the complaint to any number of people in the organization—the manager of the customer service department, the manager of the department where the product was sold to the customer, coworkers in other departments, even friends and family members. Whoever receives the account is a receiver of the communication.

## Messages

The **message** is what is said and done during an interaction. Messages are both verbal and nonverbal. Together, these message sources help us arrive at the meaning of a message. In our example, the customer's tone of voice, choice of words, general attitude, facial expression, gestures, and body posture all contribute to the customer service representative's interpretation of the message.

## Noise

**Noise** includes the physical, semantic, and hierarchical influences that either disrupt or shape the interpretation of messages. Physical noise may emanate from the environment: loud talking from the next room, opening and closing

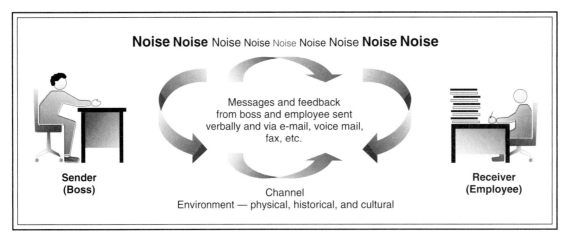

**Noise Noise** Noise Noise Noise Noise Noise **Noise Noise**

Messages and feedback
from boss and employee sent
verbally and via e-mail, voice mail,
fax, etc.

**Sender
(Boss)**

**Receiver
(Employee)**

Channel
Environment — physical, historical, and cultural

**Figure 1.3**
Updated Model
of Business
Communication

of doors, or sudden announcements over a loudspeaker that disrupt a conversation. **Semantic noise** refers to differences people have for the meanings of words: misheard or misunderstood terms, gender bias (such as saying "he" when referring to all managers or "she" when referring to all child-care givers), the perception of racial undertones (such as a fear or anxiety expressed as something "dark"), in-house or professional jargon, and culturally derived metaphors (such as the predominance of sports metaphors in North American business). **Hierarchical noise** refers to the shadings in meaning we attribute to a message based on a person's rank or status within an organization. For example, complaining to the customer service representative's supervisor rather than to the customer service representative may make the customer feel that the message has been taken more seriously.

## Feedback

**Feedback** is the activity of providing senders and receivers with responses to their communication, ideas, and identities. Initially, communication theorists viewed feedback in a very mechanical way. For example, a smile from our customer service representative could indicate acceptance of, and appreciation for, the customer's message. A frown could indicate confusion or disagreement. Quickly, however, communication researchers began to see the limitations of this either-or approach to discussing feedback. After all, a smile can be strategically deployed or faked. As researchers began studying feedback in business organizations, the complexity of the concept grew.

Feedback affects communication in an organization in a number of ways. Beyond responding to the specific words and actions of a sender, feedback can bring broader business and cultural implications to a conversation. It can help maintain the status quo through responses such as "Because that's how we have always tracked sales." It can move a situation forward through responses such as "Actually, I don't know why we track sales this way. Did you use a different method in your last company?" It may initiate change by fostering openness: "Wow, that sounds like a great system. Could you develop a plan to transition our sales tracking using your method?"

Every exchange must be considered within context. If a company is lagging behind, feedback upholding the status quo might be considered negative. However, if a company has just undertaken a major change effort, confirming the status quo may be exactly what that company needs to do to remain successful. What might appear to be negative feedback in one situation might be positive in another.

## Channels

A **channel** is the thoroughfare a message takes from sender to receiver. Channels have evolved from a simple choice between speaking and writing to complex choices from countless personal and technological possibilities. Choosing the appropriate channel for communication influences the timing, reception, and understanding of a message. For example, our unhappy customer could choose to write a letter, appear in person, send an e-mail, leave a voice message on an answering machine, make a posting to an Internet bulletin board, or call a media hotline. Each channel may reach a different audience and therefore elicit a different outcome. As a result, the choice of channel provides the customer—and the company—with varying levels of potential satisfaction and practical results.

## Context

All communication occurs within an environment. Every environment includes a particular physical situation, a cultural context, and at least two sources for communication history (the sender's and receiver's). Let's examine each of these influences in more detail.

### Physical Situation

In the workplace, the physical situation comprises the following:

+ physical space, including temperature, humidity, and noise
+ organization of the workspace, including placement of office furniture and displays of personal or professional items
+ time and timing

The physical space impacts communication partners and influences outcomes. Is the room large enough to accommodate everyone who was invited to a meeting? Are you discussing an intimate topic such as raises or reprimands in an open office space? Is the room too crowded with furniture? Is the temperature too warm or too cold for comfort? Are there distractions caused by excessive noise?

The size, location, organization, and comfort levels of the physical environment can make or break a deal, sidetrack negotiations, escalate conflict, or reduce the effectiveness of a presentation in a training program. If communication is impaired, or if distractions are present, people tend to focus on things other than what is being discussed or presented. For example, imagine that you are assigned to give a presentation to a group of potential clients. You spend weeks researching your group and honing your presentation. You book the "good" conference room two weeks in advance. The day of your presentation, you walk into the conference room to find the space is being carpeted and painted. The only conference room you can secure is the room with the tattered chairs, the broken LCD panel, and a constant temperature of about 80 degrees. Chances are good that the condition of the room will negatively impact your feelings of confidence about the presentation, as well as your audience's ability to perceive you, your company, and your product favorably.

The organization of your workspace can have an impact on perceptions of your identity, communication sensitivities, and professional competence. What does your workspace say about you? Is it a clean and neat area with well-organized shelves upon which are aligned carefully organized reference books and professional trade publications? Or is it a mess, complete with yesterday's half-eaten donut and long-cold cup of coffee? Does your desktop signal an organized approach to work, or is it the last resting place for a variety of personal objects, books, magazines, and piles of junk? Have you decorated your walls with tasteful photographs and signs of professional accomplishments, or with torn-out pages from sports magazines and personal fitness guides? Are there displays of items that could be offensive to others, such as questionable cartoons or calendars, or photographs that advertise sexuality?

The display of personal and professional items in a workspace creates impressions of your personal and professional identity. People enter your workspace and take account of it as a reflection of your interests, accomplishments, and sensitivity to a variety of cultural and gendered issues. Many businesses prohibit the display of personal items such as pictures of loved ones and pets because they believe it detracts from the business context of the workspace. In recent years, most businesses have forbidden displays of suggestive sexual materials because they potentially constitute an actionable offense under sexual-harassment laws. It is a good idea to become more conscious about the possible interpretation others may make of what you display in your workspace. Workspace displays are forms of nonverbal communication; they send clear messages about your understanding of your workplace culture. They reflect on your ability to interpret and participate in that culture.

Time and timing have dramatic effects on business and professional communication. As you undoubtedly know, some people are at their best in the morning, and others are night owls. Think about your own time preferences. Consider them when you plan a presentation or meeting or have to perform in an interview setting. Additionally, take into account the time and timing preferences of your audiences. Is it really a good idea to schedule that presentation right after the company lunch? Are meetings likely to accomplish more if they are scheduled on Monday, or on Friday afternoons? The influences of time and timing help create the atmosphere and environment for communication.

### Cultural Context

Business and professional communication also occurs within a cultural communication context: the thoughts and feelings we have in a situation, the history between the communicators, and the relationship in which the communication occurs (Wood, 1996, p. 113). For example, our friend John took an executive position with the ABC organization, a small U.S. company located in the South. John is from Canada, where religion is rarely discussed or displayed at work. The company he works for frequently makes announcements about upcoming sales events, employee illnesses or hardships, and community needs, which are followed by the statement "Any prayers you would like to offer would be appreciated." Prayer is not a requirement of the job at John's company, yet it sets a cultural context for communication within his organization.

John initially feared that, given the zeal of some religious organizations in the United States, he might have a difficult time adapting his communication to the workplace. As it turns out, he has been pleasantly surprised. Religion is certainly *a* contextual influence John encounters at work, but it is not the *only* context that influences his communication within the organization (see Figure 1.4).

As a result of his experience at ABC, John's cultural context for talk about religion in his workplace has changed. He no longer views religious talk as an intrusion. He has even said that a few times, when faced with particularly tough sales challenges, it was comforting to think about everyone back in the office pulling for him. He has begun to view the religious undertones as a part of the organizational culture that reflects a caring team spirit.

John's example shows us that cultural contexts for communication are not and should not be fixed. As we grow and learn, and as we gain insight and knowledge from new experiences, people, and situations, the contexts that influence our communication experiences evolve.

### Communication History

When we talk about **communication history,** we refer to the interpersonal history between two or more communication partners. How long have you known each other? Where are you in your relationship? What has your combined experience together taught you about how each of you is likely to respond to

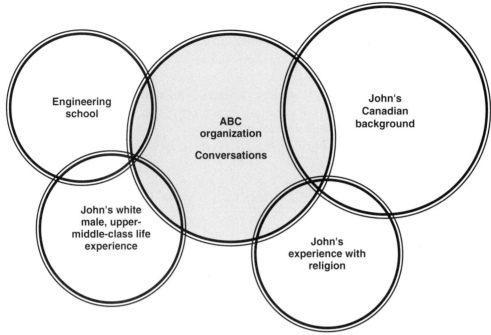

**Figure 1.4**
Overlapping Contextual
Influences That Inform
a Conversation

situations? Have you had arguments or disagreements in the past? Are there topics you knowingly avoid? Are there issues on which you are likely to agree? What intellectual, social, and personal baggage does each of you bring to communication encounters?

Communication history can determine if you are open to the opinions and observations of a communication partner, or if you become defensive or closed-minded even before hearing what the other person has to say. Your shared communication history either creates a space for potentially open communication or closes the door to it. Yet with each encounter, both positive and negative, your shared history changes. If, for example, a supervisor has a history of never asking for input at a weekly meeting and suddenly does, the group's shared history is altered from then on by that one significant event. Shared history shapes our communication, and our communication constantly reshapes that history.

## The Functions of Business and Professional Communication

*Amber hurried down the hall, her arms full of papers, reports, and folders. She was nervous about her first meeting with her new team, and she was determined to be ready. When she entered the conference room, she was relieved to find she was the first to arrive. Amber spent the next fifteen minutes arranging her information on the table in front of her. She checked her watch and waited for the others. Right before 2:00, the members of Amber's new team began to enter the room. Most carried only a blank pad. Amber was amazed at how much better prepared she was than the other members of the team.*

*Janet, the team leader, began the meeting. She asked the team members to recap for Amber their assignment and the progress each of them had made. Amber immediately cut her off. "No need, Janet. I've read all of the progress reports from the past six months." She pulled out the folder and waved it to the group.*

*Janet smiled. "I appreciate your efforts, but I think you'd benefit from hearing about the project firsthand from each team member."*

*Amber, not to be sidetracked, said, "Why don't I recap what I've read and you all can fill in any blanks? Although I'm sure you've all worked really hard on this project, I have a couple of ideas that might speed things along." Amber then launched into a twenty-minute recap of what she had read.*

*When she finished, Janet smiled and said, "Thank you, Amber, for recapping all of the ideas we have already thought about and discarded for one reason or another. Now, Chad, would you begin filling Amber in on what wasn't in the memos and reports she read?"*

*Amber's face grew hot and red. She sank as far into the back of her chair as she possibly could. Wow, had she read the memos wrong! She spent the rest of the meeting pretending to make notes and trying not to look at the rest of the team members. After the meeting, she gathered up the materials in front of her and fled back to her cube.*

Amber's unfortunate experience arose from a lack of understanding of the functions of business communication, which are to:

+ organize tasks and people
+ create identities
+ engage in sense-making and interpretations of meanings

Successful communicators realize that none of these functions occurs in a vacuum. They recognize that communication is a cumulative activity that builds understanding over time, rather than a snapshot that freezes understanding in place. Amber did not recognize these important functions of communication.

## Organizing Tasks and People

Everyone knows that a basic use for **communication** in the workplace is to convey the instructions needed to accomplish tasks. However, the need to bring people together to organize tasks and solve problems is critical for business communication success. Amber's careful preparation for the meeting showed

RNT Productions/Corbis

she did not understand this function of communication. She didn't understand that in a business context, communication is used primarily to organize tasks performed by people. Or, to put it another way, communication in the workplace is collaborative. We have to organize tasks with the help of other people.

This has not always been the case. As you will learn in Chapter 2, the organization of work in most global organizations has changed from an individual model to a team-based model. In part, this change is because of the communication influences brought about by advances in information technology, which increased the speed by which information could be organized and disseminated in and out of an organization. Technology also increased the amount of information that could be accessed. Together, these changes reduced the need to maintain many different levels of management and control of the information, as speedy and wide-ranging access to information empowered employees to make moment-to-moment decisions about their jobs. One major result of this influence of technology on the organization of work has been a new interest in group and team-based communication. Hence, individuals are seldom assigned to work alone. Companies today hire people to become team or group members, which means employees have to develop the skills associated with collaborative work and learning. In large part, this means altering the way we communicate.

Amber's example highlights what happens when we concentrate all of our communication efforts on creating meaning alone and ignore the experiences and needs of others. Amber's attempt at communication ignored everything that *wasn't* in the memos and reports she read. She ignored the team's experience. To be an effective team member at work, Amber needed to listen, ask questions, and *then* develop her ideas and present them.

## Creating Identities

Your **identity** in the workplace is constructed out of how people see and respond to you (Eisenberg and Goodall, 2001). In effect, identity is constructed out of your communication. Identity consists of three interrelated interpretations of communication:

**Organizational persona**—who we are perceived as within the organization. This may be a function of position, status, rank, years of service, or role in a company.

**Organizational credibility**—whether we do what we say we will do. This includes the values associated with being a trustworthy, honest, responsible, fair, and ethical person in the organization.

**Organizational savvy**—a person's ability to successfully negotiate political and social boundaries in an organization. In some cases this includes knowing whom to approach to get a job done. In other cases, it can mean the ability to gain new resources from unexpected sources.

Because she was a new team member, Amber's organizational persona was unknown. She had an opportunity to use her initial communication episodes to create the persona of a "team player," a "collaborative learner." Instead, her actions betrayed a team member who lacked organizational credibility and savvy. She was viewed after her first encounter with the team as a know-it-all, and it took months of hard work to prove that she could be a team player. Unfortunately, her initial communication choices seriously detracted from the identity she wanted to establish with her team.

## Sense-Making and Interpretation

In addition to creating identities and accomplishing tasks, communication helps us make sense of an organization's culture and interpret the messages of coworkers, customers, and clients (Eisenberg and Goodall, 2001; Weick, 1996). **Interpretation** is the meaning we assign to messages. The term **sense-making** underscores the idea that there is no one external reality that communication somehow "re-presents" (Hall, 1997). Instead, individual communicators construct versions of the realities they perceive and respond to based on their own past experiences, knowledge, feelings, needs, and expectations. We don't re-present reality in talk so much as we *represent* a version of it. Communication is the representational bridge that allows us to negotiate meanings, share interpretations, and collectively engage in productive, collaborative work.

When we say that employees make sense out of an organization's culture, we are saying that organizations are complex symbolic environments. As you will learn in Chapter 2, **organizational culture** consists of the histories, habits, values, and rules for conduct that make working in a particular organization feel unique. From a communication perspective, this means that it takes a lot of collaboration and communication work to produce a shared sense of culture. Getting to that shared sense of culture requires a lot of communication that builds shared understandings and meanings. Add to this cultural context the uncertainties that always exist in any business setting, and you begin to get an idea of why communication must be understood as an ongoing process of sense-making and interpretation that emerges from, and contributes to, an organization's culture.

Let's return to Amber's example. How could she have better made sense out of the culture she found herself working in? First, she should have been a much better communication-culture researcher. Too often we find that students interested in the study of business and professional communication pay attention only to the strategies and skills they can use when they are going to engage in a conversation, work on a team, or make a presentation. But there is another, very important side to studying communication in this class. You can also acquire skills as a communication-culture researcher, specifically those skills that can help you become a more adept sense-maker and interpreter of organizational cultures. How can you learn to do that? Researchers who study organizational cultures always begin by doing three things: (1) paying attention to the external environments (for example, the organization of space and people, the displays in cubes and in work areas, the style of dress worn by employees, and so forth; (2) listening to the internal talk of employees; and (3) asking questions about symbolic meanings when the meanings of expressions, sentiments, or actions are uncertain or their local interpretation is unclear. By developing and applying these communication-culture research skills, Amber would have had better information about her coworkers and the company.

Second, Amber made the mistake that too many workers new to a job make. She failed to recognize silence as an opportunity to listen. By listening, Amber could have checked her understanding of the assignment, the team members' interpretations of it, their history with the project, and the interactions of her team members. By allowing her team members to speak, she also might have gained empathy for her coworkers and their efforts, which could have helped her make better communication choices. Also, by having an appropriate communication goal—that is, being a productive team member—Amber could have made a better first impression on her team members.

What Amber needs is a lesson in making choices—conscious communication choices. From our perspective, what Amber needs is a lesson in becoming a more conscious communicator.

# Conscious Communication in the Workplace

One of the goals of this course is to make you a more conscious communicator. **Conscious communication** means being strategic in your formulation of messages and aware of the ethical and business consequences of delivering them. When we talk about **strategic communication,** we are referring to communication that is planned with specific audiences and intentions in mind.

*Consciousness* is the mental state that brings us together with others involved in a communication context. Being conscious means that we are at once "an observer, a perceiver, a knower, a thinker, and a potential actor" (Damasio, 1999, p. 10). To successfully engage in conscious communication, you need to choose, create, coordinate, and deliver your message. We will use the four-step choose, create, coordinate, and deliver **(CCCD)** process for conscious communication throughout the remainder of the book (see Figure 1.5). Let's look at each of these components in more detail.

## Step 1: Choosing a Communication Goal

**Choosing** an effective communication goal, the object you hope to achieve, requires developing an awareness of the possible messages and interpretations of messages in any business situation. When we choose a goal, we analyze the possible outcomes of a communication situation. Different messages and different audiences require different communication goals. Goals are a blending of the components and the functions of communication designed to increase the likelihood of successful communication.

An appropriate goal for interpersonal communication might not be appropriate for a formal presentation. A goal that applies to an e-mail might be inappropriate in a team meeting. Let's look back at Amber's goal. Amber's goal was to show that she had reviewed the team's progress and had the answer to their problems. Was she successful? Might she have been more successful if she had started with the goal of becoming a good team member, or the goal of understanding the team's progress, rather than jumping straight to the goal of problem solving? Amber's embarrassment was a direct result of not practicing conscious communication. She did not make a conscious effort to choose a

**Figure 1.5**

| The CCCD Process | | | |
|:---:|:---:|:---:|:---:|
| **Choose** | **Create** | **Coordinate** | **Deliver** |
| a communication strategy | your message | the communication event | the message |

goal that took into account the collaborative nature of teamwork or the team's communication history. Moreover, she skipped the creating and coordinating steps, both integral parts of conscious communication, and jumped to the end stage in the CCCD process: delivery. The result was negative for Amber and her team members.

Choosing a communication goal involves conducting a complete assessment of the following:

+ audience needs and expectations
+ likely communication outcomes
+ the criteria against which you will measure your success

Once you have chosen a goal, you can begin to create a message with your specific goal and audience in mind.

## Step 2: Creating the Message

**Creating** the message is the process of developing a presentation plan designed to reach a specific audience and carry out the strategy you developed in step 1. To a large extent, this part of the process is about organizing a message around a specific audience. You need to plan what you are going to say first, how to develop your ideas, and how to summarize and conclude your presentation. For example, in interpersonal situations you need to consider the purpose and scope of the conversation. In a meeting, you would organize your talk based on an agenda. In a formal presentation, you would use main points to support and guide the presentation.

To create a message, establish the agenda for a meeting, or plan a presentation you need to prepare in the following ways:

1. Develop a purpose for your talk (or a thesis statement for your presentation).
2. Determine the organization of your talking points (main points for a presentation).
3. Develop support for each of your talking points.
4. Craft effective introductory and concluding materials.

Once you have created your message, it is important to coordinate with other members of your team, department, or organization.

## Step 3: Coordinating with Others

Conscious communication requires input from a variety of sources. It also requires a different way of thinking about success in organizations. The old model for success in business was the Lone Ranger model (James, 1996). The Lone Ranger would ride in on a white horse to save a department or organization from disaster, and then ride back out of town into the radiant sunset. The new model for success in organizations is more the Three Musketeers model: "All for one, and one for all." For this collaborative process to work, you and the other members of your organization must trust that you will keep one another informed. You must work to create an inclusive organizational community. Follow these guidelines:

- ✦ Assemble as much information as you can about how your agenda, plan, or position fits within the mission and goals of the organization.
- ✦ Communicate with other members of the organization (teams, departments, supervisors, and managers) your need for input and feedback.
- ✦ Respect the professional and personal boundaries of others.
- ✦ Adapt your message, episode, or event accordingly.

**Coordinating** is the act of bringing together everyone required to successfully deliver the message. Coordinating with others is an ongoing organizational activity and may in some cases take place concurrently with step 2: choosing. For example, once you have determined your goals, outcomes, and criteria, you may need to check with other members of the team to ensure that any presentations representing the team reflect the team's goals. Or you may not have all the information you need to present an idea, so you may need to coordinate with other departments or team members to gather your information. As you coordinate information, you will be creating and revising your presentation.

Another important aspect of coordinating is checking to make sure that all the appropriate members of the organization are aware of the communication event. You should ensure that everyone knows where and when the event will be held. Coordinating also involves checking that all the necessary room and equipment reservations have been made. Now you are ready to deliver your message.

## Step 4: Delivering the Message

Your communication strategy is set. The research and analysis are complete. Your message is crafted. You have coordinated with other members of your team and outside departments. Now comes the time to deliver your message. The final step in CCCD, **delivery,** is really the most crucial, because in most organizations, the payoff depends on the communication performance.

Typically, students ask us three questions about the delivery of a message:

1. How much should I practice my message prior to delivering it?
2. How can I improve my performance?
3. How can I maximize feedback to my performance?

As we move through the book, we will answer these questions and develop your understanding of the CCCD process. The CCCD process is designed to maximize your communication effectiveness in any business or professional situation. In Chapter 3 we provide a detailed examination of the CCCD process. In Chapters 4 through 12, we apply the CCCD process to oral and written forms of communication in interpersonal, group or team, and public contexts.

---

### Focus on Ethics

Did Janet handle Amber's introduction to the team ethically? An important component of ethical communication is to assist others by providing the information needed to make informed choices. Were there things Janet could have done to ease Amber's first meeting with the team? How would you have handled Amber's first meeting differently?

---

## SKILL BUILDER WORKSHOP

We've all experienced moments of apprehension before giving a presentation. Even the most reticent speakers can learn to be more comfortable by following a few simple steps before giving a presentation or speaking up in team meetings. So, before you even begin preparing for your first presentation, we want to start you off with a checklist that will help you to reduce your anxiety and increase your confidence as a speaker.

**Know your topic:** When choosing a topic to speak about, pick one you know something about and that interests you. The better you know the topic, the more comfortable you will be presenting the information and answering questions after your talk. The more interested in the topic you are, the easier it will be to speak with enthusiasm. If you are asked to speak on an unfamiliar topic, find a way to relate it to your experience, or use the Internet or library to research the topic to increase your knowledge of the subject matter and your comfort level.

**Prepare your talk:** Use the CCCD method described briefly above and in detail throughout this book to prepare your talk. CCCD will help you cover all the bases, from research to delivery. Knowing that you have developed a talk that includes all the elements of a good presentation will give you confidence before you even step up to the podium.

**Practice:** One of the biggest mistakes people make when giving a presentation is to forget the vital element of practice. You can develop a perfect presentation with an amazing digital slideshow for support and have a superb introduction and closing, but if you haven't practiced, the presentation (and you) might not reach your goals. Practice, preferably in front of a few other

## Principles of Conscious Communication

One of the comments we often hear from beginning students in courses such as this one is "Why should I study communication? After all, I've been doing it all my life!" Our response has been that although almost everyone is fortunate enough to acquire an ability to communicate, not everyone learns how to communicate effectively. Still fewer people acquire the knowledge and skill to develop communication competencies specific to the workplace.

To learn about communication means more than simply doing it. It also means to study it, to acquire knowledge about it. To study business and professional communication means to read and to discuss the important ideas that have shaped our most advanced understandings about this vital skill. After careful study, application of these understandings should help improve your

people, allows you to see what points need to be honed, which lines work and which don't, and whether your great opening and closing resonate as well aloud as they did on paper or in your head. Practice also allows you to develop a naturalness with the material that takes away the stiffness of words on paper and enlivens your presentation with the fluidity of the spoken word. Every time you practice, you gain more control over your presentation and increase your confidence.

## SPEECH BUILDER EXPRESS WORKSHOP

In class, jot down a few notes about yourself for an introductory speech. Your speech should include three to five basic facts about yourself and at least two interesting facts. Give your speech to two of your classmates. Ask your classmates for feedback. What did you learn about your ability to give a speech? Did speaking off-the-cuff increase your nervousness?

Now go to Speech Builder Express. Select Introductory Speech from the menu. Write a brief speech of introduction using the outline provided. Your speech should include at least three basic facts about who you are and at least two interesting facts that will help others remember you. Your speech should be no more that two minutes long. You should include the feedback you were given from your impromptu speech in class. Practice your speech at least three times before your next class. Present your new speech to two different students. How did following an organization plan and practicing your speech change your speaking experience? Were you less nervous and apprehensive about speaking when you had a plan? Did practicing your speech help?

skills. As a result of having successfully completed a course specifically designed to improve both your understanding and skills, you should be a more conscious communicator.

To help you begin our investigation of business and professional communication, and to help you begin to think more intelligently and consciously about communication in the workplace, we offer the following list of conscious-communication principles:

- ✦ Conscious communication is mindful.
- ✦ Conscious communication displays awareness of communication as a process.
- ✦ Conscious communication respects diversity.

*Conscious communication is mindful.* Communicating mindfully means that you take into consideration the needs and expectations of others, as well as contexts (Damasio, 1999; Langer, 1989). Mindful communicators recognize that while it is important to use strategic communication to reach goals, it is equally important to reach business and professional goals ethically.

*Conscious communication displays awareness of communication as a process.* Although we use the terms *episode* or *event* to describe an act of communication in the workplace, it is more accurate to think of communication as an ongoing process. One communication event leads into another, expanding the context of communication throughout an organization.

*Conscious communication respects diversity.* Sensitivity to others includes a profound awareness of **diversity:** cultural, gender, racial, religious, and socio-economic differences. To be a mindful communicator means to research and respond intelligently to the differences you encounter in the workplace.

## Summary

Chapter 1 introduces the idea of conscious communication in the workplace. We began by exploring why communication is considered a "breakthrough skill" for the twenty-first century. We then discussed the components and the functions of communication in business and professional contexts. Next, we outlined and provided a conceptual overview of the CCCD process for improving communication at work. Finally, we provided a list of the principles of conscious communication in an effort to begin organizing your understanding of business and professional communication.

## COMMUNICATING IN PROFESSIONAL CONTEXTS ONLINE

All of the following chapter review materials are available in electronic format on either the Communicating in Professional Contexts website or CD-ROM. In addition to the multimedia case studies, activities, and numerous other learning resources you'll find on the CD-ROM, the CD is your gateway to the book's premium web content, which is not accessible via the Internet. The book's basic web content is available both with the premium content and on-line at http://communication.wadsworth.com/goodall2 and includes the chapter learning objectives and activities, key-term digital glossaries, and quizzes. The CD is also your gateway to InfoTrac® College Edition, our extensive online database of full-text articles that is fully keyword searchable and available twenty-four hours a day. Installation instructions for the CD appear on the inside of this book's back cover.

## What You Should Have Learned

The learning objectives below are available on the Communicating in Professional Contexts website, which is best accessed through the book's CD-ROM but is also available at http://communication.wadsworth.com/goodall2. Go to the Chapter 1 Resources and click on Learning Objectives.

Now that you have read Chapter 1, you should be able to do the following:

+ Discuss the relevance of studying business and professional communication.
+ Provide a basic definition of *communication* in a business and professional context.
+ Describe the term *breakthrough skills* and its relationship to communication.
+ List and describe the components of the communication process.
+ Describe the three major functions of business and professional communication.
+ Outline the CCCD process and discuss how it might apply to a formal business presentation, a job interview, and the construction of a written memo.
+ Discuss what is meant by *conscious communication* and describe its three principles.

## Key Terms

The terms below are available in a digital glossary on the Communicating in Professional Contexts website, which is best accessed through this book's

CD-ROM but is also available at http://communication.wadsworth.com/goodall2. Go to the Chapter 1 Resources and click on Glossary.

| | | |
|---|---|---|
| **business and professional communication** *(3)* | **delivery** *(17)* | **organizational credibility** *(13)* |
| | **diversity** *(20)* | **organizational culture** *(14)* |
| **CCCD** *(15)* | **electronically mediated communication** *(3)* | **organizational persona** *(13)* |
| **channel** *(7)* | | **organizational savvy** *(13)* |
| **choosing** *(15)* | **feedback** *(6)* | **receiver** *(5)* |
| **communication** *(11)* | **hierarchical noise** *(6)* | **semantic noise** *(6)* |
| **communication history** *(9)* | **human communication** *(3)* | **sender** *(4)* |
| **conscious communication** *(15)* | **identity** *(13)* | **sense-making** *(13)* |
| **context** *(4)* | **interpretation** *(13)* | **strategic communication** *(15)* |
| **coordinating** *(17)* | **message** *(5)* | |
| **creating** *(16)* | **noise** *(5)* | |

## Writing and Critical Thinking

The following activities can be completed online and, if requested, submitted to your instructor. You'll find them on the Communicating in Professional Contexts website, which is best accessed through this book's CD-ROM but is also available at http://communication.wadsworth.com/goodall2. Go to the Chapter 1 Resources and click on Writing and Critical Thinking Activities.

Choose one of the following activities:

1. Interview a manager, CEO, or business owner. Ask the person to detail his or her communication needs. Have the person rate the importance of interpersonal, organizational, team, speaking, written communication, and presentational skills for his or her employees. Describe the course you are taking. How important to the person's business are the skills you are developing?

2. Obtain a memo or report from an organization. This could be an e-mail or memo from your workplace or something available on the Internet. If you use an e-mail from an organization, be sure you have permission. Analyze the memo or e-mail using the information in this chapter. What clues did you find about the organization or writer's history and the context? What cultural clues did you find? What did your analysis reveal?

3. Working with your classmates as a group, determine the communication strategy for the following scenario:

   *Mary has worked hard for XYZ Corporation for five years. The last two years she has received outstanding performance appraisals by both her manager, Kim, and*

*Kim's director, Bob. Each year, Mary was promised a raise the next year, but because of budget cuts the raise was put off until her next review. Mary likes her job and regularly goes above and beyond her job description. This year Mary was elated to be promoted not one, but two steps. A few days after her promotion, Kim called her into her office and told her once again, because of a budget freeze, she could not give Mary the raise to go along with her recent promotion. She told Mary she had pleaded with her director, who in turn had "gone to bat" for Mary with the company president, who responded with a firm "No." Mary likes her job, but she wants that raise. Given what you have learned in this chapter, what should Mary do to make her case?*

4. The expansion of global markets since the beginning of the twenty-first century has increasingly affected relationships in the business and professional world. As sales manager of XYZ Corporation, you have been transferred to another region of the world to open new sales opportunities. In preparing for your move, choose a country (other than the U.S.) and, using InfoTrac College Edition or the World Wide Web, research and prepare a presentation for your class identifying key aspects of the culture in your chosen country and how it could impact your interactions and sales strategy. Use the "Current Model of Business Communication" explained in Chapter 1 as a guide in your research. Visit http://www.executiveplanet.com, http://www.globaledge.msu.edu, and http://www.worldbiz.com to conduct your research.

## Research and Explorations Online

The exercises below can be completed online and, if requested, submitted to your instructor. You'll find them on the Communicating in Professional Contexts website, which is best accessed through this book's CD-ROM but is also available at http://communication.wadsworth.com/goodall2. Go to the Chapter 1 Resources and click on Internet Exercises.

1. It's not your father or mother's workplace anymore. Use InfoTrac College Edition or the World Wide Web (WWW) to create a list of five changes in the workplace over the last ten to fifteen years. Consider using search terms such as *global organizations, career development, multicultural management,* or *information technology*. Compare your list to those of your classmates. Organize the list to determine the top five to ten changes you can expect to deal with in the global workplace. How many of these changes are based on communication?

2. The introduction of teams, intercultural work groups, and telecommuting makes determining the context for communication more complex. Use InfoTrac College Edition or the WWW to develop a database of information for communicating in either a team or an intercultural work group

or when telecommuting. Consider using search terms such as *intercultural communication*, *business communication*, *international business*, or *organizational change*.

3. Using InfoTrac College Edition or the web, read the article "Conscious Democracy" by Duane Elgin. He identifies characteristics of a semiconscious democracy and a conscious democracy. Discuss the pros and cons of applying these concepts to a conscious organization of the twenty-first century.

## Practicing Communication in Professional Contexts

Do you have the communication skills you need to survive in a global economy? Do you regularly use e-mail? Have you written memos or reports? Do you have specific research skills? How are your interpersonal skills? Are you prepared to communicate professionally? What are your strengths and weaknesses?

Office Team is one of the world's leaders in specialized administrative staffing, with more than two hundred offices internationally. They developed the following questionnaire to assess a candidate's ability to compete and communicate in the workplace in the year 2005 (*Canadian Manager*, 1999). The following questions will help you determine if you have the necessary people skills to be successful in the office of 2005 and beyond. For some of the questions, you may agree with more than one response. However, try to select the answer you most agree with. Circle your answers below, or you can complete the questionnaire online at http://communication.wadsworth.com/goodall2. Your total score is based on the number of questions you answer correctly.

## The Questions

1. Your colleagues have been passed over for a promotion, and you've been informed that you got it. But the announcement date becomes delayed due to your supervisor's other priorities. In the meantime, there is growing speculation among the staff, and one of your coworkers asks if you've heard anything about it. What approach do you take?

    a. Tell the colleague that you got it, but ask that he or she be discreet about it.

    b. Wait it out until your supervisor is ready.

    c. Tell a few select coworkers that you got it, but ask that they be discreet about it.

    d. Tell all coworkers involved.

    e. Tell your supervisor there is a growing discussion and you've been asked about it.

2. Your primary method of organizing work is to

    a. Continuously reestablish priorities as needed based on the requirements of the day.

   b. Complete yesterday's priority list before reviewing new assignments for the day.

   c. Try as best you can to complete one project before accepting another one.

   d. Prioritize each day's work and stick to it regardless of additional projects that may distract you.

3. Which one of the following statements best describes your beliefs or approach?

   a. I generally like to avoid conflict whenever possible.

   b. Allowing emotions to enter into business decisions is unavoidable.

   c. I'm good at logically thinking through a problem.

   d. Making a relatively quick decision is always better than waiting to make a decision.

4. Your supervisor has given you an assignment, but you're unfamiliar with certain aspects of the project in which others in the department have more experience. You

   a. Spend whatever time necessary on your own, getting at least a cursory knowledge of the unknown areas.

   b. Seek the assistance of the other experts and, in turn, offer your expertise to them.

   c. Tell your supervisor up front that you are not familiar with those aspects.

   d. Suggest to your supervisor that you handle only the familiar part.

5. Which one of the following statements best reflects your beliefs or approach?

   a. Success seems to come more easily to some people than others.

   b. If my closest friends and family agree on what's best for my career, I usually rely on their advice.

   c. My employer is in the best position to decide which career path is best for me.

   d. Career success is a direct result of my own efforts, not those of others.

6. The best way to manage people is to

   a. Make it very clear that you're in charge.

   b. Solicit input from them before making major decisions.

   c. Share your expertise by offering your direct supervision to as many people as possible.

   d. Set your goals before you begin the project and communicate them loudly and clearly to the team before getting started.

7. Which one of the following statements best reflects your beliefs or approach?

   a. When managing a project, I like all the team members to remain on task with the original approach.

   b. People with greater seniority in a company are in the best position to generate useful ideas.

   c. When managing a project, I encourage people to share differing opinions.

   d. If the majority of people believe in a certain approach, it's probably the best one.

8. Which of the following best describes the ingredients of effective persuasion?
   a. Remaining steadfast in your beliefs and not wavering.
   b. Being forceful and vocal in your opinion.
   c. Being pleasant as much as possible.
   d. Having strong listening skills.

9. One of your closest friends is in a business that you rely on as one of several vendors. You inadvertently give a little more information to your friend than you give to the other vendors. You realize that you have now given her an unfair advantage. You
   a. Explain to your friend that you shouldn't have released this information and ask her not to make it a factor in her bid.
   b. Take into consideration when evaluating the bids that your friend had more information.
   c. Give other vendors the same information and run the risk of appearing disorganized.
   d. Give information you did not give to your friend to other vendors so they also benefit.

10. Your supervisor praises you publicly on the results of a successful project. You received invaluable help on this particular assignment from a coworker who wasn't named. You
    a. Approach the coworker later and apologize.
    b. Tell your boss that credit should also go to the coworker.
    c. Weigh how important it is to bring up the coworker's involvement.
    d. Write your coworker a thank-you note.

11. Which statement most accurately reflects your beliefs?
    a. Writing will become less important due to technological advancements.
    b. Writing is a skill that is innate, not learned.
    c. An experienced writer uses large words and long sentences.
    d. An experienced writer tries to use fewer words.

12. Describe your verbal communication abilities.
    a. I'd rather walk on hot coals than speak to a large group, but I do fine one-on-one.
    b. I'm a much better oral communicator than writer.
    c. When I speak to a group, people seem to grasp my point quickly.
    d. I'm relatively talkative and not shy.

13. Which of the following best describes your approach to brainstorm meetings?
    a. I'm a risk taker and generally don't like to "follow the pack" in my thinking.
    b. I'm good at building on the ideas of others.
    c. I've always implemented ideas well and had good follow-up.
    d. I'd rather offer a feasible, well-thought-out idea than just any suggestion.

14. Which of the following statements best reflects your beliefs or approach?

    a. I believe that my employer should provide me with the training I need.

    b. I often use the Internet to research information during nonbusiness hours.

    c. I believe that a person's college/university education will provide a comprehensive source of knowledge for the balance of his or her career.

    d. If I rely heavily on my supervisor's expertise, I'll get the best training.

15. Which one of the following best describes you or your beliefs?

    a. When the going gets tough, I often make an effort to reduce tension through laughter.

    b. Good-natured teasing of others creates a less tense environment and encourages camaraderie.

    c. People who succeed in most companies tend to take their work very seriously.

    d. I've always been a good joke teller.

## Answer Key

Each question was designed to test a particular *people* skill. The skill tested by each question is listed below.

1. Diplomacy/Discretion
2. Organization
3. Problem-solving abilities
4. Team-player skills
5. Accountability/Initiative
6. Leadership
7. Open-mindedness/Flexibility
8. Persuasion
9. Ethics
10. Honesty
11. Written communication
12. Verbal communication
13. Creativity
14. Educational interests
15. Humor

### 1. Diplomacy/Discretion

a. Sorry; your supervisor wasn't ready and should make the decision on timing.

b. Problematic; your supervisor should be made aware of the staff's queries, as discussions and speculation will only grow.

c. Unfortunately, this could hurt the morale of others.

    d. Very risky; it's your manager's responsibility, not yours.

    e. Right! This is something your boss should be made aware of and be able to act on to everyone's benefit. In the 2005 office, you'll take a broader look at the company's overall welfare because you'll benefit more directly from it. Companies will offer such programs as performance-based pay and stock ownership to help retain highly skilled workers.

### 2. Organization

    a. Bingo! If new projects come in, you must evaluate their importance relative to existing priorities. In 2005 there will be more instant communication and more projects to prioritize, so this skill is crucial.

    b. Often tempting, but yesterday's work may have to wait if new projects are more urgent.

    c. Sorry; multitasking will be key in coming years—focusing on one assignment will be a luxury rather than the norm.

    d. Oops! Such rigidity will keep you from attending to potentially more urgent projects.

### 3. Problem-Solving

    a. Who could blame you? But as interaction and communication levels increase, so will the potential for conflicts. Get ready to practice better conflict-resolution skills.

    b. Sorry; in 2005 you'll have to put emotions aside. Your professional analytical abilities will be put to the test.

    c. Way to go! You have the ingredients of someone who can think clearly and analytically, which is beneficial as the pace of business increases.

    d. Not necessarily; although speed and efficiency will be important attributes in 2005, you may need more time and information to evaluate the best course of action.

### 4. Team-Player Skills

    a. Not a bad choice—this demonstrates initiative. However, you could have worked in conjunction with the others in a team-oriented manner, saving time for the overall task.

    b. Correct! As we head toward 2005, the ability to approach and help team members will be valuable, because productivity depends on continual information exchange.

    c. Sorry; to find out what you'll need to know in the office of 2005, you'll be expected to show resourcefulness and initiative.

    d. Careful; you need to show your supervisors as well as your peers that you're a team player.

### 5. Accountability/Initiative

    a. Sorry; those who believe their success rides on factors beyond their control may need to change their thinking. In 2005, those who take charge of their careers will have the greatest number of opportunities.

b. A tough one; you want to solicit input from those who care about you, yet your major career decisions should be based primarily on your own interests and goals. In 2005, being the CEO of your own career will be more important than ever.

c. Employers can help guide you, but the ultimate expert on your career growth and satisfaction is you.

d. Hurrah! Taking charge of your career, whether you're a full-time, part-time, or project worker, will bring the greatest challenge and financial rewards.

## 6. Leadership

a. Proceed with caution! The future office environment won't allow for a command-and-control management style; employees want to contribute to making decisions and offer creative solutions.

b. Right! Skilled employees will have many career options in 2005; they'll choose opportunities in which their ideas are heard. In an increasingly competitive business world, smart managers will encourage greater participation from team members.

c. Sorry; while this may seem benevolent, this choice could indicate micromanaging technologies.

d. Almost! Although sharing your vision is an admirable management trait, allowing participation in setting goals is characteristic of a good leader.

## 7. Open-mindedness/Flexibility

a. An understandable choice, but you may need to become less rigid and allow room for modification and improvements. In 2005, rapidly changing events will make flexibility a key attribute.

b. Not necessarily; whereas more senior employees have experience on their side, ideas from more recent recruits or even consultants may provide valuable, fresh perspectives.

c. Good! This approach will give you the best thinking from your team.

d. Nice try; unfortunately, peer pressure can make some employees follow the path of least resistance, not always the most productive path.

## 8. Persuasion

a. Careful; if you become too rigid in your arguments, the other individual may become defensive. You must show interest in the beliefs of others to create open lines of communication.

b. Sorry. Intimidation or being more vocal will not convince people to see things your way; it could backfire.

c. Being pleasant and courteous will certainly help your efforts, but listening carefully is an even more valuable skill in this instance.

d. Right! The most persuasive people are those who have taken on the challenge of actively listening to other individuals to best understand their perspective and motives. With increased business demands in 2005, you'll have less time to make your own case. Practice strong listening skills with coworkers and watch the results.

### 9. Ethics

    a. Caution; this may be naive, and you're not being fair to other vendors.

    b. Sorry; you're still not giving other vendors the full opportunity to compete fairly.

    c. Right! This could be embarrassing, but you'll know you've avoided giving preferential treatment to your friend. Ethics in business will remain critical in 2005.

    d. Problematic; if you give out different information, this still won't level the playing field.

### 10. Honesty

    a. A good try, but you're still accepting full credit.

    b. Excellent! Your honesty and sense of team play will be appreciated more than ever in 2005 as employees work more closely in teams and are given more autonomy to make critical judgment calls.

    c. Almost; you're moving in the right direction, but if you have doubts about whether something is ethical, chances are it is not, and you should take immediate steps to remedy the situation.

    d. A nice gesture, but you're still falling short of appropriately sharing the credit.

### 11. Written Communication

    a. Oops! There will be more e-mails than ever in 2005. Clear communication and good grammar will help you become more productive.

    b. Not really; with practice and initiative, you'll improve.

    c. Sorry; this may seem impressive, but good writers communicate clearly, not necessarily with big words.

    d. Terrific! Keeping your writing concise will make it easier to understand and will have a greater impact. As e-mail becomes more pervasive in 2005, brevity will be valued; verbosity, counterproductive.

### 12. Verbal Communication

    a. Ouch! Time to practice speaking to groups of people. You might consider joining a Toastmasters group or looking for opportunities to give speeches at your company, volunteer group, class, or other venues.

    b. A good try, but the better answer would be that you can articulate your point clearly and effectively.

    c. Good! You're able to present a clear message orally, an invaluable trait in 2005 when you must think on your feet, whether in a small or large group or during a videoconference.

    d. Close; you may have the necessary confidence to be a good verbal communicator, but making your point clearly and concisely is the next step.

### 13. Creativity

    a. You got it! In 2005, risk takers with creative ideas will be highly valued as companies compete more fiercely to come to market with innovative products and services. Are you ready to make your contribution?

    b. A step in the right direction, but innovative thinking will have to start with you.

    c. Sounds good, but original thinking will take you far in 2005.

    d. Sounds practical, but in 2005, you'll be highly valued for taking creative risks. Your thoughts may not be well defined, but they could inspire or develop into outstanding ideas.

### 14. Educational Interests

    a. Careful; companies in 2005 will invest more in training, but workers must take the initiative to constantly upgrade skills.

    b. Yes! You demonstrated the thirst for knowledge that will make you marketable in 2005.

    c. Close; a college education is certainly beneficial. But the most successful workers in 2005 will continually upgrade technical and "soft" skills.

    d. Sorry; in 2005 you'll advance more quickly if you take it upon yourself to enhance your skills and knowledge, inside and outside of the office.

### 15. Humor

    a. Good! You have an invaluable interpersonal skill that will help smooth tensions that may arise in an instant-information environment.

    b. Sorry; humor at the expense of others is counterproductive.

    c. Sounds like a valid concept, but one of the most important ingredients in career success is the ability to laugh at oneself, putting others at ease.

    d. Great for parties, but joke telling is not quite the same as light-heartedness that reduces stress in others and offers perspective on the big picture.

## Scoring

Refer to the answer key above and add up your correct responses.

### 13–15 correct answers

Congratulations! Your outstanding people skills will be an important contributor to your career success in 2005.

### 10–12 correct answers

Great. You have solid "soft" skills that will facilitate your advancement in the office of the future.

### 6–9 correct answers

Pretty good, but your interpersonal and communication skills may need some work.

### 3–5 correct answers

Start concentrating on areas you are missing. You still have time!

### 0–3 correct answers

Now is the time to develop your people skills. Your career success will depend on it! Pay close attention to the information in this course that addresses these areas.

## Your Communication Profile

Begin building your communication profile by collecting examples of good communication. These could be memos, reports, or e-mails you are particularly proud of. You could create a journal detailing conversations you have had that went particularly well. Think about communication events that went exactly as you hoped they would. Read interviews by people you respect or wish to emulate. What communication strategies do they use in their talk? How could you adapt those strategies?

# Chapter Two

## The Evolution of Communication in the Workplace

*Reality isn't what it used to be.*

—Steiner Kvale, *The Truth about Truth*

*It is no accident that most organizations learn poorly. . . . The way we have been taught to think and interact . . . create[s] fundamental learning disabilities.*

—Peter Senge, *The Fifth Discipline*

W|e begin with the above quotations because they speak to the two most important ideas in this book. The first quotation captures the challenge of explaining communication in the workplace when the realities of the workplace, and our ideas about effective communication, are experiencing great change. The second quotation identifies the main causes of recent business and professional frustrations with managing and working in times of great change: how we've been (mis)taught to think and interact. This may seem like a negative way to introduce an otherwise positive chapter, but as you will see, the best way to deal with communication in organizations during times of great change is to teach people to be more conscious communicators and reframe the workplace as a learning organization.

In this chapter we explore how we have gotten to a time and place where "conscious communication" and "learning organization" sum up the best practices associated with success and productivity in the workplace. To prepare you to better understand these terms and practices, we want to revisit a parallel evolution of two lines of thought that dominated the twentieth century: theories of organization and management, and theories of organizational communication. As a result of revisiting these theories, by the end of this chapter you will understand why and how this evolution has occurred. You will also see why "conscious communication" and the "learning organization" sum up a best-practices approach to business and professional communication.

To accomplish this task, this chapter is divided into sections that link theories of organization and management to theories of communication, following a more or less concurrent historical timeline that begins in the Industrial Revolution and ends in the present day. Using the timeline shown in Figure 2.1, we walk you through the evolution of theories of management and how these theories influenced theories of business and professional communication.

If you are making an outline for this chapter, the following divisions should shape and inform your reading:

+ Classical Management and Information Transfer

+ Human Relations/Resources and Transactional Process

+ Systems Thinking and Communication Networks

+ Organizational Cultures, Communication, and Power

+ Organizational Narratives and Dialogue

## Classical Management and Information Transfer

The classical period of management began at the height of the Industrial Revolution in the late 1800s and continued through the 1930s. The movement of people from the farm to the city and from the plow field to the factory high-

| Organizational and Communication Theory Timeline | | | | | |
|---|---|---|---|---|---|
| Classical Period— | Human Relations— | Human Resources— | Systems Theory | Cultural Theory | Learning Organizations— |
| Scientific Management and Bureaucracy | Hawthorne Studies and Maslow's Hierarchy of Needs | Maslow's Hierarchy of Needs | | | Five Disciplines |
| **1900** | **1920** | **1940** | **1960** | **1980** | **2000** |
| Communication as Information Transfer | | Communication as Transactional Process | Networks | Power | Dialogue |
| | | | | Organizational Narratives | |

**Figure 2.1**

Evolution of Organizational Management and Communication Theories

lighted this period. As more and more people entered the workplace, factory owners and store managers began to explore new and different ways to organize and manage people (Eisenberg and Goodall, 2001).

Organizational charts from this period favored a strictly vertical, top-down arrangement. At the top was a board of directors; below was a president; below the president was a series of vice presidents; below the vice presidents were department managers; below them were the supervisors; and finally, at the very bottom of the chart, were the line workers. The term for this organization by rank and status is **hierarchy.**

Classical organizational structures assigned privileges according to one's rank and status in the organization. There were two important classical approaches to managing businesses and industries: *scientific management* and *bureaucracy* (Morgan, 1986). These two theories dominated the way organizations were structured and managed during the classical period.

## Scientific Management

**Scientific management,** which emerged in the early 1900s, was defined by an engineer named Frederick Taylor (1913). Taylor believed management was a true science that should be governed by scientific principles, rules, and laws. He put forth the idea that factories and organizations should be operated as "efficient machines," modeled on the inner workings of a well-made mechanical clock. Inspired by this image of clockwork, he proposed that "time and motion" studies be conducted for every task in an organization. These studies encouraged business owners and managers to find "the one best way" (the method requiring the shortest amount of time using the smallest amount of motion) to

Hulton/Archive/Getty Images

Ford Assembly, March 1928

complete tasks. The results were used to establish standards for every job, to create an evaluation instrument that could be equally applied to every worker, and to reward (or punish) workers based on their production or performance. Tasks were divided into discrete, measurable units, and workers were trained to perform only one task, thus making replacement of sick or injured workers relatively easy. Workers were seen as merely another replaceable part in the factory machine, and there was little if any room for learning or advancement. As Henry Ford, a proud scientific-management enthusiast, once put it, "Managers think; workers work."

But what exactly did managers think about and do? During this same theoretical period, a Frenchman named Henri Fayol established the five functions of scientific management: planning, organizing, commanding (or goal-setting), coordinating, and controlling (or evaluating) (1949). According to Fayol, it was the manager's job to plan the work, organize tasks, set goals, coordinate work, and control the workforce. A person hired as a manager would be trained to perform these duties, and *only* these duties. There was no allowance for encouraging managers to learn how to do their jobs better, or even differently. Scientific principles governed the management of a plant in pretty much the same authoritative, unchanging way they were thought to rule the movement of planets or the growing of soybeans. Certainly no thought was expended on "quality improvement" when it came to managerial tasks. A man (almost all the factory managers during this period in history were men) either knew how to do the job, or he didn't!

Although scientific management was, in principle, a good theory for organizing and managing repetitive tasks done in a mechanical environment, in practice it contributed to the dehumanization of the workplace. Because workers were considered replaceable parts in a relentless machine, they were often treated as less than human. Working conditions during this period were hard, labor laws were virtually nonexistent, and management decisions were the final word. Workers could be fired, hired, or reassigned based on their sex, race, religion, attitude, or relationships to other workers.

## Bureaucracy

Although it might not seem so today, the creation of a bureaucracy was considered a more humane way of managing people in complex organizations. Max Weber, an observer of the rise of scientific management and a major sociological theorist of his day, saw bureaucracies as a means to overcome the problems of scientific management (1946). Weber believed that, managed correctly, using a set of universalisms or standards of fairness, bureaucracies would stamp out the harsh, inequitable, and often deadly conditions that arose from poor scientific management (Perrow, 1986). According to Weber (Scott, 1990), an ideal **bureaucracy** must have the following elements:

- ✦ a fixed division of labor
- ✦ a hierarchy of work responsibilities and authority
- ✦ a set of general operating rules that govern performance
- ✦ a separation of the personal lives of employees from their professional lives
- ✦ a selection process based on technical qualifications and equal treatment under the rules for operating the business

Scientific management and bureaucracy both relied on strict top-down authority structures, centralized decision making, and control of managerial power to govern the organization of work. They ignored the possibilities that workers could learn to manage, that managers could learn to become better at their jobs, or that managers and workers could learn from one another if they communicated more equitably.

That would come later. In the meantime, let's examine the dominant theory of communication that shaped scientific management and bureaucracy.

## Communication as Information Transfer

During the classical period there arose an implicit theory of communication that would later be termed the **information transfer model.** Visualize a pipeline

*(continued)*

through which information or messages pass. On one end of the pipeline is a "sender," and on the other end is a "receiver." What you have just pictured is a representation of communication that contains one or more of the following assumptions about information transfer:

+ Language transfers thoughts and feelings from person to person.
+ Speakers and writers insert thoughts and feelings into words.
+ Words contain the thoughts and feelings.
+ Listeners or readers extract the thoughts and feelings from the words (Axley, 1984, p. 429).

The information transfer model, although simplistic in its characterization of management and communication, has had a lasting influence in bureaucracies worldwide. Moreover, academic interest in how people think and process information about task-oriented communication led to the development of sophisticated research programs aimed at explaining the gaps in this complex phenomenon. This research contributed to filling the gaps in the explanatory power of the information transfer model, which in turn created the questions that led to the emergence of human relation theories of management and a new perspective on communication in the workplace.

## Human Relations/Resources and Transaction Process

Although the 1920s had been a period of extreme affluence and growth in America, in the early 1930s, prosperity quickly gave way to closed factories, massive migrations, and widespread poverty and unemployment. With little to lose, workers began to make demands for better working conditions, fairer wages, and equal treatment. Labor unions grew in popularity and power.

The poverty of the Great Depression eventually gave way to a new cycle of expansion and prosperity. Driven by the production needs of World War II, by union-sponsored demands for fairer treatment of workers by managers, and by a desire among liberal-minded journalists, academics, and industrialists for a better way to get the job done, new theories of management emerged. These new theories of management grew out of what we now term the *human relations movement* (Eisenberg and Goodall, 2001).

What made it different? The **human relations movement** viewed employees less as individual, replaceable machine parts and more as sources of group information and skill that could be developed through training and education by the organization. Two ideas were key to this movement; they were contained in the Hawthorne Studies and in Maslow's Hierarchy of Needs.

## Hawthorne Studies

In the 1930s, Elton Mayo led a team of researchers to study the way people worked at Western Electric's Hawthorne Plant in Cicero, Illinois (Mayo, 1945). Using principles drawn from scientific management, Mayo was asked to conduct research in the plant to see if productivity improved when lighting conditions were altered. What he and his research team found surprised them. The changes in productivity they witnessed had nothing to do with the lighting, but everything to do with communication with and among the factory workers. Mayo found that increased attention to the workers led to improved morale, which in turn improved productivity, a finding that became known as "the Hawthorne Effect." The researchers also found that individuals are influenced by those around them and that those group interactions could have favorable effects on work.

These two insights became the basis for a gradual change from a strictly bureaucratic to a "human relations" approach to management. The core principles of the movement emphasized the following:

- ✦ the importance of open communication and supportive relations between managers and employees
- ✦ the need for managers to take into account employees' feelings
- ✦ the need for managers to respond to the developmental needs of workers, which might be incongruent with formal hierarchies and task specialization

## Maslow's Hierarchy of Needs

During the 1940s and 1950s, a psychologist named Abraham Maslow developed the Hierarchy of Needs model to explain what motivates human behavior. The model represents a hierarchy of human needs that range from "lower order" needs, such as food, clothing, and shelter, to "higher order" needs, such as self-esteem and personal fulfillment ("self-actualization"). (See Figure 2.2.)

Maslow argued that proper motivation of employees required understanding what they were thinking about and aspiring to in their lives. Owners and managers began to understand that although a paycheck can help fulfill the lower-order needs, viewing workers as "human resources" by providing them with proper training and educational opportunities would help satisfy higher-order needs, thus making workers more productive.

Maslow's influence on managerial thinking cannot be overestimated. His work inspired other researchers to ask new questions about motivation and rewards, about the design and evaluation of performance, and about how "optimal performance" on the job might be accomplished. His work underscored the importance of what today we call "organizational learning" and "continuous improvement." He also set the academic stage for studies of "organizing for

**Figure 2.2**
Maslow's Hierarchy
of Needs

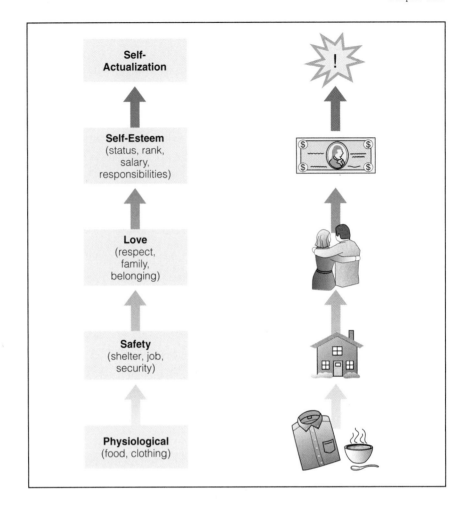

peak performance" (Eisenberg, 1990) that have led to insights about the necessary conditions for helping workers identify and meet challenges. In particular, Mihaly Cziksentmihalyi's theory of "flow" (1990, 1997) suggests that peak performances are gained when workers feel motivated to do a job that is a little above their skill level but have the training and resources to carry it out.

To understand how motivation, morale, and working in groups or teams are experienced at work, academics and professionals had to revise what they thought about communication.

## Communication as a Transactional Process

The **transactional process model** of communication emerged out of the failures of the scientific management and information transfer schools to provide a model for motivation, morale, and teamwork. Specifically, after the Hawthorne Studies, more attention was paid to the idea of communication as vital to manager–employee relations. As a result, clear hierarchical distinctions between bosses and workers were replaced with more equitable terms, such as *senders* and *receivers*. Additionally, these terms created an appreciation for how people at work perform those roles simultaneously.

The transactional process model recognizes the following statements as true:

+ All persons are engaged in sending and receiving messages (Wenberg and Wilmot, 1973).

+ Each person is constantly affecting the other (Wenberg and Wilmot, 1973).

+ Feedback, particularly nonverbal feedback, is a vital source of information (Anderson, 1999).

+ The person receiving a message, rather than the person sending the message, is the source of meaning (Axley, 1984).

Communication as a transactional process was the dominant communication model informing advances in human relations, human resources, and human potential approaches to organization and management. In an evolutionary sense, you can see how what was once a top-down, "command and control" perspective on business and professional talk gave way to a more humane and complex view of verbal and nonverbal communication. Three major areas of academic research and business practice benefited from this model: (1) interpersonal communication in the workplace, (2) team communication, and (3) leadership.

The transactional process model provides a useful general approach to understanding interpersonal and team communication in the workplace, within which new findings and advances continue to be made. However, the evolution of new theories of organization, management, and communication created yet another new way of thinking about communication in the workplace. Verbal and nonverbal communication were not only viewed as a management function or as a component of team effectiveness, but they also became more broadly associated with the process for creating the organization and becoming the substance of management. These new theories are called the *systems* and *cultures* approaches to organization and communication.

## Systems Thinking and Communication Networks

The **systems thinking** theory of business organization combines holism and interdependence. It views an organization as a system of interconnected individuals and teams. A major claim of systems thinking is that for one member of a team or organization to succeed, all members of the team or organization must succeed (Goodall and Eisenberg, 2001). These days, in the early twenty-first century, to call a company's interlocking webs of communication a "system" is to use a language that most businesspeople readily accept and many understand. A system is a way to conceptualize the dynamic set of relationships that point to a new kind of order. This order is not one made of bureaucratic hierarchies and divisions of labor but instead consists of patterns of interaction among the system's components (Farace, Monge, and Russell, 1977; Senge, 1991).

An organizational system is often envisioned metaphorically as a "family of relationships," in which the organization equates with a family and each family member's communication has some effect on—is interconnected with—every other family member's understandings, meanings, and communication. The components of a system are as follows (Eisenberg and Goodall, 2001):

+ **Environment:** Organizations do not exist as isolated entities but as integral parts of the world.

+ **Interdependence**: The organization, its environment, and the individuals and components within it are interrelated.

+ **Goals** (what the system is organized to accomplish): Goals are negotiated between the individual components, with a large influence from the system's environment.

+ **Feedback:** Feedback is an interconnected system of "loops" that connect communication and action. There are two kinds of feedback: negative, which corrects for deviations from the original goal, and positive, which finds new areas for growth and expansion.

+ **Openness, order, and contingency:** These terms refer to the notion that there is no "one best way" to organize. To succeed, an organizational system must remain open and work within its environment, in an evolving and orderly way.

One of the major contributions to communication theory provided by systems thinking was the idea of communication networks. Another was the contingent nature of decision making. A third was the importance of feedback to the health and resilience of the organizational system. Let's examine why these ideas were so powerful and how they have influenced our business and professional communication.

## The Links between Systems Theory and Business and Professional Communication

There are three direct links between the components of an organizational system and communication in it: communication flow in networks, the contingent nature of decision making (interdependence), and the importance of feedback to the health and resilience of the system. Each of these links has a direct impact on how we communicate and interpret meaning in the workplace.

## Communication Flow in Networks

When an organization is viewed as a communication system, two patterns stand out. First, some communication flows into and through the organization according to formal chains of command and through established groups and teamwork. For example, because of the devaluing of currency in the Asian economy, U.S. stock exchanges reacted swiftly and strongly. The CFO of XYZ Corporation responded to this shift in the economic environment by asking each group leader or department head to analyze how this shift would affect their products and customers. Department or group leaders worked together to incorporate their analysis into future corporate directions, which they presented to the CFO at their monthly status meeting.

Second, some communication flows into and through the organization using informal or social patterns of routine interaction that are not prescribed or authorized by the organization in a formal way. Informal patterns of interaction include talk around the water cooler and impromptu discussions in the employee lounge.

Together, these formal and informal patterns teach us a lot about how messages travel through an organization. For example, during the XYZ Corporation analysis, many employees and customers speculated on XYZ's ability to remain profitable. These conversations occurred over lunches, in parking lots, and during sales calls. Feedback from these informal interactions enlightened the formal discussion, providing decision makers with additional sources of information. In turn, formal groups reported these concerns to their superiors, who engaged a consultant to help them through the period of potential crisis.

## Contingent Nature of Decision Making

As you can see from these examples, viewing communication flow through networks in a system reveals the ongoing, dynamic nature of interaction and feedback. It also reveals why companies use a contingent approach to decision making. Rather than assume that once a decision has been made, the problem is solved, contingent decision makers understand the constant need to revise decisions based on new information and ongoing analysis of the effects of past decisions. This pattern of interaction that informs decision making is known as "interdependence." One of its major outcomes is organizational learning.

## Feedback and the Health of a System

Maintaining open lines of communication is vital to the health and resilience of an organizational system. Open lines of communication ensure that feedback—both positive and negative (or corrective)—is available to make informed decisions and enhance the productivity of an organization. Lines of communication must remain open externally and internally. In the example above, the feedback received from customers was important for channeling customer concerns to the appropriate department and planning for communication back to the customers about future plans. One of the major outcomes of this kind of systems thinking has been the development and use of continuous improvement models to monitor the quality of the organization, as well as its services or products.

Systems thinking has had a profound influence on theories of organization, management, and communication. Systems thinking is the core of Peter Senge's approach to using communication (in the form of dialogue) to build learning organizations (1994). But before we move into our discussion of conscious communication in learning organizations, we need to explain the influence of another powerful idea that has had tremendous impact on our understanding of business and professional communication: organizational cultures.

## BEST PRACTICES

### Using Formal and Informal Networks Effectively

The systems perspective provides useful tips for communicating formally and informally in an organization. Let's examine ways you can use these concepts in your professional communication.

+ Develop information and support contacts inside and outside of your workplace. Look for people who can help you plan the direction of your career and see opportunities that you might have missed if you stayed within an organizational shell.

+ Keep the lines of communication with your contacts open at all times. To do so, you need to listen carefully, respond quickly to requests, seek information when unsure, and give credit where credit is due.

+ Understand that decisions in organizations are subject to change and revision. Don't stake out a position and refuse to change because you are relying on yesterday's information; tomorrow may require a shift in decision making.

+ Never assume your company operates in isolation. Keep up with current events, changes in technology and the global economy, and shifts in your industry that will affect your company.

+ Understand that in business, change is healthy. For most people, this requires a shift in thinking: change is healthy and stagnation unhealthy.

+ Enter into all interactions from a conscious communication perspective. Be aware of the information value and potential effect of your communication on your identity, others' ability to act, and the organization's health and resilience.

## Organizational Cultures, Communication, and Power

**Organizational culture,** like a system, implies an intricate, interconnected, and purposeful pattern or order. Unlike systems, however, a culture's pattern is drawn from the metaphors and language of "community," which implies the following:

- a unique sense of place that both unites and divides members (Louis, 1979)

- histories and visions for the future, which may or may not be shared (Deal and Kennedy, 1982; Peters and Waterman, 1982)

- locally defined customs, rituals, rules, rites, and procedures (Pacanowsky and O'Donnell-Trujillo, 1983; Hofstede, 1983; Goodall, 1989)

- shared core values that, even when opposed by resistance factions, are recognized to exist (Ouchi and Wilkins, 1985; Kotter and Heskett, 1992; Shockley-Zalabak and Morley, 1994)

The culture of the organization includes the way employees dress, how they speak to superiors, the items they display in their office or cubes, and more. Culture appears to consist of the behaviors, customs, habits, stories, routines, and other meaningful events and processes that organize people (Putnam and Pacanowsky, 1983). However, cultural researchers stress the importance of understanding that culture is not a "thing," but a "happening" (Pacanowsky and O'Donnell-Trujillo, 1983).

Communication is the process by which culture is formed and transformed (Eisenberg and Goodall, 2001; Kellett, 1999). The cultural approach teaches us that communication *is* the culture. The verbal and nonverbal messages that arise from the organization's culture create the *meanings* of behavior, customs, habits, stories, routines, events, and processes that organize and inform a group of people. As the anthropologist Clifford Geertz expressed it, "Humans live in webs of meaning that we ourselves have spun" (1973).

Studying organizational cultures allows us to expand our business and professional communication knowledge to include an understanding of power, organizational storytelling, personal narratives, and dialogue. Let's examine each of these forms of contemporary business and professional communication.

## The Influence of the Cultural Approach to Power

One of the advantages of the organizational culture approach to communication has been a new understanding of the role of communication in the creation of **power**—the sources of influence derived by an individual within an organization. In part, this new understanding of power was derived from looking critically at the advice about communication provided in previous models of organizing and managing (see Deetz, 1995; Conquergood, 1991; Conrad, 1991; Mumby, 1987). Before we can understand how the cultural approach challenged these theories of power, let's review how power functioned in previous models.

## Classical Approach to Power

The classical approach to power provides what critics have labeled the *managerial view* of communication in organizations (Putnam and Pacanowsky, 1983). This means that our understanding of all communication practices, and especially of power, was rooted firmly in the idea that "rank has its privileges." Moreover, the expression of power was limited to structures created for, and functions carried out by, managers. French and Raven (1968) described the classic managerial forms of power:

*Reward power:* A supervisor can give a reward—such as a bonus, time off, or an award—based on compliance with a directive.

*Coercive power:* A boss has coercive power when employees perceive that negative things will happen if they don't comply with directives.

*Referent power:* A boss has referent power when employees do what is asked of them because they seek to emulate her or him.

*Expert power:* A boss has expert power when employees perceive a boss to have expert knowledge.

*Legitimate power:* A boss has power simply because of his or her position within the hierarchy. Employees perceive the position to be legitimately held and therefore comply with directives.

As you can see, there are times when each of these forms of power may be appropriate and useful. Power should be applied consciously and after a mindful examination of the outcome you hope to achieve.

## The Human Relations Approach to Power

In the transactional process model, the idea of power shifts from the manager's position within the hierarchy to the relationship between the manager and the employee. The employee gains power primarily by being encouraged to give feedback to the boss and to interpret his or her own meanings about the relationship and the work, and by negotiating with the organizational superior how, when, and with what resources the assigned work could be accomplished. The manager derives power from being more supportive, open, interested in the employees' feelings and thoughts, and trustworthy. Viewed this way, managers and employees use power cooperatively, and therefore more fairly.

## The Systems Approach to Power

The systems perspective encourages us to see power less as a "thing" that organizational superiors have and subordinates don't have than as a system of relationships based only in part on an employee's status in the organizational hierarchy. Systems thinking helps us account for the available uses of power in everyday exchanges between and among equals (as well as between superiors and subordinates). For example, an entry-level computer programmer with deep knowledge of an operating system has a lot of potential power in a company that requires its operating system to be in place and up and running to do business. If the system goes down, so do company profits. The programmer's power is held in relation to every other employee's ability to do his or her job. Concurrently, the programmer's success may well depend on the input about the computer system she or he receives from other employees. Viewed systemically, everyone has some available power relative to everyone else's available power.

Similarly, employees who are interpersonally close to, and whose information (feedback) is trusted by, their managers tend to be able to exert influence despite hierarchical differences. Quality of relationships and the perceived value of information mediate and often negate overt power as defined by rank and status. This principle also helps us understand the power of rumors and gossip in an organization. As sources of informal communication, rumors and gossip serve to balance power by directing and controlling information and feedback within a larger organizational system.

## The Cultural Approach to Power

The cultural perspective assumes that there is a constant struggle for power in every organization (Deetz, 1995). In organizations, people vie for attention, resources, rewards, influence, and dignity. From a cultural perspective, people and groups holding power are described as "dominant," and others seeking power are labeled "resistant" (Goodall, 1990a; Scott, 1990). One major contribution of this perspective has been the study of power as it relates to and derives from gender, race, class, and sexual orientation in organizations.

*Power and Difference*    With the advent of the cultures perspective, the model for power expanded from *overt* hierarchy, information, and relationships to *covert,* or hidden, power (Conrad, 1983; Scott, 1990). Because of sociological research, power within companies came to be viewed in relation to power in societies. In societies marked by social and economic class divisions, where differences in opportunities and evaluations of one's abilities are often based on one's race, gender, or sexual orientation, the same patterns of influence and inequity manifest in businesses and professions. Furthermore, because sociologists and anthropologists teach us to see all cultures as localized sites of struggle between those who have power and those who don't, a new language of "resistance to domination" enters organizational analysis.

Power is now understood to occur "offstage" as well as "onstage" (Scott, 1990; Goodall, 1995), which means that the lines of power extend beyond face-to-face encounters, or even beyond the workplace. For example, disgruntled or alienated employees who feel wronged may turn their work worlds upside down, and therefore regain a sense of power and equity, by casting aspersions on their bosses. In the film *American Beauty* (1999), a character facing termination from his boring job in an advertising firm confronts his superior directly, turns the power equation inside out, and wins a large settlement. In real life this is unlikely, as resistance to domination typically occurs offstage. These offstage performances may occur in break rooms, in comic asides performed behind the boss's back, in nasty e-mails to friends, in "work-hate narratives" (Goodall, 1995), and during after-work or weekend gatherings.

*Power and Democracy*    Another way of understanding the cultural perspective on power is through the application of a cooperative (or democratic) model of influence. Although this is still the exception rather than the norm in business today, the concept bears examination. Stan Deetz created a model for power and democracy in the workplace using the "stakeholder organization" (1995), in which the success of the company depends upon shared decision making at every level. Deetz outlined four steps to create such a workplace (Eisenberg and Goodall, 2001, pp. 166–167):

1. *Create a workplace in which every member thinks and acts like an owner.* When power is shared for decision making, stakeholders become more accountable to themselves, to one another, and to society.
2. *The management of the work must be reintegrated with the doing of work.* Empowering stakeholders to have control over how they perform their own jobs eliminates the need for managers or supervisors. Power is thus shared among equals.
3. *Quality information must be widely distributed.* Information is power, and power in a stakeholder organization must be shared equally. Additionally, by encouraging stakeholders to share only "real" information, this model discourages the meaningless proliferation of memos, faxes, e-mails, letters, and newsletters that reinforce existing power hierarchies.
4. *Social structure should grow from the bottom rather than be reinforced from the top.* Power is vested in all of the stakeholders, who determine every aspect of their jobs and workplace instead of taking orders from people paid to oversee and direct the work.

Now that we have studied the idea of power in relation to cultural theories of organization, let's examine two of the ways communication functions in a cultural model: *organizational narratives* and *dialogue*.

## Organizational Narratives and Dialogue

All our experiences provide us with the raw materials to construct an ongoing "story of our lives" (Bochner, 1997; Goodall, 2000; Coles, 1989). Similarly, employees and managers in businesses and professions construct "organizational narratives" to re-create and retell the important events in their working lives (Boje, 1991, 1995; Mumby, 1987; Kellett, 1999).

Theorists have labeled this perspective the **narrative** view or paradigm (Bochner, 1994; Fisher, 1987). The essential idea behind the narrative paradigm is that, communicatively, we live within the lines of the stories we tell others about our jobs, our lives, and ourselves. These narratives do not simply represent our experiences; they also help construct them. Our identities, goals, values, and passions derive from an ongoing narrative in which we each figure as a central character. How we make sense of situations and others is largely determined by the ways in which we can use the plots and lessons of our ongoing stories to render "the new" within a context of "the old" (Weick, 1995).

Four uses of organizational narratives have been studied as forms of business and professional communication:

+ *Organizational stories* (Mumby, 1987; Goodall, 1989; Boje, 1991): Individual accounts of the workplace that reveal how events occurred, how problems were solved, how heroes and heroines were created, how legends were made, and how "things are done around here." Some of these stories reveal how power works; for example, accounts of "how things are done around here" tend to repress alternative ways of doing things.

+ *Work-hate narratives* (Goodall, 1995): Individual accounts of harms, misdeeds, or violence done to employees. These stories are often told to regain equity in a situation, but they sometimes forecast acts of revenge.

+ *Narrative recovery technique* (Kellett, 1999): As a consulting tool, these stories are collected publicly from all employees in a particular department or area to "recover" the history of the organization from a personal perspective. The consultant uses key questions to prompt the narratives, including (a) What brought you to work here? (b) What are your personal joys and challenges? (c) Have there been any turning points in your relationship to this company? and (d) What vision do you have for your future here?

+ *Organizational change* (Ford and Ford, 1995; Kellett and Goodall, 1998; Kellett, 1999): Consultants, trainers, and managers all understand that productive change in organizations always begins in conversations. Because communication creates perceptions of reality, as well as constitutes systems and cultures, communication is responsible for bringing into existence ideas for change. Stories about those conversations emerge as part of the shared history—myths, legends, turning points—of any organization or profession.

## Dialogue

Conceptually, **dialogue** refers to an ongoing, open, and dynamic process in which individual communicators have a balanced chance to speak and to be heard, and in which each person makes a conscious effort to understand and empathize with the perspective, experiences, and positions of the other (Buber, 1985; Eisenberg and Goodall, 2001; Senge, 1991; Senge et al., 1994). The purposes of dialogue are to promote identity and community through empathetic understanding, to use communication to achieve mutual growth, and to search for meaningful patterns capable of effecting personal transformation and organizational change (Arnett and Cissna, 1996; Senge et al., 1994; Kellett and Dalton, 2001; Eisenberg and Goodall, 2001). As you can see, dialogue represents a unique and powerful form of communication.

H. L. Goodall (2000), working from an earlier Peter Senge (1991) model for describing types of communication, developed a continuum for conceptualizing a range of the following everyday forms of talk:

+ *phatic communication* (routine exchanges of small talk)

+ *ordinary conversation* (discussion, gossip, or information exchange)

+ *skilled conversation and professional communication* (interviews, negotiations, conflict management, informative and persuasive presentations, team presentations, argumentation and debate)

+ *personal narratives* (stories)

+ *dialogue* (deep conversation aimed at mutual growth that often requires risk taking, creativity, and suspension of critical judgment)

As this continuum reveals, dialogue is the most advanced form of communication. Viewed from an organizational perspective, dialogue requires that equitable communication opportunities are afforded to all employees (Eisenberg and Goodall, 2001). However, merely having a right to speak doesn't adequately address the quality of talk exchanged during a dialogue.

The most conscious form of communication in an organization is dialogue. As you can see from Figure 2.3, the more conscious a communicator is of talk—the more open the exchange with the other person—the more dialogic the talk becomes. Let's examine the basis for this claim in greater detail.

### Mindless Communication

Experience teaches us that we do not always behave mindfully at work or at home. Nor do we always behave in an ethical manner. In part, this is because many communication situations we face daily at work do not call for a lot of mental alertness or focused communicative activity. Communication researchers have termed these situations "phatic communication," or "small talk." In these situations, what is called for is not mindful, but "mindless" or automatic, often "scripted" responses (Greene, 1997; Goodall, 1996; Lodge, 1997).

**Mindless communication**—episodes of small talk or automatic talk—occurs most often in familiar situations. Why? Because when we are in familiar situations, speaking and listening to people we see every day, we often rely on

| Phatic Communication | Ordinary Communication | Skilled Talk | Personal Narratives | Dialogue |
|---|---|---|---|---|
| Routine, ritualized social talk | Exchanges of questions and responses, humor, ideas, and other forms of relational information | Interviews, negotiations, conflict management, presentational speaking, and teamwork | Autobiographical stories about the meaning of one's life experience | Creative, risk-taking, mutual quest for understanding and meaning |

**Figure 2.3**
Communication Continuum in a Learning Organization

past experiences, routines, rituals, or habits—what researchers call "scripted responses"—to guide our talk. We do not consciously select a strategy; we simply fall back on nonconscious routines we have used successfully. Below is a typical example of phatic communication:

SHAVONDA: Hi!
RICK: Hi.
SHAVONDA: So how are you?
RICK: Fine, and you?
SHAVONDA: Good.
RICK: So what's new in your department today?
SHAVONDA: Not much, and you?
RICK: The same. You know how it is. That's why they call it "work."
SHAVONDA: Yeah, I guess. Well, see you later.
RICK: Okay. See you.

Most of us repeat this form of small talk many times during an average day. Phatic communication is a necessary, although seldom sufficient, form of everyday business talk because it acts a kind of social lubricant that encourages a surface level of collegiality and friendliness. Furthermore, cognitive researchers suggest that mindlessness is one way the brain conserves its energy for more challenging situations. In this way, "nonconscious behavior should not be viewed as an evil" (King and Sawyer, 1998, p. 334). By behaving "automatically," we make our mental energy available for other uses.

This is not to say that relying on phatic communication or small talk is a good thing. An overreliance on mindlessness diminishes our cognitive ability to develop new scripts or creative responses and to otherwise expand the repertoire of available communication strategies we bring to new situations (Goodall, 1996). Communication ability is a skill, and like any skill, it requires practice. If all we do is rely on small talk and routine responses, we aren't using the full capacity of our communication potential. Nor are we getting much practice in developing the creative, mindful strategies that we need when phatic communication simply won't do. Nor are we always behaving ethically, because mindless activity does not allow for complex and difficult thoughts. This may help us account for why we inadvertently hurt others' feelings, or why we too often fail to appreciate how our routine actions have harmed or offended others. Finally, an overreliance on small talk probably encourages others to perceive us as friendly, but boring. For these reasons, success in business and professional communication is unlikely to occur when mindless communication dominates our everyday interactions.

Improving our conscious communication, becoming more mindful in business and professional contexts, should be a major learning goal for anyone planning an organizational career. Many of the more popular books giving advice for business communication success can be understood as reflections of the basic assumptions about conscious communication afforded by the cognitive perspective. For example, Stephen Covey's *The Seven Habits of Highly Effective People* (1990) advocates becoming more goal oriented, focused, and strategic in our dealings with others. Clearly, the knowledge and skills provided by this theoretical perspective on communication have direct relevance to developing important professional communication competencies. The next section discusses mindful, or more conscious, communication.

### Mindful Communication

A mindful approach to talk enables us to view communication consciously, as a mental and relational activity that is both purposeful and strategic. We use our heads to come up with strategies that we encode into talk designed to help us achieve desirable ends with others. When we are conscious of our communication, we become more mindful (Langer, 1990; Motley, 1992). **Mindful communication** requires the following:

+ analyzing communication situations

+ thinking actively about possible communication choices available to us

+ adapting our message to inform, amuse, persuade, or otherwise influence our listener or audience

+ evaluating the feedback we receive as an indication of how successful we were in accomplishing our purpose

But what if what is desirable for us might hurt someone else? Researchers suggest that cognitively based communication is, or at least should be, ethical (Langer, 1989). This is because we are individually responsible for our choices, our modes of adapting to listeners and audiences, and the outcomes of our actions. To become more conscious as communicators, which is to become more mindful and strategic in our dealings with others at work, should help us to become more ethical, as well.

**Focus on Ethics**

Does communication qualify as mindful if you know your message will hurt someone? Are you responsible for the outcome if your goal is achieved? What responsibility do you have to others in the workplace if you know your communication might further your career but at the same time harm the career of another?

Research shows that we can expect mindful communication to occur in specific situations (Motley, 1992):

+ *When there is a conflict between message goals.* For example, an employee may knock on a supervisor's door to ask permission to perform a task but also want to show the supervisor that he or she has taken the initiative to take on the task without being directed to do so. There is a conflict between the goals for the message — to demonstrate initiative, or to ask permission.

+ *When undesirable consequences are expected from the use of a particular message.* For example, a technical writer knows that she must inform the manager that his deadline will not be met. She also knows that he will not be pleased with this information and will likely blame her for not accomplishing the job. She thinks this will harm her career, but she also feels obligated to tell him the deadline will not be met.

+ *During time delays between messages and mental processing difficulties, such as interpreting the meaning or intention of a message.* For example, two colleagues are having lunch together and one partner seems interested in taking the relationship, which until this time has been one of friendship and collegiality, to another, possibly romantic, level. The other partner pauses for a long time before answering her colleague's last statement about his "interest" in her. She is trying to figure out what he means. He is trying to figure out why she isn't answering him.

+ *When communication situations are particularly troublesome or unique.* For example, a visiting computer engineer from Sweden arrives with gifts for the manager of a North American computer firm. The North American manager has no gifts to give in return and is clearly embarrassed. Both of them search for something to say to ease the situation.

## The Next Step: Learning Organizations

Systems thinking and understanding organizational cultures revolutionized how we view organizations and communication. Until recently, however, these concepts were difficult to apply to the actual managing of, or communicating in, a company. Peter Senge and his associates (1991, 1995) have applied systems thinking to organizational cultures through the concept of a **learning organization**—an organization marked by conscious systems thinking and an ability to continuously adapt communication to organizational, cultural, and individual changes.

## The Five Disciplines

A learning organization is characterized by five "disciplines" (Senge, 1991) or characteristics:

- **Systems thinking:** Employees and managers understand the interconnectedness of communication between and among individuals and teams, as well as their connection to organizational structures and processes. Emphasis is placed on developing a common cultural language capable of generating conscious thought about how parts relate to wholes and vice versa. Openness, trust, commitment, and respect are the relational bases for knowledge and action, and a profound bias for change characterizes systems thinking.

- **Personal mastery:** The organization recognizes that individuals learn on and off the job and that continuous learning is a responsibility of all employees and managers. By valuing open communication, organizations encourage members to share what they have learned, even—perhaps especially—when it challenges or contradicts what is taken for granted or assumed within the company. Personal mastery is another way of conceptualizing empowerment, by emphasizing the need for continuous growth and renewal as vital to the individual and the organization.

- **Mental models:** Mental models are the images, assumptions, and stories that permeate the minds of the people working in an organization (Senge, 1991, p. 235). Communication represents and shares those models with others, and it connects the images, assumptions, and stories to the organization's mission and core values. Communication also helps identify similarities and differences in ways of conceiving of connections, allowing individuals to recognize gaps between their mental models and communication practices.

- **Shared vision:** It is one thing for a company to have a vision and mission; it is another for employees and managers to own and share it. Ownership of an organizational vision and mission requires shared communication built upon a foundation of trust, openness, empowerment, and honesty. Through communication, the vision and mission are driven into local practices.

- **Team learning:** The point of team learning is conscious, coordinated action that translates shared vision, mental models, and personal mastery into systems thinking and acting. When the team learns, so do the individual team members. When the individual team members learn, they have a responsibility to share what they have learned with the team.

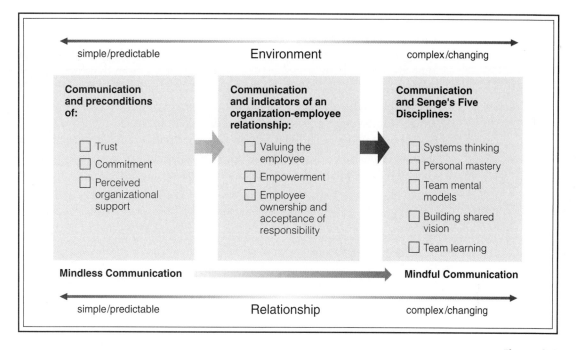

**Figure 2.4**
The Role of Communi-
cation in Learning
Organizations

Adapted from R. T. Barker and
M. R. Camarata (1998).

Each of the above characteristics points to the need for more conscious systems-based thinking and culturally adapted communication. To adapt systems thinking to any business and professional context requires a commitment to learning and a desire for continuous improvement. Both of these goals require conscious communication practices.

Randolph Barker and Martin Camarata (1998, p. 445) offer a model of communication in creating and maintaining learning organizations (see Figure 2.4). The Barker and Camarata model shows that conscious communication is central in building a learning organization. As the environment becomes more complex and changing, relationships among individual employees and managers also become more complex and subject to change. Instead of relying on simplistic communication to guide understanding, what matters is mindful communication and dialogue.

Finally, this model shows how the preconditions of trust, commitment, and organizational support influence the organization-employee relationship, which in turn directly influences the ability of an organization to practice the five disciplines required to build a learning organization.

## Dialogue and Learning Organizations

Senge and his colleagues at MIT brought the concept of dialogue to practical organizational applications. Senge realized that dialogue is the primary form of communication necessary to promote learning organizations (1991). Why?

Because when individual communicators engage in dialogue, they are encouraged to challenge existing sources of information, values, and beliefs in ways that promote learning. They genuinely listen to each other, and because of that, they learn from others' experiences. They speak from their hearts, from their accumulated and often disparate experiences, rather than from the voice of their hierarchical positions. They use their time together to consciously construct a more engaged, open, and respectful relationship.

It has probably occurred to you by now that *dialogue* and *learning organization* are terms that bring to life the ideas of organizations as systems and cultures. This renewal can be attributed to the following points:

+ Dialogue in learning organizations recognizes the systemic powers of shared information and ongoing feedback.

+ Dialogue, as the model for communication within an organization's culture, fosters more conscious forms of communication in everyday practices.

+ Dialogue respects diversity and encourages ethical conduct in ways that promote mutual learning and productive change.

+ Dialogue encourages participants in learning organizations to view their individual experiences as cultural information, and to realize that others' experiences within that same culture are likely to be distinctive, different, and vital to a fuller appreciation of the culture, the work, and the environment.

+ Dialogue in learning organizations promotes a balance between individuality and community.

+ Taking a dialogic view of the role of communication in organizations encourages us to see talk as the moment-to-moment working out of the tension between individual needs for creativity and organizational constraints (Eisenberg and Goodall, 2001, p. 41).

+ Dialogue in learning organizations values skilled talk and effective forms of communication at all levels, in all ways, each and every day.

## Why We Learn about Theories of Communication

Our experiences teaching business and professional communication courses over the years have taught us that many students, when confronted early on in the term with material in a chapter such as this one, wonder how it applies to developing their communication skills. It is a fair question, and one that we will answer for you now.

Theories, to be practical, must be applied. You may have heard the expression, first coined by the mid-twentieth-century social scientist Kurt Lewin, that "nothing is so practical as a good theory." That statement is not just something an academic would say. It is a valuable expression that speaks to a profound human truth. A theory is best thought of as "intellectual equipment" (Burke, 1989), or as a tool to enhance our understanding. However, before you can apply a theory or make it a part of your intellectual equipment, you have to develop an understanding of the theories that have guided our organizations.

By learning to think theoretically about communication in organizations, you acquire a language for describing and evaluating your personal experiences as a communicator at work. But you need to apply that language to your experiences in order to achieve the payoff. You have to incorporate what you have read into your everyday habits of mind. Use the theories as touchstones in your quest to understand the meanings of persons and things. Use them to become a more conscious, more informed communicator.

## Summary

Chapter 2 explored the close connection between theories of organization and communication. During the classical period, the ideal organization was a factory built on the model of "clockwork." Theorists such as Frederick Taylor, Henri Fayol, and Max Weber, using the concepts of scientific management and bureaucracy, built organizational structures ready-made for top-down information transfer models of communication. As these tight organizational structures and top-down approaches to communication were challenged by the effectiveness of simple human contact and a concern for workers' morale, human relations/resources and transactional process models gradually replaced them. As organizations became more complex, technological, and global, systems thinking emphasized the importance of communication networks as a way of understanding the role of groups and teams—and later, dialogue and learning—in creating and maintaining healthy and resilient systems.

Finally, renewed interest in the human side of enterprise revealed that communication was a cultural product and that understanding an organization's culture afforded rich insights about everyday values, power, and the meaning of practices. Together, the concepts of systems thinking and organizational cultures combined to reveal that communication is both formative and transformative, and that attention to developing more conscious communicators was key to building learning organizations.

From these insights and histories we learned that all communication practices are important—from small talk to dialogue. However, the more skillful we become, and the more conscious we become, the more we move toward practicing the values associated with building a learning organization through dialogue. We saw that the learning organization captures an idealized conception of communication at work capable of inspiring us to place greater value, and more directed skill development, on our daily communication understandings and practices.

## COMMUNICATING IN PROFESSIONAL CONTEXTS ONLINE

All of the following chapter review materials are available in electronic format on either the Communicating in Professional Contexts website or CD-ROM. In addition to the multimedia case studies, activities, and numerous other learning resources you'll find on the CD-ROM, the CD is your gateway to the book's premium web content, which is not accessible via the Internet. The book's basic web content is available both with the premium content and on-line at http://communication.wadsworth.com/goodall2 and includes the chapter learning objectives and activities, key-term digital glossaries, and quizzes. The CD is also your gateway to InfoTrac College Edition, our extensive online database of full-text articles that is fully keyword searchable and available twenty-four hours a day. Installation instructions for the CD appear on the inside of this book's back cover.

## What You Should Have Learned

The learning objectives below are available on the Communicating in Professional Contexts website, which is best accessed through the book's CD-ROM but is also available at http://communication.wadsworth.com/goodall2. Go to the Chapter 2 Resources and click on Learning Objectives.

Now that you have read Chapter 2, you should be able to do the following:

+ Identify and define the two theories of management associated with the classical period of organizational management.

+ Identify the communication theory that corresponds to the classical period.

+ Identify and define the two studies associated with the human relations/resources period of organizational management theory.

+ Identify the communication theory that corresponds to the human relations/resources period and the three areas of communication research that were derived from this period.

+ Identify and define the components of a system.

+ Distinguish between formal and informal networks.

+ Define the term *organizational culture*.

+ Identify at least one theory of culture in organizations.

+ Discuss the different approaches to power and how our thinking about power in organizations has evolved.

+ Discuss organizational narratives and the types of research associated with them.

+ Define and discuss *dialogue*.

+ Discuss conscious communication, to include providing the continuum for communication from mindless to mindful communication.

+ Distinguish between mindless and mindful communication.

+ Identify and discuss the five disciplines of a learning organization.

+ Discuss the use of dialogue to build a learning organization.

## Key Terms

The terms below are available in a digital glossary on the Communicating in Professional Contexts website, which is best accessed through this book's CD-ROM but is also available at http://communication.wadsworth.com/goodall2. Go to the Chapter 2 Resources and click on Glossary.

| | | |
|---|---|---|
| **bureaucracy** *(37)* | **interdependence** *(42)* | **power** *(45)* |
| **dialogue** *(49)* | **learning organization** *(54)* | **scientific management** *(35)* |
| **environment** *(42)* | **mental models** *(54)* | **shared vision** *(54)* |
| **feedback** *(42)* | **mindful communication** *(52)* | **systems thinking** *(41)* |
| **goals** *(42)* | **mindless communication** *(50)* | **team learning** *(54)* |
| **hierarchy** *(35)* | **narrative** *(49)* | **transactional process model** *(40)* |
| **human relations movement** *(38)* | **organizational culture** *(44)* | |
| **information transfer model** *(37)* | **personal mastery** *(54)* | |

## Writing and Critical Thinking

The following activities can be completed online and, if requested, submitted to your instructor. You'll find them on the Communicating in Professional Contexts website, which is best accessed through the book's CD-ROM but is also available at http://communication.wadsworth.com/goodall2. Go to the Chapter 2 Resources and click on Writing and Critical Thinking Activities.

Choose one of the following activities:

1. Select a theory of organizational management. Describe the communication theory associated with the theory you selected. How are the theories linked? Link the tenets of the theory to your own organizational experiences.

2. Analyze a memorable conversation or dialogue from a current film. Look for points of theory described in the text. How does this exercise inform your understanding of the term *conscious communication?*

3. Working with your classmates as a group, select a theory discussed in this chapter that could help resolve the following situation:

*John has recently joined your team. He does not share the team's goal or vision for completing the project required by your instructor. He shows up for meetings without being adequately prepared, and he doesn't talk unless directly spoken to. Every team meeting is a struggle to get John on board.*

Which theory best describes this situation? What does the theory suggest as an intervention? Given what you have learned in this chapter, what might you and your team members do? What theories informed your answer?

4. Interview an employee in an organization and ask her or him to describe the following: What is the environment of the company? How does information flow through the company? How do decisions generally get made? What is the mechanism for employee feedback? What benefits do they perceive as an employee working for that company? Visit the web page of that same company and compare and contrast the profile presented by the employee with the one presented to the public on the web.

## Research and Explorations Online

The exercises below can be completed online and, if requested, submitted to your instructor. You'll find them on the Communicating in Professional Contexts website, which is best accessed through this book's CD-ROM but is also available at http://communication.wadsworth.com/goodall2. Go to the Chapter 2 Resources and click on Internet Exercises.

1. Organizational theories are the foundation for many of the management styles and practices you will experience in organizations. Select one of the theories discussed in this chapter and, using InfoTrac College Edition or the WWW, find an article from a major business journal or magazine that supports the theory you selected. For example, if you select bureaucracy as your theory, enter search terms such as *bureaucracy*, *Taylorism*, or *scientific management*.

2. Enter the term *learning organization* as a keyword search on InfoTrac College Edition or the WWW. Search for organizations that use this terminology. Pick an organization from your search. How well has the organization you selected embraced the concept of a learning organization?

3. Go to the American Communication Association homepage (http://www.uark.edu/~aca/). Click on the search engine for "organizational communication" and see what websites pop up. Cruise them for information that may be relevant to your assignments in this class and other classes.

4. Visit the Learning Organizations homepage (http://www.infed.org/thinkers/senge.htm). You will find many useful (and downloadable) articles on the origins and development of learning organizations, as well as some useful descriptions of organizational applications. You will also

find links to other websites that deal with learning organizations. In particular, you should visit the Stanford Learning Organization Web and the Business Researcher's Interests: Organizational Learning and Knowledge Management.

5. *Emotional intelligence* is a term used by Daniel Goleman in his writings to describe the role of emotions in our business and professional lives. Use InfoTrac College Edition and enter "An Interview with Daniel Goleman" in the keyword search. Identify how emotional intelligence could be effective in a learning organization. To test your emotional intelligence, go to http//ei.haygroup.com.

## Practicing Communication in Professional Contexts

### Moving from Mindless to Mindful Communication

The next breakthrough skill offers a special challenge and opportunity for communication growth. Spend an entire day communicating mindfully. To do justice to this activity, you must follow these guidelines:

+ *Avoid mindless communication.* Refrain from answering questions in ritualistic, routine ways. Rather than asking, "How are you?" ask, "How did your interview go yesterday?"

+ *Connect with each person you meet in a sincere and interested way.* Don't allow your mind to wander to others in the room, the things you need to do, what's happened to you in the past, or what you are going to have for lunch.

+ *Don't give up.* When you find yourself communicating mindlessly, simply remind yourself of your goal and get back on track.

+ *Communicate ethically.* Refrain from telling "little white lies" during your conscious communication.

+ *Communicate authentically.* Do not say things just to please people if you don't mean them; speak your mind, from your heart.

+ *Analyze each communication situation for the needs and expectations of others.* Think about possible communication choices before you speak. Adapt your communication to each listener or audience you encounter throughout the day.

+ *Ask for and honestly evaluate the feedback you receive.* Use the feedback to determine how successful you were in accomplishing your purpose and as a source of corrective information capable of informing future communication choices.

Keep a journal of your "conscious communication day." Note the communication events that were conducted mindfully and those in which you lapsed into mindless communication. What did you learn from your experience?

# Chapter Three

## Preparing for Conscious Communication in the Workplace

It was only Monday, but Beth already dreaded Friday. She was scheduled to make an important presentation outlining a new advertising campaign to an important client. The audience included the client and members of his staff, her CEO, and three other people representing the creative, marketing, and finance departments of Beth's firm. Her talk was scheduled for 1:30 in the afternoon, right after her CEO, Regina, returned from what undoubtedly would be a big lunch with the client. Beth had thirty minutes available: fifteen minutes for her presentation, and the remainder for questions. "At least," she mused, "the whole thing will be over by 2:00."

Beth wasn't nervous about her advertising skills. After all, she had graduated from a good school with a strong grade-point average. She had completed two solid internships with major advertising firms. She had five years of creative experience and belonged to an exciting new team. Since joining the firm, she had excelled at every task assigned to her, earning the respect of her team members. She knew how to plan an advertising campaign, and she felt the work she had done on this project was probably her best.

She had been thrilled when her team decided she should make Friday's presentation. Their boss, Todd, the project director, who normally would make the presentation, had fallen ill and wouldn't be able to do it. When he called and asked the project creative team who should give the presentation, everyone agreed Beth should. Beth was energized by their confidence and didn't want to let them down.

Beth had to find the best way to sell the client on this advertising campaign without giving away too many of the particulars. For one thing, although the broad strokes of the campaign were solid, many of the details had not yet been worked out. For another, it was a good idea to leave some areas of the campaign relatively undefined, so that the client would feel free to offer suggestions and feel as if he had a hand in the final design. The challenge, as Orin, one of Beth's team members, defined it, was "to create a presentation that was both strategic and ambiguous, that inspired confidence in their ability to deliver the campaign yet allowed for openness to ideas from the client."

Later that day, Beth received an e-mail from Todd, who added another perspective:

The client will be entertaining bids from two other vendors, which is another good reason not to give away too many details. However, we have to sell him on the essentials—the message, our campaign strategy, the ability of our team to do the work creatively and on time, and the soundness of our budget estimates. You have to show him that selecting us to do this campaign is vital to his business success. That is really your task. Beth, we selected you to do this for us because we all have the utmost confidence in your skills. Call me after the presentation and let me hear about your—our—success.

When she read this e-mail, Beth found an important clue. She needed more information about the client's business needs. So far, she had concentrated on the advertising and creative needs of the client. Now she needed to provide the client with a business reason for hiring her firm. Quickly, Beth was learning that audiences have multiple needs and expectations.

Michael Newman/PhotoEdit

*Beth appreciated Orin and Todd's views, but her own concerns were far more basic.
From her perspective, the real issue was the oral presentation itself. How should it be
organized? What should she say, and how should she say it? What visuals should be coordinated with her talk, and how could she maximize their influence? Another concern
was how she could control the nervousness she always felt when speaking in front of
people.*

*Beth hadn't given a formal speech since she was a sophomore in college. The project
talks she had given in her advertising classes had been team presentations, and she had
usually done the introductions or conclusions, leaving the heavier work of organizing the
content to others. She had been hired for her present job in part because she was a "good
communicator," but she felt she was far more effective one-on-one, or in a team, than
when giving a talk on her own. Now she sat facing her computer screen and didn't have
a clue what to say or do. Beth needed to get organized. But how? Then Beth remembered a presentation she had attended recently on conscious communication and a process for organizing communication. Maybe now was a good time to give it a try.*

## Organizing a Communication Event

As you learned in Chapter 2, communication is closely allied with organization
(Weick, 1995). The activity of organizing is also a communication activity, and
vice versa. Your communication organizes possibilities for meaning to occur.
How well you organize — or intentionally shape — your communication has a
lot to do with how successful you will be. This is because "order" also means
"pattern" and, as the communication theorist Gregory Bateson (1992) ob-
served, "All communication is pattern recognition."

In its simplest form, the CCCD (choose, create, coordinate, and deliver) process introduced in Chapter 1 mirrors the "Think before you speak" adage many of us heard from our parents. In a more complex form, the CCCD process provides you with a powerful tool for organizing interpersonal, team, group, presentational, and public communication episodes and events. Although each of the steps in CCCD applies to all of the contexts for communication, not every step needs to be completed in the same detail for each context. For example, when speaking to a coworker about a project, we must choose our goal, create our strategy, coordinate our efforts, and deliver the message. However, we spend less time assessing the audience than we would if we were speaking to someone we didn't know or to a large group of people. Nor is it necessary to develop elaborate supporting materials or computer-assisted visual aids for a one-on-one talk with a colleague.

Throughout this chapter, we will use Beth's presentation to introduce the CCCD process. This allows us to illustrate how the process can be applied to organize a complex communication event. The example used in this chapter centers around a persuasive communication event, but in subsequent chapters you will see how CCCD can be used as a general framework to improve the communication competence for any type of communication event. Throughout the book we will demonstrate how aspects of the CCCD process can be applied to interpersonal, group, team, public, mediated, and other types of presentational communication events.

But first, we will walk you through the CCCD process using Beth's presentation. Let's begin by reviewing the four steps in the CCCD process.

1. *Choose* a goal for your message based on an intelligent assessment of the business and professional culture, the expectations and needs of audience members, the possibilities for interpretation of your intended meaning, and the likely outcomes.
2. *Create* a strategic and ethical plan for accomplishing your message goal with the targeted audience, including verbal, nonverbal, and visual appeals.
3. *Coordinate* the event or episode with other people who will have an influence on shaping a successful outcome.
4. *Deliver* your presentation after practicing it and gaining feedback on your performance.

We begin our discussion with step 1.

## Step 1: Choosing a Goal for Your Message

The first step in the CCCD process is to establish a goal for your message. To effectively define your goal, you must

1. *Assess your audience*. Determine who your listeners are, along with their needs and expectations. Think about the reasons your listeners will be

helped if they accept your ideas. It is also a good idea to examine the ways in which they—or you—may be negatively affected if the communication episode doesn't go as planned.

2. *Generate outcomes.* Determine what you want your listeners to know, believe, or do as a result of your presentation.

3. *Establish criteria for measuring success.* Determine how you will know if you have been successful in attaining your goal.

In most business and professional settings, these tasks involve interpreting information from a variety of sources. Let's see how Beth accomplished each of these tasks.

## Assessing Audience Needs and Expectations

When assessing the needs of the audience, many speakers mistakenly assume that their own needs should be of utmost importance. Unfortunately, the **audience needs and expectations** and those of the speaker are rarely the same. Successful communicators recognize that although it is important to know what you personally expect to get out of giving a presentation, it is even more important to understand what your listeners should gain or expect to gain from it. After all, listeners are our clients and customers in business and professional communication environments. As in every other aspect of doing business, meeting the needs of our customers is a primary goal.

To meet her client's needs, as well as the expectations of her boss and coworkers, Beth should put herself in her client's shoes and identify the reasons he would agree or disagree with her presentation. To help her determine what these reasons might be, she should ask:

+ What ideas and strategies have worked in the past with this particular audience? Has anyone in my firm dealt with this audience before? What can I learn from them?

+ What reasons, authorities, examples, and "truths" does this audience regularly use to justify his position in reaching his goals? Is there some way to gain access to past advertising campaigns used by this client, or statements the client has made about why he chose a particular campaign or firm?

+ What information can I gain from written or electronic sources to help me better understand our client? Do any recent publications quote or feature the client? Does the client's company maintain a website with useful information about their culture and values? Do I have friends or business contacts who might know valuable information? Can and should these be incorporated into my presentation?

Collecting this information can help Beth determine how the client might comparatively evaluate her campaign against any competitor's. Once she comes up with the reasons the client may agree or disagree with her presentation, she can

- create arguments within the presentation that satisfy the needs and expectations of the client,

- insert the client's reasoning and values or beliefs into the presentation, and

- plan to articulate the information gained from research during the question-and-answer session.

While Beth thinks through her presentation from the client's perspective, she also needs to consider what the client may see as objections to or potential problems of the campaign. Here again, Beth should spend time coming up with the scenarios that could occur if the client doesn't accept her reasoning. She can use this information either by offering a section toward the end of the presentation to articulate and overcome possible objections, or by including responses to objections in her question-and-answer session.

*Thinking back on Todd's advice and the meeting with her team members, Beth identified two distinct audiences for her presentation: the client, and the members of her own firm. Each would be coming to the presentation with very different needs and expectations.*

*To address the needs of her client, Beth decided (a) she must convince the client that her firm has a valuable idea for the advertising campaign, and (b) the initial presentation should allow for creative input from the client. If her talk made it seem that their advertising company had it all figured out, this could suggest to the client that they were unwilling to listen to input or work with him on details.*

*To address the needs of her CEO and team members, Beth thought she must demonstrate the close working relationship between the client and the project team. She also needed to sell herself and her team as a friendly, open, cooperative group that knows its stuff. To do this, she would have to present herself as a professional and knowledgeable team player.*

*Beth created the following worksheet of audience needs and expectations.*

| **Step 1:** CHOOSING A GOAL—Audience Needs and Expectations | |
|---|---|
| **Audience** | **Needs and Expectations** |
| Client | • Find an advertising firm that balances the creative needs of the project with the company's business needs (i.e., budget, time constraints, competition concerns). <br> • Commit to a creative team that best represents the product, is open to ideas, and can work well with the company during this project. |
| Firm | • Sell the client on the concept of the campaign without giving away too many details. <br> • Convince the client that the firm's message, strategy, team, and budget are better than the competitors' (without knowing the details of either competitor's campaign). |

*(continued)*

| Step 1: CHOOSING A GOAL—Audience Needs and Expectations (*cont.*) | |
|---|---|
| **Audience** | **Needs and Expectations** |
| Beth | ✦ Make a professional-quality presentation within an advertising/sales environment by meeting the goals of the firm.<br>✦ Satisfy and, if possible, favorably impress the boss and the other members of the firm by representing them successfully. |

## Determining the Possible Communication Outcomes

The **outcome** of a communication event is what you achieve as a result of speaking. Four general communication outcomes can be used to shape a goal statement for a business and professional presentation:

1. *Inform* listeners about an idea, process, or concept.
2. *Persuade* listeners to accept, purchase, value, or act on the information presented.
3. *Entertain* listeners.
4. *Build a business relationship* with listeners.

In some contexts, only one communication outcome will guide the preparation of the talk. Every day, people communicate with the goal to inform, *or* to persuade, *or* to entertain, *or* to build relationships. In other situations, there are multiple likely outcomes. For example, Beth knows that her job is to both inform and persuade her client, but she also realizes that her talk will be instrumental in building a business relationship between the client and the firm. This knowledge has direct implications for how Beth interprets her goal, organizes her presentation, assembles supporting materials, and answers questions.

Beth also needs to determine what her own communication outcome should be. Is she most interested in being seen by her client as a competent provider of information? As an effective salesperson? As an informative and entertaining speaker? As the kind of person the client would want to work with on a project? Beth added an outcomes column to her worksheet.

After reviewing all the possible audiences, needs and expectations, and outcomes, Beth decided to focus on the second entry under her firm's needs and expectations: "Convince the client that the firm's message, strategy, team, and budget are better than the competitors' (without knowing the details of either competitor's campaign)." Beth believed that if she made this the main priority of her presentation, all the other outcomes would be met.

## Establishing Criteria to Measure Success

Specifying **criteria** for measuring success means thinking about the desirable statements, behaviors, or actions that you want to receive from your audience

| **Step 1:** CHOOSING A GOAL—Outcomes | | |
|---|---|---|
| **Audience** | **Needs and Expectations** | **Outcomes** |
| Client | ◆ Find an advertising firm that balances the creative needs of the project with the company's business needs (i.e., budget, time constraints, competition concerns).<br><br>◆ Commit to a creative team that best represents the product, is open to ideas, and can work well with the company during this project. | ◆ *Inform* the client about the campaign concepts.<br><br>◆ *Persuade* the client that the firm is better equipped to handle his advertising needs than the other firms he has investigated.<br><br>◆ *Build a business relationship* that results in a commitment to Beth's firm. |
| Firm | ◆ Sell the client on the concept of the campaign without giving away too many details.<br><br>◆ Convince the client that the firm's message, strategy, team, and budget are better than the competitors' (without knowing the details of either competitor's campaign). | ◆ *Persuade* team members and supervisor that Beth's ideas are based on solid research and creative efforts that present the best campaign possible.<br><br>◆ *Build on the team's relationship* so they feel they have successfully met the client's creative and business needs.<br><br>◆ *Inform* through feedback that Beth's presentation hit the mark. |
| Beth | ◆ Make a professional-quality presentation within an advertising/sales environment by meeting the goals of the firm.<br><br>◆ Satisfy and, if possible, favorably impress the boss and the other members of the firm by representing them successfully. | ◆ *Convince* Beth that she did the best job possible.<br><br>◆ *Build on her relationship* with her team to successfully implement the ideas presented to the client. |

during and after the presentation. Specifying these criteria will help you determine if you have reached your personal and business goals. It is also an excellent way to learn from a communication event or episode. By establishing criteria for an event and measuring the success of your communication against them, you learn how your communication may or may not have met the needs and expectations of your audience. As we saw in Chapters 1 and 2, positive and corrective feedback can and should help us to improve our communication skills.

What would Beth need to hear to know that she had provided the client with all the information he needed to make a decision? Or that she had made an effective presentation? Or that the client would be interested in pursuing a working relationship with her company? Learning to articulate these evaluative standards will help Beth reach her goal. She added a criteria column to her worksheet.

| **Step 1:** CHOOSING A GOAL—Criteria | | | |
|---|---|---|---|
| **Audience** | **Needs and Expectations** | **Outcomes** | **Criteria** |
| Client | ◆ Find an advertising firm that balances the creative needs of the project with the company's business needs (i.e., budget, time constraints, competition concerns).<br><br>◆ Commit to a creative team that best represents the product, is open to ideas, and can work well with the company during this project. | ◆ *Inform* the client about the campaign concepts.<br><br>◆ *Persuade* the client that the firm is better equipped to handle his advertising needs than the other firms he has investigated.<br><br>◆ *Build a business relationship* that results in a commitment to Beth's firm. | ◆ Shows interest in the ideas presented and favorably compares the concept to those presented at competing firms.<br><br>◆ Commends the firm on their ideas, teamwork, and attention to the client's needs.<br><br>◆ Agrees to the concept and is interested in discussing the terms set forth in the presentation. |
| Firm | ◆ Sell the client on the concept of the campaign without giving away too many details.<br><br>◆ Convince the client that the firm's message, strategy, team, and budget are better than the competitors' (without knowing the details of either competitor's campaign). | ◆ *Persuade* team members and supervisor that Beth's ideas are based on solid research and creative efforts that present the best campaign possible.<br><br>◆ *Build on the team's relationship* so they feel they have successfully met the client's creative and business needs.<br><br>◆ *Inform* through feedback that Beth's presentation hit the mark. | ◆ The team nods and smiles throughout the presentation.<br><br>◆ The CEO supports Beth during the presentation, interjecting only to emphasize or clarify a point being made.<br><br>◆ Her team congratulates her on her performance.<br><br>◆ Her boss thanks her for her hard work. |
| Beth | ◆ Make a professional-quality presentation within an advertising/sales environment by meeting the goals of the firm.<br><br>◆ Satisfy and, if possible, favorably impress the boss and the other members of the firm by representing them successfully. | ◆ *Convince* Beth that she did the best job possible.<br><br>◆ *Build on her relationship* with her team to successfully implement the ideas presented to the client. | ◆ She is confident and calm throughout her presentation.<br><br>◆ She walks away knowing she did a good job.<br><br>◆ She doesn't second-guess her information, presentation, or ability. |

To prepare for the first presentation in this class, we suggest making a worksheet like Beth's. Fill it out as you develop your presentation. Clearly defining your audience, outcomes, criteria, and goals will help you to be successful in class as well as in the workplace.

## Step 2: Creating a Strategic and Ethical Message

The second step in the CCCD process is to create the message. To create a successful message capable of accomplishing the goals outlined in step 1, you must do the following:

1. Determine the thesis of your message.
2. Determine the organization of the main points for the body of your talk.
3. Support each of your main points.
4. Create transitions for each of your main points.
5. Develop an effective introduction and conclusion.

Obviously, if you are communicating interpersonally, you may not need to write down your purpose, main points, supporting materials, transitions, and introduction and conclusion. However, you do need to consider each of these elements before you speak. Many professional communicators use the term *talking points* to refer to items organized for a one-on-one or group discussion. Communicating consciously requires you to be mindful of the process of communicating effectively with others in all communication contexts. Let's follow Beth through the process of creating her presentation.

### Creating a Thesis Statement

Beth needed to turn her goals into a general thesis statement that would guide the development of the presentation. After reviewing her Step 1: Choosing a Goal worksheet, Beth wrote the following purpose on her Step 2: Creating the Message worksheet under "Purpose and Thesis Statement."

| Step 2: CREATING THE MESSAGE—Purpose | | | |
|---|---|---|---|
| **Introduction** | | | |
| **Purpose and Thesis Statement** | **Main Points** | **Support** | **Transitions** |
| ✦ To provide compelling information about a new advertising campaign theme, strategy, and budget with the intention of persuading the client that the firm can do the best job. | | | |
| **Conclusion** | | | |

The **purpose** is a general statement that defines the primary goal for your message. Beth's next step was to use the purpose to create her thesis statement.

A **thesis statement** is a simple declarative sentence that (a) introduces your audience to your message and (b) announces your intentions. In most business and professional contexts, the thesis statement sets up expectations among listeners that they will use to evaluate the effectiveness—and truthfulness—of your message. For this reason, it was vital that Beth not misrepresent herself or her goals for the presentation.

For example, because she wanted the presentation to sufficiently motivate the client to sign a contract with her firm, she needed to focus on the persuasive intent of her presentation. But she also didn't want to overdo it. She wanted the client to buy her campaign because it met his needs and expectations, and because it would do a better job for him than other campaigns offered by her competitors.

Beth had to condense all of these thoughts and feelings into a simple declarative sentence. To do this, she envisioned speaking directly to her client. Then she wrote on her worksheet what she would say to him one-on-one, as if they were engaged in a business conversation.

| **Step 2:** CREATING THE MESSAGE—Thesis Statement | | | |
|---|---|---|---|
| **Introduction** | | | |
| **Purpose and Thesis Statement** | **Main Points** | **Support** | **Transitions** |
| ◆ To provide compelling information about a new advertising campaign theme, strategy, and budget with the intention of persuading the client that the firm can do the best job.<br><br>◆ I will present to you our concept that we believe will help you reach your product sales goals and open your product to additional markets, while remaining within the budget guidelines you specified. | | | |
| **Conclusion** | | | |

Beth translated her informational and persuasive goals into a simple thesis designed to show how she planned to meet the listener's needs and expectations. Developing a clear and concise thesis statement would help Beth determine a preferred organizational pattern for the body of the presentation.

## Determining the Main Points of the Message

Generally speaking, business and professional presentations contain two to four major points. The number of points depends on the organization pattern that best accomplishes your purpose. However, research has demonstrated that if you use more than four main points, the chances are very good that listeners will forget some of them (Ehninger, 1974). Let's examine in more detail the relationship between your choice of organization pattern and the number of main points that best accomplishes it.

Four basic organization patterns can be used to structure a presentation:

+ **causal**—offering a cause and effect

+ **problem–solution**—stating a problem and a solution

+ **chronological**—detailing the sequence of events

+ **topical**—outlining the main ideas surrounding the problem or issue

Some thesis statements naturally lend themselves to causal or problem-solution reasoning. Others require a chronological sequence that provides a historical overview and development of an idea. Others suggest that a logical series of topics be presented to guide listeners' understanding.

Beth needed an organizational pattern that captured the major points she planned to cover. She considered using causal but drew a blank. Then she considered problem–solution. This pattern had merit, because she could approach the development of her presentation as the solving of her client's problem: how to select an appropriate advertising campaign. But did this format allow her to present her ideas about the theme, or the implementation strategies, or even the budget? She decided it didn't. The chronological sequence also had appeal. She could use it to describe the evolution of her team's ideas about the proposed campaign, ending with a vision of how the client's sales would increase as a

| Basic Organizational Patterns | | |
|---|---|---|
| **Two Main Points** | **Three Main Points** | **Four Main Points** |
| + *Causal Pattern* Cause>>>Effect  + *Problem–Solution* Problem>>>Solution | + *Chronology* ◇ Past ◇ Present ◇ Future | + *Topical* ◇ Basic idea ◇ Implementation of the idea ◇ Budget for implementation ◇ How it all works |

**Table 3.1**
Organizational
Patterns for Messages

result of the advertisements. But on further reflection, she rejected this pattern because she favored a softer sales approach, one that would allow the client to ask questions at the end. She wanted *his* vision, not hers, to be the last word. Finally, she chose the topical pattern because it would allow her to develop her ideas about the theme, the campaign, and the budget logically, from the customer's point of view.

Next, Beth developed a preview statement containing the best progression of her main points, as they evolved from her thesis statement. The preview prepares listeners for the informational content of the message by giving them advance notice of what they will be hearing. Using her topical pattern as a guide, she jotted down her main points.

| **Step 2:** CREATING THE MESSAGE—Main Points | | | |
|---|---|---|---|
| **Introduction** | | | |
| **Purpose and Thesis Statement** | **Main Points** | **Support** | **Transitions** |
| ◆ To provide compelling information about a new advertising campaign theme, strategy, and budget with the intention of persuading the client that the firm can do the best job.<br><br>◆ I will present to you our concept that we believe will help you reach your product sales goals and open your product to additional markets, while remaining within the budget guidelines you specified. | ◆ First, I will describe our concept and explain why we believe it will appeal to your target market.<br><br>◆ Second, I will provide a timeline of how we will implement the concept.<br><br>◆ Third, I will outline our proposed budget, which I'm sure you will find well within your prescribed parameters.<br><br>◆ Finally, I will answer any questions or discuss ideas you may have. | | |
| **Conclusion** | | | |

Beth's work on her presentation thus far had produced a specific purpose and a general topical plan for accomplishing it. What Beth did was translate the topics she knew must be covered into a topical pattern that would lead listeners from an understanding of the information (her first three main points) they would need to make a decision, to a subtle persuasive appeal (her fourth main point) for gaining the business. She felt the natural collaboration between presenter and client during a question-and-answer session would provide her with the best opportunity to respond to specific needs and satisfy his expectations.

Her next task was to expand on and support the main points in the body of her talk. To accomplish this task, she outlined the subpoints for each main point. She added these subpoints to her worksheet.

| **Step 2:** CREATING THE MESSAGE—Subpoints | | | |
|---|---|---|---|
| **Introduction** | | | |
| **Purpose and Thesis Statement** | **Main Points** | **Support** | **Transitions** |
| ◆ To provide compelling information about a new advertising campaign theme, strategy, and budget with the intention of persuading the client that the firm can do the best job. <br><br> ◆ I will present to you our concept that we believe will help you reach your product sales goals and open your product to additional markets, while remaining within the budget guidelines you specified. | ◆ *First, I will describe our concept and explain why we believe it will appeal to your target market.* <br> ◇ Concept <br> ◇ Connection to target market <br><br> ◆ *Second, I will provide a timeline of how we will implement the concept.* <br> ◇ October–January <br> ◇ February–April <br> ◇ May–August <br><br> ◆ *Third, I will outline our proposed budget, which I'm sure you will find well within your prescribed parameters.* <br> ◇ Total budget <br> ◇ Cost breakdowns by category <br> ◇ Justification for budget <br><br> ◆ *Finally, I will answer any questions or discuss ideas you may have.* <br> ◇ Request for questions <br> ◇ Request for business | | |
| **Conclusion** | | | |

By outlining the subpoints derived from the main points in her speech, Beth knew exactly what additional information she needed to provide. She also began to see where in her presentation she would need to use supporting materials.

## Developing Supporting Materials

Supporting materials add interest, visual impact, and credibility to your message. How many presentations, team meetings, or group discussions have you attended where the speaker droned on and on, mostly repeating the same main points over and over again? Is it any wonder that the audience's attention began to wander shortly after the speaker began talking? In today's high-tech, visually driven world, few people will sit still long enough to listen to anyone who isn't an incredibly captivating speaker, or who doesn't use interesting and engaging graphics to support the verbal message. In this section, we will discuss two types of support you can use to increase the impact of your message: verbal support and visual support. At the end of each subsection, we will review the types of support Beth selected for her presentation. We begin with verbal support.

### Verbal Support

Often, business messages contain complex new ideas or concepts. Verbal support can make complicated messages or ideas clear. They can add punch to a message and credibility to concepts that might fall outside your audience's field of experience or expertise. There are four types of verbal supporting materials to use when developing the oral content of your message:

- ✦ facts and statistics
- ✦ testimony or authoritative sources
- ✦ examples
- ✦ narratives or personal stories

*Facts and Statistics*    **Facts** are sources of basic, empirically verifiable information. **Statistics** are basic, empirically verifiable, numerical representations of information. By "empirically verifiable," we mean that the statistics or statements represented as facts are drawn from credible sources and may be checked out by audience members. Facts and statistics have benefits and drawbacks. If used effectively, they offer quick, credible support for your message. They are often overused, though, and as a result, people in business environments have developed the attitude that "you can find a statistic to support any position"—which, by and large, is true.

Nevertheless, facts and statistics can lend persuasive impact to your presentation. The following principles will help you use facts and statistics effectively.

+ Use statistics only from credible sources.

+ Be sure that any statistics you use can be validated independently.

+ Limit the use of statistics. Don't use more than one or two facts or statistics for each main point.

+ Tie your statistics to your audience. Don't use a furnishing industry statistic in a talk about auto parts unless there is a direct and obvious connection.

+ Use graphics to illustrate your statistics.

*Testimonies and Authoritative Sources*   If appropriate to your topic and taken from a source recognizable to your audience, testimonies and authoritative quotations add instant credibility to your talk. Like facts and statistics, testimonies and authoritative sources have both benefits and drawbacks.

If the audience is familiar with the person offering the testimony, or believes the citation comes from a credible source, these forms of support may prove compelling. On the other hand, given the diverse views of most audiences, it may be difficult to locate a quotation from a source that has universal appeal. One person's idol—Bill Gates, Jesse Jackson, or Sandra Day O'Connor—may be disregarded by another. In general, when using testimonies and authoritative sources, do the following:

+ Use quotes only from sources your audience will find credible.

+ Make sure the citation ties directly to your topic. Don't name-drop simply for the sake of name-dropping.

+ Cite only the information that is necessary to make your point. Don't use a long, confusing quote if only one sentence is needed.

+ Tie your citation to your audience. Don't quote a furnishing industry executive in a talk to managers of auto parts stores unless there is a direct and obvious connection.

*Examples and Narratives*   Examples and narratives provide memorable elaboration for main points and subpoints. Although extremely effective forms of support, they may require time to develop, a higher level of confidence and competence on the part of the speaker, and a close, personal identification between the listeners and the example or story used.

Presentational speakers using examples and stories often require additional rehearsal time to find the most effective method of phrasing, modulations in tone of voice, and strategic placement of internal pauses. Used well, examples and narratives humanize information and build rapport between a speaker and an audience.

Many speakers limit their use of personal stories or narratives to attention-gaining material for the introduction and leave-taking material for the conclusion. By contrast, examples can be effective when used throughout the talk, and they are particularly effective as support for the main points and subpoints in the body of a speech. To effectively use examples and personal narratives, follow these guidelines:

- ◆ Carefully choose examples and narratives with regard to the cultural, professional, gender, racial, and socioeconomic considerations of your audience.
- ◆ Make sure the story or example is memorable (you may want to try it out on friends or coworkers prior to using it in a presentation).
- ◆ Try to use fresh examples and stories—ones that haven't been heard by the listeners before.

Beth had to determine how much time she was willing to devote to each topic. To make that decision, she considered—from the audience's perspective—how much verbal support each topic would require and what specific types of support might do the best job. She reviewed her worksheet and added the following types of verbal support to each main point.

| **Step 2:** CREATING THE MESSAGE—Forms of Support | | | |
|---|---|---|---|
| **Introduction** | | | |
| **Purpose and Thesis Statement** | **Main Points** | **Support** | **Transitions** |
| ◆ To provide compelling information about a new advertising campaign theme, strategy, and budget with the intention of persuading the client that the firm can do the best job. | ◆ *First, I will describe our concept and explain why we believe it will appeal to your target market.*<br>  ◇ Concept<br>  ◇ Connection to target market<br>◆ *Second, I will provide a timeline of how we will implement the concept.*<br>  ◇ October–January<br>  ◇ February–April<br>  ◇ May–August | ◆ *Concept—fact and examples*<br>  ◇ Two examples of successful campaigns from the same target market<br>◆ *Target Market—statistics*<br>  ◇ Current numbers representing the size of the market and target demographics<br>◆ *Timeline—fact and examples*<br>  ◇ Which media we will use and examples of how they will be used at each stage in the campaign | |

*(continued)*

| **Step 2:** CREATING THE MESSAGE—Forms of Support *(continued)* | | | |
|---|---|---|---|
| **Purpose and Thesis Statement** | **Main Points** | **Support** | **Transitions** |
| ◆ I will present to you our concept that we believe will help you reach your product sales goals and open your product to additional markets, while remaining within the budget guidelines you specified. | ◆ Third, I will outline our proposed budget, which I'm sure you will find well within your prescribed parameters.<br>◇ Total budget<br>◇ Cost breakdowns by category<br>◇ Justification for budget<br>◆ Finally, I will answer any questions or discuss ideas you may have.<br>◇ Request for questions<br>◇ Request for business | ◆ Budget—statistics, authoritative sources, and examples<br>◇ Total budget—statistical breakdown<br>◇ Cost breakdown—statistical breakdown of each category and statements from clients illustrating the cost savings compared to other firms<br>◇ Justification—review examples for each phase and show quality vs. cost<br>◆ Questions and request for business—examples and personal narrative<br>◇ Review examples to illustrate points brought up during the question period<br>◇ Describe my experience with the firm, my clients, and why I think the concept and the firm are the best investment for the client | |
| **Conclusion** | | | |

## Visual Support

The old cliché "A picture is worth a thousand words" simply no longer holds true. Visual messages bombard us. In an average day, we see 3,500 advertisements, including commercials, billboards, print ads, brand names, and webpage banners (Jhally, 1997). Only a few years ago, it was considered cutting edge to enter a meeting, flip open your laptop, and begin a slideshow presentation. Now most business people have developed a "Been there, done that" attitude to most presentational software special effects. Face it: words and pictures that morph, fade, and slide off a screen are interesting the first few times we witness them. After that, they may join the crowd in an already visually overloaded day.

That said, there is still an important place for well-developed, relevant visual materials that are used to support a message. Visual supports range from traditional flip charts, physical objects, and storyboards to more advanced slideshow presentations, models, and demonstrations. Each type of visual support should be understood in relation to its audience and context to make its use more effective. In Appendix A, the Visual Support Reference Guide, we provide a comprehensive list of the types of visual support, the appropriate audiences for them, do's and don'ts for display, and practical advice for using them.

Before selecting the type of visual support you will use, you should follow these steps:

+ *Determine the visual needs and professional expectations of your audience.* For example, engineers generally expect fairly technical visual support in the form of schematics or technical drawings, whereas a group of nurses would rather see live demonstrations of new techniques.

+ *Preview the meeting or presentation location.* An engineers' meeting in a conference room wired for Internet hookups could easily use forms of computer technology to produce and display visual support.

+ *Be aware of the time constraints.* A well-prepared and rehearsed slideshow may not add additional time constraints to your presentation. However, a presentation that depends heavily on the Internet must allow for web pages that load slowly during peak hours of use and the likely impatience of the audience during those information display delays. You might consider saving pages before the presentation, in case you have problems with your connection.

+ *Determine the method that best adds visual quality, not quantity, to the message.* Showing a client the blueprints for every building ever designed by an architect may have less impact than showing one well-executed design, a model, and a picture of a building that matches to the building needs expressed by the client.

*Beth was lucky. She worked for a company and in an industry that afforded her the technology and the knowledge to create powerful visual messages to enhance her presentation. She decided to make use of both traditional and advanced types of support. To set the agenda for the presentation, lay out the main points and timeline for the campaign, and highlight the factual and statistical support of the talk, she would use a digital slide presentation. To showcase the concept, she would use traditional storyboards (large pieces of poster board with artwork representing each phase of the project). This would allow her to break up the visual portion of the presentation and avoid having her audience stare at the same projection screen for thirty minutes.*

*Beth now had most of the elements she needed for a strong presentation. This CCCD process was really making it easy to plan, organize, and develop her message. What was next?*

## Making Transitions

**Transitions** are devices that help audience members listen more effectively. Think of a transition as an internal signpost that provides directions to the audience members about (a) upcoming changes in the point being made, or (b) internal movements in reasoning that will occur in the speech. They may also serve as previews or reviews of material and as internal summaries.

The lack of good transitions creates four types of listening problems:

1. Confusion can occur when a speaker has moved to a new point but the listener hears what is being said as support for the last main point.
2. Boredom can occur when the speaker relies on the same device repeatedly, such as saying, "Next."
3. Listeners will perceive speakers as less effective because of the overuse of unplanned transition-fillers, such as "okay," or "you know," or "well."
4. Listeners may become lost or disoriented in the message due to the lack of a consistent reminder about the order used to develop the ideas.

To avoid these problems, speakers make use of several types of transitional devices, as illustrated in Table 3.2.

*Beth realized that several places in her presentation called for effective transitions. She added them to her worksheet, being careful to vary the type of transition.*

*Beth was almost finished with her presentation worksheet. All that remained for her to accomplish was writing an introduction and conclusion.*

## Developing an Effective Introduction and Conclusion

Beginnings and endings in oral communication are uniquely interrelated. In part, this is because structurally, they surround the body of a talk, serving to preview and review its key points. Within North American culture, we have learned to expect to hear in the ending of a presentation some reminder of what we heard during the beginning of it. A good presentation is circular; it returns to where it began, giving the audience a feeling of closure and completeness.

To accomplish this, the introduction and conclusion should wrap around the main points of the presentation by developing a complete thematic package. Occasionally, the theme for a presentation arises before the presentation is developed. More often, the theme evolves from the main points of the presen-

**Table 3.2**
Types of Transitional
Devices

| When you need to: | Use this type of transition: |
|---|---|
| Introduce or preview topics in the speech | First, second, and third<br>One, two, three<br>A, B, C |
| Signal topic changes in cause–effect, problem–solution, and chronology patterns during the body of the speech | "Now that we have seen how X occurred, let's examine its influences on Y."<br>"Now that we understand the problem, it is time to explore solutions."<br>"The past has provided us with X. The present has given us Y. If you are like me, you are wondering what the future holds." |
| Offer extended explanations of key definitions or ideas | For example . . .<br>To illustrate . . .<br>Simply put . . .<br>Allow me to clarify . . .<br>In other words . . . |
| Alert listeners to spatial relationships | Think of the face on a clock. At one o'clock we see X; at four o'clock we find Y; at eight o'clock we locate Z.<br>To the east . . . ; to the west . . .<br>Alongside, behind, in front of, next to, below, above. |
| Remind your audience of your main points prior to moving to your recommendations | "We have seen that there are three causes of our problem. They are: 1, which is caused by X; 2, which is brought about by Y; and 3, which is generated by Z. Now let's see what a solution should include and how we can work to implement it." |

tation, which is why we suggest writing the introduction and conclusion last rather than first.

An effective introduction should do the following:

+ *Gain the listener's or audience's attention.* There are many effective ways to gain attention:

   + Ask an interesting question directly related to the theme of your speech.

   + Use a startling statement or an appropriate quotation.

   + Relate a personal experience that ties into the topic.

   + Tell a brief story that develops suspense or makes a humorous point.

   + Use a captivating or startling image.

+ *State a thesis.* Explain in a clear and concise manner the topic of your presentation or the basis of your message.

+ *Preview the main points in the body of the speech.* Outline the main points in your presentation using signposts to alert the audience or listener to topical divisions. For example: "First, I will discuss the concept we have developed. Second, I will discuss the time frames associated with the concept. Third, I will go over the budget estimates associated with the project. Finally, I will answers any questions you might have."

+ *Offer an inducement.* Explain to listeners what benefit will accrue to them—what they will learn that they don't already know, or what they will be able to do that they can't already do—as a result of their participation in the speech.

| **Step 2:** CREATING THE MESSAGE—Transitions | | | |
|---|---|---|---|
| **Introduction** | | | |
| **Purpose and Thesis Statement** | **Main Points** | **Support** | **Transitions** |
| + To provide compelling information about a new advertising campaign theme, strategy, and budget with the intention of persuading the client that the firm can do the best job. | + *First, I will describe our concept and explain why we believe it will appeal to your target market.*<br>⋄ Concept<br>⋄ Connection to target market<br><br>+ *Second, I will provide a timeline of how we will implement the concept.*<br>⋄ October–January<br>⋄ February–April<br>⋄ May–August<br><br>+ *Third, I will outline our proposed budget, which I'm sure you will find well within your prescribed parameters.*<br>⋄ Total budget<br>⋄ Cost breakdowns by category<br>⋄ Justification for budget | + *Concept—fact and examples*<br>⋄ Two examples of successful campaigns from the same target market<br><br>+ *Target Market— statistics*<br>⋄ Current numbers representing the size of the market and target demographics<br><br>+ *Timeline—fact and examples*<br>⋄ Which media we will use and examples of how they will be used at each stage in the campaign<br><br>+ *Budget—statistics, authoritative sources, and examples*<br>⋄ Total budget— statistical breakdown | + *Introduction*<br>⋄ Preview the flow of the talk<br><br>+ *Concept*<br>⋄ Simply put, the concept will allow us to reach the target market by . . .<br><br>+ *Timeline*<br>⋄ Now that you have seen the concept, I would like to take a few minutes to discuss the timeline.<br><br>+ *Budget—statistics, authoritative sources, and examples*<br>⋄ Of course, a timeline this rigorous requires an investment . . .<br><br>+ *Questions and request for business*<br>⋄ Review main points<br>⋄ Return to introduction<br><br>*(continued)* |

| Step 2: CREATING THE MESSAGE—Transitions (continued) | | | |
|---|---|---|---|
| **Purpose and Thesis Statement** | **Main Points** | **Support** | **Transitions** |
| • I will present to you our concept that we believe will help you reach your product sales goals and open your product to additional markets, while remaining within the budget guidelines you specified. | • Finally, I will answer any questions or discuss ideas you may have.<br>  ◇ Request for questions<br>  ◇ Request for business | • Budget—statistics, authoritative sources, and examples (cont.)<br>  ◇ Cost breakdown— statistical breakdown of each category and statements from clients illustrating the cost savings compared to other firms<br>  ◇ Justification— review examples for each phase and show quality vs. cost<br>• Questions and request for business— examples and personal narrative<br>  ◇ Review examples to illustrate points brought up during the question period<br>  ◇ Describe my experience with the firm, my clients, and why I think the concept and the firm are the best investment for the client | |
| **Conclusion** | | | |

Conclusions also have more than one function. An effective conclusion provides a review of the main points in the body of the presentation, as well as a sense of closure by returning in some way to the attention-gaining device used in the beginning of the talk.

*Beth thought about how to introduce her presentation. She knew her thesis and preview statements accomplished their business purpose, and she knew what inducement she could offer—the advertising campaign that would ensure the business success of this new product. What she didn't know was how to creatively grab her audience's attention. Until she had that firmly in mind, she also had no ending for her speech.*

*She decided to try out several approaches. Because the speech already included a lot of statistics and quotations from authorities, she ruled out these attention-gaining devices. She tried to put herself in the listener's position, and when she did so, she saw that the presentation lacked variety. Perhaps she should begin with a startling image? Perhaps some humor? No. The startling image might distract attention from the concept, and humor was always a bit risky with an unknown client. She remembered the CCCD speaker saying that for humor to be effective, she needed to understand the sense of humor of the client and try out the material on a similarly disposed listener beforehand. What if she and the client didn't agree on what was funny? Worse yet, what if she and the CEO of her firm didn't agree? That could be devastating to the whole presentation. You never get a second chance to make a good first impression!*

*She finally decided to use a personal story. As a fairly recent hire, she decided to use her experience trying to decide whether or not to accept a job with this company as a kind of comparison to how the client was deciding whether or not to buy this campaign. The central issues of company credibility, cultural and personal fit, how it would be to work with people on her team, and the value they placed on personal input were all likely issues for the client, as well. Beth could begin and end the presentation on a personal level that might help sell the idea. She added these entries to her worksheet.*

| **Step 2:** CREATING THE MESSAGE—Introduction and Conclusion | |
|---|---|
| **Introduction** | ✦ Personal narrative about choosing the company.<br>✦ Statement of thesis.<br>✦ Preview of main points.<br>✦ After listening to my presentation, you will clearly see that our company has the ideas, the team, and the resources to make your product a success across America. |

| **Purpose and Thesis Statement** | **Main Points** | **Support** | **Transitions** |
|---|---|---|---|
| ✦ To provide compelling information about a new advertising campaign theme, strategy, and budget with the intention of persuading the client that the firm can do the best job.<br><br>✦ I will present to you our concept that we believe will help you reach your product sales goals and open your product to additional markets, while remaining within the budget guidelines you specified. | ✦ *First, I will describe our concept and explain why we believe it will appeal to your target market.*<br>  ◇ Concept<br>  ◇ Connection to target market<br><br>✦ *Second, I will provide a timeline of how we will implement the concept.*<br>  ◇ October–January<br>  ◇ February–April<br>  ◇ May–August | ✦ *Concept—fact and examples*<br>  ◇ Two examples of successful campaigns from the same target market<br><br>✦ *Target Market—statistics*<br>  ◇ Current numbers representing the size of the market and target demographics | ✦ *Introduction*<br>  ◇ Preview the flow of the talk<br><br>✦ *Concept*<br>  ◇ Simply put, the concept will allow us to reach the target market by . . .<br><br>✦ *Timeline*<br>  ◇ Now that you have seen the concept, I would like to take a few minutes to discuss the timeline.<br><br>(continued) |

## Step 2: CREATING THE MESSAGE—Introduction and Conclusion (*continued*)

| Purpose and Thesis Statement | Main Points | Support | Transitions |
|---|---|---|---|
| | ✦ *Third, I will outline our proposed budget, which I'm sure you will find well within your prescribed parameters.*<br>◇ Total budget<br>◇ Cost breakdowns by category<br>◇ Justification for budget<br>✦ *Finally, I will answer any questions or discuss ideas you may have.*<br>◇ Request for questions<br>◇ Request for business | ✦ *Timeline—fact and examples*<br>◇ Which media we will use and examples of how they will be used at each stage in the campaign<br>✦ *Budget—statistics, authoritative sources, and examples*<br>◇ Total budget— statistical breakdown<br>◇ Cost breakdown— statistical breakdown of each category and statements from clients illustrating the cost savings compared to other firms<br>◇ Justification— review examples for each phase and show quality vs. cost<br>✦ *Questions and request for business— examples and personal narrative*<br>◇ Review examples to illustrate points brought up during the question period<br>◇ Describe my experience with the firm, my clients, and why I think the concept and the firm are the best investment for the client | ✦ *Budget—statistics, authoritative sources, and examples*<br>◇ Of course, a timeline this rigorous requires an investment . . .<br>✦ *Questions and request for business*<br>◇ Review main points<br>◇ Return to introduction |
| **Conclusion** | ✦ Review main points.<br>✦ Choosing an advertising firm is much like choosing a place of work. Because we will be working together closely, it is important that you trust the people you work with, believe in their abilities, and find their ideas exciting and creative. I know I've found the right company; I'm sure you will feel the same. | | |

*When Beth was finished, she had a solid strategic plan for her presentation. She was ex-cited about the meeting and confident she would do herself, her team, and her company proud. What a difference the CCCD process had made! Now she needed to meet with the other members of her team to ensure that her message coordinated with their goals.*

## Step 3: Coordinating with Others

Conscious communication is mindful of the needs and expectation of others. When we say "others," we go beyond just the audience; we refer to everyone who might be impacted by the communication event. Our friend Menyon, the director of technology for a large global apparel firm, made a statement that sums up the coordinating stage of conscious communication: "It doesn't mat-ter if I am promoted, or if I look good, as long as the company can move ahead and meet its goals. As long as the company is moving ahead, I am moving ahead, because I own stock . . . [and] have a stake in the company. My job is to ensure that everyone has the information they need to keep the company mov-ing ahead."

Menyon's attitude epitomizes the Three Musketeers approach to communi-cating in organizations, mentioned in Chapter 1. She has learned that for a project to succeed is for her to succeed, and she can't do that by working alone and keeping information to herself. To be truly successful in today's business en-vironment, Menyon has learned that she must provide information to others who may be able to use it, gain feedback from them, and coordinate her com-munication efforts.

Her statement also recognizes that the communication process moves a company forward. Without communication, Menyon's company—any com-pany—would come to a grinding halt. Sharing what we know (or what we are doing, or what we think was said or heard, or what direction we are taking on a big project or a group initiative) is vital for our own growth, as well as for the growth of the company.

Coordinating our communication also allows us to gain vital insight (feed-back) we cannot get working alone. Feedback tells us that we are on the right track and in sync with the goals and mission of the group, team, department, and company. It allows us to rehearse our message, to try it out on others before making a mistake. With corrective feedback, we learn to edit our errors, mod-ify our information, and become more effective with others.

In addition, coordinating means making sure everyone who should be in-cluded in a communication event is notified of the event. It means asking for feedback from those who can help make a communication event successful. In Beth's case, this meant the other members of her team.

*Beth sent out an e-mail asking her team members to attend a dry run of her presenta-tion. She explained in the e-mail that she was looking for feedback and wanted to catch*

## SKILL BUILDER WORKSHOP

### ORGANIZING YOUR SPEECH

Have you ever listened to a speaker and at the end of the presentation realized you had no idea what the talk was about? Have you ever listened to a speaker who seemed to just ramble incoherently, moving from one point to another without any idea of how to connect his or her thoughts? Have you heard a speech by someone you admired, only to walk away wondering how that person got to where they were? What do all these speakers have in common? They all lack an organizational plan for their talk.

As a speaker, you might have exciting new ideas that you can't wait to share with your audience, but without a organizational plan, your ideas will fall short. In Beth's example above, we used the CCCD worksheets to develop a plan for Beth's presentation. In Step Two: Creating the Message, we lay out all of the elements for Beth's talk. These elements can also be organized online using Speech Builder Express.

### SPEECH BUILDER EXPRESS WORKSHOP

Open Speech Builder Express. Select Persuasive Speech from the menu. Using Beth's example, complete the outline in Speech Builder Express. This process familiarizes you with the elements of a solid presentation and with the process of organizing a talk. In class, discuss the process with your group. How did using an organizational tool help with the organizational process? Why is it important to become familiar with tools such as the CCCD worksheets and Speech Builder Express *before* you have an assignment or have to prepare your first presentation?

*any flaws before the client heard the presentation. After sending her e-mail message, Beth looked over the presentation one last time and turned off the computer. She was really looking forward to getting some feedback tomorrow, but for now she needed a break from the project.*

*The next day, Beth arrived at the conference room thirty minutes early to set up everything and walk through her presentation once on her own. When her team members assembled, Beth began by reminding them she was looking for feedback. "I want to make sure that I've covered all the bases and that the presentation is solid," she said. "If anything is missing, please tell me."*

*"Like we wouldn't," someone said. Everyone in the room laughed.*

*Twenty minutes later, Beth sat down. "Well?" she asked. "What's the verdict?"*

*"Great job!" and "Nicely done" echoed from the group.*

"Really fine job, Beth," Orin said. "But I do have a few notes I'd like to share."

"Great," Beth said, smiling. The group spent the next forty-five minutes going over the notes Orin had made, polishing the presentation. When they were done, Beth really felt the presentation was the best it could be and thanked the team for their help.

Before she left that afternoon, she confirmed with the office coordinator that the room was booked for the next day and that all the standard arrangements for coffee, tea, and other refreshments were set. After running through the presentation a few more times that night, she would be ready.

---

### Focus on Ethics

Orin provided Beth with valuable feedback that Beth and the other team members used to improve Beth's presentation and the chances that her team would win the client's business. Let's suppose for a minute that Orin felt slighted that Beth, a newer member to the team, had been asked to give the presentation instead of her. Orin could see the improvements that needed to be made to strengthen the presentation but chose not to share them with Beth and the team. Why should she? If Beth was such a hotshot, shouldn't she be able to find the flaws and weaknesses in her own presentation?

Did Orin have an obligation to share her observations with Beth and the team? If Orin hadn't shared her observations and the client chose another firm, would the failure be Beth's, Orin's, or equally shared? Think back on the definition of *mindful communication* in Chapter 2. Would Orin be communicating mindfully if she failed to share her observations. What are the ethical implications of Orin's actions if she fails to communicate mindfully with Beth and the team?

---

## Step 4: Delivering the Message

The payoff for a presentational event is the actual delivery of the speech in front of the intended audience. The first three components of the CCCD process ensure that you will have a professionally developed outline with strong supporting materials. These steps will help you develop an interesting, informative, and structured message appropriate for your audience and aligned with your personal goals. However, even the best message, with strong verbal and visual support and clear goals, will suffer if delivered poorly. The last component in the CCCD process—delivery—begins with your need to practice.

### Practice, Practice, Practice

How many times have you listened to someone speak and felt that their message was good but something was missing? Try as you might, you couldn't quite put your finger on it. Chances are good what was missing was practice. Few of us are naturally eloquent. Fewer still feel really comfortable giving a speech without any preparation—which is why practice is essential to delivering an effective message.

There are no research studies demonstrating an optimal amount of preparation and rehearsal time for presentations. However, most teachers of speech communication agree that the amount of practice time needed depends on these factors:

+ the amount of prior speaking experience
+ the number and complexity of presentational aids
+ familiarity with the topic and audience
+ confidence regarding speaking abilities
+ the degree of formality of the occasion or context

Rehearsal of a message is not limited to presentational speaking. If you are meeting with a boss or a coworker, take a few minutes before you talk to consider what you will say. Take into account your communication history, the norms of the organizational culture, and how your goals may or may not mesh well with his or hers. If you anticipate conflict, try out your message with someone who will give you honest feedback before you speak with your boss or coworker.

In group or team meetings, think carefully before you interject. Think about how you will say what you want to say, keeping in mind the needs and expectations of your team members. Practice your message in your head before you speak.

We have found that most people feel more confident if they practice a formal presentation at least three time before delivering it. For important presentations (those that will get you noticed within an organization), you may want to practice more often, and before an audience of friends, spouse, or coworkers before you go public. This practice should be done with an outline or from limited notes (see Chapters 12 and 13 for an extended discussion). Each practice session should be timed (so that adjustments to the length of the speech can be made, if necessary), and the speaker should try to make less and less use of the outline or notes each time. As you acquire experience as a presenter, the amount of time you need to prepare will lessen, sometimes dramatically. But no professional we know presents an effective speech without some preparation.

Beth took this step seriously. Not only did she practice the presentation before her team members to gain their feedback, but she practiced again at home that evening. She knew that with a little extra practice she would feel confident the next day rather than nervous and anxious. Practicing your presentation will help you achieve four speaking characteristics that make the difference between a good presentation and a great presentation: fluency, naturalness, vivacity, and nonverbal competence. If you don't practice, your audience will immediately see that your talk lacks these characteristics. Let's look at each of these characteristics in more detail.

## Fluency

**Fluency** refers to the smooth or effortless articulation of a speech. With practice, fluency naturally increases. You know what you intend to say, in what order, and as you practice, a comfortable speaking style emerges, helping you to sound more fluent. Practice helps you avoid saying "um" or "ah" or "like, you know," or any other form of speech that will make you appear less articulate. You will no longer connect sentences with "and" or "so." These speaking crutches go away and are replaced with natural vocal pauses, rather than stumbling for words and filling spaces with "and" or "uh."

Achieving fluency allows you to focus on the flow of ideas rather than on specific words. When you speak fluently, your message is clear and you deliver it smoothly and with confidence.

## Naturalness

**Naturalness** refers to an easy, genuine manner of speaking. Although your aim is not to re-create the Oprah Winfrey show, think about how natural she appears when speaking before a large audience. Natural speakers draw us into the message, making us feel a part of the presentation. They are fluent in their subject and comfortable talking about it.

You should aim to be yourself. Avoid affectation; your attitude toward your audience should always be one of collaboration and equality, not superiority and distance. You should stand up straight, be precise yet poised, and reflect a positive, helpful posture toward your listeners. By analogy, think of how you speak with a group of friends or business colleagues in a public place.

## Vivacity

Every day in boardrooms, conference rooms, and training facilities all across America, people are forced to sit and listen to seemingly endless streams of flat, lifeless, boring talk. **Vivacity** refers to the energy and enthusiasm used when speaking. High-energy speakers display a positive attitude toward their topics and their audiences, which has an infectious quality. This energy comes through in their enthusiasm for the subject and the opportunity to tell the audience about it.

However, do not confuse being vivacious with being overly emotional or falsely passionate. In most cases, audiences will reject the ideas of overly emotional or passionate speakers because they don't seem reasonable.

## Nonverbal Competence

**Nonverbal competence** refers to the ability of a speaker to (a) maintain an appropriate level of eye contact with listeners; (b) use gestures without making them appear repetitive or redundant; (c) use purposeful body movement, particularly during verbal transitions in the speech; and (d) incorporate visual aids smoothly in the presentation. The more confident you become in voicing your speech, the more attention you can place on these aspects of effective delivery.

Practice helps you develop each of the characteristics described above. With ample practice, your delivery will be fluent, natural, vivacious, and competent. Your nonverbal cues will reflect a level of assurance that can come only when you feel confident and prepared.

## How Beth Fared

*After the client left, Beth's team members gave her a round of applause.*

*"Wow!" Orin said. "You really did well."*

*"Great job!" Todd said from the conference-room speakerphone. "I couldn't see the visuals, but I don't think I could have done better! I can finally get some rest and stop worrying about this account. Thanks, Beth."*

Beth was thrilled with the results. The CCCD process worked just as the speaker had said it would. The presentation she had dreaded provided her with an opportunity to help her team land an important new client. She knew she would never give another talk without using CCCD.

## Summary

In this chapter, we introduced the CCCD process as the framework for developing conscious communication. We used Beth's example throughout the chapter to illustrate the four components of CCCD: choose, create, coordinate, and deliver. We briefly explained that although at first glance the CCCD process might seem a bit detailed for all types of communication events and episodes, in the following chapters we will show how you can apply CCCD to any type of communication event.

The discussion of CCCD in this chapter laid a foundation for the chapters to come. The use of the worksheets and the process Beth used to set communication goals, make choices, coordinate with team members, and deliver her message will reoccur to varying degrees throughout the book. Exposing you to these ideas early on in the text serves two purposes: (1) You can begin to use the framework immediately, for your first presentation assignment in class; and

(2) You have a firm grasp of the framework that informs the remainder of the chapters.

We will build on this framework to increase your understanding of what it takes to be a conscious communicator in the workplace. You will find that the CCCD process will work effectively for business and professional communication in the workplace, for both formal and informal speaking events.

## COMMUNICATING IN PROFESSIONAL CONTEXTS ONLINE

All of the following chapter review materials are available in electronic format on either the Communicating in Professional Contexts website or CD-ROM. In addition to the multimedia case studies, activities, and numerous other learning resources you'll find on the CD-ROM, the CD is your gateway to the book's premium web content, which is not accessible via the Internet. The book's basic web content is available both with the premium content and on-line at http://communication.wadsworth.com/goodall2 and includes the chapter learning objectives and activities, key-term digital glossaries, and quizzes. The CD is also your gateway to InfoTrac College Edition, our extensive online database of full-text articles that is fully keyword searchable and available twenty-four hours a day. Installation instructions for the CD appear on the inside of this book's back cover.

## What You Should Have Learned

The learning objectives below are available on the Communicating in Professional Contexts website, which is best accessed through the book's CD-ROM but is also available at http://communication.wadsworth.com/goodall2. Go to the Chapter 3 Resources and click on Learning Objectives.

Now that you have read Chapter 3, you should be able to do the following:

+ List and explain the steps in the CCCD process.
+ Discuss how the CCCD process reflects the principles of conscious communication.
+ Use the CCCD worksheets to outline a basic presentation for your class.
+ Provide feedback to others about their presentations, using the CCCD process as your guide to what a professional presentation should include and accomplish.
+ Explain how to choose communication goals.

- ◆ Explain why the body of a message should be created prior to the introduction and conclusion.
- ◆ Discuss why it is important to coordinate your communication event or episode with others prior to the actual delivery of it.
- ◆ Discuss strategies for improving delivery style and effectiveness.

## Key Terms

The terms below are available in a digital glossary on the Communicating in Professional Contexts website, which is best accessed through this book's CD-ROM but is also available at http://communication.wadsworth.com/goodall2. Go to the Chapter 3 Resources and click on Glossary.

| | | |
|---|---|---|
| **audience needs and expectations** *(66)* | **naturalness** *(91)* | **thesis statement** *(72)* |
| **causal pattern** *(73)* | **nonverbal competence** *(92)* | **topical pattern** *(73)* |
| **chronological pattern** *(73)* | **outcome** *(68)* | **transitions** *(81)* |
| **criteria** *(68)* | **problem–solution pattern** *(73)* | **vivacity** *(91)* |
| **facts** *(76)* | **purpose** *(71)* | |
| **fluency** *(91)* | **statistics** *(76)* | |

## Writing and Critical Thinking

The following activities can be completed online and, if requested, submitted to your instructor. You'll find them on the Communicating in Professional Contexts website, which is best accessed through the book's CD-ROM but is also available at http://communication.wadsworth.com/goodall2. Go to the Chapter 3 Resources and click on Writing and Critical Thinking Activities.

1. Think about your class and instructor as an audience for your presentations. What needs and expectations do they have? How should their needs and expectations influence your choice of communication goals? Of communication content? Of style? Of delivery?

2. Compare what you have learned in your English classes about writing outlines for papers with the advice given in this chapter about completing CCCD worksheets for an oral presentation. What are the similarities? What are the differences? What does this teach you about the relationship of oral to written style?

3. Think of an upcoming communication episode. Using the worksheets, devise a conscious communication plan. Try it out! What influences, if any, did the CCCD process have on your communication episode? How did CCCD improve your effectiveness?

4. Working in groups, complete step 1 of the CCCD worksheet for the following scenario:

   *The CEO of your growing company is about to make a final decision on buying a new software product for handling and tracking your company's sales, billing, customer service, and production needs. Since this product will affect several departments in your company, as well as current customers, the CEO has assigned your group to develop a presentation that will include a product overview for each of the different groups described below and solicit their feedback.*

   With your group, complete step 1, Choosing a Goal, from your CCCD worksheet. Identifying the goal for each group, assess the specific audience needs, concerns, and expectations, and determine the possible outcomes and how you will identify criteria for success of your presentation.

   + Group 1: Data entry/computer group. This group will have to spend several weeks converting current customer records to the new format.

   + Group 2: Customer support group. This group will have to change its method for entering customer issues but ultimately will have a better method for tracking this data.

   + Group 3: Operations. Most members of this group have been with the company more than ten years and are comfortable with the current, but high-maintenance, manual system of entering data to produce widgets.

   + Group 4: Sales. This group will receive their commission reports sooner but will have to complete additional paperwork on each customer.

   + Group 5: Long-term customers. This group's orders will become automated. Automation may result in faster order receipt, but customers will have to install new software (at their own expense) on their systems.

   + Group 6: Corporate board of directors. This group knows nothing about the system currently in place. They only know the new system will have a high initial expense.

5. Visit a spokesperson for your university (try the university relations department) or a spokesperson for an organization to which you belong and ask the speaker these questions: How do you collect information on their audience? How do you prepare for your presentations? How do you determine the success of a presentation? What is your greatest concern when giving a presentation, and how do you deal with that concern?

## Research and Explorations Online

The exercises below can be completed online and, if requested, submitted to your instructor. You'll find them on the Communicating in Professional Contexts website, which is best accessed through this book's CD-ROM but is also available at http://communication.wadsworth.com/goodall2. Go to the Chapter 3 Resources and click on Internet Exercises.

1. Visit at least one website that specializes in oral communication. For example, you might try http://www.toastmasters.org. This site contains information on making effective oral presentations. What advice is given? How is that advice reflected in our CCCD process?

2. Visit http://www.eloquent.com, a site dedicated to providing audio and video transcripts of current business and professional speeches and presentations. You will notice that there are also some search features available, as well as outlines for some of the presentations. Use the CCCD system to critique one of the downloadable presentations available on this website.

3. Visit http://www.entrepreneur.com and enter "seven presentation pitfalls" in the search field. Identify the errors Mr. Lyden made in his first presentation. Now assume you are Mr. Lyden preparing for the second presentation. Using the CCCD worksheet, develop a conscious communication plan to maximize your opportunity for a successful presentation and outcome.

## Practicing Communication in Professional Contexts: Completing the CCCD Worksheets

CCCD is a new "breakthrough" process for organizing communication events. Now that you have been introduced to the process, you are ready to apply what you have learned. However, keep in mind that we will be building on and developing your skills throughout the course. In this skill-building exercise, we want you to begin using CCCD.

Using the CCCD worksheets (in Appendix A or online under Student Resources, Worksheets for Chapter 3, at the Communicating in Professional Contexts website), prepare for your first in-class presentation. Your instructor will provide details on the assignment.

Critique at least one of your classmates' presentations using the CCCD worksheets as an evaluation guide. You can download a copy under Worksheets for Chapter 3 at the Communicating in Professional Contexts website. Did the speaker complete all of the steps in the worksheets? For example, were the speaker's main points clearly defined? Did they tie into the speaker's stated thesis? Discuss your critique with the speaker. Help one another develop goals to improve your next speeches.

## Communicating in Professional Contexts in Action!

Improve your own presentation skills by watching, listening to, critiquing, and analyzing the scenarios featured on this program. After completing an analysis for each communication scenario and answering the questions provided, you can compare your work to our suggested responses. Now is a good time to try out your CD-ROM!

# Chapter Four

## Listening in the Workplace

**B**en couldn't believe his boss was making him sit through a workshop on listening. *"Listening, of all things," he grumbled to himself. "What could you possibly learn about listening by sitting in a workshop? This is such a waste of time!"*

*Ben thought about the pile of work on his desk: the new engineering project he had just been assigned, and calls he had to make that afternoon. Then there was his date that evening—he didn't want to be late for it. This employee development stuff was going to set him way back.*

*"Hmmm," he mused, "maybe I can sneak out at the break and no one will notice."*

## Becoming a Conscious Listener

As we have seen in the previous chapters, often when we think we are communicating effectively, we may not be. This is equally true of **listening,** the process of hearing and interpreting messages. Listening is an integral part of the communication process. Think about it for a moment. How many of us truly listen? How many times has someone said to you, "You're not *listening* to me, are you?" One reason we haven't developed our listening skills is the fast pace of our culture. We don't seem to have time to listen; we're too busy talking, and if we aren't talking, we're formulating what we are going to say next.

Our failure to listen is also because of the lack of formal listening training we receive. Judith Pollack, president of Language at Work, has described the problem this way: "We spend 80 percent of our time communicating, but we only receive training in the speaking, reading, and writing aspects. We *never* really receive training in listening, except at the hands of our teachers and parents" (Jones, 1999, p. 15). Patrice Johnson, director of Spectra Incorporated in New Orleans, emphasized the importance of investing in listening training. She said, "I think listening is getting attention now because organizations don't have the luxury of redundancy. In the past, large dinosaur organizations had plenty of people to do rework, unnecessary work, and so forth. Failing to listen and the errors that it caused could be managed" (Salopek, 1999, p. 58). Now, however, many CEOs, training managers, and business owners think of listening as an important, even crucial business skill.

Conscious listening, much like conscious communication, can be understood using a continuum (see Table 4.1). The continuum shows the spectrum of listening ranging from hearing to conscious listening, or "listening to the whole," which emerges out of dialogue (Senge et al., 1994, p. 20). Let's look at the listening continuum in more detail.

| Hearing | Informational Listening | Critical Listening | Self-Reflexive Listening | Conscious Listening |
|---|---|---|---|---|
| Listener processes a signal from a speaker. | Listener identifies the signal as words. Moves from hearing to listening. | Listener deliberates on what is said, exploring the logic, reason, and point of view of the speaker. | Listener reflects on how what is said applies to his or her life. | Listener becomes open to the speaker's point of view. |
| **Mindless Listening** . . . . . . . . . . . . . . . . . . . . . . . . . . . . . . . . . . . . . . . . . . . . . . . . . . . . . **Mindful Listening** | | | | |

**Table 4.1**
Listening Continuum

## Hearing

**Hearing** is the passive and physical process of listening. We may hear a speaker's words, but we don't necessarily understand their meaning. Hearing is simply what happens when a message vibrates our eardrums and causes a signal to move to the brain. At the physical level, our ability to listen can be affected by outside elements that may hamper our ability to hear, including noise and physical and technological diversions.

### Noise

Imagine you are at a job fair in a crowded hotel conference room. You finally have the attention of the head of personnel for a company you have been trying to interview with for months. However, the noise in the room keeps you from hearing the hiring information you need in order to target your résumé effectively. **Noise** is any sound that disrupts or interferes with the delivery of a message. Noise can cause a listener to become frustrated or confused, or to give up on the message altogether.

### Physical Diversions

Have you ever tried to listen in a room that is too hot or too dark? A **physical diversion** is any physical element that disrupts or interferes with the delivery of a message. A few years ago, we were asked to sit in on training sessions at a software development company. The head of training had received a number of complaints from trainees about the material and the trainers. The head of training changed the trainers and revised the materials, but the complaints continued. Oddly enough, trainees complained only when the training was done at the home office. One hour into a training session there, we knew exactly why the trainees were unhappy. The room where the training sessions were held was a medium gray color. The lights in the main part of the room were kept dim so that the trainees could see the large LCD screen at the front of the room. The temperature was a balmy 78 degrees. The problem wasn't the materials or the trainers. It was the room! The physical space lulled the trainees to sleep and kept them from listening or learning.

### Technological Diversions

A **technological diversion** is any technological element that disrupts or interferes with the delivery of a message. How many times have you initiated a conversation, only to have the phone or doorbell ring? Because we work in a home-based office, this happens to us many times a day. After using call waiting for only two weeks, we called the phone company and canceled the service. This "revolution in the way people use the telephone" distracted and annoyed our callers. Even if we did manage to keep the first caller on the line, by the time we returned to the call, our listener was distracted or frustrated and no longer focused on our message.

*"Okay," Ben thought. "That makes sense. Hearing is the physical part of listening. Noise and other things can block it. So what?"*

## BEST PRACTICES

## Overcoming Blocks to Hearing

1. Hold conversations in spaces where noise is not a problem. If you are in a crowded or noisy space, try the following:
   + Move to a quieter space, if possible.
   + Make an appointment to call or see the person when you will be back in your office and can concentrate on the conversation. Be sure to secure the information you need to contact the person at a later date (phone number or e-mail address).

2. Make adjustments to the physical space:
   + Move closer to the front in dim rooms. Adjust the temperature.
   + Hold the speaker or meeting manager accountable for the physical space. If you attend regular meetings in the same room and every week you fall asleep or freeze during the meeting, bring it to the attention of the person who arranged the meeting.

3. Be conscious of technological distractions:
   + Don't take other calls, read your e-mail, or open your mail while someone is talking to you. Give others your full attention.
   + Be honest if someone begins a conversation during a time when you know you will be distracted. Tell the coworker, "This is not a good time for us to talk. I am really distracted right now and will not be able to give you my full attention. Can we schedule another time to talk about this?"

**Figure 4.1**
The Listening Cycle

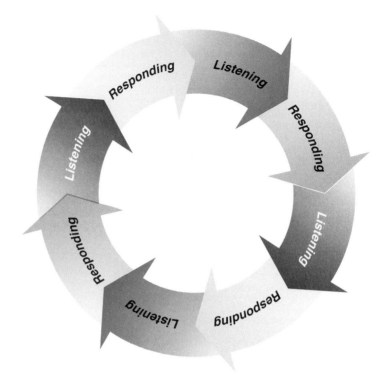

## Informational Listening

**Informational listening** describes the stage when a message begins to be interpreted by the listener. At this stage in the listening process, we assign meaning to the words we hear and we listen for information. Many people conduct much of their business communication at this stage of the listening process, getting caught up in a cycle of listening and responding, without moving on to the next stage, critical listening (see Figure 4.1).

At this level, our ability to listen and gain information can be influenced by internal elements, such as cultural, gender, and language differences. Another factor that may interfere with listening is our communication history with the person speaking. Let's look at each of these factors in more detail.

### Cultural Differences

Cultural differences affecting communication can include the slang used by a younger or older generation, the language and tonal accents used by another nationality or race, the regional differences in language style, and the jargon used in a certain profession or industry. All too often, we focus on the cultural differences of the speaker and forget to listen to the message itself. In business, where diverse cultures abound, this can become a serious communication problem.

Consider the situation of Rasheed, a highly qualified, motivated programmer at a software development company. Rasheed was new to the United States, as well as to the company, but he churned out more lines of code than almost anyone else. When he spoke, however, his voice was barely above a whisper. In meetings, members of the development team would talk over one another, excitedly working through ideas. Rasheed struggled to be heard, but often he gave up out of frustration. He wasn't used to the team's raucous organizational culture. Unfortunately, the team was losing out on a valuable perspective on the project. After a few weeks, Rasheed confided his concerns to another team member, Sandra. She suggested to the team that Rasheed raise a manila folder whenever he had a point to make. The tactic worked well. Not only did the team listen more carefully to Rasheed, they began to listen more carefully to one another.

## BEST PRACTICES

### Working with Non-Native Speakers

- ✦ Pick one member of the group or team as the liaison for the non-native speaker.
- ✦ Encourage the non-native employee to put comments, suggestions, or other input in writing. Generally, non-native speakers have a better command of the written language.
- ✦ Repeat sentences back to the speaker, clarifying your understanding, one sentence at a time.
- ✦ Be patient. It is just as frustrating for the non-native speaker as it is for you. Becoming frustrated or angry will heighten the speaker's anxiety, which will make it more difficult for you to understand each other.

Cultural barriers also can present themselves in less obvious ways. An older male boss may ignore the suggestions of a younger male employee simply because he thinks the younger man is too inexperienced to know what he is talking about. Even clothes can present cultural barriers to listening. When talking to a sales clerk, have you ever found yourself distracted by the clerk's multiple earrings, or choice of earring location? Have you found others distracted by *your* nonverbal presentation of self? How you look and present yourself in a business setting can distract from your ability to communicate, by impeding others' ability to listen.

## BEST PRACTICES

### Removing Cultural Barriers to Listening

- ✦ Mentally acknowledge nonverbal distraction before you begin a conversation. By making yourself aware of the distraction and acknowledging it, you reduce the interference it may cause.
- ✦ Concentrate on the speaker's words and their meanings rather than allowing yourself to become distracted.
- ✦ Acknowledge cultural differences. When dealing with someone significantly older or younger, realize that you are coming from very different positions but you each have something to offer.

### Gender Differences

We've all heard John Gray's statement, "Men are from Mars and women are from Venus." We know that numerous studies point to the differences in the way men and women communicate. Understanding why men and women communicate differently can go a long way toward explaining how men and women listen. Noted communication researcher Deborah Tannen explained the differences this way: "Men communicate to report, and women communicate to build rapport" (Tannen, 1990).

Let's look at this statement from a listening perspective. If men are communicating to *report* knowledge, they probably are not as attuned to receiving feedback or gathering additional information or viewpoints. Men in business often view communication as a simple process of delivery, as one-sided communication events intended to impart knowledge.

If women are communicating to build *rapport* (create mutual understanding), they are more receptive to feedback and to the responses of others. Women generally are considered empathetic listeners. Not only do the words they hear affect them, so do the perceived feelings of the speaker. Openness to feedback and empathetic listening create a view of communication as conversation, as exchanges that are used to further relationships.

Gender differences also seem to occur in the way men and women process conversational cues. Women tend to use and process conversational cues such as "Oh, really?," "Hmmm," and "That's interesting" as means of moving the conversation along. These cues signal they are listening and engaged. For men, these same cues may signal agreement or submission. Men often view such cues as prolonging a conversation when only a quick decision is needed. Women become frustrated by most men's inability to listen rather than react. Becoming aware of the gender differences in listening can help to overcome gender-related misunderstandings and frustrations in the workplace.

PhotoDisc

## BEST PRACTICES

### Overcoming Gender-Related Listening Differences

Become aware of the differences in the way men and women tend to communicate and listen. Reading one of the books or articles on gender and communication suggested in the References will help you become more aware of these differences.

+ Be sensitive to the differences in communication. Listen carefully, regardless of a person's gender.

+ Use summaries and questions to ensure that you have heard what was said.

+ Don't assume that conversational cues such as "Hmmm" or "Uh-huh" signal agreement.

### Language Differences

A Canadian friend of ours occasionally will say something that is absolutely clear to her, but not to us. These twists of language happen across generations, cultures, and industry groups. Often, language differences occur because an industry or generational group has given a new meaning to a word or phrase. For example, the Internet has generated a new and evolving lexicon in the English language. The word *web*, which to most people has always meant something a spider uses to catch food, now can be used to refer to an intricate woven relationship between sites on the Internet. *Surfing*, which once required water and a surfboard, now can mean looking for information or entertainment opportunities on the Internet.

## BEST PRACTICES

### Surmounting Language Barriers

If you are in a meeting and cannot check your understanding of a term or phrase, write the phrase down. After the meeting, clarify the meaning with another team member or the person speaking.

If you are in a conversation and someone uses a phrase or term you don't understand, ask for clarification. Too often, people assume that asking for clarification will make them appear unsavvy or out of the loop. By not asking for clarification, you set yourself up to make mistakes or have future misunderstandings.

Keep your own jargon and language differences under control. Using the latest term might lead to miscommunication that costs you or your company time and money.

Communication History

Have you ever noticed that you tune out certain people *before* they begin to speak? Have you ever considered why you respond this way? Chances are it is because of your **communication history,** the cumulative record of communication events between the participants in a conversation.

Communication history can interfere with listening in many ways. For example, some people just seem to waste your time. Others want to talk about issues you have no interest or stake in. Some people have the communication style of a battering ram; they hammer their point home over and over again. Others communicate only to complain. Their communication revolves around negative messages about how much work they have to do, how unfair the company is, or how bad their personal relationships are. Two distinct problems characterize these dysfunctional communication styles:

1. The speaker views the listener as a passive receptor who is there to absorb whatever message the speaker chooses to send.
2. The speaker assumes that talking is more powerful or important than listening.

As we will see later in this chapter, both of these positions weaken a speaker's ability to communicate effectively. Unfortunately, sometimes in business you have to communicate with these people to gain important information, which might mean wading through a certain amount of overload or negativity first.

## BEST PRACTICES

### Dealing with Communication History Barriers

- ◆ Begin any conversation by setting parameters. For example, "Gee, Mahoan, I'm sorry I can't talk. Hunter needs these figures for a meeting in fifteen minutes."

- ◆ Don't avoid someone who has information you need because of your communication history. Acknowledge your history and ask for the information. For example, "I know we normally talk about your job when we meet, but today I would like to focus on our project. If you need to talk about your job, we could schedule lunch later in the week."

- ◆ If communication history, or someone's communication style, continues to block your ability to get information, find a new source for the information, or discuss the problem with your boss. You may not be not the only one dealing with the problem; it might be affecting your entire team, department, or company.

*"Not bad," thought Ben. "I can use some of these tips. Maybe this listening stuff even explains why I've had a hard time talking to some of the women in the engineering group. I know of at least two people this will make a real difference with—who knows, maybe it will even work with Mr. Spencer. If I have to listen one more time to his list of complaints about young people and how his generation was so much better at everything, I'll go nuts. Next time I have to talk to him, I'll begin by acknowledging that I know things are being done a bit differently but I think we can work together to ensure the project's success. It's worth a try to see if it will help me deal more productively with him. Maybe I should stay after the break and find out what critical listening is."*

## Critical Listening

Many people get bogged down in the cycle of listening and responding. Most of us are skilled in phatic communication and informational exchanges, but often we lack skill in **critical listening**—the ability of a listener to deliberate on what is said by exploring the logic, reason, and point of view of the speaker.

It is only when we reach the critical listening stage that we can begin to reflect on the credibility of the speaker, the message, and the motivation behind the talk. Before we can reflect on the impact a message has on us personally, we have to evaluate the qualities of the message.

### Speaker Credibility

When we examine a speaker's credibility, we are evaluating the personal and professional qualifications a speaker brings to a communication event. The qualifications a speaker needs in an interpersonal communication event may differ from those required for a formal presentation. For example, if your boss, a twenty-nine-year-old with an MBA from the Wharton School of Business and no actual work experience, offers you advice on dealing with a client you have been working with for five years, how would you view her advice? If the same advice came from an account executive who had worked with the client for eight years before you took over the account, would you view the suggestions differently? On the other hand, if the MBA boss presented a workshop on a new way of creating a monthly sales report that saves time, would you respond more positively to her advice?

Not all speakers are credible in every communication situation. Each situation, event, and speaker must be considered individually.

### The Message

When we speak, it is important to back up what we say with support. When we listen, we are listening for the supporting evidence or data a speaker uses to add credibility to a message.

You should listen for the following:

+ *Facts and statistics.* Are the facts and statistics offered reliable? Do they come from respected sources? Do they support the speaker's claims, or have they been used simply for effect?

+ *Examples.* Are the examples clear and relevant? Or have they been added to make the material seem more interesting? Do you recognize an example as something that holds true for the topic? Can you identify with the example?

+ *Personal appeals.* Are the personal appeals used to gain your compliance appropriate for the message and the speaker? Are the appeals being used in place of a strong and clear factual appeal?

### Motivation

**Motivation** is the force or reason that drives us toward an action. All talk is rooted in the motivation to reach a goal. For example, we may speak to take up a department's cause, support a program slated to be cut, or rouse a group to action. Even passing along task information is rooted in a motivation—the need to ensure that a job gets done.

When you evaluate a speaker's motivation, you must listen for the speaker's stake in the message. What does the speaker have to gain? Is the speaker's motivation similar to yours? Or is the speaker acting from a selfish position?

When you speak, evaluate your own motivation. What do others hear you say when they listen to your message? Are your motivations appropriate for the message? Will you be perceived as working for the good of the team, or only for yourself?

> *After the break, Ben sat reflecting on what he had heard. He was beginning to understand why he had been the only one from his team chosen to attend the Listening in the Workplace workshop. He didn't like to admit it, but he could see that he had not been a very effective listener. He needed to make some changes, and this workshop was really going to help him do it.*

## Self-Reflexive Listening

So far, our listener has heard what was said, mined the message for useful information, and evaluated the credibility of the person speaking. Now it is time to reflect on the message. **Self-reflexive listening**—listening for how what is said applies to a listener's life—allows us to integrate and then move beyond the first three stages of the listening process. By reflecting on what is said and how it will affect us, we move closer to conscious listening. When we listen self-reflexively, we are listening for the ways a message reflects our identity at work, our personal goals, our understanding of an issue or problem, and our sensitivity to the needs of others.

### Identity

When we listen self-reflexively, we hear and reflect on the meanings of what others say about us. Listening to what others say about us, our work, our values, and our work ethic provides us with insight into who we are in the workplace. The words and metaphors people use to describe us—"He's a real go-getter"; "She's the brightest bulb in the accounting department"; or "That's the toughest team I've ever had to work with"—create our work identity. How do people at work describe you? What are the adjectives commonly used when people talk about you or your work? Does this talk accurately reflect who you are or want to be in the workplace?

### Personal Goals

Listening for the personal goals of the speaker gives us insight into the speaker's motivation. Listening self-reflexively allows us to think about how our personal goals align with those of the speaker. Is this a person you want to do business with, or are the speaker's personal goals outside of your personal or ethical boundaries? Are your personal goals aligned in such a way that together you could bring about change or close a sale that you could not accomplish separately? Listening for personal goals helps you identify people who can help you succeed and those who do not share your ethical, moral, or business values.

### Understanding

Listening self-reflexively provides you with an opportunity to evaluate how well you understand a person, problem, or situation. Too often in business situations, we are concerned with how well *other* people understand a problem. It is much easier to be critical of another's position without really evaluating our own understanding. Listening self-reflexively allows us to listen to the verbal cues that signal *our* understanding of a problem or situation. Cues from others, such as "I really think you are on the right track" or "I'm not sure you see the whole problem," signal how well we grasp their message and intention.

### Sensitivity

Listening with **sensitivity** means taking into consideration the speaking differences of your communication partners. Becoming a sensitive listener requires listening for, and awareness of, the differences that arise from racial, gender, cultural, socioeconomic, and other factors that contribute to how we evaluate meanings and messages. It means that we are aware of how these differences affect our ability to listen and integrate the message into our thinking.

## Conscious Listening

The final stage on the listening continuum is **conscious listening,** openly listening to the speaker's point of view, which emerges out of dialogue. Conscious listening occurs when all of the communication partners involved in a communication episode or event listen for and reflect on how talk affects the whole group, team, or company. Peter Senge has described this conscious listening as the "deeper patterns of meaning that flow through a group . . . that build a subtle awareness of collective thought that profoundly transforms our experience of what is possible" (Senge et al., 1994, p. 20).

Conscious listening transforms us from individuals into relational partners or a collective group moving forward together. Conscious listening, like dialogue, takes into account the shared vision, goals, and values of a relationship, group, team, or organization. Conscious listening results in new alternatives that we would not have seen had we not listened consciously.

Conscious listening is a vital business skill. It opens us to the views of others, presents possibilities we would not see if we didn't listen consciously, and creates a level of understanding that helps move our relationships, teamwork,

## BEST PRACTICES

### Listening Consciously

+ Stop talking. You cannot listen at any level if you are talking.

+ Stop reacting. You cannot listen consciously if you are focusing on what you are going to say next.

+ Listen for feelings. It is easier to be empathetic if you understand how someone feels. Rather than focus on the content, take a minute to focus on the feelings of the speaker.

+ Listen for cues about yourself. What is the listener saying about you? Does it ring true?

+ Listen for motivation. What motivates the speaker to feel this way, react this way, take this position?

+ Listen for intention. What does the speaker really want to happen as a result of having spoken?

+ Listen for position. Is compromise possible, or is the speaker unmovable?

+ Listen for benefits. How will this benefit you, your company, or your client?

+ Recap what was said as calmly as possible. Use phrases such as "I heard you say that . . ." or "It seems that you want . . ."

+ Ask for confirmation. Ask questions such as "Do you feel I have a handle on the situation now that we've talked?"

+ Suggest alternatives that work for both the individual and the whole. "We could ask Paula to reschedule the meeting so that you will have more time to prepare. Or we could tell the group that your report is preliminary, because you were given the assignment yesterday, but they can begin to analyze the information. And let's go ahead and let everyone know your final report will be available on Friday."

and the organization forward. Now that we have a better understanding of listening in the workplace, let's look at listening within specific business contexts.

*After the workshop, Ben stayed to talk with the speaker and to thank her for the information. He was amazed at how much there was to learn about listening, something he obviously had not been doing very well. Now he was determined to become a conscious listener in all his business and personal communication encounters.*

## The Importance of Listening in Business and Professional Contexts

Developing conscious listening skills should be a goal for anyone in business. In fact, in many business situations we discover that listening is our job. How well we listen in these situations, the level at which we listen, and the outcome of our listening will all have a direct impact on our success in our chosen business or profession. This section addresses the role of listening in a few typical business situations.

### Listening in Meetings

Meetings require a combination of listening skills. Although in meetings we listen mainly for information, it is also important that we follow the listening continuum up through critical, self-reflexive, and conscious listening. How well we listen can provide us with important information and an opportunity to share knowledge and receive feedback.

### BEST PRACTICES

#### Listening in Meetings

+ Set a positive example. Sit up, be quiet, and take notes. There is nothing worse than someone whispering, squirming, talking, or otherwise disrupting a meeting, class, or presentation.
+ Don't pass judgment. You will continue to encounter your share of boring, disorganized, or unskilled speakers. Your job, however, may depend on the information you get from the speaker. Listen for information; downplay the presentation style.
+ Take good notes. Outline the speech or talk using the CCCD components. Try to determine the speaker's purpose, thesis, preview, main points, support, and conclusion.
+ If possible, review the material later with the speaker or other members of the audience to verify or modify what you heard.
+ Follow up on any points that need clarification or action.

### Listening in Conflict Situations

Listening in conflict situations requires well-developed listening skills—along with patience. Often when we find ourselves in conflict situations, we become defensive. However, the conflict may be situational, not personal. We need to learn to listen to the speaker's reactions to and feelings about the situation, rather than concentrate on our own anger, defensiveness, or need to counterattack.

## BEST PRACTICES

## Listening in Conflict Situations

- ✦ Relax and take a few deep breaths. Step back from the person who is speaking so that you gain control over your personal space. Stepping back physically can also help us to step back mentally.

- ✦ Don't become defensive when the speaker focuses on you rather than on the situation. Keep your thoughts and words focused on the situation, not the person. Remember, not everyone knows how to listen consciously.

- ✦ Acknowledge the conflict. If you know in advance that a conflict is brewing, begin the conversation with, "I know we have different views. I would like to hear yours before we go any further. Then please listen to what I have to say."

- ✦ Listen for areas of compromise. Most conflict resolution arises out of compromise, not consensus.

- ✦ Listen for signs of escalation of the conflict. If this happens, say, "I think we are becoming overly emotional. Perhaps we should meet later to discuss this."

- ✦ Recap what the speaker said. Show you were listening critically by recapping the speaker's motives, supports, and appeals. Show you were listening self-reflexively by acknowledging your role, from the speaker's perspective, in the conflict. Show you were listening consciously by pointing out the areas of compromise and alternatives for moving forward.

## Listening to Complaints

One of the things Kanika disliked most about working for a company was the amount of time she had to spend listening to coworkers', managers', and clients' complaints and problems. Now that she works as an independent consultant, she finds she gets much more accomplished because she doesn't have disgruntled people streaming into her office every day. Kanika's attitude might appear negative at first, but it is important to understand the difference between someone in the workplace who has a legitimate complaint and the chronic complainer who nibbles away at our time and energy.

### Legitimate Complaints

Legitimate complaints come from clients, customers, or members of your organization and address specific issues or problems. These types of complaints should be listened to with care and handled quickly and efficiently. To handle a legitimate complaint, follow these steps:

1. Listen carefully. Allow the person to have his or her say.

2. Remain neutral. When listening to a complaint, keep in mind that the complaint is not an attack; it is a request for acknowledgment.
3. Listen empathetically. Think about how the situation or problem has affected the person.
4. Repeat the person's statement of the problem. Let the person know that you understand the problem or situation from his or her perspective.
5. Ask what the person would like to have happen.
6. Explain your position.
7. Follow up in any reasonable way to ensure the person's satisfaction.

### Chronic Complainers

Chronic complainers complain about everything: the company, their manager, their assignments, and their coworkers. They rarely ever take action on a problem. Instead, they spend their time complaining. Listening to chronic complainers can zap our energy, create feelings of distrust toward group or team members or the organization, and take time away from important organizational activities.

---

**Focus on Ethics**

Sarah's manager, Maria, requires everyone to attend a weekly meeting to discuss the status of their department. Sarah admires and respects Maria, viewing her as a mentor and an excellent manager. But she can't stand the tedious weekly meetings. Maria reads each person's status report out loud and then asks if anyone has any questions or concerns about what each person is working on. Sarah understands the importance of everyone working together and knowing what other members of the team are doing. But she wonders if there is a better way of communicating everyone's status other than reading to them.

Should Sarah voice her concerns to Maria? Would you speak to Maria directly? Would you discuss the problem with everyone in the department and then confront Maria at the next meeting? Or would you simply head to the nearest coffee shop before the meeting and keep your thoughts to yourself?

Are barriers to good listening the responsibility of the listener, or the speaker?

---

## Listening When Asked for Help

Occasionally, whether you are a manager, coworker, or team member, someone will come to you for help on a project or for career advice. When this happens, listening is the most vital skill you can use to ensure you give the best help possible. How we listen can determine how well we understand the problem, the person's needs, and the feelings that may be contributing to the situation.

Try to understand what people expect from you. Are they looking for advice, a sounding board, a chance to vent, or the information they need to make

## BEST PRACTICES

### Dealing with Chronic Complainers

+ Acknowledge their complaints and their feelings about the situation.

+ Explain that although you understand the situation must be frustrating, you cannot spend any more time discussing it.

+ Offer positive actions the complainer can take to resolve the situation.

+ When confronted by the complainer again, explain that you are in the middle of a task and now is not a good time to discuss the problem. After you refuse to listen to the complaints a few times, most complainers will get the message and either begin complaining to someone else or take action.

## SKILL BUILDER WORKSHOP

### DEALING WITH CHRONIC COMPLAINERS

Every time Ben gave Sam a new assignment, Sam complained. At first Ben didn't mind, because Sam always did a great job and turned in his work on time. After almost a year of constant complaining, though, Ben was starting to get a knot in his stomach every time he asked Sam to do something. He knew had to find a way to talk to Sam that would end the complaining. He decided that he would script the conversation ahead of time, using tips he had learned at the workshop, for dealing with chronic complainers.

### SPEECH BUILDER EXPRESS WORKSHOP

Open Speech Builder Express. Select Persuasive Speech from the menu. Think about the last conversation you had with a chronic complainer.

Use the tips above to construct a conversation that could have acted as a guide for dealing with the situation. In retrospect, if you had scripted the major points of the conversation ahead of time, how would the outcome have been different?

Note: Speech Builder Express (SBE) is intended for constructing entire speeches. However, it is a tool that adapts well to conversations, too. Some parts of SBE may not apply to every exercise. For example, when scripting conversations, the sections on visual aids can be left blank.

an informed decision? Often people will come to you for help and their words will say one thing but what they want is something entirely different. Listening can help you pick up on the clues that are vital to understanding exactly what someone needs.

We have discussed the differences in communication styles between men and women. These differences also apply to the way men and women tend to approach requests for help. Men generally listen to the problem and then immediately provide a course of action. Women generally listen to the problem, ask questions, and ask how the speaker feels about what is happening. Women tend to be concerned about the feelings of the person asking for help, whereas men tend to be concerned with addressing the problem and moving on. Each style has its benefits; each gender can learn from the other.

You should follow certain procedures when people ask for your help:

1. Let them speak. Don't interrupt or offer quick solutions.
2. Ask them what form they want the help to take. Ask if they want advice, assistance, analysis, a solution, or simply your support.
3. Offer the help they ask for if you feel comfortable giving it.
4. Keep the conversation to yourself. When people ask you for help, they are doing so because they trust you. Don't abuse their trust by telling others about their request if it should be kept private.
5. Offer support after the conversation is over. Follow up with their request and see how they are doing.

## Summary

Learning to be a conscious listener is important for two reasons: listening can help you avoid mistakes and misunderstandings, and it can help to move your business and professional relationships forward. Listening allows us to gather important information, empathize with coworkers and clients, gain a deeper understanding of situations, and reflect on our place within a specific communication context.

In this chapter, we discussed listening as a skill vital to the workplace. We introduced the conscious listening continuum and the types of listening: hearing, informational listening, critical listening, self-reflexive listening, and conscious listening. We learned that although listening occurs in many forms, conscious listening is the kind of listening we should all strive to do in our business and professional interactions. We also offered a number of tips for dealing with specific listening situations and contexts.

• • • • • • • • • • • • • • • • • • • • • • • • • • • • • • • • • • • • • • •

 COMMUNICATING IN PROFESSIONAL
CONTEXTS ONLINE

All of the following chapter review materials are available in electronic format on either the Communicating in Professional Contexts website or CD-ROM. In addition to the multimedia case studies, activities, and numerous other learning resources you'll find on the CD-ROM, the CD is your gateway to the book's premium web content, which is not accessible via the Internet. The book's basic web content is available both with the premium content and on-line at http://communication.wadsworth.com/goodall2 and includes the chapter learning objectives and activities, key-term digital glossaries, and quizzes. The CD is also your gateway to InfoTrac College Edition, our extensive online data-base of full-text articles that is fully keyword searchable and available twenty-four hours a day. Installation instructions for the CD appear on the inside of this book's back cover.

## What You Should Have Learned

The learning objectives below are available on the Communicating in Profes-sional Contexts website, which is best accessed through the book's CD-ROM but is also available at http://communication.wadsworth.com/goodall2. Go to the Chapter 4 Resources and click on Learning Objectives.

Now that you have read Chapter 4, you should be able to do the following:

+ Identify and define the five types of listening.
+ Explain the conscious listening continuum and provide two important characteristics of each type of listening.
+ Explain why listening is a skill that is vital to the workplace.
+ Distinguish between hearing and listening.
+ Describe possible blocks that may keep someone from hearing a message.
+ Draw the listening cycle associated with informational listening.
+ Describe the four barriers that may occur with informational listening.
+ Describe the qualities you should evaluate when listening critically.
+ Discuss the four components of self-reflexive listening.
+ Explain conscious listening and why it is important in the workplace.
+ Follow the tips for listening in meetings.
+ Listen in conflict situations.
+ Listen to legitimate complaints and handle chronic complainers.
+ Listen when asked for help.

## Key Terms

The terms below are available in a digital glossary on the Communicating in Professional Contexts website, which is best accessed through this book's CD-ROM but is also available at http://communication.wadsworth.com/goodall2. Go to the Chapter 4 Resources and click on Glossary.

## Writing and Critical Thinking

The following activities can be completed online and, if requested, submitted to your instructor. You'll find them on the Communicating in Professional Contexts website, which is best accessed through this book's CD-ROM but is also available at http://communication.wadsworth.com/goodall2. Go to the Chapter 4 Resources and click on Writing and Critical Thinking Activities.

Choose one of the following activities:

1. Spend an entire day focusing on your listening skills. Take the time, for each communication event you encounter, to go through each stage of listening. Listen for information critically, self-reflexively, and finally consciously. Write down your listening experiences. What did you learn about yourself as a listener? What did you learn about conscious listening?

2. Evaluate a specific listening situation. What was the context? What were the speaker's motives? Was the speaker credible? What did the person want?

3. In your group, share an experience where either conscious listening or a lack of good listening skills had an impact on your personal or professional life. Ask your group members for feedback. What would they have done differently in the situation?

4. Read the statements below and take a position on each issue. Now, working in a group, each person is to discuss his or her position, with a goal of reaching group consensus on each issue. Before providing a new response, each participant must recap the previous speaker's statement.

   ✦ Some lyrics in rap music should be banned because they incite violence.

   ✦ Women are better suited to be caregivers than to be corporate executives.

   ✦ The grading system at our school should be a simple pass-fail rather than letter grades.

   When all participants have responded, discuss the process, focusing on the Best Practices outlined in the chapter. Discuss with your group which points were most difficult to accept and which were easier. What did you learn about your own listening behaviors, both verbal and nonverbal, that block your ability to listen consciously?

5. An unknown author once said, "I know that you believe you understand what you think I said, but I'm not sure you realize that what you heard is not what I meant." Prepare a short discussion on how this quote relates to the chapter on listening.

## Research and Explorations Online

The exercises below can be completed online and, if requested, submitted to your instructor. You'll find them on the Communicating in Professional Contexts website, which is best accessed through this book's CD-ROM but is also available at http://communication.wadsworth.com/goodall2. Go to the Chapter 4 Resources and click on Internet Exercises.

1. Track down one of the listening sites on the WWW. Share with your group or class some of the exercises you found on the site. For example, the International Listening Association, at http://www.listen.org, lists links to other sites, articles on listening, and listening exercises.

2. Enter the terms *business communication, listening* as a keyword search on InfoTrac College Edition or the WWW. Search for articles that use this terminology. Pick an article from your search that discusses listening in a business context. How would you do in the organization or context discussed in the article?

3. Go to the American Communication Association homepage at http://www.uark.edu/~aca/. Type *listening* into the search engine and see what websites pop up. Cruise these sites for information that may be relevant to your assignments in this class and other classes.

4. Using InfoTrac College Edition, visit the International Listening Association website (http://www.listen.org) and complete the Listening Self-Assessment, in Listening Resources. Based on your scores, in what areas do you show strengths, and what areas are challenges? Choose one challenge area and, using the guidelines in the chapter, become a conscious listener for at least one week. Maintain a journal of your progress and the results of using these new behaviors. How did your conscious listening affect your interactions with others? How did others respond to your conscious listening? Prepare a short presentation to share your experience with the class.

5. Using the Goodall CD and InfoTrac College Edition, read the article "Seeking Silent Type: Be It Business or Pleasure, Good Listening Skills Can Go a Long Way." Now view the group presentation on the Goodall CD connection. Analyze and discuss the importance of conscious listening among the group members during their presentation. What effect would the presentation have had on you as an audience member if the team members interrupted or corrected one another during the formal presentation?

## Practicing Communication in Professional Contexts
### Moving from Mindless to Mindful Communication

Working in a group, complete the following exercise. This process allows you to work consciously through the exercise at an experiential level, then at an evaluative level.

### The Process

1. Pick one member of the group to tell the story narrated below. (If your class is not working in groups, read the story to a friend and complete the remaining steps of the exercise.)

2. Go around the group and give each person three minutes to expand the story.

3. As each person speaks, listen to the personal narratives, facts, history, and other elements interjected into the story.

4. After the last person has spoken, leave the group without discussing the story further.

5. Write an essay describing what you heard and your listening experience. (See additional instructions below.)

### The Story

*Enrique was excited about his promotion to area sales manager at GHS. He had worked hard to reach his goal of becoming a sales director by age thirty. The company was growing and expanding, which meant he had more opportunity ahead of him. Shortly after his promotion, the regional sales director, Hal, asked him to fly to the home office in Tampa for a regional sales meeting. The meeting would be on Monday; however, Hal wanted Enrique to fly in on Saturday so that he could go "golfing and hang out with the guys."*

*Later that day, when Enrique was talking to Mary, the area sales manager of another district, he mentioned that he was arriving in Tampa on Saturday. Mary asked why, and Enrique told her Hal had invited him to go golfing. Mary . . .*

Group member one speaks for three minutes, adding to the story.
Group member two speaks for three minutes, adding to the story.
Continue until all the group members have added to the story.

### Your Essay

Outside of class, write a three-to-five-page paper about your experience. How did gender, language, culture, and communication history affect what you heard? How did listening play a part in the development of the story?

# The Power of Verbal and Nonverbal Communication in the Workplace

E very morning on his way to work, Lawrence listened to talk radio. He switched between a National Public Radio news-oriented format and a local talk show featuring a feisty pair of hosts who engaged callers in a discussion of the "question of the day."

Most mornings, the questions were about people's personal or work relationships, and sometimes about personal relationships with coworkers. Lawrence found the NPR broadcasts interesting and informative, but more often than not he listened to the talk show, because he believed it revealed how people really are.

Lawrence considered himself a student of "how people really are." He had studied psychology, sociology, and communication as an undergraduate at his state university and was now enrolled in a weekend MBA program. He worked as the assistant manager of human resources for a large bank, a job that allowed him to combine his interest in people with his love of business. His favorite books were of the self-help and motivational varieties, especially ones by best-selling authors who talked about how to deal with people at work and in personal relationships.

Lawrence saw himself as a positive, empathetic, high-energy person who excelled when working one-on-one with other employees, trying to help them solve work-related problems. He believed that he worked well in small-group or team situations, where he could use his knowledge of people to bring out the best in them. Because of his experiences as a college debater, he felt very comfortable and confident in presentational speaking situations. All in all, Lawrence considered himself a well-rounded communicator.

Lately, however, his sense of himself as a good communicator who could handle any situation had been challenged at work. The previous week, he had overheard some coworkers talking about him in unflattering terms. They described him as being a person who is all flash and no real substance. They made fun of his positive attitude, his high level of energy, and his always-present smile. One coworker even joked about the way he dressed, calling his style "imitation GQ."

These comments had stopped him cold in his tracks. Were they really talking about him? The more he overheard of their conversation, the clearer it became. Not only were they talking about him, they were making fun of the way he spoke and dressed. He stood in the hallway, hidden from view, with a growing sense of anger mixed with fear that gradually gave way to embarrassment. He walked back to his office alone and shaken.

With all his study of "how people are," with all his confidence about his communication skills, he didn't know what to do. Should he charge back down the hall and make a scene? Pretend he hadn't heard them? Act cool, as if nothing of importance had occurred? Try to get even?

As he reflected on his experience, he decided to use it to his advantage. He apparently needed to rebuild his image at work. If he was being perceived as a shallow person, all flash and no substance, what could he do about it? Maybe his clothing was part of the problem. And his big smile. On the other hand, maybe it was the other people who had the problem. After all, what was so bad about having a positive attitude at work? Or being well dressed? Or smiling? Why should he trust the opinions of people who talked badly about him behind his back?

The talk show he was listening to this morning featured the question "What do your coworkers do that makes you nuts?" The first caller claimed that she wasn't being taken seriously by her coworkers. Lawrence turned up the volume. He listened for a while to her woes: she had good ideas, but other people stole them and she never got credit for the work she did. Within minutes, the hosts began imitating—cruelly, Lawrence thought—her high-pitched voice and her somewhat whiny conversation style. The caller became quiet, and Lawrence felt a little sorry for her.

The second caller complained that coworkers were spreading rumors about him in his organization but he was at a loss about what to do. He felt that if he denied the accusations, he would look guiltier. If he didn't say anything about them, he looked bad, too. Lawrence nodded. The hosts asked what the rumors were about. The caller hemmed and hawed, then finally admitted that the company was in the process of being bought out by a competitor. He was in charge of a department that was due to be downsized, and everyone thought he was negotiating a side deal with the new owners. "Well, are you?" asked one of the hosts. "Who, me?" came the reply. It was instantly apparent that the caller was not going to give a straight answer to the question—which probably meant, Lawrence mused, that the caller didn't give straight answers to any questions. That was his problem. His coworkers were spreading rumors because there was an absence of truth being told. Lawrence had seen it before.

The third caller reported that she was the victim of repeated sexual harassment at work, and that even though she had filed a complaint, nothing was being done about it. To make matters worse, everyone she worked with now gave her the silent treatment, as if she were the person who had done something wrong by reporting it. "Maybe they fear for their jobs if they associate with a whistle-blower," one of the hosts offered.

"Yeah, maybe," the caller replied. "I'm thinking about quitting," she admitted.

"Don't do that!" shouted one of the hosts. "You haven't done anything wrong!"

The caller sighed loudly. "You know," she said, "it just shouldn't be like this. I wish I knew what to do."

Lawrence, being well trained in dealing with sexual harassment issues, knew the woman was being unfairly treated and found himself aggravated that the human resources department at her company wasn't doing its job properly.

Finally, a woman called in to say that there was this nice guy at work, an assistant manager, whom everyone was down on lately. They talked badly about him behind his back. They made fun of how he dressed, how he talked, and even the books he read. This angered her, because she knew he was a dependable, hard worker who always had a smile on his face and a positive attitude toward his coworkers. She thought some of his coworkers were jealous of him because he was going back to school to get his MBA, *which meant he would eventually get a big raise and a promotion. She didn't know whether to tell him what was going on behind his back. She was also a bit ashamed that she hadn't said anything when people were slamming the guy.*

*Lawrence froze. He recognized the caller's voice. This person worked down the hall from him, in computer services. He had no doubt whom she was referring to. She was talking about him! He listened to this show because it revealed "how people really are." Now he was hearing how he really was, or at least how some others saw him.*

*As Lawrence turned onto the avenue where his office was located, the hosts were saying it was "too bad" coworkers were acting that way, but they had to wrap up the show. They encouraged the caller to "talk to the man." Then, in their talk-show wisdom, they summed up the complaints they had heard during this hour as proof that "the people we work with are basically the same people we went to high school with, only older, uglier, bolder, and meaner." This line was accompanied by the standard laugh track, and then the show ended.*

*But for Lawrence, the day was just beginning.*

## Communication of Self in the Workplace

In this chapter, we examine the relationship of communication to our work identities and the concept of power. As Lawrence learned, what we say and do in the presence of others largely determines who we are, or our identities. In turn, our identities determine how much power we have to influence others and outcomes. To develop positive identities and have influence at work, you need to understand the role verbal and nonverbal communication play in how others see you. As you will learn, issues of identity and power relate to how conscious we are of our presentation of self in verbal and nonverbal communication situations.

Lawrence's experience shows us that other people's perceptions of our verbal and nonverbal communication create our identity at work. Identity is the response we get from others to what we say (verbal communication) and do (nonverbal communication) (Mead, 1934; Goodall, 1983; Wood, 1997). In this way, we can only partially control our identity at work. Those with whom we exchange verbal and nonverbal communication have a great deal of impact on our workplace identity. To gain more personal control over others' perceptions of our identity requires us to become more conscious of our communication.

How can we do that? By becoming more aware of the influence of our verbal and nonverbal communication in the workplace and choosing strategies for improving our image. Table 5.1 shows the connection between awareness and identity in the conscious communicator.

| Verbal and Nonverbal Awareness Continuum | | |
|---|---|---|
| **Unaware** | **Moderately Aware** | **Aware** |
| Communicator uses:<br>◆ unclear, ambiguous phrases.<br>◆ no strategies for upward and downward communication.<br>◆ exclusive, disconfirming messages.<br>◆ unsupportive messages.<br>◆ communication that detracts from professional credibility.<br>◆ communication that displays little or no awareness of the relationship between power and words.<br>◆ communication that displays no awareness of gender differences in talk. | Communicator:<br>◆ uses a mixture of clear and ambiguous phrases.<br>◆ attempts to apply upward and downward communication strategies.<br>◆ uses a mixture of inclusive and exclusive messages.<br>◆ attempts to use supportive messages.<br>◆ uses communication that doesn't detract from professional credibility.<br>◆ is aware of the relationship between power and words.<br>◆ applies knowledge of gender differences in talk. | Communicator uses:<br>◆ clear, strategically unambiguous phrases.<br>◆ strategies for upward and downward communication.<br>◆ inclusive, affirming messages.<br>◆ supportive messages.<br>◆ conscious verbal communication that enhances professional credibility.<br>◆ communication that demonstrates the relationship between words and power.<br>◆ communication that displays a respect for the differences in the way men and women communicate. |

**Mindless** . . . . . . . . . . . . . . . . . . . . . . . . . . . . . . . . . . . . . . . . . . **Mindful**

**Table 5.1**
Awareness Continuum

## Developing Awareness in the Workplace

We need to become more conscious of our overall verbal and nonverbal impact in the workplace. We need to pay closer attention to our word choices, behaviors, appearance, and style of dress. We need to actively seek out feedback from others to our communication in interviews, interpersonal exchanges, group and team meetings, and presentations. By showing others our interest in their responses to what we say and do, we encourage them to share information with us about our identity at work.

We also need to become better monitors of the influence of our behaviors on others. By **monitoring,** we mean two things: (1) checking the accuracy of your perceptions regarding how the messages you believe you sent were actually interpreted, and (2) questioning the cultural and contextual factors that may lead to different perceptions about your communication.

## Monitoring Our Assumptions about Communication

It may seem odd that we are often our own worst enemies when it comes to communicating mindfully at work. But the truth is that too often we operate mindlessly, allowing our stereotypes, cultural biases, assumptions about the meanings of words, and routine perceptual filters to control our daily communication.

Most of us operate mindlessly because we live as if our assumptions about verbal and nonverbal meanings are essentially the right ones. For example, we assume that we were reared the right way, that our religious and political beliefs are correct, and that our thoughts and feelings about what others say are justified. It is as if we assume that our life — which is also to say our culture, gender, age, socioeconomic level, and race — is the center of the known universe and that everything and everyone essentially revolves around us. The problem with this belief in our rightness is that it may lead us to treat others unfairly or create inequity in the workplace.

## The Principle of Workplace Equity

**Equity** is the principle that we should be treated fairly by others and, in turn, should treat them fairly. Think of equity as the golden rule that governs the choosing and creating of verbal strategies for workplace communication.

The concept of equity is based on four key assumptions (Walster, Walster, and Bershied, 1978; Wilson and Goodall, 1991):

1. *People work for rewards.* **Rewards** are what people derive from their work (money, identity, power, support, companionship, a skill set) in relation to what it costs them (physical labor, mental and emotional stress, loss of free time, time away from family, subordinating personal goals, dealing with difficult people, harassment). When what they get out of going to work balances with what it costs them to be there, they feel a sense of equity. Some days are better than others, but overall there is a sense of fairness, of justice in their work lives.

2. *People seek empowerment.* When people believe they are being rewarded fairly, they tend to do a good job and feel good about the work they perform. Workers who feel a sense of equity also tend to feel empowered. **Empowerment** is the process of enabling and motivating employees, mainly by removing roadblocks, which builds feelings of personal effectiveness and control. When employees feel they are heard and their input is valuable, their performance improves. They actively seek better ways to perform tasks and get along with people because, in the end, what is good for the business is good for them.

3. *People become stressed when they feel they are treated unfairly.* When people find themselves in a state of inequity, they become stressed. Inequity may be caused by unequal pay for doing the same job as others, unfair treatment by coworkers or bosses, or a sense that the company doesn't care about the welfare of the worker as much as the worker cares about the welfare of the company. The stress brought on by feelings of inequity impairs

the job being done. The more inequity felt, the more stress experienced, and the worse the job becomes.

4. *People experiencing stress will try to restore equity.* When people experience stress brought on by feelings of inequity, they will try to restore equity in one of three ways: (a) *seeking mental equity* (making excuses for the bad treatment, forgiving the wrongdoer, assuming an attitude of moral or intellectual superiority); (b) *seeking actual restitution* (doing less work, slowing down the work of others, stealing property); or (c) *seeking narrative equity* (talking badly about the workplace; engaging in gossip and rumors designed to lessen the influence of the perceived wrongdoer; telling work-hate stories).

In many ways, the equity principle can be applied directly to choosing communication strategies in the workplace. Your overall goal should be to select strategies that encourage others to treat you equitably and that demonstrate your interest in treating others equitably.

## Making Conscious Choices about Verbal Communication

Making conscious choices about communication is a central way in which you can become a better workplace communicator. It also may improve your communication skills at work. Why? Because most people's verbal communication at work can suffer from these types of problems:

+ a lack of clarity or a misuse of ambiguity
+ an inability to distinguish communication strategies for upward or downward communication in the organization
+ a failure to distinguish between inclusive (affirming) and exclusive (disconfirming) message strategies
+ a failure to distinguish supportive from nonsupportive messages
+ an inability to conceive of verbal communication as a way of enhancing professional credibility
+ a lack of awareness of the relationship of our words to power
+ a lack of awareness of gender differences in talk

In the following sections we describe in more detail each of these challenges to verbal communication in the workplace.

## Clarity and Ambiguity

**Clarity** means providing messages in the clearest, least ambiguous way. **Ambiguity** means expressing oneself in terms that are unclear or open to multiple interpretations. One of the most frequently given pieces of advice for the workplace is to communicate clearly. As you learned in Chapter 2, the underlying theory of communication informing this advice is the information transfer model. The idea, simply put, is that if a sender can find the clearest, least ambiguous way to say something, the chances are greater that the receiver will hear and understand it as it was intended. The problem with this conception of communication is that regardless of how clear the message may be, people still interpret the meanings of words differently.

Does this mean that clarity shouldn't be a goal of effective communication? Absolutely not. It does mean that, even if you choose and plan a message that you think is clear, your audience may not hear exactly what you communicated. Assume that miscommunication is likely, and ask for feedback on what message your listener actually heard. When you behave this way, you gain power over the meanings others attribute to your communication.

## BEST PRACTICES

## Communicating Clearly

+ *Clarify the received messages to avoid misunderstandings.* Have you ever missed a meeting because you wrote down the wrong date or time? You may have jotted down "Tuesday" under the assumption that it was next Tuesday, not this Tuesday, only to find that you were wrong. To avoid misunderstandings, check the accuracy of what you think you heard rather than assume you are right.

+ *Avoid abstraction.* The goal should be to reduce possible misunderstandings by becoming more specific in your language usage. Instead of saying, "We've got a problem; we need to talk," which may set off alarms for your coworkers, say, "We have a problem with the e-mail system this morning, so we'll need to call a meeting to exchange ideas about getting it fixed." Remember, the closer your language comes to representing the specific reality you are trying to describe, the less abstract it will be.

+ *Watch your use of jargon.* Every organization, profession, age group, and culture develops its own verbal shorthand, known as "jargon." Used inside the group, these terms save time. Outside the group, these terms are often incomprehensible, which increases the likelihood of misinterpretation or misunderstanding. When you select a goal for a message, consider whether you should adapt your language usage to the needs and expectations of your audience or listener.

+ *Avoid the use of inflammatory language.* Too often we punctuate our workplace communication with expletives, harmful expressions, or words that demean the character, efforts, or abilities of others. When this happens, conflict can occur. If inflammatory language is used during an ongoing conflict, the conflict tends to escalate.

> ◆ *Avoid cultural and gender biases in everyday speech.* Many of the words
> and expressions we use are culture specific, and very often our style of
> speaking (and listening) is gender specific. For example, the statement
> "That dog don't hunt" may communicate clearly in Alabama, but its mean-
> ing will probably be lost on someone from Japan. Similarly, gender and
> communication specialists often distinguish between men's tendency to com-
> municate in a "reporting" style (for instance, "I'm just telling it like it is")
> and women's tendency to use a "rapport-building" style (Tannen, 1990).
> Taking gender and cultural differences into account is an important element
> of becoming a more mindful communicator in the workplace.

## Upward and Downward Communication

A nationwide survey of employees who have changed jobs points to a correlation between employee turnover and supervisor relationships. The majority of
those surveyed cited a bad supervisor, not low pay, as the main reason for job
change (*Greensboro News and Record*, May 30, 2000). Our guess is that we
would find poor communication skills at the core of the breakdown in the su-
pervisor-employee relationship.

Although a number of organizations have flattened hierarchical structures
and empowered employees, most companies still equate hierarchical position
within a company with power. Put simply, the higher up you are on the organizational ladder in terms of title, position, seniority, or salary, the more authority you have to exert influence on those whose position is understood to be
hierarchically lower. As you learned in Chapter 3, power that is associated with
position in an organization is referred to as *legitimate* power.

In everyday communication, power among levels of legitimate authority in
organizations is greatly influenced by choices made about the style and content
of talk. This means that how you choose to speak to organizational superiors
(anyone higher than you on the ladder) and subordinates (anyone lower than
you on the ladder) can determine how they respond to your identity, requests,
directives, and commands. Speech used with organizational superiors is called
**upward communication.** In general, the following communication choices
tend to enhance employees' power and identity with superiors:

◆ balancing politeness with a clear task orientation

◆ balancing friendliness with respect and deference to authority

◆ balancing self-interest with company needs

◆ asking for feedback on the accomplishment of tasks

◆ avoiding sexist, racist, or classist remarks

Speech used with organizational subordinates is called **downward communication.** In general, the following communication choices tend to enhance employees' power and identity with subordinates:

+ listening openly to employees' communication

+ responding honestly to inquiries and requests

+ asking for information prior to evaluating a situation or problem

+ providing feedback on tasks

+ avoiding sexist, racist, or classist remarks

+ balancing personal and professional respect with a task orientation and accountability

## Inclusive and Exclusive Messages

Organizations are cooperative settings. To work usually means to work with other people, using communication to coordinate objectives and activities and to share meanings. For this reason, your identity at work derives from generalized observations about how you deal with people. Are you open to the ideas of others? Do you seek feedback? Are you interested in what others think and feel about issues? Do you share credit (or blame)?

Evaluations such as these reflect what communication scholars refer to as "inclusive and exclusive" message strategies. The basic idea is that how you treat others at work is part of an overall goal you have for using talk in your life. In political terms, one way to conceive of the difference is to think about democratic versus autocratic strategies. **Inclusive message strategies** are democratic because they reveal your interest in fitting in with the group or business culture, taking into account the thoughts and feelings of others, soliciting contributions from others, and actively valuing differences in opinion as a way of maximizing the available information needed to carry out a task. Examples of inclusive strategies include actively coordinating your goals with coworkers' goals, asking for and being willing to give feedback about tasks, soliciting the opinions of others on a project, and avoiding seeking sole credit for good ideas or work.

By contrast, **exclusive message strategies** reveal an autocratic communication style. Exclusive strategies are revealed in a "me first" pattern of behavior. Examples of exclusive strategies include seeking individual credit for ideas or work, requiring compliance from others, attempting to forge close allegiances with selected others who can advance your personal goals or career (often without feeling any equitable obligations or sense of reciprocity), pitting one group or person against another, and demonstrating a lack of interest in the opinions of others, particularly others whose opinions or background may differ from your own.

We choose to behave inclusively or exclusively. As a result, others evaluate our patterns of behavior accordingly. People who reveal an inclusive pattern tend to find that others work with them in achieving goals, affirm preferred identities, and cooperate with them in accomplishing tasks. They tend to be more integrated into formal and informal communication networks, thus improving their opportunities to gain and give feedback. They tend to be valued as team players by managers and coworkers. By contrast, people who reveal an exclusive pattern tend to find themselves more isolated from others in the workplace, which often translates into feeling less connected to formal and informal networks. Because they are not interested in the opinions of others and do not seek feedback, they leave themselves, their motives, and their actions open to suspicion, misinterpretation, and criticism. As a result, those who use exclusive message strategies tend to have less influence in the workplace and less control over interpretations of their identities.

## Confirming and Disconfirming Messages

People are sensitive to the responses others give to their talk. One way in which we monitor our work identities is by evaluating the responses we get as being either confirming or disconfirming. Confirming responses support and enhance the identities we seek:

"I appreciate the work you did on this project."
"I think that's a great idea!"
"You're a wonderful employee."

Using the equity principle discussed earlier, you can see how positive, confirming messages influence coworkers, subordinates, and superiors to reciprocate. Confirming messages also may inspire them to repeat exemplary performances or even encourage them to believe they are capable of higher qualities of work.

By contrast, disconfirming messages attack the very heart of workers. Disconfirming messages deny or harm our identities:

"I can't believe anybody in this company would do such a stupid thing!"
"This is incompetent work."
"I'll never forget that you made this mistake."
"I can't believe I ever trusted you to carry out this task."
"You are a fool!"

Using the equity principle, you can see what is likely to happen when disconfirming messages are given to coworkers, subordinates, or superiors. The targeted individual will probably retaliate by seeking some form of restitution for the perceived harm done to her or his identity.

So how should you communicate verbally to people who have made mistakes on the job? When engaging in corrective communication, it is important to limit the discussion to the task and not attack the person. Whenever possible, frame the error within a more general statement that affirms the worker's identity. In this way, you separate the mistake from the identity of the person who made it, and you show others that you treat people fairly and responsibly on the job. As you can imagine, these verbal choices will also enhance perceptions of *your* identity.

That said, sometimes emotions get the better of us. When stressed, many people say or do things they later wish they hadn't. Another important form of verbal communication in any workplace is the *sincere apology*. Equity may be restored when a sincere apology is given.

## Supportive versus Nonsupportive Messages

Closely related to inclusive and confirming message strategies are the mindful goals of using communication to provide support for others. As we have pointed out, because the workplace is a cooperative setting, people value others who try to support them. **Supportive messages** communicate concern and respect for others and indicate cooperation. Supportive messages include the following:

- ✦ offering to help out on a project
- ✦ listening
- ✦ doing nice things for your coworkers
- ✦ showing respect for others' views and feelings, as well as for the general condition of the workplace
- ✦ demonstrating concern for the welfare of coworkers

By contrast, the use of nonsupportive messages closely relates to exclusive, disconfirming communication. **Nonsupportive messages** are associated with an inflated ego and self-centeredness. They communicate disrespect of others and lack of cooperation:

- ✦ appearing aloof and behaving in a superior manner with coworkers
- ✦ refusing to be of assistance on a project when asked
- ✦ withholding information
- ✦ not listening
- ✦ disrespecting others and the condition of the workplace
- ✦ lacking concern for the welfare of coworkers
- ✦ not being a team player

Individuals who choose to be supportive in their dealings with others at work tend to encourage others to treat them equitably in return. Individuals who behave in nonsupportive ways also encourage a sense of equity from others: unsupportive behavior tends to reap more unsupportive behavior. In terms of constructing an identity in the workplace, supportive messages tend to encourage others to affirm your identity and, at the same time, provide corrective feedback when necessary. After all, being supportive sometimes means pointing out ways that communication may be improved or errors corrected. In this way, support does not always mean affirmation. Supportive messages, however, go a long way toward encouraging others to help you obtain your goals.

## Enhancing Personal and Professional Credibility

One of the first theorists of human communication, Aristotle, pointed out in his classic treatise *The Rhetoric* that the goal of all public talk should be the improvement of one's character with one's peers. Today, we describe that goal for talk as "the enhancement of personal and professional credibility."

*Credibility* refers to the authority and trust listeners or audiences give to speakers. If we believe that an individual is a good person, knowledgeable about a topic, and trustworthy, we tend to pay more attention to what he or she says. We also tend to be more easily influenced by the person. For this reason, advertisers promote their products with testimonies given by credible spokespersons. Credibility is often associated with celebrity, which may be a cultural by-product of living in a media-influenced age. However, the fact remains that we are persuaded most by people we find credible.

In the workplace, employees find that by developing their own personal and professional credibility, they also influence others to affirm their identities. Credibility is a goal for communication that is enhanced by the following actions:

+ becoming informed and knowledgeable about the work assigned to you, which includes being an information resource for others and providing people with the information they need, when they need it

+ behaving in a trustworthy manner by keeping secrets and confidences, looking for the good in situations and in others, and not spreading gossip and rumors

+ being open, honest, and authentic in your dealings with everyone

+ demonstrating that you are capable of being a friend as well as a coworker by showing respect and caring for others on the job

+ doing what you say you will do, which means becoming reliable as a person and as a professional

+ graciously accepting criticism and corrective feedback from others, and using these messages to improve your performance

+ accepting personal responsibility for your actions and not blaming others for your problems, challenges, or mistakes

## Verbal Communication and Perceptions of Power

Communication is the basis for identity, and it is also the source of personal and professional power. Forms of organizational and institutional power are tied to one's status and hierarchical position at work. For example, a manager has the power to organize work teams, set objectives, and evaluate workers. Similarly, forms of cultural power derive from an individual's wealth, perceived attractiveness, or family lineage.

But there is a form of power that is not tied to status or cultural hierarchies and that directly relates to communication. This is the communication power that refers to the perception others have of your ability to use words and actions to obtain workplace results that would not have occurred otherwise. In this way, communication power is a rhetorical or narrative quality attributed to you by listeners, audiences, coworkers, or managers because of what you say and do.

### Gendered Talk

Research has shown that women and men can differ in the ways they tend to communicate, construct meanings, and derive implications or evaluations from communication (see Tannen, 1994; Wood, 1997, for review). For this reason, we say that all talk is "gendered." **Gendered talk** refers to the differences between the ways men and women tend to communicate.

Generalizing about gendered talk in the workplace is difficult. For every generalization, there are clear exceptions to the rule. However, research studies have shown the following to be true (Wood, 1997):

+ Women generally use talk to build rapport in relationships; men generally use talk to make reports to others.

+ Women's style of talk tends to be more expressive (rich with words intended to deepen understanding and meaning); men's style tends to be more instrumental (clipped responses, intended to provide direction).

+ Women's communication style tends to be more tentative; men's style tends to reflect more certainty.

+ Women tend to use talk to create and maintain relationships; men tend to use talk to gain control over situations and others.

For reasons that should be clear from the above list of gendered differences, we suggest that women and men can improve their communication in the workplace by meeting halfway. For example, avoid the assumption that your intentions or meanings are clearly shared. Avoid talk that stereotypes another's talk or that connotes inferiority due to gender (such as "Only a woman would . . ." or "Guys always think . . ."). Think about the gender implications of communication *prior* to speaking. Lastly, be willing to switch styles when the situation calls for it.

## Verbal Lie Detectors

Do you know when someone is telling the truth? Here are some tips that may help you detect when someone is trying to deceive you.

+ Response time—the time between the end of a question and the start of a reply. Liars take longer and hesitate more.

+ Distancing—not saying "I," but talking in the abstract (for example, liars might say, "One might believe . . .").

+ Uneven speech—stuttering while trying to think through the lie. Liars might also suddenly talk quickly, attempting to make a sensitive subject appear less significant.

+ Gap filling. Liars are too eager to fill in the gaps of conversation. Liars keep talking when it is unnecessary, as if a silence signifies that the other person does not believe them.

+ Raised pitch. Liars raise their voices unnaturally. Instead of the pitch dropping at the end of a reply, it is lifted in the same way as asking a question.

+ Message insecurity. Liars are unsure of their message, which leads to an increase in stuttering, slurring, and Freudian slips.

From Adrian Furnham, 1999, "Gesture Politics," *People Management* 6, 52.

Your workplace identity is based on the responses you get from others to what you say and do. However, you can have some control over how others respond to you by making wise choices about message strategies designed to help you accomplish your personal and professional goals. By communicating inclusively and affirming others' identities and efforts, by showing support for others, by striving to become credible as a person and as a professional, by being more aware of cultural and gender biases in talk, you limit the possible negative responses others can make. You gain greater control over their perceptions of you and of your chances of reaching your goals with their help.

## Nonverbal Communication and Perceptions of Meaning

Nonverbal communication is the natural counterpart of verbal communication. Nonverbal means "without words," and nonverbal communication refers to all of the resources beyond what you say that contribute to the meaning of a message. Unless you are physically removed from your listeners or audience (for example, talking on the phone or using e-mail), what is interpreted as meaningful in your interaction will be informed by what you say—and by how you look when you say it. Researchers have found that between 65 and 70 percent of the social meaning of communication is conveyed nonverbally (Birdwistell, 1970; Philpott, 1983). Researchers also have established that if there is a discrepancy between what you say and how you look when you say it, most listeners will believe your nonverbal actions over your verbal ones (Andersen, 1998).

In this section we want to examine the sources of nonverbal communication in business and professional contexts. Throughout our discussion, we want you to understand that although "actions speak louder than words," in most cases actions work *with* words to produce meanings. The discussion in this section centers around the nonverbal communication that is commonly accepted within corporate America. If you find yourself dealing with other cultures, you should familiarize yourself with the nonverbal expectations and taboos of those cultures.

## Your Workspace

In Chapter 2 we discussed the importance of keeping your work area neat, free from clutter, and clean. We also stressed the importance of artifacts, the personal and professional items that mark a territory as our own. We encourage the use of artifacts that attest to your accomplishments—decorating your office space with diplomas, certificates, and awards. We discourage the display of personal items, and under no circumstances should you display anything that has suggestive sexual content. Our basic message is to treat your workspace as an extension of your professional self. Become conscious of the way your office area and artifacts communicate to others.

## Clothing and Personal Appearance

You've undoubtedly heard the expression "You never get a second chance to make a good first impression." But have you ever asked why that is true? The answer is that most humans make initial evaluations of others based on stereotypes, and stereotypes are largely derived from the size and shape of our bodies, the clothing we wear, and perceptions of our level of physical attractiveness (Andersen, 1998). Of course we know we should avoid stereotyping and that evaluations made on the basis of stereotypes can be wrong, but most of us engage in it routinely every day. There is no place in our lives where stereotyping is more evident than in the formation of initial impressions. According to uncertainty-reduction theory (Berger and Calabrese, 1975), nonverbal cues are read and interpreted against stereotypes to reduce the uncertainty in initial interactions. In other words, as tennis star Andre Agassi put it, "Image is everything."

What does research about personal appearance teach us? For one thing, our culture values and rewards people who are tall, physically fit, appropriately

## BEST PRACTICES

### Creating the Optimal Workspace

+ Keep displays of your personal life to a minimum. One family photograph is enough. Don't clutter your office with items that may suggest you'd rather be doing something else.

+ Prominently display diplomas, awards, certificates, and other professional accomplishments.

+ Clear your desk and empty your trash prior to leaving work for the day.

+ Be aware of the messages you are sending when you display personal items in your workspace. Keep personal collections at home. Your workspace is not the area to show off your car magazines, stuffed toys, or collection of cat photographs.

The books highlighted below will help you to create the optimal workspace. Putting time and effort into the appearance of your workspace sends a clear nonverbal message to those around you that you are in control and ready for whatever needs to be done.

+ *Taming the Office Tiger,* by Barbara Hemphill (Kiplinger Books, 1996). This book is considered by many large companies, including 3M and Xerox, to be the definitive book on organizing your workspace. *Taming* provides tips for managing a filing system, organizing your computer, using to-do lists, and knowing when to use piles. It also provides a list of essential tools for any office and tips for managing your voice mail.

+ *Practical Feng Shui at Work,* by Simon Brown (Barnes & Noble Books, 1998). Feng shui is based on the principle that everything has energy, so that how you arrange your space either enhances or detracts from your energy. By positioning your desk and other materials in the optimal place, you can create an office that energizes you and helps you achieve your goals. Feng shui also addresses issues such as clutter, which practitioners believe saps your energy and your ability to accomplish tasks and move forward.

dressed, well groomed, and physically attractive (Andersen, 1998, p. 31). Anyone who has watched television commercials can attest to the fact that the sale of body-building equipment, makeup, perfumes, clothing, beer, and even soft drinks depends on how well the ad communicates messages of success, popularity, and happiness. Commercials rarely stress the intrinsic worth of being healthy, fashionable, or fit (Jhally, 1997). We live in a postmodern world that glorifies images rather than substance.

In business and professional settings, the norms for our cultural ideals also apply. Every few years, one of the major TV news programs does a segment on

## BEST PRACTICES

### Dressing Successfully in the Workplace

+ Never dress noticeably better than your boss or your peers. Your boss may wonder if you are moonlighting or after his or her job. Your peers may feel you are trying to show them up.

+ Savvy businesspeople understand that for men, casual dress means khakis or, depending on the organization, nice jeans with a nice golf shirt. Women have a harder time achieving a "business casual" look but should dress down without trying to look like "one of the boys." Avoid tight jeans, shorts, and other apparel that works against your ability to be taken professionally.

+ Men and women should keep jewelry to a minimum. Too much jewelry can be distracting and, in some cases, physically limiting. The wrong kind of jewelry can alienate people.

+ The reality is that everything in the competitive workplace counts. Our goal here is simply to make you aware.

job interviews. Invariably, these shows pit a physically fit, well-groomed, attractive, and well-dressed applicant against an overweight, unkempt, unattractive, and sloppily dressed applicant. Both applicants have résumés reflecting exactly the same work experience and qualifications. Not surprisingly, the attractive applicant is consistently hired. The unattractive applicant is treated rudely and is rejected on the basis of appearance. Noted communication theorist Peter Andersen has pointed out that "appearances can be deceiving, but that fact is almost beside the point. A communication perspective recognizes that subjective impressions by receivers are all that really matter" (1998, p. 31).

What should you do to "dress for success" on the job? Ethnographic studies have shown the advantages of researching the physical appearance, clothing, and hairstyles associated with people doing the job you are applying for (Goodall, 1989; Goodall and Phillips, 1985). Before applying for a position with a firm, ask for a company tour. Pay close attention to how people dress. Ask yourself if your appearance and clothing choices are a match for this organization. In most cases you will find that human resources people and managers tend to hire people who fit the attitude, appearance, and style of their company (Wilson and Goodall, 1991). Even in the "business casual" workplace, there are limits; going beyond those limits may send the wrong signal.

Once you are on the job, become more conscious of how your clothing choices fit into the norms of the organization. Unless you are interested in making a personal statement (perhaps at some risk to your career), it is a good idea to opt for a look that doesn't attract too much attention. As a headhunter once explained it to us, "I tell my clients that the most subversive people in any organization tend to be the most conservatively dressed. That way they can be subversive without looking like revolutionaries. The difference is whether they really want to change things, or just look like they do."

---

### Focus on Ethics

Miranda is up for a big promotion she has been working toward for more than a year. She works hard, meets deadlines, stays late, and comes to the office early. Miranda is convinced there isn't anything that could hold her back.

Ryan respects Miranda's work and her work ethic. He recognizes that she is the most dedicated researcher in his division. She deserves the promotion she has worked so hard for, but Ryan isn't sure he wants to promote her. A promotion to analyst would mean that Miranda would have to meet with government officials and even an occasional senator. Ryan has no qualms about Miranda's ability to present crucial information; he just isn't sure how seriously others would take her. From what he has seen, Miranda's entire wardrobe consists of sweaters with seasonal or holiday scenes on them, khakis, and tennis shoes. She doesn't dress like someone with a high-security clearance and a job handling sensitive government information.

As a researcher who rarely interacted with anyone outside the department, Miranda could wear whatever she wanted. Ryan had guys who came to work in shorts and flip-flops, and nobody cared. But even the guys knew that when they decided to get on the analyst track, it was time to clean up their act and dress professionally.

Does Ryan have a responsibility to discuss an appropriate dress code with Miranda before he makes his decision? Should the way Miranda dresses hinder her career advancement? Is it ethical to deny someone a promotion simply because he or she needs a makeover? Does Miranda have a responsibility to dress in a professional manner?

---

## Voice

The human voice is a powerful instrument of meaning. Learn to listen critically to how you speak, and monitor the match between your vocal characteristics and the attitude, intention, or emotion you want to convey. Such monitoring is vital to communication effectiveness. How many times have you heard or used the expression "It's not what you said; it's how you said it"? What came across was not the words that were spoken, but an interpretation of the words derived primarily from the sound of the voice, or what communication theorists call *paralanguage*. Paralanguage is a powerful form of nonverbal communication because it conveys to listeners a communicator's attitude, intentions, and emotions. Consider the following list of sources of paralanguage in light of your own experiences in responding to others' speech:

+ *pitch* (highness or lowness of the voice)

+ *tempo* (speed at which the message is delivered)

+ *intensity* (when words are vocally accented, or spoken softly, or with particular emphasis)

+ *range* (the ability of the speaker to vary the pitch, tempo, and intensity of what is expressed verbally)

+ *resonance* (richness or weakness of tone)

+ *volume* (the loudness or softness of the voice)

+ *articulation* (the precision with which words are spoken)

+ *rhythm* (the relative flow and punctuation of the voice)

+ *pauses* (the frequency and duration of silences between words, phrases, or sentences)

+ *dysfluency* (punctuation of a message with expressions such as "er," "um," "you know," and "like")

Overall, these sources of paralanguage tell us a lot about the attitudes, intentions, and emotions we use to construct what we call the *meaning* of a message. Consider, for example, how we determine if someone is enthusiastic about a project or nervous about doing a presentation. Or whether someone we asked to carry out instructions will actually do so. In all of these cases, our evaluation is based on the articulation and tempo of the voice, the relative authoritative resonance we hear, smoothness or interruptions in flow, and whether there are too many or too few pauses. How we speak shapes how others interpret our messages.

There is a caveat. Although all of us believe we can evaluate a person's voice with great accuracy, research has revealed important cultural and gender differences. For instance, men who use a wide vocal range and often vary their pitch may be perceived as feminine and aesthetically inclined, whereas women using a similar pattern are perceived as dynamic and extroverted (Richmond and McCroskey, 1995). Similarly, some women and many young people tend to tag their sentences with vocal inflections ("uptalk") that turn a declarative statement into a question. For example, "I'm having lunch with Paul? We'll talk about the project?" may be intended as two statements of fact, but the vocal cues suggest they are two questions.

## Body Movement, Facial Expressions, and Eye Contact

The study of body movement, including facial expressions, eye contact, and gestures, is known as **kinesics.** The specific study of the eyes as a source of communication is called **oculesics.** Together, these forms of nonverbal communication dominate the research literature and provide interesting and useful resources for the conscious communicator in business and professional settings.

Of all of the forms of nonverbal expression, the most important source of information is the face, especially the eyes. Research shows that we seldom manifest distinct or recognizable facial expressions when we are alone (Kraut and Johnson, 1979). But the face becomes expressive when we are with other people, and humans have learned to be very attentive to even small differences in facial expression and eye contact.

We also learn how to manage our true feelings using our facial expressions. Researchers have shown that as we mature, we learn to "manage facial affect" by deploying five "display rules" (Andersen, Andersen, and Landgraf, 1985; Ekman, 1978; Bugental, 1982). Those display rules are as follows (from Andersen, 1998, p. 36):

+ *simulation:* showing feelings when we have no feelings

+ *intensification:* showing more feelings than we actually have

+ *neutralization* or *inhibition:* showing no feelings

+ *deintensification* or *miniaturization:* showing fewer feelings than we actually have

+ *masking:* covering a feeling with an expression of a feeling we are not actually experiencing

Children do not learn to manifest these display rules until preschool or during their elementary school years. Mastery of them occurs only in adulthood.

One of the negative consequences associated with failing to express our true feelings is an increase in adverse psychological reactions, feelings of stress, and disease (Buck, 1979). In the workplace, we limit the ability of others to respond when we limit our nonverbal cues. By managing our facial cues, we deprive others of valuable communication information.

The eyes provide the clearest case of meaning associated with nonverbal communication. Why? Because when we talk to someone, we tend to locate their self right behind the eyes. We establish eye contact to make contact with others. According to research (Kendon, 1967), eye contact performs eight potential nonverbal actions:

1. Regulates interaction by signaling turn taking
2. Monitors interaction by receiving information from others
3. Signals cognitive activity, because eye contact is typically broken when individuals are thinking about complex issues
4. Expresses involvement in the interaction
5. Reveals intimidation through intensive staring, particularly when combined with negative facial expressions
6. Reveals flirtation

7. Reveals attentiveness
8. Displays the level of participative immediacy of listener involvement and attention

## Benefits of Making Eye Contact

There are seven benefits to making good eye contact:

1. It inspires trust. Would you make a major purchase from a salesperson who didn't look you in the eye?

2. It automatically gains confidence. Hold a firm gaze and you will be perceived as being more businesslike, serious, and self-assured.

3. It buys you time. If you've lost your train of thought, if you don't know what to say next, or if you've been caught off guard, eye focus is your best weapon of defense. You'll seem deep in thought—even a bit mysterious—but can use a pause to collect your thoughts, take a deep breath, and plan your next move.

4. It quietly keeps control. If people in a meeting are ignoring you, talking over you, or otherwise usurping control, use eye contact to redirect them. Simply stop speaking and fix your eyes on them until they notice you (and they will). Be sure to keep a neutral expression so you don't come across as a sour-faced schoolteacher scolding pupils. Once you've regained control, hold it.

5. It deftly wields power. Who isn't drawn in by a silent person with a strong gaze? If your eyes aren't focused on a person, you may be giving up power. Are you silent and looking down? You may be viewed as bored or subservient. Are you looking away or out the window? You may be seen as a daydreamer.

6. It effectively stifles stage fright. When you focus your eyes on one person at a time for varying lengths of time, you instantly reduce a large audience to a series of one-on-one conversations.

7. It effortlessly puts others at ease. People on the receiving end of good eye contact benefit, as well. You can help others feel at ease and open up.

Adapted from Guiliano (1999).

Researchers also have discovered that the eyes communicate through pupil dilation. Our pupils dilate (enlarge) when we are aroused by, interested in, or attracted to another person (Andersen, Todd-Mancillas, and DiClemente, 1980). Most people are relatively unconscious of this signal and in many cases attribute positive responses to something else—a pleasant facial expression or a nice smile.

Eye movement is a controversial area of nonverbal communication research because results have been inconsistent. However, there is a general belief that the eyes move right or left during cognitive activity, and there is a tendency, at least in males, to move the eyes to the left when employing visual or spatial right-hemisphere thought and to look right when employing linguistic cognition.

In business and professional settings, just as in everyday life, facial expression and eye contact communicate potentially useful information about ourselves and others. In our experience as consultants, we often find that people who display positive, affirming, and inclusive facial expressions and who maintain eye contact tend to win allies and attain a reputation for being good to work with or for. They are perceived as being easy to be around, and they seem to send a general nonverbal message of openness to and interest in others. How do they do this? In our experience, they are skilled in maintaining eye contact with listeners and using eye contact as a source of information about the emotional responses of others; using positive, affirming head nods to indicate listening to as well as appreciating the information being shared; and smiling easily and genuinely.

We tend to believe that the eyes are the source of truth about character and intention. Given that chronic liars tend to be very good at maintaining eye contact while telling lies, this is probably not as good an indicator of character as we believe it is. We also believe that smiles and affirming head nods are signs of interest, attention, and respect. However, in other cultures, such as Asian cultures, head nods merely mean that a message is being heard, not necessarily agreed with. These differences suggest that easy generalizations probably are not warranted.

## Nonverbal Lie Detectors

Just as there are verbal indicators that someone is being less than truthful, nonverbal cues also may give liars away. Check the speaker's nonverbal behavior for the following:

+ Too much squirming. Shifting around in one's seat signals a desire not to be there.
+ Too much, rather than too little, eye contact—liars tend to overcompensate.
+ Microexpressions—flickers of surprise, hurt, or anger that are difficult to detect.
+ An increase in comfort gestures. These often take the form of self-touching, particularly around the nose and mouth.

From Adrian Furnham, 1999, "Gesture Politics," *People Management* 5, 53.

Nevertheless, becoming a more conscious communicator means monitoring your own and others' facial expressions and eye contact. It is important to become aware of the nonverbal messages you may be sending others with your face, eyes, and body. To do well in business and professional settings, you need to be mindful of the potential meaning of these nonverbal messages at least as much as you are mindful of your own and others' verbal content. You must also be mindful of cultural and gender differences that may affect your verbal and nonverbal communications with others.

## Space

**Proxemics** is the study of interpersonal space and distance (Andersen, 1998). What do we know about the relationship of nonverbal communication to spatial relationships? Researchers have identified three broad categories of meaning: territoriality, crowding and density, and personal space.

### Territoriality

Humans are territorial creatures. Think about your desk in a classroom, or your room in your residence. How do you feel when someone invades your space? What do you do about it? Researchers have found that we use nonverbal communication to signal our boundaries, or markers of the edges of our territories (Sommer, 1969). We may leave our books or clothes on chairs or in rooms, or we may place backpacks on tables. In dating relationships, partners often leave behind personal items as if to signal to others that they are currently occupying this space, and perhaps to ward off potential intruders.

### Crowding and Density

It has become a cultural cliché to say "I need my space." But in fact, research shows very clearly that this is true. When we feel crowded—in classrooms, rock concerts, or offices—we tend to become measurably stressed. In cases of extreme crowding, people have been shown to become pathological and engage in criminal conduct.

### Personal Space

As we walk through life, we feel that we own a certain degree of space around us at all times. We call this area our **personal space,** and research indicates that we feel violated, uneasy, stressed, and potentially violent if anyone other than an intimate encroaches on it (Hall, 1968; Anderson, 1999). Our sense of the extent of our personal space varies from culture to culture—what a Canadian thinks is close may seem distant to someone from Turkey. Hall (1968) maintained that in North America we have four "zones of interaction":

+ *Intimate zone*—from the edge of our skin to about eighteen inches away from our bodies. We allow into this zone only close friends, intimates, and family members.

+ *Casual or personal zone*—from about eighteen inches to four feet away from our bodies. This is the space we reserve for most conversations and social engagements with friends and family members.

+ *Social-consulting zone*—from four to eight feet. This is the zone we reserve for most business transactions with shop clerks and sales personnel, and with teachers, ministers, lawyers, and other professionals. This is also the zone we use most often in team or group meetings and with anyone with whom we want to signal a "business-only" relationship.

+ *Public zone*—eight feet and beyond. This space is reserved for public speakers, celebrities, and executives.

Most people regard these distances as almost sacred. This means that we protect them, and we regard invasions of them to be culturally, if not personally, offensive. For people interested in becoming more conscious of their business and professional communication, it is wise to keep these distances in mind.

## Touching

The study of touching as a form of nonverbal communication is called **haptics.** Researchers (Heslin, 1974) have identified five basic types of touching behavior, which we have organized below from least to most intimate:

+ *Functional-professional*. This is the form of touching that we expect from physicians, massage therapists, coaches, tailors, hairstylists, and other professionals who must invade our personal space and lay hands on us to do their jobs.

+ *Social-polite*. The handshake is the most obvious example of this form of casual, yet meaningful, touching. Other forms include the social hug and the pat on the back, or placing a hand for a moment on the forearm of another person.

+ *Friendship-warmth*. This category ranges from the outer limits of social-polite touching to the edge of love-intimacy touching, and for this reason it is the most common and most ambiguous in our culture. As Andersen put it, "Too much touch or touch that is too intimate conveys love or sexual interest, whereas too little touch may suggest coldness and unfriendliness and arrest the chance for relational escalation" (1998, p. 47).

+ *Love-intimacy*. This is touching we reserve for those closest to us, and research indicates that it is unique to each person. Usually, this touching is nonsexual, but it may become sexual with the appropriate partner in the right setting. Studies show that when this type of touching occurs, the result is "increased psychological closeness and warmth" (Andersen, 1998, p. 47).

+ *Sexually arousing.* This is the most personal and most intimate form of touching shared by humans. Research indicates that it is also the most arousing and most anxiety-producing form of human contact. For this reason, it requires "mutual consent, a high level of attraction, and a desire to stimulate and be stimulated by one's partner" (Andersen, 1998, p. 47).

As with other forms of nonverbal behavior in the workplace, it is important to become aware of the messages that may be communicated by touching. As a conscious communicator, you must be mindful of the potential meaning of such nonverbal messages.

## Harassment and Communication in the Workplace

Thus far in this chapter, we have been concerned with functional forms of verbal and nonverbal interaction. In this section we describe a dysfunctional form of communication that is all too common in the workplace: harassment. The Equal Employment Opportunity Commission (EEOC) tracks the following forms of harassment and workplace discrimination: race, sex, national origin, religion, age, and disabilities. Based on EEOC guidelines, harassment includes slurs about sex, race, religion, ethnicity, or disabilities; offensive or derogatory remarks; verbal or physical conduct that creates an intimidating, hostile, or offensive work environment; and creating conditions that interfere with the individual's work performance.

In the remainder of this section, we will concentrate on sexual harassment, a form of harassment that is prevalent in the workplace. Much of the information and many of the tips provided in this section can be applied to the other forms of harassment listed above.

### What Is Sexual Harassment?

In the context of the workplace, **sexual harassment** is any form of sexually explicit verbal or nonverbal communication that interferes with someone's work. The Civil Rights Act of 1964, additional legislation in Congress, and federal, state, and local court decisions have addressed two types of sexual harassment. The first type, **quid pro quo** ("this for that") harassment, is based on the threat of retaliation or the promise of workplace favoritism or promotion in exchange for dating or sexual favors. In recent years, this category has been interpreted to refer to suggestions and innuendoes as well as explicit quid pro quo comments. The second type of harassment, a **hostile work environment**, is created through sexually explicit verbal or nonverbal communication that interferes with someone's work or that is perceived as intimidating or offensive. It is im-

Steven Lunetta/PhotoEdit

portant to note that the behavior doesn't have to be intentional to create or contribute to a hostile work environment. Offhand remarks or casual displays of sexually explicit materials count. So do remarks that the sender may think of as "compliments."

Sexual harassment can occur between people of the same sex or of the opposite sex. Although usually associated with the negative behavior and activities of men in the workplace, it also may be litigated when men are the alleged victims and women are the alleged perpetrators. The Equal Employment Opportunity Commission reported that between 1990 and 1996, formal sexual harassment complaints jumped 150 percent (see http://www.eeoc.gov/stats/harass .html). Sexual harassment has become so pervasive in North American society that many for-profit and nonprofit companies, as well as most government agencies and schools, have implemented policies, mandatory seminars, and workshops to train employees in how to recognize and prevent it.

Sexual harassment, although clearly recognized as a problem in North American organizations and culture, is not viewed similarly in other cultures.

Latin and Mediterranean cultures, for example, do not regulate physical contact or suggestive language usage in professional settings. Because of such differences, many intercultural misunderstandings can occur in the workplace. As we've pointed out already in this chapter, it is a good idea to understand that our assumptions about the rightness of our communication acts are largely culturally determined.

## How Can Harassment Be Avoided?

The best defense against a sexual harassment charge is to carefully monitor your own verbal and nonverbal communication. Be courteous and polite at all times. Take other employees' feelings into consideration when you speak to them. Recognize that women and men often respond differently to comments about appearance, suggestions about behavior or attitudes, and sources of humor.

Do not engage in sexual commentary, jokes, or banter about others' appearance or clothing. Do not bring sexually explicit photographs, magazines, objects, or calendars to your workspace. Around people you know to be especially sensitive to issues of harassment, be especially careful about your conduct. Trying to excuse yourself for an offensive statement or gesture is embarrassing and hurtful to your credibility at work; losing your job or having to spend months in litigation is far more damaging to your sense of self and career.

We all share an obligation to make the workplace a safe and productive environment for everyone. Toward this end, avoiding verbal and nonverbal communication likely to be perceived as offensive is the only right thing to do.

## What Should You Do if You Are a Victim of Harassment?

Even though there are laws against sexual harassment, knowing exactly what you should do when you feel victimized is not always easy. One of the common problems experienced by harassment victims is the belief that either nothing will be done about it or that saying anything about it may cost them their jobs (Claire, 1998). Unfortunately, both of these scenarios can occur. The machinery of the judiciary is often slow, and victims of harassment may be forced to spend months or years in court trying to gain a settlement.

This does not mean you are defenseless. Nor does it mean that you should keep quiet about harassment. What you should do is be conscious of the steps the courts have determined a victim of harassment should pursue:

1. *Confront the harasser and ask him or her to stop the offensive behavior.* This advice is often the hardest to follow. If you fear the harasser, consider writing her or him a letter expressing your concerns or asking a friend to intervene on your behalf. However, it is vital to confront the person with the charge and to document the outcome. Failure to do so can result in a less viable legal position.

2. *Keep a diary in which you record the dates, times, and places of offensive or harassing actions.* In many cases, simply informing a harasser about the problem is enough to stop unwarranted comments or actions. However, if it persists, it is important to record, in as much detail as possible, further incidences of harassment. You are establishing a pattern of harassment, which is much harder for the harasser to defend against in court.

3. *Complain about the harasser within the channels prescribed for such action by the policies of your employer.* Become familiar with the policies regarding employee appeals in your organization. Follow them to the letter. Most companies ask that complaints against employees be made to a supervisor, who may then channel them to a personnel committee, union, or mediator for resolution. It is also important to decide what actions you want taken on your behalf. Will you be satisfied if the harasser stops harassing you? Or do you feel that additional remedies are required—a public apology, a job transfer, coverage of medical expenses?

4. *File a legal complaint with the federal EEOC or with your state agency for workplace discrimination.* You are entitled to file a complaint and to have legal representation. For people who elect to pursue this option, it is a good idea to schedule a meeting with an EEOC representative to discuss your case.

Sexual harassment is a crime. It is very serious business. It doesn't matter to the courts how you may personally feel about it, or whether your words were intended to offend or be complimentary, or how other people may have responded to similar jokes, suggestions, or touching. Being labeled as a convicted harasser will likely have lifetime negative consequences. Think carefully about these consequences *before* you engage in any activity that may be perceived as potentially harassing.

## Summary

This chapter explored the dimensions of verbal and nonverbal communication at work. We began by detailing the relationships among verbal communication, identity, and power. In these sections we focused on how important it is to engage in conscious decisions about verbal behavior, to monitor the effect of one's choices on others, and to be receptive to feedback about verbal communication. We then turned our attention to nonverbal communication. In these sections we focused on the powerful influences nonverbal actions have on the interpretation of meanings. We concluded this chapter with a discussion of sexual harassment as a special form of dysfunctional communication involving both verbal and nonverbal components.

# Chapter Five

# COMMUNICATING IN PROFESSIONAL CONTEXTS ONLINE

All of the following chapter review materials are available in electronic format on either the Communicating in Professional Contexts website or CD-ROM. In addition to the multimedia case studies, activities, and numerous other learning resources you'll find on the CD-ROM, the CD is your gateway to the book's premium web content, which is not accessible via the Internet. The book's basic web content is available both with the premium content and on-line at http://communication.wadsworth.com/goodall2 and includes the chapter learning objectives and activities, key-term digital glossaries, and quizzes. The CD is also your gateway to InfoTrac College Edition, our extensive online data-base of full-text articles that is fully keyword searchable and available twenty-four hours a day. Installation instructions for the CD appear on the inside of this book's back cover.

## What You Should Have Learned

The learning objectives below are available on the Communicating in Profes-sional Contexts website, which is best accessed through the book's CD-ROM but is also available at http://communication.wadsworth.com/goodall2. Go to the Chapter 5 Resources and click on Learning Objectives.

Now that you have read Chapter 5, you should be able to do the following:

+ Discuss how we make conscious decisions about verbal and nonverbal communication in the workplace.

+ Discuss the role of monitoring in conscious communication.

+ Discuss the principle of workplace equity.

+ Describe the difference between upward and downward communication.

+ Explain the differences between inclusive and exclusive messages.

+ Discuss the differences between supportive and nonsupportive messages.

+ Explain how we can use verbal and nonverbal communication to enhance personal and professional credibility.

+ Describe a few types of verbal power displays.

+ Discuss differences in the ways men and women tend to communicate.

+ List the types of nonverbal communication that may occur in the work-place.

+ Discuss the impact of clothing and personal appearance on professional identity.

+ Discuss how eye contact affects nonverbal communication.

- ✦ Discuss proxemics and why the concept of personal space is important to communication in the workplace.

- ✦ Discuss haptics and the types of touch that are appropriate and inappropriate in the workplace.

- ✦ Discuss the two types of sexual harassment recognized by the courts.

- ✦ Discuss ways to avoid sexual harassment.

- ✦ Describe what to do if you are a victim of sexual harassment.

## Key Terms

The terms below are available in a digital glossary on the Communicating in Professional Contexts website, which is best accessed through this book's CD-ROM but is also available at http://communication.wadsworth.com/goodall2. Go to the Chapter 5 Resources and click on Glossary.

| | | |
|---|---|---|
| **ambiguity** *(127)* | **haptics** *(145)* | **personal space** *(144)* |
| **clarity** *(127)* | **hostile work environment** *(146)* | **proxemics** *(144)* |
| **downward communication** *(130)* | **inclusive message strategies** *(130)* | **quid pro quo** *(146)* |
| **empowerment** *(126)* | | **rewards** *(126)* |
| **equity** *(126)* | **kinesics** *(140)* | **sexual harassment** *(146)* |
| **exclusive message strategies** *(130)* | **monitoring** *(125)* | **supportive messages** *(132)* |
| | **nonsupportive messages** *(132)* | **upward communication** *(129)* |
| **gendered talk** *(134)* | **oculesics** *(140)* | |

## Writing and Critical Thinking

The following activities can be completed online and, if requested, submitted to your instructor. You'll find them on the Communicating in Professional Contexts website, which is best accessed through this book's CD-ROM but is also available at http://communication.wadsworth.com/goodall2. Go to the Chapter 5 Resources and click on Writing and Critical Thinking Activities.

Choose one of the following activities:

1. Look at the area of your dorm room or apartment you use for studying, or your office, cube, or desk where you work. What nonverbal messages does your workspace send out? Are they the messages you want others to receive? Investigate the references in this book or go to the bookstore to find resources to help you get your work area in shape. Ask for books on clutter, feng shui, organizing, or space management.

2. Briefly write about a communication event that had a significant nonverbal component. The event you choose can be placed in either a professional or educational setting. What was memorable about the encounter?

Did your behavior help or impair your ability to resolve the situation? What would you do differently now that you have read this chapter?

3. Spend a day of conscious, positive communication with the following goals in mind: clarity, inclusion, supportiveness. As you go through the day, be aware of how you use power and gender in your talk. Write a short essay about your experience. What did you notice? Did people respond to you differently? How did you feel at the end of your positive-communication day?

4. Select an e-mail or a memo you recently received from a business associate or a friend that had an unclear message. Specifically identify what aspects of the e-mail or memo were ambiguous or unclear. Consider ambiguous terms such as "ASAP," "soon," and "maybe," as well as the tone of message. Meet with the person for clarification. Write a short essay describing the difference in your perception of the message and the sender's intended message. Also discuss the benefits or disadvantages of meeting with the person face-to-face rather than continuing the written communication.

## Research and Explorations Online

The exercises below can be completed online and, if requested, submitted to your instructor. You'll find them on the Communicating in Professional Contexts website, which is best accessed through this book's CD-ROM but is also available at http://communication.wadsworth.com/goodall2. Go to the Chapter 5 Resources and click on Internet Exercises.

1. Write a sexual harassment policy for a fictitious company. When you have finished, go to InfoTrac College Edition or the WWW and find examples of real policies. What did you leave out? What would be the result of using your policy?

2. Using the search engine on InfoTrac College Edition or the WWW, type in "gestures" as a keyword search. Look for information on offensive gestures. These could be gestures other cultures find offensive or gestures that could be considered harassing. Pick one of the resources you located and summarize the information for your class or group. Include the web address so that your classmates can use the resource in the future.

3. Use InfoTrac College Edition or the WWW to find information on "dressing for success" for the workplace. Create a shopping list of the items that you need to dress for success. Keep in mind the type of work you will be doing and the culture you will be working in.

4. Go to www.isabellemori.homestead.com/tests.html and complete the intercultural assessment. Write a short essay on what you learned about intercultural relations and why it is important to be aware of and sensitive to cultural verbal and nonverbal differences in today's global economy.

## Practicing Communication in Professional Contexts

As a professional, you will be called upon to attend meetings of professional groups or civic organizations. These groups provide us with opportunities to network, gain information about our profession or industry, and practice our communication skills.

Attend, either individually or with your group, a meeting of your local Toastmasters organization (or you may choose to attend another civic or professional meeting). You can use the Internet to locate meeting times and places in your community (for example, the Toastmasters International website is http://toastmasters.org).

This is your opportunity to be a "fly on the wall." Carefully watch the public and interpersonal communication events that occur during the meeting. What verbal and nonverbal cues did you notice people using to deal with communication diversity? How did males and females differ? What cues were used to deal with cultural diversity? How did the older members of the group communicate with the younger members of the group? What cues did you find yourself using?

Take two examples from the meeting and apply the information in this chapter to the examples. How would those participating in the communication event you selected have benefited from what you have learned? Discuss your experience with the class.

## Communicating in Professional Contexts in Action!

Working with a group, watch a film or a video of a speech with the sound suppressed. Each member of the group is to independently write down their impression of the nonverbal messages and emotions being conveyed by the speaker and their overall impression of the speaker based on nonverbal cues.

Be specific in identifying the nonverbal cues that help form your impression. The group then shares their impressions, identifying the body language cues that affected their impressions. After the discussion, rewind the video and replay it with audio.

How accurate were your evaluations?

Did the nonverbal message match the verbal message? If there was a discrepancy between the nonverbal behaviors and the spoken words, what suggestions would you give the speaker to enhance the connection between the verbal and nonverbal language?

# Information Technology
# and Conscious Communication

**J**en's morning routine always begins with turning on her computer. Then, while waiting for the startup program to run, she checks her phone messages. She has learned to appreciate callers who keep their messages short and to the point. It drives her crazy when callers drone on and on, forgetting to give a return phone number or name, then requesting she call them right back.

By the time Jen finishes the chore of voice mail, her computer is up and running and it is time to check her e-mail messages. This morning, at least three are flagged with red exclamation marks, meaning that they are urgent. But experience has taught her that maybe one is actually important and the other two really aren't urgent at all. She'd like to give the senders the benefit of the doubt and assume they simply forgot to turn off the "high priority" option. Chances are, though, the senders figured that because she would check the urgent messages first, flagging them improved their chances of getting a quick response.

As Jen finishes reading the urgent e-mails, Tanisha pops her head into Jen's cubicle and announces, "Meeting in five minutes, Jen. Be sure to bring your PDA." Five minutes! What should she do first? Answer the urgent phone messages, or the urgent e-mails? And what about the remaining messages in her inbox?

When Jen picks up her PDA—the electronic personal digital assistant that the company encourages employees to use for making notes and linking with word processing and calendar programs to save time and money—she realizes that she has begun to resent it and the other forms of technology invading her life. These days, her PDA, e-mail, cell phone, desktop computer, and voice mail ensure that she is never very far from communication with coworkers, clients, suppliers, friends, and family. Heading out the door, she thinks, "Welcome to another day in information technology hell."

This chapter is about information technology and conscious communication in the workplace. We aim to help you begin thinking about information technology as a communication tool and improve the way you use it. Imagine yourself as Jen. Given that some of the same technology-based pressures and challenges she faces probably shape your life, this shouldn't be too hard. Now imagine that your goal in reading this chapter is to gain more control over your time by making better use of technology to communicate in the workplace. Accordingly, we will focus on improving the results you get from initiating and responding to technologically mediated messages.

We begin by framing our discussion of technology as an extension of what you have already learned about the relationship of communication to power, to gender, and to systems and cultures of organization. We move on to a brief discussion of the types of information technologies currently in use in organizations, and our conscious-communication approach to making better decisions about using them. We then offer a practical section on doing web-based research. We conclude this chapter with some words of advice about how much technology you need and how much information about technology you really need to know.

Jose Luis Pelaez, Inc. /Corbis

## Information Technology and Communication

We want to begin our exploration of information technology with an intriguing thesis developed by an information scientist named Dan Lacy (1995). According to Lacy, if world history is viewed from a communication perspective, the societies that communicated information the farthest and the fastest gained power and dominated each era.

For example, consider our human evolution as communicators from, as Lacy puts it, "grunts to gigabytes." Among our ancient ancestors, hunters who could gesture and grunt in ways that gained the cooperation of other hunters were able to pool their resources, hunt larger game, and better organize themselves for survival. Similarly, we can see how the invention of the Phoenician alphabet and rules for grammatical usage led to the Phoenicians' dominance in their epoch and to the later ancient Greek construction of a system of logical reasoning. In turn, these advances led to the systematization of rules for conduct and laws for societies.

Power and the domination of a given society were not solely gained, nor maintained, by peaceful means. Roman generals and Chinese warlords used messengers to hand deliver plans of attack to their armies, thus greatly improving their ability to coordinate battles. The printing press, radio, television, computers, and satellites have significantly improved the widespread distribution of information and the speed with which it can travel, and they have determined which nations or multinational corporations control our destinies. As

Lacy has put it, the nation or company that can send messages the farthest and the fastest wins.

## The Downside to Information Technology

One downside to Lacy's worldview is that there are losers in every era — those people, nations, or companies that cannot compete. They fall behind in their ability to access and process important information. They do not learn at the speed and from the diverse cultural sources required to maintain current knowledge and skills. These days, because information is a commodity of primary value in a global economy, the effects of falling behind in information technology have never been more potentially devastating. As Barnet and Cavanaugh (1994) expressed it, we are rapidly becoming a world made up of Global North and Global South, where those in the northern hemisphere have access to information technology and economic resources for the development and deployment of information, and those in the southern hemisphere don't. Companies with well-developed information technology systems and the economic resources to train people to use them become more powerful, and those who rely on outdated modes of accessing and processing information find they can no longer compete.

Our hope for the future is that those of us in the Global North who are privileged to have access to information technologies and economic resources will find ways to build new bridges to those societies who are less fortunate. Such humane gestures are unlikely in business, however, as global competitiveness works against any form of altruism.

But even if humane gestures triumph, simply providing the technology is unlikely to be enough. We must also provide intelligent ways of deciding which technologies are needed to carry out meaningful tasks, and which technologies are less useful or merely redundant. We must combine our ability to provide material resources with better instruction about becoming more conscious and ethical in our professional uses of those resources. To do that means acquiring a new perspective on the relationship of information technology to business and professional communication.

## Revising Our Approach to Information Technology

Do you ever feel controlled by technology? Like Jen, do you sometimes feel overwhelmed by the sheer number of messages you have to respond to? By the pressure to respond to all of them? Do these concerns interfere with your desire and your ability to respond to those messages thoughtfully?

When organizations provide employees with information technology resources — pagers, answering systems, and computers, as well as the training to use them — they do so because they believe these tools will empower workers to organize and manage work on the workers' own schedules. What they seldom realize is that they may also be contributing to the employees' sense of **information overload.** When too many forms of communication intersect at one time, we have difficulty making decisions and responding.

Of course, in a success-oriented, individualist culture such as ours, making these resources available carries the implicit message that you should never *not* be working. A television commercial for an investment-banking firm drives this point home. In the commercial, a police officer pulls over a car and, upon discovering the identity of its driver, suggests that instead of playing golf this afternoon, the driver should go back to the office. Why? Because last year, the driver was in only the top ten, not the top five, of all investment bankers. The policeman pulls the golf bag out of the back seat of the car and returns to his patrol car, leaving the driver somewhat bewildered but obviously feeling guilty. Guilty — of what crime? Of not working when he could have been.

Increasingly, we have given up more and more of our leisure time for the allure, as well as the demands, of work. Women often cite this pressure as a reason for leaving organizational life in order to pursue alternative careers that give them more time for themselves and their families (*Utne Reader*, 1997). Working out of the home often affords more time, and more control over the demands made on them, than does working in a company. But for some women and men, opting for a work life constructed out of a home office means only trading the intrusions of information technologies at work for those that now reside in the home office.

## Information Technology and Gender Differences

We have learned in previous chapters that women and men tend to differ significantly when it comes to communication. But for a long time, researchers did not see a correlation between gender differences and perceptions or uses of information technology. Recently, however, important new questions have been asked that highlight how gender differences can be used to better understand decisions about information technology in the workplace (Geffen and Straub, 1997; Matheson, 1991; Witmer and Katzman, 1997).

Gender differences impact the introduction and diffusion of information technologies. Women tend to experience greater levels of anxiety than men do when it comes to implementing new information technologies, and user-friendliness matters more to women than to men. But women tend to adopt characteristically masculine usage patterns once the technology is in place (Matheson, 1991; Geffen and Straub, 1997, p. 397).

Women tend to place information technology within a social context. They have a greater need for "a technological medium to convey 'the presence' of the communicator —her feelings and thoughts" (Geffen and Straub, 1997, p. 397). Women tend to want to express themselves in a medium that allows for greater elaboration of their reasons and feelings, whereas men tend to focus primarily on the instrumental function of mediated speech.

Men and women perceive the modes of communication differently; for example, women tend to perceive e-mail communication as less useful than men do (Tannen, 1994b; Geffen and Straub, 1997). Women and men may have differing perceptions of the "social presence" of e-mail. More misunderstandings may take place between women and men who communicate via e-mail, because of the different perceptions of the social meaning of words used in that technological context. This may help explain why women tend to use more graphic accents (such as smiles and frowns) in e-mail than men do (Witmer and Katzman, 1997).

Organizations planning to introduce new or updated information technologies should take into account gender differences. Additionally, men and women should learn to recognize that differences in gender may significantly influence perceptions of meaning associated with e-mail, as well as other forms of mediated speech. Marketing specialists make use of this research when putting together focus groups designed to help implement new technologies in the workplace or provide feedback to systems and software designers about user impact and usage.

## Information Technology and Conscious Communication

How can we better think about, make decisions about, and use the rich information-technology resources available to us? In an informal ethnographic study conducted for this text, we considered the types of personalities typically associated with usage patterns in organizations we've consulted with. The results are displayed in Figure 6.1.

Figure 6.1 shows a range of usage patterns for information technologies, based in part on preferences for communication mode and in part by personality. At the left side of the continuum, we represent people who are least likely to use or respond to technology: "Luddites." A **Luddite** is a person who refuses to adapt to new forms of technology. (The term comes from workers in 19th-century England who destroyed machines that they thought would threaten their employment.) Typically, people who fail to adapt to technological advances fall behind in their ability to compete successfully, so Luddite behavior is not a good choice for people who work in a business and professional environment.

In the middle of the continuum, we represent a range of users—from the compulsive personality to the employee who just tries to cope day in and day out with information overload. Employees in the middle of the continuum may try to limit the time they spend sending and receiving mediated messages, thus risking being thought rigid. Or they may try to make better-informed decisions about channels for exchanging messages but sometimes find themselves unable

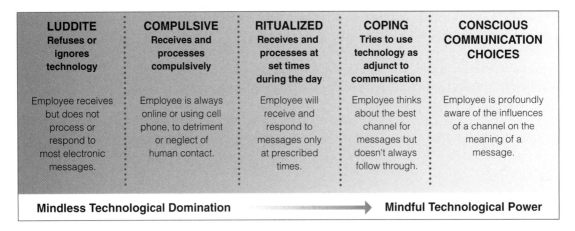

| LUDDITE | COMPULSIVE | RITUALIZED | COPING | CONSCIOUS COMMUNICATION CHOICES |
|---------|------------|------------|--------|----------------------------------|
| **Refuses or ignores technology** | **Receives and processes compulsively** | **Receives and processes at set times during the day** | **Tries to use technology as adjunct to communication** | |
| Employee receives but does not process or respond to most electronic messages. | Employee is always online or using cell phone, to detriment or neglect of human contact. | Employee will receive and respond to messages only at prescribed times. | Employee thinks about the best channel for messages but doesn't always follow through. | Employee is profoundly aware of the influences of a channel on the meaning of a message. |

**Mindless Technological Domination** ⟶ **Mindful Technological Power**

**Figure 6.1**

Conscious Communication and Technology Continuum

to carry out their decisions. As you can see, as you become a more conscious communicator, you grow less willing to allow information technologies to control your time or the channels you use to create, maintain, or change relationships with others.

On the far right of the continuum, you see people who make conscious decisions about which technology to use for maximum communication effectiveness with minimal intrusion on their lives. To become a mindful, more conscious user of communication channels, we must adapt our thinking about selecting appropriate channels and consider likely outcomes when selecting technology. Conscious users of technology understand the need to include relational and contextual information when communicating using technology. To reduce the possibility of misunderstanding in communication with coworkers or clients, mindful communicators may limit the amount of information shared via e-mail and phone messages, and they may make more time for personal contact.

Ideally, the more conscious you become of the influences of technology on communication in business and professional relationships, the more power you gain to define how and when you will select and use technology. When used wisely, technology is a catalyst for change. Robert H. Buckman, vice chairman of Buckman Laboratories International, has put it this way: "If you want to change your company, radically increase the span of communication for each individual. Let each person use a computer to communicate with anybody in the company—or anywhere else in the world—without any barriers, real or imagined. When you change a person's span of communication, you also change their span of influence—you expand their power. The more you allow each person to grow in terms of information and power, the more you grow the entire organization (1997)."

In the following section, we provide advice about using technology to change your span of communication.

## Types of Information Technologies

Huber (1990) uses two broad categories to define types of communication technologies currently available to organizations:

1. *Computer-assisted communication technologies*, including forms of image transmission (for example, facsimiles, modems, videoconferencing), e-mail and voice mail, and computer networks.
2. *Computer-assisted decision-aiding technologies*, including online management information systems, information retrieval databases, and expert systems or programs.

In the following sections, we will describe the first type of technology, which deals directly with communication. We will discuss how to make informed communication decisions about using specific types of technology and provide tips to increase your mediated communication efficiency.

### Computer-Assisted Communication Technologies

As recently as twenty years ago, the word *technology* was not part of the daily lexicon and desktop computers were considered a luxury. However, fax machines and phone systems were beginning to dominate offices as high-tech business solutions. Today, fax machines, although still widely used, are considered old technology. Many people use the fax as a last resort when a "hard-copy signature" is required or if the intended recipient of the message doesn't have e-mail software that allows attachments.

As modems became faster, PCs more prevalent, and e-mail more sophisticated, sending documents via e-mail became an important business solution. Now it is becoming commonplace to attend meetings by sitting in front of your "computer cam" and sharing information across a computer network with team members located hundreds, even thousands of miles away. Now that you have read Chapter 4, it should be clear how important it is, in many professional contexts, to have the ability to see the person sending an e-mail or attending a meeting electronically. These images provide real-time clues to meanings and the context of verbal feedback. In addition, high-technology and scientific firms often use videocams to facilitate communication among members of a diverse and multilingual workforce.

Videoconferencing, although becoming increasingly more widespread, has yet to catch on the way its creators had hoped. In part this is because people prefer face-to-face contact (Long, 1987), and in part it is because there are often time delays in message transmission, making the exchanges seem artificial in ways that interfere with communication.

In all of these applications, more informed choices about implementing and using technology can be made by following these conscious communication principles:

+ The quality of the image is likely to convey an impression about the credibility of the sender as well as the importance of the message. Choose high-quality images that represent the best interests of you and your company.

+ Ask whether using image-based transmissions of messages contributes anything of value. For example, if diversity in your workforce means that people who do not share a common language will be asked to communicate, could the availability of facial images facilitate shared meaning?

## Electronic and Voice Mail Systems

Almost everyone who interacts in a business and professional environment routinely uses voice answering systems, pagers, and e-mail. However, fewer people know how to make decisions about the communication dimensions of these channels. In the story at the beginning of the chapter, Jen was unhappy when callers left overlong voice messages and didn't supply a name or return phone number. She also was displeased when she saw "urgent" markers by e-mail messages that she had learned from experience were probably not urgent at all.

Making clear and conscious choices about how and when to use voice mail and e-mail will ensure that your message is well received and acted upon. Abusing voice mail and e-mail puts your messages at the mercy of the delete button. Below, we offer tips for using voice mail and e-mail effectively.

## BEST PRACTICES

### Using Voice Mail and E-mail

#### Using Voice Mail

**Voice mail** is any message left on a telephone answering system. Think of voice mail as a rough equivalent to a business memo.

+ Be clear and concise.
+ Give relevant information, such as the date and time of the communication, and the name of the sender and intended receiver.
+ Limit the message to two or three sentences. If additional information or clarification is needed, the receiver can call you back.
+ Include the specific date and time a response is required, if necessary.
+ Do not ramble or mix information or purposes.

## Using E-mail

**E-mail** is electronic mail transmitted to or from your computer almost instantaneously anywhere in the world. Think of e-mail as a virtual conversation rather than a long essay.

- Use short, concise statements that offer opportunities for feedback.

- Follow the assumption that each partner to an e-mail will have at least one turn in the conversation to make a point or respond to the other person's information.

- Don't cry wolf. Don't mark every e-mail message urgent. Eventually, your audience will catch on and stop reading your e-mail.

- Invite follow-up in the form of person-to-person contact, letters, or a phone call, so that the communication partners can facilitate more detailed exchanges.

- Convey emotion. If a posted message appears to have ambiguous meanings or if it could cause an unwanted emotional response, use an "emoticon" to signal the mood or effect intended. For example, a smiley face [ :) ] after a sentence may signal humorous intent; a wink and smile [ ;) ] can indicate "This is just between us," or a sense of irony; a frown [ :( ] can indicate displeasure or unhappiness.

- Have easily recognized participants. Attaching a "signature file" to your e-mails helps recipients locate you through other communication channels—phone, fax, physical address, and virtual address via e-mail, homepage, or website.

## What E-mail Is and Isn't

- An e-mail isn't a novel; it is a business message. E-mails should be concise and to the point. This should help eliminate the need for follow-up phone calls or other e-mails to clarify what you meant.

- It isn't a fight; it's a form of public communication. Avoid "flaming" others with critical comments, slurs, or personal attacks. If you have a problem with someone, resolve the problem in person.

- It isn't junk mail; it's e-mail. Avoid sending unsolicited e-mails by making sure that the content is likely to be of value to the recipient. "Spam" (the Internet term for junk mail) is seldom appreciated and, after the first one from a particular source, is usually deleted unread.

- It isn't a private love letter; it's a public document. There is no such thing as private e-mail. Even if the message is deleted, it can be accessed from the hard drive or network system. For this reason, think of everything that you send as potentially readable by your boss.

---

**Focus on Ethics**

Jen receives jokes from her friends via e-mail every day. At first it was fun, but now the amount of joke e-mails she receives is out of control. Leith is the worst. Some days, he sends five or more e-mails with jokes. She has asked him to stop, but Leith continues to send the jokes to everyone in the department. Even though she's learned to delete the e-mails rather than read them, they still take time out of her day.

How should Jen handle the joke e-mail issue? Should she explain to Leith again that she no longer wants to receive joke e-mails? She would love to just block all his e-mails, but if she does she might miss something important. Should Jen address the problem with her manager and ask that he or she create a policy about circulating jokes via e-mail on company computers? Jen doesn't want to be a tattletale, but she's drowning in joke/junk e-mail.

---

## Computer Networks

Computer **networks** are two or more computers connected either locally (within a company or building) or widely (across different geographic locations) by cable, phone lines, or satellite. Unlike e-mail and voice mail, computer networks do not facilitate direct communication. Instead, these forms of technology facilitate communication indirectly. Local Area Networks (LANs), Wide Area Networks (WANs), and the Internet allow us to access files, e-mail, the World Wide Web, and documents stored in another computer, in another room, or even in another part of the world. Perhaps the biggest impact networks have had on business and professional communication is **telecommuting:** working from your home or another remote site, away from your company's primary location, but connected by telephone, fax, and computer.

Telecommuting, commuting to work along the "information superhighway," has created a number of communication challenges. How do you communicate, build relationships, deal with conflict, or solve problems with members of a team who have never met face to face? Although telecommuting has certain advantages (freedom regarding your time and empowerment to do work your own way), the disadvantages (removal from everyday organizational life, lack of person-to-person contact, uncertainty about your place in the organization's culture) are only now being addressed from a communication perspective.

**Virtual communities,** where participation in the issues of the day can be more democratic and more deliberative, are springing up on the Internet and within organizations to address the feelings of isolation often associated with telecommuting. These communities bring together like-minded people or members of a team to work through problems, share ideas, and resolve conflict.

An interesting offshoot of these communities is the **netiquette** that has emerged from their interaction. *Netiquette* is the term used to describe appropriate manners when participating in online discussions. The basic rule is to "think before you type and lurk before you leap" (Trenholm, 2000, p. 323). Netiquette encourages community members to use appropriate entrance and exit rules; check FAQs (frequently asked questions) that are posted on a website, to avoid redundant questions; and avoid "flaming" others when in disagreement with them.

## E-mail and Chatroom Shorthand

FWIW—For what it's worth

FUBAR—Fouled up beyond all recognition

GD&R—Grinning, ducking, and running (after a snide remark)

GTG—Got to go

INAL—I'm not a lawyer (but . . .)

IDK—I don't know

IMHO—In my humble opinion

IYKWIM—If you know what I mean

IYKWIMAITYD—If you know what I mean and I think you do

LOL—Laughing out loud

OTF—On the floor

OTOH—On the other hand

PMFJI—Pardon me for jumping in (a polite way to get into a running discussion)

PMJI—Pardon my jumping in

RTFM—Read the "fascinating" material (usually in anger)

POS—Parent over shoulder

TIA—Thanks in advance

TPTB—The powers that be

TTFN—Ta-ta for now

ROTFL—Rolling on the floor laughing

RSN—Real soon now

SOHF—Sense of humor failure

SWALK—Sealed with a loving kiss

SPAM—Stupid person's advertisement

WRT—With respect to

WYSIWYG—What you see is what you get

YMMV—Your mileage may vary

YWIA—You're welcome in advance

Jim DeBrosse, Cox News Service, reprinted in *Greensboro News and Record*, September 24, 1999.

## Videoconferencing

Often, you will find yourself assigned to a work team or group whose members may not work in the same city, state, or even country. In many cases, virtual teams rely on **videoconferencing** to hold meetings or present ideas. In videoconferencing, two or more participants at different sites conduct a conference by using computer networks or audio and video equipment. As the cost of

## BEST PRACTICES

## Videoconferencing

### Before You Begin

1. Reserve the videoconference facilities for the day of your presentation and for one or two practice sessions if necessary.
2. Learn to use the equipment. Ask the technology support person at your company to go over all the equipment with you. Ask questions and be sure you understand how everything works. Ask someone who frequently uses the equipment to attend your practice session and give you advice for using the equipment more efficiently.
3. Determine your potential audience in advance. If possible, find out the names of those attending the conference and their affiliations.
4. Keep in mind that videoconferencing is a visual medium. Therefore, *you* become a visual aid. Wear bright colors that project well on screen. Keep your hair, jewelry, and other accessories simple so they do not distract your audience. Make sure the room you are presenting in is free of visual clutter.

### When Conferencing

1. Present an agenda for the meeting. This could be on a digital slide, or you could e-mail the agenda to your audience in advance.
2. Vary the images on the screen: you, a digital slideshow presentation, back to you, other members of the team at your location (this is possible if you have a cameraperson at your facility or if there are multiple cameras in the room), back to you.
3. Use confident, energetic, and engaging body language. Just because you are speaking into a camera doesn't mean there is no audience.
4. Look into the camera! Don't forget that people are watching. Don't walk out of camera range and continue to talk while your audience stares at a blank screen.
5. Adjust your speech and movement for the time lag that may occur between you and the remote audience. Speak more slowly than normal. Enunciate carefully. Vary the quality of your voice so that your presentation isn't flat or boring.

travel increases, many companies find that videoconferencing is an economical way to provide long-distance training or bring a company together for meetings when its employees are spread across many time zones.

However, without planning and practice, videoconferencing can be confusing and intimidating. Using CCCD (choose, create, coordinate, and deliver) to plan the components of your presentation and adding in elements for videoconferencing will help ensure your success. The tips in the box above were developed with help from Diane Howard's work on videoconferencing. Howard teaches students and professionals how to present information in a videoconference environment.

## News You Can Use: Doing Web-Based Research

In addition to opening up opportunities for telecommuting and networking, another major advantage of the Internet is that it provides us with access to information quickly and relatively painlessly. One disadvantage is that distinguishing quality information from the rest of the stuff out there can prove time-consuming and frustrating. In this section we want to recommend ways of using the Internet that can help you to distinguish among qualities of information available on websites. All of the websites we include are maintained and updated under Student Resources, HyperContents for Chapter 6, at the Communicating in Professional Contexts website at the Wadsworth Communication Café (http://www.wadsworth.com/communication_d). First, some general guidelines:

+ *Check out your school's library for information about search engines that are unique to your institution.* Librarians are usually the most up-to-date professionals to consult when it comes to Internet research. Many universities sponsor collaborative Internet-based research programs that allow users to electronically search professional journals, magazines, newspapers, and reference sources. In some cases, users can print entire articles and abstracts from these sources at no charge.

+ *Use your school's homepage to begin navigating the Internet.* Most universities and colleges in North America sponsor websites with practical links to libraries, research institutions, academic departments, and alumni and student organizations. These sites provide useful search advice and help the novice user become acquainted with what the Internet can offer.

+ *Contact the Communication Institute for Online Research (CIOS) to begin your research project.* Go to http://www.cios.org/ and follow the links. This is a very easy-to-use, impressive site designed for students.

Next, we want to offer advice about finding valuable information posted on websites:

+ The best, official information in any field of study or profession is likely to be found on the homepages of the professional organization's website. Check out the National Communication Association (http://www.natcom.org/) or the Academy of Management (http://www.aom.pace.edu/). The American Communication Association website (www.uark.edu/~aca) offers an online journal and comprehensive links to research sites associated with the communication field. For an interesting, eclectic resource, check out the Western Connecticut State University site at http://www.wcsu.ctstateu.edu/~wiss/online.htm.

+ Bulletin boards and discussion groups provide formal and informal sources of information, and many sponsor archives that can be searched with keywords or topics. For comprehensive listings of available groups, see http://www.tile.net/ and http://groups.yahoo.com.

+ Popular information relevant to any field of study can usually be found on the websites for commercial magazines and newspapers. They often sponsor searchable archives. For good examples, check out the *New York Times* online (http://www.nytimes.com/), *BusinessWeek* magazine (http://www.businessweek.com/), or Microsoft's online magazine *Slate* (http://www.slate.com/).

+ Although often unreliable as sources for information, individual homepages can be unique, artistic, or alternative resources. You can access them by knowing the electronic address of the homepage, or by using an Internet search engine.

+ Information on any topic can be found through search engines such as Google, Yahoo!, Excite, Netscape, AltaVista, or Ask Jeeves. Our personal favorite is Ask Jeeves (http://www.ask.com/), because you can type your question in natural language and the engine will provide several alternative interpretations of the meaning of your wording, each with its own set of links.

## How Much Technology Do I Need?

Often, when consulting, we encounter people who do not have the technological skills to keep up with changes in their industry. Their lack of skills frustrates them, their colleagues, and their customers. However, we also regularly encounter the "techno geek," the person who has every gadget, software program, and electronic toy ever made. Sitting with a techno geek in a meeting can be quite painful when the person attempts to juggle a pager, a cell phone, a laptop, a PDA, and other devices. As with most areas of our life, there needs to be a balance.

In our experience, the most successful users of technology are those who pick a few tools that are appropriate for their jobs and become very proficient with the tools they selected. What does this mean, exactly? We will use ourselves as an example. We are writers. We write books, and we write articles. When we do consulting, we write reports and analyses for our clients. Many of our writing projects require graphics and special layouts and design. We also need to keep in touch with our clients on a regular basis, so we need voice mail and e-mail.

## BEST PRACTICES

### Surfing the Net for Information: A Practical Guide

1. Access a search engine and type in the most succinct keywords you think identify the sites you want to visit. The sites will appear in a rank order determined by your keywords and the search engine's evaluators. For example, let's assume you want to find up-to-date information on e-commerce. One possible source of information is trade magazines with sites on the Internet. For our purposes, let's say you want to visit *BusinessWeek* online. Type in "BusinessWeek magazine."
2. Once the relevant sites are identified, click on the site you want to visit. If the site contains a lot of graphics, it may take a while to appear on your computer screen, depending on your connection speed. The *BusinessWeek* site is professionally created, so graphic content on its homepage is limited to small items that load fairly quickly. In a few seconds, you will see the entire page. Links generally appear in blue or as underlined text. To explore a topic, click on a link. Or you can use the search engine for the site to locate e-commerce information within the *BusinessWeek* archives.
3. Let's say that a story on e-commerce is available on the *BusinessWeek* homepage. When you click the link, it takes you to Intel Corporation's site about starting e-commerce companies, complete with stories from startups. On the Intel site, a link at the bottom of the page takes you to a list of other information resources about e-commerce.
4. **Bookmark** the site you found. Bookmarking allows you to save the site address for future reference. Click the Bookmarks button on the toolbar at the top of your web browser. Clicking the Bookmarks button while you are on a particular web page automatically prompts you to add the bookmark to a folder. The next time you want to visit this site, click on the Bookmarks button, find the name of the Intel or *BusinessWeek* site, and click on it.

To accomplish our tasks, we have become very proficient in using Microsoft Word, PageMaker, a number of graphics programs, Microsoft Outlook, and the Internet. Because one of us travels to client sites and prefers to be mobile, she primarily uses a laptop. Because one of us primarily works in an office at school or at home, he prefers a desktop computer. We don't do extensive calculations, need spreadsheets, or require extensive database support. Therefore, we have not invested time or money in this type of software. However, we keep the versions of the software we do use current and our skills with them up-to-date.

How much and what type of technology you need depends on several factors:

+ *Your business or profession.* Why spend hours or weeks learning a piece of software you will never use? Find out which software is commonly used in your chosen field and learn it—now. Accountants need to be proficient with spreadsheet and tax accounting software. Cartologists (mapmakers) need to know CAD/CAM software. Learning the dominant software for your industry ensures that you will be able to communicate your ideas in the proper format when you need to.

✦ *The standards set by your industry.* Each industry differs slightly on the specific types of hardware and software that are used. For example, Word-Perfect, which is equipped with templates and standard phrases that assist with the creation of legal forms and documents, is still preferred by many law firms. Graphic artists and designers almost exclusively use Macintosh computers. Microsoft Word is widely preferred in business environments. These standards have evolved over time and change slowly. Stick with the technology that is the standard in your industry.

✦ *The amount of time you are willing to invest in learning.* "Continuous learning," "lifelong learning," and "learning organizations" are phrases you will hear again and again throughout your business or professional life. These terms are especially relevant when it comes to technology in the workplace. Technology changes every day, and it is difficult to keep up with progress in software, hardware, and networking. Invest in and learn only those technologies you are willing to continually use.

## Summary

This chapter served as an introduction to technology and communication in the workplace. As we proceed through the book, we will introduce software programs and skills that are used for specific types of communication. We believe it is important to understand how technology impacts your communication in the workplace. To foster that understanding, we looked at the use of technology in business and professional settings and offered tips for using technology more efficiently.

• • • • • • • • • • • • • • • • • • • • • • • • • • • • • • • • • • • •

 COMMUNICATING IN PROFESSIONAL
CONTEXTS ONLINE

All of the following chapter review materials are available in electronic format on either the Communicating in Professional Contexts website or CD-ROM. In addition to the multimedia case studies, activities, and numerous other learning resources you'll find on the CD-ROM, the CD is your gateway to the book's premium web content, which is not accessible via the Internet. The book's basic web content is available both with the premium content and online at http://communication.wadsworth.com/goodall2 and includes the chapter learning objectives and activities, key-term digital glossaries, and quizzes. The CD is also your gateway to InfoTrac College Edition, our extensive online database of full-text articles that is fully keyword searchable and available twenty-four hours a day. Installation instructions for the CD appear on the inside of this book's back cover.

## What You Should Have Learned

The learning objectives below are available on the Communicating in Professional Contexts website, which is best accessed through the book's CD-ROM but is also available at http://communication.wadsworth.com/goodall2. Go to the Chapter 6 Resources and click on Learning Objectives.

Now that you have read Chapter 6, you should be able to do the following:

+ Provide a brief history of the evolution of technology in the workplace.

+ Describe the downside to technology.

+ Discuss the gender differences associated with technology.

+ Explain how we can use technology consciously.

+ Describe the relationship between power and spans of communication.

+ Describe the two types of information technology.

+ Discuss the advantages and disadvantages of telecommuting.

+ Provide tips for using voice mail and e-mail effectively.

+ Discuss virtual communities and their use in the workplace.

+ Walk through the process for doing web-based research, including providing sites that you could use.

+ Discuss the three elements used to decide how much technology you need in your chosen field.

## Key Terms

The terms below are available in a digital glossary on the Communicating in Professional Contexts website, which is best accessed through this book's CD-ROM but is also available at http://communication.wadsworth.com/goodall2. Go to the Chapter 6 Resources and click on Glossary.

| | | |
|---|---|---|
| **bookmark** *(169)* | **netiquette** *(165)* | **virtual communities** *(164)* |
| **e-mail** *(163)* | **networks** *(164)* | **voice mail** *(162)* |
| **information overload** *(158)* | **telecommuting** *(164)* | |
| **Luddite** *(159)* | **videoconferencing** *(165)* | |

## Writing and Critical Thinking

The following activities can be completed online and, if requested, submitted to your instructor. You'll find them on the Communicating in Professional Contexts website, which is best accessed through this book's CD-ROM but is also available at http://communication.wadsworth.com/goodall2. Go to the Chapter 6 Resources and click on Writing and Critical Thinking Activities.

Choose one of the following activities:

1. You have to set up an important meeting for your group. The meeting will be Monday, October 25, in Conference Room 7 at 9:00. Each participant needs to be prepared to give a brief update on his or her progress. At the end of the meeting, you will be giving Dension, the foreign exchange student assigned to your group, a going-away party. Write an e-mail that includes the above information.

2. You consistently receive incoherent voice mail messages from Carl. Whenever Carl calls, he mumbles, forgets to leave complete information, or rambles on about three or four unrelated topics. How do you address the problem with Carl?

3. You are one of the first in your department chosen for the new telecommuting project. The prospect of working at home excites you, but you worry that you may be overlooked for future promotions or special projects. What steps can you take to ensure that you remain part of the company culture?

4. As you are a recognized conscious business communicator, the president of your company has approached you and asked for your advice on the quickest and most effective way to send crucial information to all employees in the company. Some company divisions are not in your physical location, and some employees telecommute. Prepare a report for the president identifying the advantages and disadvantages of the use of the technologies discussed in the chapter to enhance the reception and understanding of her message. Of the following scenarios, are there any for which you would advise not using electronic information technology?

   + the need for employees to contribute an additional 10 percent to their company health insurance next year

   + a potential employee cutback due to a downturn in the economy

   + announcement of a new multimillion-dollar contract awarded to your company

   + relocation of some company departments to better align with their customer base

   + your company's merger with another company

   + your recent promotion to vice president of public relations

   + accepting applications for telecommuting

5. In groups, discuss the ethics of personal use of office equipment and technology (telephones, e-mail, Internet).

## Research and Explorations Online

The exercises below can be completed online and, if requested, submitted to your instructor. You'll find them on the Communicating in Professional Contexts website, which is best accessed through this book's CD-ROM but is also available at http://communication.wadsworth.com/goodall2. Go to the Chapter 6 Resources and click on Internet Exercises.

1. Your boss asked you to find information about a competitor. You need to research the company on the WWW. The company's name is InvoiceLink. Use the Internet to provide your boss with information about the company's products and history.

2. You are desperately looking for a new job. You have tried Barron's and other professional newspapers and have networked with everyone you know, to no avail. Yesterday, someone mentioned using the employment bulletin boards on the Internet. Use the Internet to find the job descriptions for five jobs in your chosen field. You can use sites such as the Monster Board (http://www.monster.com) or Career Builder (http://www.careerbuilder.com).

3. Go to http://www.netlingo.com on the Internet. Familiarize yourself with the terms listed on the site. Pick three terms that you have not heard before but that you think you and your classmates should know to be computer literate in the workplace. Share the terms and their definitions with your class or group.

4. Your boss is considering offering telecommuting as an option for employees. Before she does so, she has asked you to research the pros and cons of your company offering this option. Enter the keyword *telecommuting* in InfoTrac College Edition or on the WWW and prepare an up-to-date list not only of the pros and cons of telecommuting but also a profile of the employee who would be most suited for this option.

5. Your boss has recently had a problem with computer viruses and has heard about "firewalls" but doesn't have a clue what they are or how they can protect his computer. Visit http://www.interhack.net/pubs/fwfaq/ and provide a short summary of the functions of firewalls.

## Practicing Communication in Professional Contexts

We have talked about technology as an important communication tool that creates a span of communication. For this breakthrough skill development, we would like you to begin investigating the technology associated with your profession or chosen career. What software products are standard in your industry?

What computer skills do you need in order to communicate your ideas effectively? What is the learning curve associated with these skills? What steps would you have to take to become proficient?

Create a technology plan that includes the following information:

+ the type of software used in your chosen field

+ your current level of proficiency with that software

+ the learning curve to reach the level of proficiency that is standard for your industry

+ the steps you need to take to learn to use the product

+ the classes or training available through your current job, at your school, or at community colleges or training locations in your city

+ the benefits of learning the software now rather than waiting until you have begun a job or are looking for a job in your field

+ the costs involved in becoming a proficient user of the technology

+ the costs involved if you *don't* learn the technology

# Exploring Interpersonal Communication

A s José sat listening to Marie, the human resources representative for Hamilton Hospital, he was amazed at how lucky he was to find a nursing position with this hospital. Hamilton offered great benefits, and it had this incredible program for new employees. Rather than make them sit through boring presentations on the company's 401(k) or medical plans, they were teaching him skills he could actually use before he even set foot into his new department or started working with patients.

Marie explained that their workshop would be organized around a process called "CCCD," which would teach them how to choose productive communication goals, create appropriate messages, coordinate within relational communities, and deliver messages in ways that would build and strengthen their professional interpersonal relationships. Marie told them that by the end of the workshop, everyone would have developed skills to help them succeed interpersonally in the workplace. José was so impressed with Marie's easy communication style and her message, he was eager to hear more.

## Choosing: Strategies and Ethics for Relational Development at Work

"Choosing" is the process of defining the strategies and goals for your interpersonal behavior. However, before we can begin choosing strategies, we must look at how we use talk to create relationships with others at work. What is the "work" of talk in building professional relationships?

In a practical sense, the "creating" stage of relational communication is about how we make decisions that will guide our choices of words and actions with others in the workplace. From first impressions to last goodbyes, the work we do to manage our relationships involves balancing strategies for obtaining our goals with the ethical dimensions of workplace conduct. This begins with first impressions.

### First Impressions

How do we form first impressions of people? The term we use to describe this complex process is **perception.** *Perception* refers to how we process and interpret cues from a person's outward appearance, voice, and language usage.

How does perception work? According to cognitive psychologists and communication scholars (see Andersen, 1993), we use **schemata,** or mental pattern recognition plans, that "help us identify and organize incoming information" (Trenholm, 2000, p. 50). Sarah Trenholm, a communication scholar, suggests that we use three basic patterns to develop first impressions: person prototypes, personal constructs, and scripts.

#### Person Prototypes

We tend to characterize individuals by their physical and behavioral resemblance to an existing category of person. These categories are **person proto-**

**types.** In everyday usage, we call person prototypes *stereotypes*. For example, we can recognize "student," "college professor," "politician," "business person," "cowboy," "artist," or "evangelist." If you can quickly form a mental representation of a type of person, you are relying on the person prototype schema.

Although stereotypes help us identify people by their relationship to our idealized images of a role or category, they also encourage us to ignore or miss important details that separate uniqueness among individuals from categorical generalizations. Because person prototypes form a basis for first impressions, they also influence how we choose to communicate with others. We tend to seek out contact with people who fit stereotypes we associate with positive images and roles, and we avoid contact with people we associate—fairly or unfairly—with negative images and roles. Although it is true that you should "never judge a book by its cover," we often do.

## Personal Constructs

If stereotypes represent basic patterns of person and role definition, **personal constructs** may be thought of as representing specific evaluations we make of others based on our assessment of their personal communication habits and behaviors. For example, we tend to evaluate others as being "hard charging" or "easygoing," as "neat and clean" or "sloppy," as "nice" or "mean."

The important thing to remember about personal constructs is that they are our personal preferences. Of the wide variety of clues we can pay attention to, each of us typically uses only a few to figure out others. For this reason, two people may meet a third person and come away from the interaction with different interpretations of the third person's identity and behavior.

> *Marie asked the workshop group to think about five people they worked closely with on their previous job. Then they had to write the names of those five people on a piece of paper. After each name, they had to write down a series of adjectives to describe the person. José wrote:*
>
> *Kathryn—head of nursing, feminist, rigid*
>
> *Larry—doctor, sharp dresser, witty*
>
> *Eric—director of finance, bottom-line, heartless, athletic*
>
> *Rod—lab tech, young, useless, trouble, slacker, black clothes*
>
> *Vikki—fellow nurse, smart, team leader, motivating*
>
> *Marie asked the group to think about what their lists indicated about their personal constructs. "Do you tend to classify people by their physical or psychological characteristics? By their clothing? By their sense of humor?" she asked. Then Marie said to the group, "How might you do if others used these same personal constructs to evaluate you?"*
>
> *José noticed the first thing he wrote down was the person's job title. "I wonder," he thought, "what it says about me that I think of everyone by how they fit into the*

*hierarchy first, before anything else? Maybe I should get to know people first, before labeling them."*

## Scripts

First impressions often occur during *phatic communication*, the patterned sequences of talk that we use every day. Another term for phatic communion is **scripts.** Scripts allow us to behave effortlessly, mindlessly, while we appear to be engaged in a conversation. Because we know how to act during a scripted performance, we tend to evaluate others based on their compliance with — or alteration from — our preferred lines in the script. However, we need to be careful about applying our script to others and thereby denying them opportunities for creativity and uniqueness of expression. To counter this powerful influence, we need to become more mindful during these scripted performances.

> *Marie asked the group to think about their scripts. Jose had to laugh when he thought about where he previously worked. He always found it funny that, every day, his co-workers walked through the halls of the hospital saying "Hi, how are you?" to everybody, knowing full well no one cared. And he thought, "I am as guilty as the next person."*
>
> *"As you can see," Marie said, "first impressions are a natural part of how we acquire general information about others, but also, because they are drawn from stereotypes, personal preferences, and scripts, they have the potential to be unreliable. It is a good idea to remember these things when forming a first impression of someone else."*
>
> *Then Marie asked the group, "What can you do to make a better first impression? What strategic choices can enhance your presentation of self to others in a business or professional setting?"*

Several strategic choices enhance the impression we make during our first encounters with others. Follow these guidelines when meeting someone for the first time:

- Establish eye contact, smile, and offer a firm handshake.
- Speak clearly and avoid using nicknames during initial encounters. This holds true whether you are introducing yourself or someone else.
- Listen carefully for the other person's name when being introduced. Repeat the name to yourself a couple of times or use a mnemonic device to remember the name. For example, you can remember someone named McDonald if you think of the restaurant chain or the children's song.
- Listen carefully to what is being said and respond clearly and succinctly when asked a question.
- Maintain a positive business attitude.
- Have a sense of humor. Smile and be pleasant.

+ Maintain an appropriate social distance during the interaction. Do not be a close talker. Keep space between you and the other person.

+ Exchange business cards for future contact, if appropriate.

+ Leave when the conversation is over; professional people have work to do.

## Establishing Expectations and Boundaries

Although first impressions set the patterns of communication, how we construct our relationships is heavily dependent on the way we interpret the contexts and boundaries surrounding a communication event. To complicate things further, these interpretations are influenced by our experience, which in turn defines our expectations, which in turn limit our communication because of the limits of those perceived boundaries. In many ways, our ability or failure to communicate effectively in interpersonal communication events is a vicious circle. (See Figure 7.1.)

*When Marie asked for volunteers for a demonstration, José raised his hand. Marie took José aside and gave him a card with the details of a communication event on it. José would be playing the role of the head resident in charge of the ER. Today he would be meeting a new employee. When the employee introduced himself, José was supposed to give him a complete brush-off.*

*José sat down at the desk in the front of the room while Marie instructed the other volunteer, Max, about his role. Marie gave Max a card with his script and told him to pretend he was knocking on a door and then begin.*

*"Hi, I'm Max, the new ER nurse. HR told me you were expecting me. I'm really excited about being here," Max read from his card.*

*"Who? Oh, yeah. Look, I don't have time to show you around today. The ER is swamped. You'll just have to wait until things slow down and try not to get in the way." José then turned around and acted as if he was walking away.*

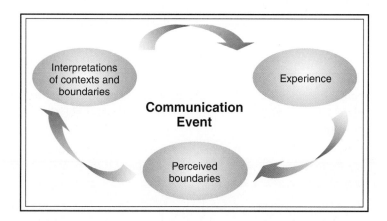

**Figure 7.1**
The Cycle of Interpersonal Communication

*Max looked around dejected and then went back to his seat.*

*"Max," Marie said, "how did that make you feel?"*

*"I didn't like him at all. If that had been a real situation, I would have thought I'd made a huge mistake coming to this hospital," Max said.*

*"Yeah," said José. "I can't imagine how he would feel about working with me. How could you trust anyone who acted that way?"*

*"Exactly," Marie said. "It would take a long time for Max to feel comfortable. Even if José's behavior was an anomaly, this first interaction would taint every encounter Max had with him thereafter."*

Expectations and boundaries have an effect on peer relationships in the workplace. Research suggests that we use three general categories to define peer relationships at work (Fritz, 1997; Kram and Isabella, 1985):

- *Information peers:* people of more or less equal status with us but with whom we share low levels of trust and disclosure, little emotional support, and little personal feedback.

- *Collegial peers:* people of more or less equal status with us and with whom we share a moderate level of trust, disclosure, and expression of self. For example, with these peers we may engage in "career strategizing, job-related feedback, friendship, some information sharing, confirmation, and emotional support" (Fritz, p. 30).

- *Special peers:* people of more or less equal status with us and with whom we share high levels of disclosure, intimacy, and confirmation. With our special peers, we feel free to express ourselves fully, openly, and directly.

Our perceptions of the people we work with, and our responses to them, may be limited by the peer categories we place them in. For example, we have a higher level of self-disclosure with collegial peers than we have with information peers, and our highest level of self-disclosure is reserved for the people we consider our special peers.

Organizational relationships are also limited by rules, policies, and cultures (Gilsdorf, 1998):

- **rules:** assumptions and formal pronouncements about proper communication among employees

- **policies:** explicitly developed guidelines regarding conduct in the workplace. Often these guidelines are stated in a company's policies and procedures manual

- **cultures:** evolved standards for communication practices that may be unique to the organization and must be acquired through observation and experience

*Marie told the group, "Rules can be stated or just taken for granted. In our company, for example, it's taken for granted that humor flows among peers but rarely between em-*

*ployees and superiors. But we routinely hold meetings in which the CEO must appear before all employees and answer any question honestly. This has become an important part of our organizational culture."*

*Marie gave everyone a copy of the hospital's policies and procedures manual. She suggested that they read the manual that evening and make a list of any questions they had. The HR director would spend an hour or so going over their questions the next day. Marie described the manual as the basis for shared policy and procedure understanding within the organization.*

## Behaving Ethically

Knowing that organizational relationships are defined by expectations and limited by boundaries, policies, rules, and cultures can help you become more strategic and ethical in your selection of communication practices. You improve strategic skills by focusing communication goals on what individuals can fairly provide, and by being mindful of the limits that operate within your relationship. You improve ethical skills by communicating within these established boundaries.

Although it may appear obvious that relationships in the workplace—and the workplace itself—should be governed by conscious ethical decision making, the fact is that the harsh realities of a global marketplace often pit the ethical interests *against* the business interests of organizations. There are numerous examples of companies that, when faced with a choice between making a profit and doing the right thing, have chosen the bottom line. Tobacco company executives, for example, have admitted they knew the health risks associated with cigarette smoking, yet they continued to cover them up.

However, public vigilance via the Internet, combined with investigative reports from responsible journalists, has encouraged more ethical conduct from organizations. Furthermore, "whistle-blowers" (Redding, 1993) have been more willing to speak publicly about unethical, immoral, and illegal business activities.

*After the break, José was ready to hear more about strategic choices for relational development in the workplace. Marie brought up the topic of ethics.*

*"Let's look at the relational level of ethical conduct and decision making in the workplace," she said. "Much of our ethical understanding is based in an organization's culture and values. For example, in the film* Glengarry Glen Ross, *the sales representatives in a company openly use unethical practices with customers that mirror the treatment they receive from their own management. The employees dish out to the customers what the managers have dished out to them."*

*Marie mentioned another example. "In the film* Working Girl, *the main character expresses her belief that misrepresenting herself to her superiors was justified in her company because she was being forced to play by rules she had no hand in making. Was her behavior unethical? Perhaps, but watching the film, you see that the character is working within the boundaries set by the organization culture."*

Unfortunately, ethical decisions are seldom easy. This is because "doing the right thing" often depends on where you stand in relation to an issue or problem. The main character in the film *Working Girl* engages in what many would consider unethical conduct, but she sees her choices as necessary because women from working-class backgrounds have limits placed on their opportunities in American corporate life. The maniacal sales manager in *Glengarry Glen Ross* believes harsh methods are required to motivate a sales force because his own job depends on their performance. As some economic philosophers, such as Milton Friedman, have pointed out, if the point of running a business is to make money for investors, then shouldn't our ethical code be derived solely from that primary objective? If so, wouldn't any decision that reduced profits for investors be considered an *unethical* decision?

Ethical decision making and conduct can be rendered even more problematic on a global economic scale, because an organization's cultural values may also be shaped by national norms. For example, North American firms often complain that they are disadvantaged when dealing with companies from nations that allow—and even encourage—the payment of bribes or the giving of expensive gifts to enhance business opportunities. On the global stage, what may seem obvious and ethical in one culture may well be illegal or unethical in another. Is it better to lose business while maintaining high ethical standards, or to compromise those standards by paying bribes and giving gifts that may enhance profits?

Communication ethicists point out that in reducing arguments about ethical conduct to "the ends justify the means" reasoning, people fail to acknowledge Gandhi's truth: "Means are ends in the making." The "ethical urgency" that ought to be used to guide decisions about conduct is, therefore, that you don't know how things are going to turn out (Bracci, 1999). In *Working Girl*, the main character's decisions may seem acceptable because of how things turned out for her, but in everyday business life, we cannot predict the results of our actions. We should therefore make decisions about ethical conduct based on what the consequence of behaving this way is likely to be.

To do that, we need to build our ethical practices on a solid foundation of core communication values. Ethical communication practices begin with an organization's need to clarify its underlying workplace values within the context of national norms and practices. For example, research indicates that in North American business culture, there are a number of most desirable organizational values associated with ethical communication practices (Harshman and Harshman, 1999, p. 30):

+ Trust one another.
+ Treat others with respect.

+ Recognize the value of each individual.

+ Keep your word; do what you say you will do.

+ Tell the truth; be honest with others.

+ Act with integrity.

+ Be open to change.

+ Risk failing in order to get better.

+ Learn; try new ideas.

The above list of productive organizational values reinforces the central notion that relational ethics are part and parcel of our everyday communication in organizations. There is no communication event or episode that does not reflect an ethical attitude or stance, or a strategic decision that cannot be informed by a conscious consideration of its ethical implications. For this reason, the National Communication Association has adopted the following ethics code.

## NCA Credo for Ethical Communication

### Adopted November 6, 1999

Questions of right and wrong arise whenever people communicate. Ethical communication is fundamental to responsible thinking, decision making, and the development of relationships and communities within and across contexts, cultures, channels, and media. Moreover, ethical communication enhances human worth and dignity by fostering truthfulness, fairness, responsibility, personal integrity, and respect for self and others. We believe that unethical communication threatens the quality of all communication and consequently the well-being of individuals and the society in which we live. Therefore we, the members of the National Communication Association, endorse and are committed to practicing the following principles of ethical communication.

We advocate truthfulness, accuracy, honesty, and reason as essential to the integrity of communication.

We endorse freedom of expression, diversity of perspective, and tolerance of dissent to achieve the informed and responsible decision making fundamental to a civil society.

We strive to understand and respect other communicators before evaluating and responding to their messages.

We promote access to communication resources and opportunities as necessary to fulfill human potential and contribute to the well-being of families, communities, and society.

We promote communication climates of caring and mutual understanding that respect the unique needs and characteristics of individual communicators.

*(continued)*

We condemn communication that degrades individuals and humanity through distortion, intimidation, coercion, and violence and through the expression of intolerance and hatred.

We are committed to the courageous expression of personal convictions in pursuit of fairness and justice.

We advocate sharing information, opinions, and feelings when facing significant choices while also respecting privacy and confidentiality.

We accept responsibility for the short- and long-term consequences for our own communication and expect the same of others.

Balancing strategies for creating effective relationships at work with the appropriate ethical standards is a constant challenge for all communicators. In our view, learning to think of ethical conduct in terms of likely relational outcomes rather than solely as an "ends-means" justification is a good way to practice conscious ethical conduct. These principles hold true whether you are communicating face-to-face, in a conference call, or over the Internet.

*"If you are ever in doubt about whether some action is ethical," Marie told her workshop group, "you can always fall back on the Golden Rule: Do unto others as you would have them do unto you. It's simple, but it works."*

### Focus on Ethics

A number of websites devoted to personal accounts of ill treatment of employees have popped up. These sites provide employees strategies for whistle-blowing and for overturning sources of corporate hierarchy and domination. The question is, are their recommendations ethical?

## Creating: Messages That Reflect Self, Other, and Context

*"Now we are ready to move on to the second step in the CCCD process—creating goal-oriented messages that are adapted to the needs and expectations of others within specific contexts," Marie told the group. "Anyone want to guess how we go about doing that?"*

*"We just talk and hope for the best?" José said. The others laughed.*

*"No," said Marie. "We use tools that help us create a message that meets the needs of our audience within a specific context. For the next hour, I will describe both the intellectual and practical tools you need to use to create strategic and ethical messages in workplace relationships. Let's begin with equity."*

To create strategic messages in the workplace, we make use of the following concepts:

- ✦ equity
- ✦ self-disclosure
- ✦ risk-taking
- ✦ feedback
- ✦ dialectics
- ✦ dialogue
- ✦ conflict resolution

## Equity: Principles of Everyday Exchange

In Chapter 5 we introduced the idea of equity as a principle that guides most workplace interactions. We defined equity as the principle that we should be treated fairly by others and in turn should treat them fairly. We asked you to think of equity as the golden rule governing the choosing and creating of verbal strategies for workplace communication.

To refresh your memory, let's reexamine the four key assumptions that inform equity theory (Walster, Walster, and Bershied, 1978; Wilson and Goodall, 1991):

1. *People work for rewards.* We all attempt to maximize our outcomes. In relationships at work, we try to obtain our personal, social, and professional goals by gaining the cooperation and support of others.
2. *People seek equity.* We all want a sense of fairness and justice to guide our relationships with others.
3. *People become stressed when they feel they are being treated unfairly.* If we find ourselves in an inequitable relationship, we feel tension, stress, frustration, or even anger. We cannot overcome these ill feelings until we restore equity in the relationship.
4. *People experiencing stress will try to restore equity.* We may restore equity mentally, socially, or physically.

As you can see, the equity principle can be applied directly to choosing communication strategies in the workplace. Your overall goal should be to select ethical strategies that encourage others to treat you equitably and that demonstrate your interest in treating others equitably. When you do so, you uphold the principle of *reciprocity*.

Sources of inequity in workplace relationships include the following:

- ✦ lying, cheating, or stealing
- ✦ misrepresenting yourself, your goals, or your methods

+ not speaking up for a colleague who is wrongly accused or who is held accountable for something that isn't her or his fault

+ not supporting the work of someone who regularly supports you

+ allowing someone else to pick up the check for lunch or dinner without offering to do the same for them next time

+ failing to volunteer to help someone meet a deadline even though this person has volunteered to help you in the past

+ failing to disclose your personal feelings about an issue or idea after you have asked someone else to disclose their personal feelings

+ being chronically late for meetings and events

+ trying to claim credit for work done by a group or team

+ ingratiating yourself with superiors at the expense of others with whom you work

+ withholding information from others that may benefit them

+ spreading rumors or gossip about others

+ telling someone else's secrets

Once we recognize equity as a powerful tool for building rewarding professional and business relationships, we can tip the scales toward ethical and equitable behavior. We also can use this new knowledge of equity as a way of evaluating and critiquing our own and others' communication choices.

> *"Have you ever found yourself sitting in a meeting and listening to someone who was describing their recent surgery in frightening detail?" Marie asked.*
>
> *"Hello, we work in a hospital!" said José with a laugh. "But even when I'm not working, I seem to be a magnet for people who want to tell me things I really don't want to know. I don't tell other people personal things about myself. Why do other people feel that they can tell me anything about themselves?"*
>
> *"Is it that you dislike hearing about other people's personal lives, or is it that you feel a lack of equity? If you aren't disclosing and others are, possibly you feel that things are out of balance," Marie offered.*
>
> *"Hmmm. I never really thought about it like that," José said.*

## Self-Disclosure and Risk-Taking

George Caspar Homans (1961) proposed that all human relationships can be partially understood as exchanges of goods, services, sentiments, and time. Ideally, these exchanges should be equitable, because relative value for goods, services, and sentiments is always understood between people as something that should be fairly traded, and it is generally understood that the amount of time one person puts into a relationship needs to be reciprocated by the other partner.

Given this theoretical framework, self-disclosure and risk-taking have commodity value in workplace relationships:

+ If I offer disclosures about myself to you, I expect that you will, in return, disclose about yourself to me.

+ If I take risks in our relationship, I am also encouraging you to take risks in our relationship.

As if guided by a marketplace metaphor, we "trade commodities" in our relationships. We understand the values we attach to those commodities. We operate under a principle of reciprocity and equity in making those trades or exchanges.

However, it is important to point out that self-disclosure and risk-taking, although potentially powerful resources for building close relationships, can create risks in business and professional relationships. **Self-disclosure** means providing personal information within a conversation. Telling your coworkers the intimate details of your life provides them with ways of understanding how your personal history informs and shapes your workplace identity. It also provides information to people who may not have your best interests in mind. Imagine, for a moment, if the details of your most reckless behavior on a weekend or vacation became common knowledge at work. Before you disclose, think about

PhotoDisc

## BEST PRACTICES

### Monitoring Disclosures

#### Your Disclosures

+ Disclose personal information only to people you know well and trust. Remember, trust must be earned.

+ Before you disclose something, stop and think about how information you disclose might be used.

+ Never disclose personal information to anyone who may use it against you.

+ Never disclose anything that may be interpreted by others as potentially damaging to your reputation or character, nor encourage others to. This includes all potentially illegal, immoral, or unethical conduct, no matter how it was motivated, how funny it was, or what the outcome may have been.

+ Don't disclose information someone told you in confidence.

#### Responding to Disclosures

+ Keep in mind, you are not a licensed therapist or counselor. If people who need emotional support begin disclosing unwanted or troubling information to you, the best thing you can do for them is help them find their way to a trained professional.

+ If someone you work with begins disclosing personal information at a level you are not comfortable with, say, "I'm sorry, but there are some things about you I'd rather not know." Or "While I sympathize with your situation, I would like to keep our relationship on a professional level."

+ Remember that self-disclosure is expected to be reciprocal. If others disclose information about themselves to you, they will expect you to disclose information about yourself to them.

whether or not you really want your coworkers—and your superiors—to know these things about you. Chances are you probably don't.

When communicating in the global workplace, you should bear in mind that people from other cultures may be uncomfortable with the level of self-disclosure and risk-taking that many North Americans routinely offer. Your goal when creating messages should be to adapt your talk to the needs and expectations of others.

## Asking For and Giving Feedback

**Feedback** means providing others with an evaluation of the effectiveness of their actions. Feedback is a valuable source of information that allows communicators to adjust their talk to situations and to other people. Skilled communicators seek out feedback because it provides them with an evaluation of how well their messages achieved their goals, what modifications may need to be made, and what they may want to consider doing to become more effective. Asking for feedback is an important tool for the development of your communication skills. Giving feedback, however, can be problematic. Not everyone wants feedback. This may be because most people are simply not skilled in providing good feedback, so our reactions to feedback tend to be negative.

Research by Trenholm and Jensen (1992) suggests the following five rules for giving feedback:

+ *Own your message*. Use the pronoun "I" to begin statements that evaluate the performance of others. Avoid using generalizations such as "everyone thinks" or "we all know" to preface your remarks. As long as you make it clear that *you* are the one providing the feedback, you are showing ownership (and responsibility) for what you say.

+ *Avoid apologizing for your feelings*. Don't preface feedback with a disclaimer such as "It might just be me, but I thought what you said in the meeting was ill-timed." This sort of disclaimer gives the impression that you are apologizing for the feedback, or that you are the one at fault, not the person to whom you are offering the feedback. You are also downplaying the corrective effect of the message, which may be counterproductive. Say what you mean. Notice how different the impression would be if the sentence started, "I thought what you said in the meeting was ill-timed."

+ *Make your message specific and behavioral*. Don't mask your feedback by being vague or ambiguous. The idea is to give someone useful information about their communication. To do that means specifying precisely what behaviors are being targeted. Focus on behaviors that may be modified or changed rather than on general mental states or attitudes. For example, you could say, "You didn't return my call yesterday, and as a result I didn't get the information I needed to finish the budget report." This kind of statement explains the behavior that caused the problem and opens up possibilities for a discussion of what needs to be done in the future.

+ *Verbal and nonverbal behaviors should support each other*. Avoid trying to smile while expressing frustration, anger, or resentment, because the message your expression gives may be quite different from what you say. As we pointed out in Chapter 5, when there is a discrepancy between nonverbal and verbal messages, we tend to believe the nonverbal.

+ *Avoid evaluating and interpreting your communication partner unless he or she asks you to*. Useful feedback avoids promoting defensiveness. Unsolicited feedback can easily be viewed as criticism, thereby encouraging your partner to become defensive or to argue against what you are offering.

*"Feedback," Marie explained, "is essential to personal, team, and organizational learning. It provides us with valuable information about the processes and outcomes*

*of our communication, which is to say, about our choices for strategic and ethical messages."*

*"You know," said José, "now that you've explained it, I understand why people often don't respond the way I had hoped when I try to help them. It wasn't necessarily that I was trying to give them feedback; it was the way I was giving the feedback."*

*"Yeah," said Max, "and I think I will be able to think differently about people giving me feedback in the future. Maybe this will even help with my wife." Everyone laughed.*

*"Within any work group, and even in a marriage," Marie said with a smile, "how we learn from feedback will be a guide to how open others are likely to be with us in the future. When we combine all the elements we have discussed so far, we are moving closer to a dialectical approach to interpersonal communication or dialogue. Let's take a quick break and then talk about these concepts."*

## Dialectics and Dialogue

A **dialectic** generally refers to the interaction of two arguments that are by nature oppositional. The term *relational dialectics* (Rawlins, 1984; Baxter, 1988; Baxter and Montgomery, 1996) refers to the interaction of two opposing arguments or forces—called *tensions*—operating within the boundaries of the same relationship. Interpersonal researchers have identified three primary sources of relational dialectics:

+ *Autonomy-togetherness dialectic.* To be in a relationship often means to spend time and to share information together. However, no matter how much you enjoy spending time with another person, sometimes you just want or need to be by yourself.

+ *Novelty-predictability dialectic.* All relationships form patterns. In time, these patterns become predictable. Because relationships are at least in part predictable, they can be safe and comfortable and serve as islands of sanity in an otherwise stressed world. However, we also want our relationships to be novel, to offer excitement, adventure, and opportunities to experience and learn from new places, people, and things.

+ *Expressive-protective dialectic.* This dialectical tension informs how we make decisions about sharing information about ourselves with our relational partners and coworkers. There are times when we freely disclose, and there are times when we prefer not to share what we consider private.

With all of these sources of dialectical complexity operating in our relationships, how can we make space for dialogue? More importantly, how do we make space for talk within the autonomous, predictable, and protective environments of the workplace?

**Dialogue** is communication that focuses on mutuality and relational growth rather than on self-interest. Dialogue is "more concerned with discovering than with disclosing, more interested in access than in domination" (Anderson, Cissna, and Arnett, 1994, p. 2). Peter Kellett (1999) has applied the idea of relational dialectics to creating dialogue in organizations:

+ *Focus on mutuality.* Both partners to a dialogue should use the experience to learn and to grow; each communicator should consciously try to help the other person.

+ *Discover rather than disclose.* Communicators should ask questions aimed at improving understanding of the other's position, standpoint, and perspective. Avoid unnecessary self-disclosures that deflect attention from mutual growth.

+ *Be more interested in access than in domination.* Communicators should avoid strategies designed to one-up or demean the perspective offered by the other person. Each person should remain open to differences of opinion, values, and beliefs. The exchange of talk should be aimed at uncovering those differences for the purpose of mutual understanding and growth.

*"The key word here," Marie said, "is growth. We need to encourage dialogue that helps us to grow individually within our jobs, and as an organization. When you are faced with a confrontational situation, you should focus on the question, How will this situation help me to grow?"*

*"That's good long-term advice," José said. "But what do you do when you have a real problem with somebody?"*

*"I won't kid you; we aren't perfect," Marie replied. "Conflict occurs here. Let's talk about some ways to work through conflict when it does happen. Often, we find that workplace conflict occurs when two people have incompatible goals," Marie explained. "For example, consider how you feel when you want to attend a professional advancement seminar but your boss schedules a mandatory task-force meeting during that week. Such conflicts are normal in the operation of any business and can usually be resolved by both partners engaging in a problem-solving session aimed at negotiating a creative solution. Can anyone think of possible solutions for this scenario?"*

*"Maybe I could provide my boss with input in advance that could be used at the task-force meeting," said Max.*

*"That's a possibility," said Marie. "Anyone else?"*

*"Maybe I could take a break from the seminar and do a conference call during the task-force meeting. That way, I wouldn't miss out on either," said José.*

*"That might work, as well. The point is that you and your boss get together with the goal of solving the problem," said Marie. "But as we know, not all conflicts are so easily worked out. Before we discuss more ways to work through conflict, let's look at some less desirable strategies many of us tend to use."*

## Working Through Relational Conflict

**Conflict** refers to the feelings or perceptions of imbalance that arise in a relational setting. A number of strategies help us temporarily avoid or postpone a confrontation, but they will not help resolve the conflict (from D. Johnson, 1993, pp. 205–7):

+ *withdrawing:* walking away, changing the subject, or ignoring the conflict

+ *accommodating:* giving in immediately simply to end the conflict

+ *compromising:* giving up part of what you want in exchange for your communication partner also giving up part of what he or she wants

+ *avoiding or postponing:* failing to engage in communication designed to address the conflict, or suggesting that the conflict be addressed later

Although each of the above strategies may be appropriate in a given context, each provides a less than optimal way of working through the conflict. For example, by withdrawing, or by avoiding or postponing conflict, relational partners may build up resentments that surface in other situations. By accommodating and compromising, relational partners may create an imbalance in their relationship that influences other aspects of their talk and work. Of all the strategies available for working through a conflict, only a problem-solving dialogue stands a good chance of producing a win-win situation.

That said, it is also true that "conflicts experienced in organizations are often related to deeper processes" (Kellett and Dalton, 2001). For example, conflicts can be based on deeper systems of meaning related to the politics in an organization (Cheney, 1995), differing perceptions of "the reality" of an issue that inform competing values and narratives (Mumby, 1993), or deeper organizational processes and themes (Smith and Eisenberg, 1987). To get at these systemic or cultural conflicts, it is helpful to ask the following questions (from Kellett and Dalton, 2001):

+ *Where does the conflict come from?* Who and what is producing the disagreement? Is there a history of disagreements between the communicators?

+ *How is it being managed?* Who avoids it, and who wants to engage in it? What goals are being sought by the participants?

+ *How do other people react to the conflict?* Is it perceived as "something new" or "nothing new"? What negative work-related consequences can be associated with the conflict? What personal consequences follow from it?

+ *How does it affect key organizational functions?* How does the conflict influence productivity? How does it influence openness? Honesty? Learning? Dialogue?

+ *How does it manifest systemically in other organizational practices?* Are stress levels higher for those with similar conflicts? Are discussions routed around these key participants? Is there a loss of potential important feed-back? Are denial and blaming strategies spread to other conflicts? If the conflict is gender-, class-, or race based, are other work relationships nega-tively impacted? How?

*Conflict* is often described as a "neutral" organizational term (Eisenberg and Goodall, 2001). This is because some level of conflict is natural to all group- and team-based activities (Fisher, 1984) and because conflict, when properly managed, can lead to productive, insightful, and creative learning opportuni-ties (Goodall, 1990). Managing a conflict requires admitting you have one and then being willing to work through it using a problem-solving approach. By contrast, conflicts that are hidden, repressed, avoided, or denied tend to build resentment and frustration, as well as create additional problems within the organization.

## Coordinating: Making Relational Communities Work

*"Now that we've developed skills for creating positive, effective messages," Marie said, "it is time to talk about the third component of CCCD—coordinating. When we work in any organizations, we are constantly coordinating with others. In order to coordinate our communication effectively, we need to become more aware of the goals, needs and expectations, schedules, and informational concerns of others. For the next hour or so, we will examine some of the major influences on relational management in the work-place, including differences brought about by culture and gender."*

## Negotiation of Cultural Differences

Today's global workplace poses new challenges for communicators and for ed-ucators. As Lovitt and Goswami (1999) have pointed out, until very recently, most textbooks and training tools for multinational business environments stressed the importance of learning as much as possible about other cultures. This included studying the history, politics, religion, economic structure, edu-cation, linguistics, and technology of a culture, as well as the "do's and taboos" of communicating with people representing that culture. More recent research (Scollon and Scollon, 1995; Perkins, 1999) indicates that only certain cultural factors, such as "ideology, face systems, forms of discourse, and socialization" (Scollon and Scollon, p. 126), actually influence business and professional communication. Moreover, shared language usage and standards for evaluating communication among professional categories—engineers, accountants, tech-nical writers, technicians—may outweigh other cultural factors (Webb and Keene, 1999).

The important thing to remember is that learning about other cultures is a good way to build a repertoire of intercultural and cross-cultural communication skills, as well as to show respect and appreciation for other cultures. Educating oneself about world cultures is a rich enough subject to last a lifetime, but there are some practical ways to begin exploring how cultural differences may influence communication. With this goal in mind, we would like to begin with a basic difference between individualist and collectivist cultures (Triandis et al., 1988).

*Individualist cultures,* such as the dominant culture of the United States, revere the individual person and expect individuals "to make their own decisions, develop their own opinions, solve their own problems, have their own things, and, in general, learn to view the world from the point of view of the self" (Samovar, Porter, and Jain, 1991, pp. 73–74). People in individualist cultures value democratic relationships and are less influenced by status or hierarchy when dealing with others. *Collectivist cultures,* such as the dominant culture of China, revere the common good over self-interest, value group and family identity over individual achievement, and tend to respect vertical status hierarchies. As you can well imagine, relationships between representatives of these distinct cultures could be very difficult. However, each partner learning more about the communication rules and cultural norms of the other person can significantly reduce the negative influences of these cultural differences. Table 7.1 outlines several rules or strategies for collectivist-individualist interaction.

Arthur Bell (1992), Jurgen Bolten (1999), and Judi Brownell (1999) have built on the work of Triandis and others to suggest that when persons from different cultures interact, a "third" or "transaction" culture is created. Bell elaborated:

> When you and your own cultural background come into contact with persons of another culture, something new emerges—a middle ground, called a "transaction culture." In this new middle ground, sensitive and often unstated rules and understandings guide behavior. That is, if a member of Culture A interacts with a member of Culture B, neither the cultural rules of A nor those of B are the sole guide for behavior. Instead a mixed set of rules—middle Culture C—develops for the purposes of the interaction.
>
> For example, consider the cultural rules that would guide a business conversation between you and a manager from Japan. You would not speak and act entirely as you would when conversing with American co-workers, nor would the Japanese manager hold fast to Japanese conversational rules and behaviors. Both of you would consciously and subconsciously bend your own cultural habits and assumptions to accommodate the communication needs of the others. (pp. 452–53)

| Rules Collectivists Should Follow When Interacting with Individualists | Rules Individualists Should Follow When Interacting with Collectivists |
|---|---|
| 1. Don't expect to be able to predict an individualist's attitudes and behavior on the basis of group affiliations. Although this works in your country, individuals have their own ideas. | 1. Expect collectivists to abide by the norms, roles, and obligations of their groups. If group membership changes, expect members' values and personal styles to change, as well. |
| 2. Don't be put off when individualists take pride in personal achievement, and do not be too modest yourself. | 2. Do not disclose personal information unless asked. Feel free, however, to disclose your age and salary. |
| 3. Expect individualists to be less emotionally involved in group affiliation than is the norm for you. Do not interpret this as coldness or as a personal defect. | 3. Do not criticize collectivists or openly refuse their requests. Expect them to be more sensitive to loss of face than you are. |
| 4. Do not expect persuasive arguments that emphasize cooperation and conflict avoidance to be as effective as they are in your culture. Do not be offended by arguments that emphasize personal rewards and costs. | 4. Persuasive arguments based on authority appeals or on the good of the group will be more effective than those based on personal rewards. |
| 5. Do not interpret initial friendliness as a signal of intimacy or commitment. Expect relationships to be good-natured but superficial and fleeting according to your own standards. | 5. Spend a great deal of time getting to know others. Be patient, expect delays, and do not adhere to a rigid timetable. |
| 6. Pay attention to written contracts. They are considered binding. | 6. Do not be surprised if plans are changed after everything was seemingly agreed upon. Do not be surprised if negotiations take a lot longer than you consider necessary. |
| 7. Do not expect to be respected because of your position, age, sex, or status. Do not be surprised if individualists lack respect for authority figures. | 7. Let others know your social position, job title, and rank. A collectivist has a strong need to place you in an appropriate niche in the social hierarchy. |
| 8. Expect individualists to be upset by nepotism, bribery, and other behaviors that give in-group members an advantage over others. | 8. Gift giving is important, but do not expect to be paid back immediately. |
| 9. Do not expect to receive as much help as you would in your own country. After initial orientation, you may be left to do things on your own. | 9. Remember that for collectivists, family and social relationships are extremely important. Expect collectivists to take time off from work for family matters. |
| 10. Do not expect an individualist to work well in groups. | 10. Do not expect to be afforded as much privacy as you may be used to. |

From Harry C. Triandis, Richard Briskin, and C. Harry Hui, "Cross-Cultural Training across the Individualism-Collectivism Divide," *International Journal of Intercultural Relations* 12 (1988), pp. 269–98.

**Table 7.1**
Rules for Collectivist-
Individualist Interaction

## Negotiation of Gender Differences

By the end of the twentieth century, the proportion of female managers in the United States was 45 percent, an increase of 35 percent since 1984. Women now account for almost half of all managers. Management is no longer a male-intensive occupation, making it possible that the managerial role is no longer associated with predominantly masculine characteristics (Powell and Graves, 2004).

Women and men exhibit generalizable differences in communication styles. Confusion about these styles can interfere with the message. Learning to coordinate your communication style with that of the opposite gender can help you to negotiate a successful outcome.

Women tend to use what Deborah Tannen has called a "rapport-building" style, whereas men tend to use a "report-making" style. These differences in style, as well as differences in language and meaning, contribute to relational communication challenges in the workplace. For example, the fact that men tend to interrupt women speakers may be explained by research findings, but research findings should not be used to excuse this form of rude behavior. Similarly, the fact that women tend to use more qualifiers ("I think maybe"; "I guess"; "maybe just a little bit"; "kind of"), disclaimers ("It might be beside the point, but . . ."; "Don't get upset with me, but . . ."), and tag questions ("You know?") should not diminish the need for users of such weak syntax to more carefully monitor their speech.

Another relational challenge occurs because not all women and men adhere to these gross stereotypes. Some women are report oriented, and some men are rapport oriented. Some men use annoying tag questions, and some women routinely interrupt anyone who happens to be speaking. Simply categorizing individuals by these general findings can be very misleading. Labeling a pattern as a "genderlect" (a gender dialect) may help us to understand these differences, but it doesn't necessarily help people communicate more effectively with each other.

Most communication scholars agree that the single most important skill for us to develop is flexibility (Wood, 1997; Tannen, 1994; Trenholm, 2000). When we become aware of the way we talk and learn effective strategies for communication, we begin to override our automatic impulses and replace bad communication habits with habits that will serve us better in the workplace (Tannen, 1990, p. 95). Doing this makes us more mindful communicators.

*"In other words," Marie explained, "to communicate effectively across cultures and genders requires both partners to be somewhat knowledgeable about each other's culture and communication rules, but also able to suspend the rigidity of them. We need to become more conscious, mindful communicators. Part of being mindful is learning how to deliver your message. Delivery is the fourth step in the CCCD process."*

*José glanced quickly at his notes and the outline of the CCCD process. "Choose, create, coordinate, deliver," he repeated to himself.*

*"We can view delivery in two ways," Marie continued. "Delivery can be dramatistic or pragmatic. Let's spend a few minutes looking at both forms of delivery and how we can take a mindful approach to delivering interpersonal messages."*

## Delivering: Improving Relationships at Work

Delivery of interpersonal messages can be viewed as dramatistic or pragmatic (Eisenburg and Goodall, 2001). Viewed dramatistically, all relationships are cultural performances, and the delivery of your communication role in those performances is central to the ongoing story, or narrative, of the workplace. Viewed pragmatically, how well we learn to adapt our communication to the needs and expectations of relational partners will determine the quality of those relationships and our levels of satisfaction within them. Either way, skill in building relationships at work means becoming mindful of our continual need to learn from those relationships and to improve them.

To become a more mindful communicator in workplace relationships, we recommend that you do the following:

+ Become more conscious of your goals for communicating with others and their goals for communicating with you.
+ Recognize that communication has consequences—avoid mindless talk, careless comments, gossip, rumors, sexual banter, and innuendos.
+ Always be mindful of the equity principle in workplace relationships—always be conscious of the exchanges and commodity values that operate within them.
+ Accept responsibility for your own communication in relationships—own what you say and do.
+ Be open to feedback from others—use the feedback to improve your relational performance.
+ Accept conflict as a natural part of any human relationship—when it occurs, try to use problem-solving to resolve it, but recognize that not all conflicts are resolvable.
+ Treat others with respect and honesty—take into account the ethical dimensions of your decisions and the influence those actions may have on your relationships and communities.
+ Be mindful of cultural and gendered differences in relationships.
+ Use communication to build flexibility and freedom into your interactions with others.
+ Always be on the lookout for ways to improve your communication with others—never stop learning.

*"Okay," said Marie, "that's it! Now you are all ready to go into the workplace and develop healthy, productive, mindful relationships. Right?"*

*"I don't know if I can change all my bad relationship habits overnight," José said, "but you certainly have taught me a lot about relationships in a short period of time. I know that I'll spend a lot more time thinking about what I'm going to say and how I'm going to say it than I did in the past."*

*"Yeah," said Max. "Just having CCCD to fall back on will help me to organize what I'm going to say, especially in difficult situations. Thanks, Marie."*

## Summary

In this chapter, you learned how you could use CCCD to organize interpersonal communication. We examined the process of choosing strategies that further goals while communicating ethically. We also examined the importance of first impressions and learned ways to improve the impressions we give and monitor those presented by others. Next we discussed expectations and boundaries and how we rely on these elements to help us define interpersonal situations and our responses to them.

Throughout this section, we discussed the ethics of interpersonal communication. By listing the ethical practices we believe are important in the workplace, we laid a foundation for developing ethical responses in the workplace. We discussed tools for creating ethical messages while maintaining equity in relationships, and we learned to balance self-disclosure in our communication.

We discussed dialectics in the workplace and ways to use dialogue to resolve issues of dialectics. In our discussion of conflict, we talked about the typical responses to conflict and provided a list of questions designed to help you manage conflict in the workplace.

We then discussed how cultural and gender differences affect coordinating a message in the workplace. Finally, we discussed delivery of a message as a way to improve work relationships. The goal of this chapter was to help you communicate more effectively in your personal relationships in the workplace.

· · · · · · · · · · · · · · · · · · · · · · · · · · · · · · · · · · · · · · · · · ·

## COMMUNICATING IN PROFESSIONAL CONTEXTS ONLINE

All of the following chapter review materials are available in electronic format on either the Communicating in Professional Contexts website or CD-ROM. In addition to the multimedia case studies, activities, and numerous other learning resources you'll find on the CD-ROM, the CD is your gateway to the book's premium web content, which is not accessible via the Internet. The book's basic web content is available both with the premium content and online at http://communication.wadsworth.com/goodall2 and includes the chapter learning objectives and activities, key-term digital glossaries, and quizzes. The CD is also your gateway to InfoTrac College Edition, our extensive online database of full-text articles that is fully keyword searchable and available twenty-four hours a day. Installation instructions for the CD appear on the inside of this book's back cover.

· · · · · · · · · · · · · ·

## What You Should Have Learned

The learning objectives below are available on the Communicating in Professional Contexts website, which is best accessed through the book's CD-ROM but is also available at http://communication.wadsworth.com/goodall2. Go to the Chapter 7 Resources and click on Learning Objectives.

Now that you have read Chapter 7, you should be able to do the following:

+ Explain the importance of first impressions.

+ Discuss how person prototypes and personal constructs affect your first impressions.

+ Explain how scripts undermine opportunities for creative or unique expression.

+ Use information about expectations and boundaries to improve your relationships.

+ Explain how rules, policies, and culture impact our communication.

+ Discuss the importance of communicating ethically.

+ List ways that we can communicate ethically.

+ Define *equity* and how it is applied in the workplace.

+ List sources of inequity in the workplace.

+ Discuss how risk-taking and self-disclosure enhance communication.

+ Explain the concept of feedback and how it can be used to improve communication.

+ Discuss the concepts of dialectics and dialogue.

+ List negative reactions to conflict.

+ Discuss how conflict can be handled in the workplace.

+ Explain how we can adjust our message delivery for cultural or gender differences.

## Key Terms

The terms below are available in a digital glossary on the Communicating in Professional Contexts website, which is best accessed through this book's CD-ROM but is also available at http://communication.wadsworth.com/goodall2. Go to the Chapter 7 Resources and click on Glossary.

| | | |
|---|---|---|
| **conflict** *(192)* | **perception** *(176)* | **schemata** *(176)* |
| **cultures** *(180)* | **person prototypes** *(176)* | **scripts** *(178)* |
| **dialectic** *(190)* | **personal constructs** *(177)* | **self-disclosure** *(187)* |
| **dialogue** *(190)* | **policies** *(180)* | |
| **feedback** *(188)* | **rules** *(180)* | |

## Writing and Critical Thinking

The following activities can be completed online and, if requested, submitted to your instructor. You'll find them on the Communicating in Professional Contexts website, which is best accessed through this book's CD-ROM but is also available at http://communication.wadsworth.com/goodall2. Go to the Chapter 7 Resources and click on Writing and Critical Thinking Activities.

Choose one of the following activities:

1. Think about a communication situation you recently experienced that resulted in unresolved conflict. How did you handle the situation? Based on the conflict section in this chapter, how could you have handled the situation differently? Write a narrative of the situation, using what you have learned.

2. Ask the members of your group, friends, or peers at work to describe their first impression of you. Make a list of the words that recurred in the descriptions. Is this the impression you want to project? Develop a plan for changing the first impression that others form of you.

3. In your group, have each person disclose something about himself or herself that the group didn't previously know. Be careful about what you disclose. Reread the section on disclosure and think carefully about what you want this group to know about you. How did the disclosures change your impression of your group members? Was the information disclosed appropriate? Why? Has your impression of each group member grown more or less favorable? Discuss the nuances of disclosure in your group.

4. Write an essay identifying the strategy you most often use in conflict. Can you identify it as any of the behaviors listed in the chapter? If so, consider and identify some of the factors that may have contributed and continue to contribute to this. These may include factors such as culture, gender, family background, position of power, rewards, and punishment. What do you see as your strengths and your challenges in employing your conflict behaviors? Are the outcomes typically satisfactory, or unsatisfactory? If unsatisfactory, what strategies can you use to create a more positive outcome?

5. Partner with someone you do not know and, without exchanging any information, write a description of your partner based on nonverbal and first impressions. Include in your description the car you would imagine they drive, a vacation spot you think they would enjoy (mountains or water), and their favorite animal. Then have a conversation with each other for two minutes and, following your conversation, again working independently, delete or add any new descriptive information. After completing your list, share and discuss the original and revised list each of you has completed. What verbal and nonverbal cues were used to create the impression, and how accurate were your perceptions?

## Research and Explorations Online

The exercises below can be completed online and, if requested, submitted to your instructor. You'll find them on the Communicating in Professional Contexts website, which is best accessed through this book's CD-ROM but is also available at http://communication.wadsworth.com/goodall2. Go to the Chapter 7 Resources and click on Internet Exercises.

1. Go to the Conflict Resolution Resource Center website at http://www .conflict-resolution.net/index.cfm. Click on the Articles link. Select one of the articles from the site. Read the article and summarize it for your group. Share the information on conflict with your group members.

2. In the search engine of one of the major online bookstores (http://www .amazon.com or http://www.bn.com), enter the term *"business ethics."* Pursue the books that are listed. Read the summaries of the books. Consider reading one of the books from the list to enhance your knowledge of workplace ethics.

3. Review your recent e-mails. Think about how you are using self-disclosure in an e-mail setting. Is your self-disclosure equitable? Or do others disclose considerably more or less than you do? What can you do to make your electronic disclosure more equitable?

4. Go to a search engine and enter the term *Johari Window*. Based on the information you find, prepare a short presentation about the effect of disclosure on workplace communication.

## Practicing Communication in Professional Contexts

Have each group member prepare a three-minute talk about him- or herself. Keep in mind the principles of CCCD covered in this and the preceding chapters. In your group, take turns giving your talks. Refer to the Communicating in Professional Contexts website at the Wadsworth Communication Café (http://www.wadsworth.com/communication_d/) for copies of the CCCD worksheets. Each member of the group should give feedback to at least one other person. Your feedback should follow these guidelines:

+ Use the word "I" so that you own your message.
+ Avoid apologies.
+ Be specific.
+ Avoid conflicting verbal and nonverbal behaviors.

This exercise is designed to prepare you for the group and presentation exercises to come.

## Communicating in Professional Contexts in Action!

Using the Goodall CD-ROM, watch the team presentation on http://www
.giftlist.com, and watch the presenters as they research a company and prepare a
persuasive presentation that would entice potential investors. They were required to use the CCCD worksheets to complete the assignment. In addition
to the CCCD worksheets, the students were required to create and use a Power-
Point presentation within their talks. One of the challenges of the presentation
was coordinating the talk with the PowerPoint slides and with each speaker.

How were their interpersonal skills? Apply the concepts that you learned in
this chapter to the clip, and critique each team member's presentation. Some
items to consider are your first impressions as they approached the podium,
their credibility based on nonverbal behavior cues, their fluency in delivery,
and your perception of their preparation for the presentation.

Roger Persson

# Interviewing and Conscious Communication

**L**ing sat at his desk, surprised at how much better he felt now that he had contracted with a consultant to help him staff the new technical writing department he was responsible for developing. As director of customer service for Bilin.com, an Internet startup, Ling handled everything that "impacted customers both internally and externally." Two weeks ago, he found out this included the documentation, online help, and training materials required for the various software systems Bilin.com develops and uses. The problem was, Ling didn't know anything about writing documentation or hiring technical writers.

Carmen, the head of the quality assurance group, soon came to the rescue. In her previous job at a different company, Carmen had worked with a technical communication consultant who helped her define and staff the documentation and training group there. She gave Ling the consultant's name and number and suggested he give Valerie a call.

Now, sitting at his desk a week later, Ling thought about his meeting with Valerie, the consultant he had just hired. "What a strange interview," Ling thought. "I feel like I was the one being interviewed! I have to get better at this now that I have all this responsibility."

On the way back to her office, Valerie thought about her newest consulting job. She was excited to be working for a smaller company again, doing what she did best—hiring and training writers and building a department. Yet she could tell from her meeting with Ling that this was going to be a lot of work. Ling didn't have a clue about interviewing, the job requirements for technical writers or trainers, the requirements for a documentation department, the components of a documentation set, or anything else that would be needed to get the department up and running. That was the downside. The upside was that Ling seemed to be a nice, easygoing guy who didn't mind admitting what he didn't know and didn't try to snow Valerie. He was honest about his inability to hire and develop a writing staff on his own. He had been very up front about the budget and staffing resources that were available. Valerie found that honesty a big plus.

## Conducting Conscious Interviews

Conscious interviewing assumes there is a back-and-forth, give-give exchange of ideas, questions, and information on the part of the interviewer and interviewee. In many ways, watching a good interview is like watching a good tennis match. Each participant is responsible for upholding his or her end of the game. Each must return information in order for the interview to continue. The worst interviews happen when one or both participants drop the ball. Game over. Nobody wins.

In this chapter, we will follow Ling and Valerie to demonstrate how conscious communication works when we conduct interviews. We will also examine how the CCCD process works in a variety of interviewing contexts. While the main example is that of an employment interview, other examples, tips,

| Interrogation | Persuasive or sales interview | Informational interview or focus groups | Employment interview | CONSCIOUS COMMUNICATION CHOICES |
|---|---|---|---|---|
| Interviewee is grilled about a grievance filed by a customer or a co-worker. Typically one-sided and biased. | Interviewer appeals to the values and needs of the interviewee to make a convincing pitch or appeal. Typically one-sided, can be manipulative. | Employee will receive and respond to messages only at prescribed times. | Employee thinks about the best channel for messages but doesn't always follow through. | Give and take of information by participants who are informed and goal oriented. |

**Mindless Interviewing** ➔ **Mindful Interviewing**

**Figure 8.1**
Conscious Communication and Interviewing Continuum

and questions will be presented to explore the different types of interviewing you may encounter in the workplace. The basic types are indicated in the conscious communication and interviewing continuum provided in Figure 8.1.

Before you begin an interviewing process, it is important to identify the type of interview you are conducting. Are you trying to fill a position, solve a problem, or gather information? Let's examine the types of interviews in more detail.

## Interrogation

From the perspective of the conscious communication continuum, with its scale of mindless to mindful communication, the most mindless form of interviewing is **interrogation.** An interrogation is a one-sided interview that usually concentrates on the negative aspects of a situation or an employee's behavior. Although interrogation may sound ominous and out of character in the business world, you might be surprised how often managers interrogate rather than interview employees when there is a problem. While there may be a rare occasion when an interrogation would bring results, we don't recommend using this technique if your goal is to build rapport, gain information, or develop consensus.

## Persuasive or Sales Interviews

At its core, a **persuasive interview** is a sales call. Most people recognize it as such. How many times have you been sitting home in the evening and received a call from a telemarketer who first apologizes for disturbing you and then rushes to inform you, "This is not a sales call; I only want to ask you a few questions." The first time you hear this pitch you think, "Sure, I can answer a few questions," but then you find yourself listening to a ten-minute sales pitch. The persuasive or sales interview is usually one-sided and can be manipulative.

Royalty-Free/Corbis

## Performance Reviews

A **performance review** is a review or critique of an employee's work and job performance. Performance reviews are designed to give employees feedback on their performance, reward good performance, set expectations for improvement, and solve any problems that an employer thinks may be inhibiting good job performance. While they are often classified as interviews, rarely are performance appraisals conducted in the give-give manner of a true interview. Nor should they be. The performance review is the employer's, manager's, or team leader's opportunity to let employees know how they are doing. Although there should always be room for a brief period of question and answer, in a performance review, the manager imparts most of the information, and the employee listens and takes notes. After the employee has had an opportunity to evaluate the information provided in the review, the employee should be allowed to offer additional information or evidence, if necessary.

## Information Interviews or Focus Groups

A person, group, or organization uses an information interview to gather specific information, further understanding, or test a concept or idea. Information interviews can take the form of exit interviews, legal investigations, medical histories, surveys, polls, news interviews, research interviews, or personal or organizational histories. A focus group is a group assembled to help explore an idea or test a product or concept.

## BEST PRACTICES

# Performance Reviews

### Employer

*Before the Review*

+ Ask for a written evaluation from the employee of his or her performance.

+ Carefully read the employee's evaluation *before* you complete your evaluation.

+ Review (if a record exists) the employee's past two performance reviews.

+ Outline the areas of the employee's performance that exceeded expectations, met expectations, and fell short of expectations for the appraisal period.

+ Indicate areas that have fallen below expectations over the past two review periods.

+ Outline a course of action for the employee to follow that will meet expectations.

+ Document the course of action in a memo for both you and the employee to sign.

*During the Review*

+ Present the evaluation to the employee beginning with areas that exceeded expectations, followed by those that met expectations, and ending with those that were below expectations.

+ Keep the focus on the employee's job performance and team and group interactions.

+ Avoid making vague references to the employee's "attitude" or other subjective references.

### Employee

*Before the Review*

+ Prepare a written evaluation of your work prior to the manager's evaluation.

+ If you are not asked for a self-evaluation, check with your manager two weeks before your review date and request the opportunity to provide a self-evaluation.

+ In your evaluation, give an honest assessment of your performance. Include the areas where you believe you went above and beyond the requirements of the job and the areas where you need improvement.

+ Outline goals for the next review cycle. The goals you outline should reflect your individual and team goals.

+ Submit a well-thought-out, well-reasoned, organized appraisal of your work.

*During the Review*

+ Listen, listen, listen. By now, your manager knows what you think. Listen carefully to everything he or she has to say.

+ Take notes.

+ Be gracious when given praise or high marks for doing well.

+ Acknowledge areas you know need improvement.

+ Ask for a period to reflect on and respond to areas that may be in dispute.

*(continued)*

**Employer**

*During the Review (continued)*

+ Present the course of action for improvement.
+ Ask the employee if he or she has questions.
+ Offer the employee a brief period to think about the evaluation and respond either in writing or in person.
+ Ask the employee to sign the review memo documenting the course of action. Indicate that you will expect the memo to be signed by the employee by a specific date and that nonresponse on the part of the employee indicates agreement with the memo as is.

*After the Review*

+ Follow up on the memo if the employee has not signed it by the date specified.
+ Continue to document problems as they arise, but don't harp on problems that have been discussed and solved.
+ Praise the employee for changes and progress made.
+ Follow up with additional reviews as needed at three-month intervals.

**Employee**

*During the Review (continued)*

+ Walk away from the review without being defensive, negative, or closed to suggestions offered by your manager.

*After the Review*

+ Spend some time honestly thinking about your review.
+ Don't talk about the review with co-workers or vent only your side to friends and family.
+ Submit a well-thought-out, well-reasoned, organized assessment of your review if you believe any areas were unfair.
+ Indicate areas of agreement and areas that seem unfair or too harsh. Suggest ways to remedy the disagreement. Indicate that you are willing to work on your performance as well as working toward an amicable conclusion.
+ Give your manager an opportunity to respond.

Information interviews can be one-on-one or with a group:

+ One-on-one: for example, a team leader interviews an employee who has quit to determine if there were problems on the team, or a sales manager interviews a customer about changes to a product.
+ With a group: for example, focus groups can be used to explore a new Internet concept, or professional groups can be polled at a meeting about regulatory changes.

## BEST PRACTICES

## Information Interviews

### Interviewer

- ◆ Determine the purpose of the interview.
- ◆ Conduct any research necessary to familiarize yourself with the interview subject.
- ◆ Set clear goals for the interview.
- ◆ Create limits for the interview, including the number of participants, the questions to be asked, and the time frame for the interview.
- ◆ Select participants for the interview who have knowledge of or experience with the subject.
- ◆ Develop a clear structure for the interview.
- ◆ Prepare the interviewees by explaining the process you will use for conducting the interview.
- ◆ Follow up with a thank-you e-mail, phone call, or note. Or, if appropriate, send the interviewee a thank-you gift.
- ◆ Prepare the final report.
- ◆ Present the final report.

### Interviewee

- ◆ Confirm the purpose of and the process for the interview before the interview begins, if the interviewer does not provide an orientation.
- ◆ Think carefully about your answer before speaking.
- ◆ Don't elaborate unless you are asked to.
- ◆ Don't be an interview hog. If you are a member of a focus group, don't always be the first to speak. The interviewer is interested in everyone's opinion.
- ◆ Don't try to be funny or entertaining. Focus groups are expensive to conduct, and interviewers will not appreciate wasting time.
- ◆ Don't attempt to bias the other members of the group. Each member of a focus group is selected to provide a balanced view of the product, concept, or service under investigation. It is not your job to sway the members of the group to your side.

The goal, the purpose of the interview, the persons interviewed, and the limits of the interview should be clearly defined before the interview begins. Information interviews that stray beyond these set limits are rarely effective and can be frustrating for the persons being interviewed.

## Employment Interviews

**Employment interviews** are the most common forms of interviews. Many of you have already experienced an employment interview—or you soon will. The employment interview's purpose is to create a match between employee and employer that meets all or most of the goals each party brings to the table. Thus the participants must do the following:

+ Spend time clearly defining their goals and expectations prior to the interview.

+ Be honest about their goals and expectations to ensure a good fit.

+ Approach the interview from an informed position that allows information to flow back and forth.

+ Make an informed choice based on all the available information.

The goal of an employment interview should never be to "find a warm body to fill the position" or to "get a job, any job." If these are the goals, the outcomes will surely be dismal for both parties.

The remainder of this chapter focuses on using the CCCD process to conduct an employment interview.

## Choosing: Setting the Parameters for the Interview

*Successful employment interviews are governed by a number of parameters. Valerie knew this, and before she and Ling could proceed, she needed to lay out those parameters for him. She explained each of the pieces that had to come together before they could interview the first applicant. The main pieces were goals and job descriptions.*

Goals help you determine the qualifications you are looking for in job candidates, along with factors such as the number of team members required, the job title for each position, and the mix of team members. Job descriptions help you tailor the skill set and experience to the specific job—for example, the number of years of experience a person must have, the types of experience needed, or the specific tools required. These elements allow you to develop a framework for a positive and productive interview for you and the applicants.

### Setting the Goals for the Interview

If you are the interviewer, an obvious goal is to find the best-qualified person to fill the position. However, you may also find that a number of secondary goals, once identified, will help you narrow the field of applicants and result in a better fit for your organization. For example, are you looking for a spit-and-polish professional, or someone who is more a khaki-pants-and-golf-shirt type? Do most of your team members have four-year or graduate degrees, or is the team a mix of interns and technical and degreed people? What qualities do you or your team members value most—hard work, a sense of humor, creativity? What have previous team members lacked that kept them from fitting into either the team or the corporate culture? These are the types of questions we will examine during the choosing phase of interviewing.

*Valerie learned about conscious interviewing in an article she read and in a workshop she attended at a Society for Technical Communication (STC) conference. She began reflecting on her goals for the technical-writer interviews she would soon conduct:*

1. *Help Ling identify the qualities he is looking for in a writer that go beyond having the skills needed to do the work.*

2. *Educate Ling about the process of writing and the required knowledge base.*

3. *Find a manager and writing team that can work well together within the given culture.*

*Valerie then sent Ling an e-mail (see Figure 8.2).*

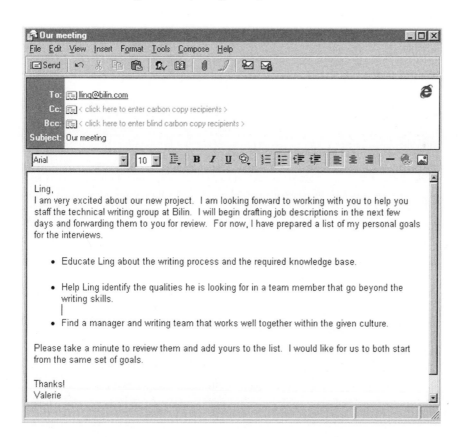

**Figure 8.2**

Ling,
I am very excited about our new project. I am looking forward to working with you to help you staff the technical writing group at Bilin. I will begin drafting job descriptions in the next few days and forwarding them to you for review. For now, I have prepared a list of my personal goals for the interviews.

- Educate Ling about the writing process and the required knowledge base.

- Help Ling identify the qualities he is looking for in a team member that go beyond the writing skills.

- Find a manager and writing team that works well together within the given culture.

Please take a minute to review them and add yours to the list. I would like for us to both start from the same set of goals.

Thanks!
Valerie

**Figure 8.3**

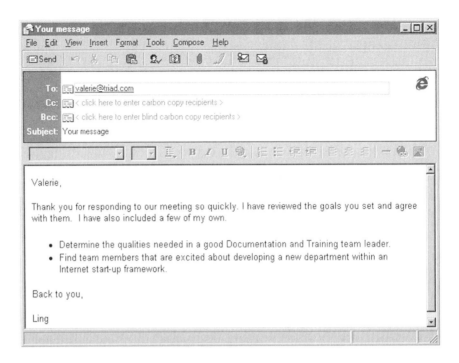

*After reflecting on Valerie's goals, Ling replied, listing the goals he had in mind. (See Figure 8.3.)*

*Valerie and Ling met a few days later to narrow down the goals for the interviews. The first goal they identified was to fill four positions: documentation and training team leader, technical writer, curriculum development specialist, and trainer/curriculum development specialist. For each of the positions, they identified additional goals:*

1. *Documentation and Training Team Leader: must have the ability to hire and develop team members, manage documentation and training projects, and be an enthusiastic spokesperson for the team within the organization.*

2. *Technical Writer: must have a solid history of technical writing within a software environment, must have a wide skill set, must be a self-starter who has demonstrated high levels of responsibility on previous projects.*

3. *Curriculum Development Specialist: must have a solid history of curriculum development within a software environment, must be able to work closely with the technical writer to develop training materials that work with the documentation set.*

4. *Trainer/Curriculum Development Specialist: must have an excellent training style, must have a solid history of curriculum development within a software environment, and must be able to work closely with the technical writer to develop training materials that work with the documentation set.*

## Developing a Job Description

Large corporations usually develop detailed **job descriptions** that minutely specify all of the individual duties and responsibilities that make up a particular job. Smaller companies such as Ling's may not go into such detail. A job description for an open position usually includes experience and education requirements and the salary range for the position. This brief description is the basis for the job announcement that will appear in print ads or online job boards. These job announcements or brief job descriptions set the basis for the interviewing questions and allow potential applicants to determine if there is an initial match with the company.

> *Valerie and Ling carefully scripted each job description to identify the broad qualities they were looking for. Valerie suggested they concentrate their efforts initially on the team leader's position. This would allow them to hire the team leader and have the team leader participate in hiring the other members of the team.*

Just as the résumé is the first impression you have of a job applicant, the job description you place in the newspaper and trade publications or on the Internet is the first impression prospective employees have of the job and your company. When you write a job description for a job announcement, you should follow these guidelines:

- Keep the description as short but informative as possible.

- Provide a list of at least three qualifications for the position.

- Identify the city and state the job is located in. Online job banks allow users to search by city and state. Not providing this information may narrow your pool of candidates. Providing this information may help eliminate applicants who will not relocate to your area.

- Provide a clear contact for the applicant, along with contact information. If you are using an online job bank, be sure to provide an e-mail address. If you don't want to use your own e-mail address, have your company establish one that is used specifically for job applications—for example: applications@bilin.com.

*Using these guidelines, Valerie and Ling developed the following job description for the documentation and training team leader position:*

### Job Title: Documentation and Training Team Leader

*Description: Internet startup located in Greensboro, NC, looking for enthusiastic individual to join our growing company. We are seeking a team leader with 5 to 7 years of team, leadership, and knowledge-based experience. The D&T team leader will be responsible for hiring, leading, and developing a team of 5 to 7 writers, curriculum developers, and trainers. Primary responsibilities will be to determine the documentation and training set and schedule for each release, schedule*

*training for new clients, provide ongoing internal training for the organization, and*
*manage the training facility.*

*Send resumes to: applications@bilin.com. Please put* D&T *leader in the*
*subject line.*

*Once they had the job description, they decided where to place the announcement. They*
*had a number of options, each with advantages and disadvantages. A few of the options*
*they considered are described below. (You can also go to these sources to look for job*
*announcements.)*

### Local Newspapers

An ad in the local paper typically limits the applicants to the delivery area of
the paper. The advantage of this option is that you will receive applications
from people living in the immediate area who will not have to arrange a move
to take the job, which means less lag time and no moving expenses. Also, this
is a relatively inexpensive option for placing announcements. A disadvantage
is that a large number of qualified people in your industry may not live in your
area, so you may be choosing from a limited pool of applicants.

### University Career Placement Centers

Career placement centers are a great place to locate entry-level and experienced applicants who have returned to college to pursue a degree. Concentrating on colleges in your area ensures that the applicants will be readily available
to interview or to accept a position without incurring travel costs.

### Professional Associations and Trade Publications

Organizations such as the Society for Technical Communication, the Internet
Developers Association, the International Television Association, and the
American Academy of Audiologists all provide job databanks that help pair job
applicants with organizations. The advantage of placing an announcement
with a professional organization is that you are targeting a very specific group
of people with very specific skills. The disadvantage is that chances are slim the
person you find will be located in your city, which means you may have to pay
moving expenses for higher-level positions.

### Online Job Databanks

Online services such as those found at http://www.job-hunt.org, http://www
.careerbuilder.com, http://www.monster.com, and http://www.jobbankusa.com, provide a wide range of announcement opportunities. Some of the online services
serve a specific industry or profession. For example, http://www.brainbuzz.com
concentrates on placing network engineers and developers. The cost for placing an announcement with an online databank varies. The advantages are that

you reach a broad range of potential applicants very quickly. In many cases, as soon as you hit Enter key on the form, the job announcement is online. The disadvantage is the same as with professional organizations and trade publications; the ideal candidate may not live in your area.

### Headhunters

With this option, you essentially pay someone to screen potential applicants. Headhunters can save you a tremendous amount of time, but their services are very expensive. They often charge as much as 25 to 30 percent of the position's annual salary if they place someone with your company.

> *Valerie and Ling examined their options and decided to place an ad in the local paper and with the online job databanks of the Society for Technical Communication and the American Society for Training and Development. While they waited for résumés, they turned their attention to preparing interview questions.*

## Creating: Scripting the Interview

Good interviews put participants at ease and allow information to flow between participants. This type of interview seldom takes place without a well-established interview plan or script. An **interview script** is a plan of questions used for the interview. An interview script should contain questions that accomplish the goals listed on page 211.

Once the general script is created, it will need to be adapted to each individual interviewee. This type of interview is called a *semi-structured interview*. The interview script establishes the main questions that will be asked within each segment of the interview, but it leaves the interview process open for follow-up and response questions. See the sample on page 216.

### Ethical Interviewing

The interview script should not contain illegal or inappropriate questions. It also should not ask questions that require an interviewee to justify his or her race, religion, marital status, age, sex, or sexual orientation. The chart on page 217 describes some of the questions you can and can't ask. Valerie and Ling used this structure to develop the questions they would use in the D&T team leader interviews.

## Coordinating: Setting Up the Interview

Interviews should not occur in a vacuum. When a team member is hired, he or she will work with people throughout the organization. It is important that new

## Sample Interview Script

| | |
|---|---|
| Establish rapport | These questions should put the interviewee at ease and break the ice. Examples are:<br><br>◆ How was your flight?<br>◆ Did you have trouble finding us? |
| Define the interviewee's experience | These questions arise from the cover letter, résumé, and references. Examples are:<br><br>◆ I see that you majored in communication. How has your major prepared you for this job?<br>◆ Tell us a little about your current position.<br>◆ What are two things about your current job that you find challenging?<br>◆ What are two things about your current job that you dislike?<br>◆ What has been your biggest accomplishment at your current position?<br>◆ What will you miss most about the company you work for?<br>◆ Of all the jobs you have had, which has been the best fit and why? |
| Clarify the requirements for the position | These questions zero in on the requirements for the position. Examples are:<br><br>◆ This position requires hiring and developing a team of writers and trainers. How would you go about doing that?<br>◆ In this position, you will be required to manage a team. What qualities do you think are important in a team environment?<br>◆ As a manager, you will be required to report the progress of your team. How do you feel about providing regular status reports?<br>◆ An important function of this position is liaison to other teams. What skills do you have that will facilitate this function?<br>◆ How would this position further your career goals? |
| Present the organization | These questions open a discussion of the organization. Examples are:<br><br>◆ What do you know about Bilin.com?<br>◆ How do you feel about working for an Internet startup, coming from such an established company?<br>◆ Bilin is a small, young company and we can't offer the benefits some organizations can. Is that a problem?<br>◆ We have just signed three major contracts, which has tripled our deliverables overnight. To meet our schedules, we know that we have to work extremely long hours. Is there anything to prevent you from working long weeks when necessary? |
| Provide closure | These questions signal the interview is ending and allow for a final opportunity to clarify information. Examples are:<br><br>◆ Do you have any additional questions?<br>◆ If offered the position, when could you start? |

## Ethical Interviewing

| Topic | What you can't ask | What you can ask |
|---|---|---|
| Marital Status | Are you married? How long have you been married? Are you divorced? Are you single? Do you go by your maiden name? Does you husband (or wife) mind you traveling? | This position requires a good bit of travel. Is there any reason you cannot travel? <br><br> Have you ever used another name for any reason? |
| Children | How many children do you have? How old are your children? Is day care a problem for you? | Our company has an excellent onsite day care program. Would you like to visit the day care center? |
| Citizenship | Are you a US citizen? What country were you born in? How long have you lived in the United States? Do you have a green card? | Do you speak any languages other than English? Your Arabic is very good. How long have you spoken the language? <br><br> Our company requires employees to provide proof of citizenship or legal work papers after they are hired. Will this be a problem? |
| Race | You have the nicest eyes. Are you Asian? | There are no questions in this area that are appropriate. |
| Age | How old are you? When did you finish high school? I love getting my AARP discount. Have you applied for your card yet? | There are aspects of this job that require the operator to be over 18. Can you provide proof of age? |
| Physical Attributes | How long have you had a weight problem? Do you find it difficult to carry out functions of your current job? | This position requires a lot of physical activity. Do you have a handicap or physical condition that would keep you from performing any part of the job? <br><br> Do you have any physical liabilities that may require special equipment or accommodations? |
| Military Service | Have you ever served in the military? | I see that when you were in the Navy, you were a telecommunications expert. How do you think these skills apply to this position? |
| Criminal Record | Have you ever committed a crime? Have you ever been arrested for anything? | Have you been convicted of a felony? Before you answer, I need to inform you that the information you provide may disqualify you for this position. |

hires fit within the organizational culture and meet the expectations of those outside as well as inside the group.

*Ling and Valerie knew that they would need to include others in the interview process. They decided to include the following managers:*

✦ *Quality Assurance Manager, Carmen: Valerie emphasized the relationship the D&T team would need to have with QA. She decided that including Carmen in the interview process would be a good way to start this relationship.*

✦ *Implementation Manager, Tom: Ling suggested that training and implementation would follow each other closely and that the training team might need technical support from the implementation team.*

✦ *Human Resources Manager, Keisha: Company protocol required Keisha to be included in the interview process.*

*After determining who would be included in the interviewing process, they devised an interview schedule:*

*Ling: welcome and orientation—ten minutes*

*Ling and Valerie: first question session—forty-five minutes*

*Carmen: QA question session—thirty minutes*

*Tom: Implementation question session—thirty minutes*

*Keisha: HR question session—thirty minutes*

*Ling: follow-up questions and closing—twenty minutes*

*With the interview plan and schedule in place, they were ready to begin interviews. Now all they needed were the résumés.*

### Focus on Ethics

You are conducting a joint interview with a colleague who keeps asking inappropriate questions. The colleague asks gender-based questions, directly asks an interviewee his age, and implies that overweight applicants are a waste of his time. What do you do? Is your primary ethical obligation to the interviewee, your colleague, or your company?

## Delivering: Ready, Set, Interview

*After Ling began to receive responses to the job posting, he and Valerie set up a time to meet and go over the résumés. Ling was eager to hire someone and wanted the team leader in place within three weeks. Valerie was concerned that things might not happen as quickly as Ling hoped they would. She cautioned Ling to look for the best-qualified candidate who was a good fit for the company and had the right attitude.*

*Having spent years hiring writers and trainers, Valerie knew this could be a difficult and time-consuming process.*

*The good news was that from the résumés, they had identified five good candidates for the position. The problem was, Ling's budget would allow them to bring in only three candidates to interview for the team leader's position. They decided to conduct phone interviews to screen the candidates and narrow down the field.*

## Conducting Phone (Screening) Interviews

Phone interviews are an excellent way of narrowing down the possible candidates for a job. From a phone interview, you can get a general idea of the personality, energy level, and knowledge base of an individual. Obviously, though, you cannot see the person.

*Ling and Valerie decided to start with Anna, whose strong résumé highlighted her twelve years of documentation and training experience. She currently worked as part of a D&T team that, on paper, appeared similar to the team Ling hoped to develop. Ling placed her at the top of the list. Valerie, however, had a couple of reservations. Anna's job experience appeared complete, yet she had changed jobs frequently in the past seven years. Missing from her skill set were some software products that Valerie thought were key for the position. They set up a phone interview with Anna for 2:00 the next day.*

---

### BEST PRACTICES

## Phone Interviews

- ✦ Make sure that there are no distractions when you conduct or participate in a phone interview.
    - ✦ Reserve a conference room so that you will not be interrupted.
    - ✦ Have the interviewer call you at home, rather than try to have the conversation at work.
    - ✦ Turn off call waiting! The last thing you want to do is ask the interviewer to hold while you answer another call.
- ✦ Speak clearly and loudly enough to be heard, especially if the call is being conducted over a conference phone.
- ✦ Wait until each speaker finishes before beginning to speak. Answer all questions completely.
- ✦ Clarify any questions you don't understand.
- ✦ Smile. When you smile, your voice is more confident and friendly.

*Ling and Valerie met in the conference room and dialed Anna's number, using the speakerphone option on the conference room telephone so that they both could hear Anna and speak to her. Anna answered the phone, saying "Hello" in a soft voice.*

*"Anna, I am here with Valerie, our consultant," Ling said, after introducing himself.*

*"Hi, Anna," Valerie said.*

*"Hi," Anna said softly.*

*Ling jumped right in, asking Anna about the information on her résumé and the duties of her current job. Anna answered each of his questions completely, but very softly. A couple of times, Ling had to ask her to speak up or repeat what she had said.*

*Valerie asked Anna about some of the software she used on various projects and then asked her about software she didn't see on Anna's résumé. Anna explained that most of her positions had used the same software over the years and she really didn't need additional tools. She felt that sticking to what she had always used was more efficient.*

*Ling then addressed the issue of job changes. Anna explained that she had worked in the textile industry and been downsized a couple of times. She then found a job with a company that made machine engines. She was doing technical writing, but the work was very limiting, and she felt she was writing the same thing over and over, that she was stuck. So after only thirteen months in her current position, she was looking again. She was very eager to find a position with a growing company in a growing industry.*

*Ling thanked Anna and told her they would be in touch. After hanging up, Ling asked Valerie what she thought.*

*"Well, I'm not sure if she doesn't like talking on the phone or if she is always that timid, but I found listening to her very trying. I can't believe you had to ask her to speak up four times. What did you think?" Valerie asked.*

*"I hate to say it, but I knew after the first four questions that she wasn't going to work out," said Ling.*

## Summary

This chapter examined the different types of interviews and the uses for each. It also introduced the concept of conscious interviewing and used the employment interview as an example of how we can implement conscious interviews, primarily from the interviewer's perspective. We also followed Ling and Valerie through the process of developing goals, a job description, and an interview script. The chapter went over the importance of asking questions that are fair and nonintrusive but that elicit the information needed to qualify a candidate for a position. Finally, we discussed phone interviews. The next chapter examines the interviewing process from the interviewee's perspective.

## COMMUNICATING IN PROFESSIONAL CONTEXTS ONLINE

All of the following chapter review materials are available in electronic format on either the Communicating in Professional Contexts website or CD-ROM. In addition to the multimedia case studies, activities, and numerous other learning resources you'll find on the CD-ROM, the CD is your gateway to the book's premium web content, which is not accessible via the Internet. The book's basic web content is available both with the premium content and on-line at http://communication.wadsworth.com/goodall2 and includes the chapter learning objectives and activities, key-term digital glossaries, and quizzes. The CD is also your gateway to InfoTrac College Edition, our extensive online data-base of full-text articles that is fully keyword searchable and available twenty-four hours a day. Installation instructions for the CD appear on the inside of this book's back cover.

## What You Should Have Learned

The learning objectives below are available on the Communicating in Profes-sional Contexts website, which is best accessed through the book's CD-ROM but is also available at http://communication.wadsworth.com/goodall2. Go to the Chapter 8 Resources and click on Learning Objectives.

Now that you have read Chapter 8, you should be able to do the following:

+ Describe the major types of interviews.
+ Discuss the difference between a mindful and mindless interview.
+ List the steps in conducting a performance review.
+ Discuss the do's and don'ts for information interviews.
+ Discuss the choices that need to be made for a conscious employment interview.
+ Create a job description.
+ Set goals for an interview.
+ Create a script for the interview.
+ Establish an interview schedule.
+ Conduct a phone interview.

## Key Terms

The terms below are available in a digital glossary on the Communicating in Professional Contexts website, which is best accessed through this book's CD-ROM but is also available at http://communication.wadsworth.com/goodall2. Go to the Chapter 8 Resources and click on Glossary.

| | | |
|---|---|---|
| **employment interviews** *(210)* | **interview script** *(215)* | **performance review** *(206)* |
| **interrogation** *(205)* | **job descriptions** *(213)* | **persuasive interview** *(205)* |

## Writing and Critical Thinking

The following activities can be completed online and, if requested, submitted to your instructor. You'll find them on the Communicating in Professional Contexts website, which is best accessed through this book's CD-ROM but is also available at http://communication.wadsworth.com/goodall2. Go to the Chapter 8 Resources and click on Writing and Critical Thinking Activities.

Choose one of the following activities.

1. Write a job description for your current job or a job you previously had. If you haven't had a job, write a job description for your ideal job.

2. Write an interview script for the job description you wrote in Activity 1.

3. In pairs, answer the interview questions for the job description and interview script. Or have a friend ask you the interview questions.

## Research and Explorations Online

The exercises below can be completed online and, if requested, submitted to your instructor. You'll find them on the Communicating in Professional Contexts website, which is best accessed through this book's CD-ROM but is also available at http://communication.wadsworth.com/goodall2. Go to the Chapter 8 Resources and click on Internet Exercises.

1. Enter the word *interview* in your search engine. Our search resulted in 114,625 hits. Scroll through the list of sites. Open some of the online interviewing sites and browse. Two of the sites we found were http://www.careercc.com and http://www.ukans.edu/cwis/units/com2/via.

2. Narrow the search by entering *interview questions* in the search engine. Open a few of the sites with interview questions. Print out the questions you find. Could you answer these questions? If not, begin to develop answers to the typical interview questions you find.

3. Search for a website that represents a professional organization associated with your major. Scroll through the job listings.

4. Create a concept and prototype of a product that you would like to market to college students. Be as creative as you wish in your product design.

Use the WWW to research guidelines for conducting a focus group by entering the keywords *focus group* in your search engine. Have a group of class members act as a focus group panel for your product. Write a report about your research on focus groups and the format of questions most effective in soliciting information. What feedback did you receive from your panel to help you determine whether your product is suitable or unsuitable for the marketplace? What have you learned about being the moderator of a panel?

5. Enter *360 degree feedback* in your search engine or in InfoTrac College Edition. Write a report on the results of your research and the pros and cons of conducting this form of feedback.

## Practicing Communication in Professional Contexts

### Handling Team Interviews

Often, you will be asked to conduct an interview with two or more people. Let's consider the following scenario:

*Ling and Valerie ask Tom, the implementation manager, to sit in on an interview with a prospective employee. The applicant, Jan Chin, is a young Asian American woman who is well qualified for the position. During the interview, Tom asks questions that are both illegal and inappropriate, many having nothing to do with Jan's ability to perform the job. Which of the following should Ling and Valerie do?*

   a. Ignore Tom and continue the interview.

   b. Apologize for Tom, make excuses about how hard he has been working, and continue the interview.

   c. Stop the interview, ask Tom to leave, and continue the interview.

   d. Stop the interview, leave the room with Tom and ask him not to return, then continue the interview without him.

After the interview, which of the following should Ling and Valerie do?

   a. Forget about what happened.

   b. Confront Tom about his behavior during the interview.

   c. Speak to Tom and then Tom's boss about his behavior.

   d. Bring up their concerns with the human resources manager.

Select the answer you think is the best action for each situation. Write an explanation for your choices. Discuss your choices with the class or within your group.

# The Job Search and Conscious Communication

A fter working as a technical writer for eight years, Shannon had finally finished her graduate degree and wanted to advance in her profession. She liked the people she was working with, but she didn't think she was being given all the responsibility she could handle. In the four years at her current job, she had performed every duty within her department. In the last year, she had planned and coordinated the writing and delivery of documentation for a number of high-profile clients. She had developed and delivered a number of training courses. She had even done the job of her boss, Lisa, the documentation and training manager, while Lisa was on maternity leave.

When Lisa returned to work, she praised Shannon for doing a great job. They both knew that Shannon was ready for more responsibility, but it was clear that no management positions would be opening up in the company. So Shannon decided to look for a new job. She was excited at the prospect.

## Conducting a Conscious Job Search

Every day, people across the country look for jobs. Some will accept the first job they are offered. Some will accept a job that they aren't thrilled about, figuring it's better than what they have been doing. Some will search for a job consciously and find a *great* job.

What makes the difference between the person who takes the first job offered and the person who finds a great job? The conscious job search. In this chapter, we will outline the process for conducting a conscious job search, including preparing for and participating in an interview. But first, look at the job search continuum in Figure 9.1 to see the difference between mindless and mindful job searches.

Before beginning the job search and interview process, it is important to identify the type of position you want. Are you looking for a management

**Figure 9.1**
Conscious Communication and Job Seeking Continuum

| Idle job seeker | Interested job seeker | Focused job seeker | Conscious job seeker | CONSCIOUS COMMUNICATION CHOICES |
|---|---|---|---|---|
| Job seeker goes through databanks or the newspapers, sees an interesting job and sends out a stock résumé. | Job seeker finds a job announcement, changes the résumé to target the job, sends résumé. | Job seeker researches possible jobs, narrows list to positions he or she really wants, targets résumé, sends. | Researches jobs, narrows possibilities, researches the company, targets the résumé, dresses for the interview, asks the right questions, gets the job. | Job seeker is in control of the job search, seeks the information necessary to target the résumé and interview, accepts the position that is right for him or her. |

**Mindless Job Seeking** ⟶ **Mindful Job Seeking**

position, or a trainee job? Do you need flexible hours? Are you hoping to travel? The first step in the conscious job search is to set your job goals.

## Choosing: Setting Your Job Goals

The choosing process helps you set the parameters of your job search. Before you write your résumé, apply for a position, or schedule an appointment for a job interview, you must set **job goals.** Job goals can be expressed as the type of position you want and the outcomes you want from your employment. You can start by identifying the following elements:

- ✦ types of positions you would enjoy
- ✦ benefits you expect from a position
- ✦ your salary requirements
- ✦ types of employers you would like to work for
- ✦ types of industries you would like to work in
- ✦ lifestyle you expect from the position

### Job Research

The research stage is crucial for finding not only a job, but the *right* job. Without research, you are not aware of the job possibilities available or the limitations and benefits of a particular position. How do you know which job is right for you? How do you know which company will be a good fit? How do you begin a conscious job search? How do you set clear job goals? The first step is research. However, job seekers often overlook this crucial step in the job search process. What can research do?

- ✦ *Research can focus or broaden the types of jobs you are applying for.* Often, seasoned job seekers will continue to apply for the same job over and over, thinking, "That is what I do." Rather than use research to find related jobs or a similar job in a related industry that might be more fulfilling and interesting, they continue to do the same old thing; only the company actually changes. At the other extreme, some new job seekers attempt to apply for anything and everything without a lot of thought for the duties, responsibilities, or salary associated with a particular job. Research helps you focus on the types of jobs you really want to do, eliminating those that don't fit your expectations.

- ✦ *Research can provide you with important job parameters.* Knowing important parameters such as the educational and experience requirements, associated salaries, and travel requirements for a particular type of job will save you the time of applying for jobs you are under- and overqualified for and will keep you from omitting crucial elements from your résumé.

+ *Research can help you identify potential industries and employers.* Often, job seekers fail to target industries and employers that may offer great job opportunities. Research helps you identify industries or employers you may not have realized need your services.

+ *Research can help you define what you can contribute to a specific company.* The bottom line with interviewers is the question "What can you do?" At the heart of this question lies a second question: "How will you make my job and life easier?" Without research, you cannot sell yourself to a prospective employer.

+ *Research can impress an interviewer.* Interviewers are impressed when you take the time to research their company. Speaking intelligently about a company's products and services shows interviewers that you are interested in not just a job, but a job with *their* company.

How do you begin? There are a number of starting places for job research:

+ the Internet—to find job boards, view a company's website, view online profiles and prospectuses, locate news articles, and consult professional organizations

+ company employees—to gather insider information on a specific organization

+ company tours—to gather information on work habits, dress code, and departmental interaction

+ friends and relatives—to gather insider perspectives

+ campus recruitment office—to determine the success rate of other grads who have been placed with a particular company or to research and schedule appointments with companies that are interviewing on campus

You can use one or more of these tools to effectively research possible jobs.

## Internet Research

The Internet has revolutionized the job search process. Using the Internet, you can search for job openings, research a company and its key employees, gather details about the products or services an organization provides, locate examples of résumés targeted to a particular industry or specialty, and determine if you and the company are a good fit.

First, consult a few of the hundreds of job boards that have sprung up on the Internet. Some of these boards offer a wide variety of jobs that cut across a variety of industries—medical, technical, high-tech, retail, and many others. Other job boards offer postings specific to a particular industry. For example, a number of them provide listings only for high-tech development positions. Within the high-tech area, there are boards that list jobs only for JAVA programmers.

## Company Employees

Company employees are a valuable source of information. If you know some-one working in a company or industry that interests you, give him or her a call. Take the employee to lunch and ask questions about the company. Here are some areas to ask about:

organizational structure
departmental ties, conflicts, and strengths
work environment
company future
dress codes

However, when talking with current company employees, it is important to keep in mind that you are gaining only one person's perspective. It may be nec-essary to balance what is said with the other information you gather about the company.

## Company Tours

Company tours are often available at large companies such as CNN, BMW, and Warner Brothers. Even some smaller companies — the ice cream maker Ben & Jerry's, for instance — offer daily tours. These public tours can be very useful for gathering information about an organization to help you determine if this is a place where you want to work. While on a tour, pay close attention to the in-teraction of employees, the dress code, and the working environment.

If a public tour is not offered, you might call the human resources depart-ment and ask for a tour of the organization. You can explain that you are inter-ested in the company as a potential employee. Many organizations will not pro-vide a tour, however, because of the private nature of their products or services. For example, many banking and financial institutions would view a request for a tour with suspicion and would deny your request.

## Friends and Relatives

Many of us know someone working for exactly the company we want to work for. Or we may live in a city or town where there are only one or two large com-panies. Friends and relatives working in these companies can provide a wealth of knowledge about the company, the industry, and the people we might be working with.

## Campus Recruitment Office

The campus recruitment office can be an excellent source of information about prospective employers, dressing for an interview, targeting résumés, and more. College students looking for a job should visit their college recruitment office at least once. The college recruitment office may be able to put you in touch with alumni working for a company that interests you.

*A number of Shannon's friends worked as technical writers across the country. Over the past few months, she had been querying them about their jobs. The happiest among them, Jen, was working for an Internet company in Seattle. She loved the fast pace and the change the company was always going through. Also, Jen was always being asked to do things that, although writing related, weren't strictly writing tasks.*

*Shannon decided to track down the job boards that listed openings for technical writers and managers in the high-tech area. She scrolled through the technical communication listings at* http://www.monster.com *and the job board at the website of the Society for Technical Communication (*http://www.stc.org*). There were a number of jobs that Shannon qualified for, but she wanted more than a repeat of her current position. She was looking for a job that would allow her to grow her career.*

*These are the job goals Shannon set:*

+ *to work for an Internet company*

+ *to find a management position*

+ *to work with both documentation and training*

*Scrolling through the STC job board, she noticed a listing for a documentation and training team leader (below). The job description seemed to be just what she was looking for. Shannon printed a copy of the job description. She wanted to find out more about*

---

| **Job Title:** | **Documentation and Training Team Leader** |
| --- | --- |
| **Description:** | Internet start-up located in Greensboro, NC, looking for enthusiastic individual to join our growing company. We are seeking a Documentation and Training team leader with 5–7 years of team, leadership, and knowledge-based experience. The D&T team leader will be responsible for hiring, leading, and developing a team of 5–7 writers, curriculum developers, and trainers. Primary responsibilities will be to determine the documentation and training set and schedule for each release, schedule training for new clients, provide ongoing internal training for the organization, and manage the training facility. |
| **Contact:** | Send resumes to **applications@bilin.com**. Please put D&T leader in the subject line. |

**< back >**                                                                 **< next >**

*the company that had posted the opening. In this case, the listing included the company name. Many of the listings she read didn't have a company name or contact, which would have made additional research difficult until she received a response to a letter of inquiry.*

## Hint

If a job listing interests you but does not include the company name or contact information, send a general inquiry letter or e-mail. This allows you to elicit more information from the company before sending a résumé. For example:

*Hello!*

*I just finished reading your posting on monster.com. I am very interested in the position you posted. However, I would like more information before submitting my résumé. Any additional information you could provide about the position and the company would be greatly appreciated.*

*Sincerely,*
*Shannon Green*

*Shannon entered "bilin.com" in the search field on her web browser and hit Enter. A number of possible matches appeared. A couple of the entries were articles that detailed the company's plans to go public later that year. One entry was for the company's website. She decided to check out the website first. After clicking through the site and reading about the company's products and services, Shannon was getting excited about the job. The website was laid out really well, but the writing definitely needed help. The products seemed interesting, something lacking in her current position. Best of all, Bilin was an Internet-based company, an area Shannon really hoped to get into.*

*Next, Shannon read through the articles she downloaded from her search. Most of what she read was very positive. Bilin.com had started as a business-to-consumer company but recently made the jump to business-to-business. Even though their entrance in the business-to-business market came late in the game, the limited competition in this area meant that getting a late start had not really hurt them. One article announced a partnership with two large companies, a move analysts said would help with their upcoming initial public offering (IPO). The final article listed Bilin.com as one of the best Internet startups to work for.*

*Sold! Shannon couldn't wait to structure her résumé for Bilin.com.*

# Creating: Putting Together a Winning Résumé

Let's start this section with a personal story. After Sandra finished her graduate program, she decided to stay at home with our son Nic. Four years later, after Nic started school, Sandra found that she had a good bit of free time and little to fill it. One afternoon, Bud came home ranting about how difficult it was to get a job and how his students were really struggling in the slow job market. Sandra challenged his point of view and boldly said, "Oh, come on! I could get a job tomorrow if I wanted, and I've been staying at home with a child for the last four years." Of course Bud took Sandra up on her challenge. He dared her to find a job in the current market.

A few days later, Bud brought Sandra a job announcement from the Internet. A consulting firm located in Tampa, Florida, was looking for someone to develop documentation and training materials for a client in South Carolina.

Sandra researched the company, targeted her résumé, wrote a snazzy cover letter explaining her absence from the job market, and faxed the résumé to the number on the announcement. Exactly one day later, the president of the company called Sandra. He loved her cover letter and résumé. Her past experience spoke for itself, and he was also impressed that she clearly understood the changes that had occurred in the marketplace and that she was equipped to adjust to those changes. He informed Sandra that although the project manager in South Carolina was looking for a technical writer for a specific customer, *he* was looking for someone to develop a documentation and training department for the entire organization. This was something, according to Sandra's résumé, she had done in the past. Would she like the job? The salary and stock participation blew her away, and best of all, she could work from home. She immediately accepted the job.

We tell you this story for two reasons:

1. Bad résumés get thrown in the trash; good résumés will get you an interview; great résumés can make an important lasting impression.
2. Résumés *can* open doors you may not know exist within an organization.

## Selecting the Format

A **résumé** is a formal statement of who you are. It is part autobiography, part work history, and part sales presentation. The primary goal of a résumé and cover letter is to compel the reader to call you for an interview. If you currently have résumés out and you aren't receiving calls for interviews, revise your résumé immediately.

Years ago, before computers became so widely available, we would spend hours on our résumés, have professionals review them, and pay to have the final résumés typeset. We would get twenty or thirty copies printed and send them out. Not anymore. Now, because computers and high-quality printers are so prevalent, there is no excuse for *not* tailoring a résumé to a specific job or employer. Even job seekers with little or no experience will benefit from tailoring their résumés. Tailoring the résumé may require you to do the following:

+ Change the format based on the type of industry or organization you are applying to. For example, a technical writer applying to an engineering firm might use a traditional format; however, that same writer might use a contemporary format for an Internet firm and an artistic format to apply for a position at a new magazine.

+ Highlight accomplishments that match the job requirements.

+ Change the language of the résumé to match the jargon of the industry you are applying to.

+ Change the tone of the résumé from informal to formal, based on the type of industry you are applying to.

Consider the following résumés Shannon could have used for the positions she found in her search.

### Traditional Format

The traditional format is very conservative and straightforward. It is the least creative résumé style. This format should be used for very conservative organizations, such as law firms, banks, and accounting companies. An example is shown on the next page.

### Contemporary Format

The contemporary format leans toward the conservative, but it allows the writer to include accomplishments that deserve mentioning. This format works well for managers or those who wish to move into a management position. This is also a good résumé for advertising, marketing, and high-tech professionals. An example is shown on page 234.

### Artistic Format

The artistic format is used by job seekers who need to display their creative or individual talents. It allows the writer to highlight talents or creative abilities, which may be difficult to fit into a traditional or contemporary format. This format works well for artists, musicians, and actors who need to showcase their creative side. An example is shown on page 235.

*Shannon decided to use the contemporary format for her résumé. She liked the fact that it highlighted both her work experience and her accomplishments, something she felt would be important to a fast-growing Internet company. Now all she had to do was write a cover letter.*

**Shannon Green**

790 Snowgoose Cove
Middletown, MD 25678
210-555-5555
sgreen@middletown.com

*Goal:*  To find a writing position with an established engineering firm that allows me to use my experience and education to the fullest.

*Education*

*1993–1996*  Master of Science in Communication from the University of Maryland.

*1989–1993*  Bachelor of Arts in English from Maryland State.

*Work Experience*

*May 1996–current*
*Senior Technical Writer*

*Computer Consultants, Inc.*
*Middletown, MD 25678*

Duties include developing documentation, online help, and training materials for a variety of companies. Work required learning a number of custom software packages and developing custom materials.

*June 1993–May 1996*
*Technical Writer*

*First Bank of Maryland*
*Middletown, MD 25678*

Duties included developing documentation, online help, and training materials for teller software packages.

*June 1990–June 1993*
*Work Study*

*The Graduate School*
*Maryland State*

Duties included preparing graduate student packages for prospective graduate students and editing master's theses.

*References available upon request.*

Traditional Format

## Two Words Never to Use on a Résumé

*Entry level.* These words raise red flags for those who are in charge of the screening process. You will be screened, never to be heard from again. Avoid using these two words, not only on your résumé, but also in your job search language, written and spoken. Companies are not looking for entry-level employees. They are looking for employees who can contribute to the growth and development of the organization.

Adapted from Job Search Info at www.collegegrad.com (2000).

## Shannon Green

**Home**                                              **Business**
790 Snowgoose Cove                                    Computer Consultants, Inc.
Middletown, MD 25678                                  Middletown, MD 25678
210-555-5555                                          210-555-5552, ext. 789
sgreen@middletown.com                                 shannon.green@ccinc.com

*Goal:*   To find a writing position with a growing Internet company that allows me to grow and develop my
          skills and move into a management position.

### Professional Experience

| | |
|---|---|
| ***May 1996 – current***<br>*Senior Technical Writer* | ***Computer Consultants, Inc.***<br>*Middletown, MD 25678*<br><br>Duties include developing documentation, online help,<br>and training materials for a variety of companies. |
| *Accomplishments:* | Learned over 35 software packages in the last four years to develop<br>customer documentation and training. Guided the development and delivery<br>for the last nine projects including: selecting the writing and training<br>team, developing the project plan, assigning the resources, and delivering<br>documentation and training. Each project was delivered on time and<br>within budget.<br><br>*Received five outstanding reviews and pay raises over the last four years.* |
| ***June 1993–May 1996***<br>*Technical Writer* | ***First Bank of Maryland***<br>*Middletown, MD 25678*<br><br>Duties included developing documentation, online help, and training<br>materials for teller software packages. |
| *Accomplishments:* | *Received TIP (Team Initiative and Performance) award from three separate<br>branches for the training I wrote.* |
| ***June 1990–June 1993***<br>*Work Study* | ***The Graduate School***<br>*Maryland State*<br><br>Duties included preparing graduate student packages for prospective<br>graduate students and editing master's theses. |
| *Accomplishments:* | *Asked to remain on in a full-time position after graduation.* |

### Education

*1993–1996*   Master of Science in Communication from the University of Maryland. GPA 4.0
*1989–1993*   Bachelor of Arts in English from Maryland State. GPA 3.8

*References available upon request.*

Contemporary Format

# Shannon Green

<table>
<tr>
<td>

**Home**
790 Snowgoose Cove
Middletown, MD 25678
210-555-5555
sgreen@middletown.com

</td>
<td>

**Business**
Computer Consultants, Inc.
Middletown, MD 25678
210-555-5552, ext. 789
shannon.green@ccinc.com

</td>
</tr>
</table>

*Goal:*   To find a writing position that allows me to mix my creative talents and professional expertise.

*Agent:*   Marilyn Timmons, 17000 Park Avenue, New York, NY 10028.

## Writing Competitions and Awards

| | |
|---|---|
| *New York Literary Magazine* May 2000 | Juried Award, Short Story Competition |
| *Maryland Writing Contest* December 1999 | Juried Award, Short Story Competition |
| *Coyote Journal* June 1999 | Judges Award, Short Story Category |

## Books and Publications

I currently have one book, *Tales From My Heart,* and three short stories with my agent.

## Professional Experience

| | |
|---|---|
| **May 1996 – current** *Marketing Writer* | **Computer Consultants, Inc.** *Middletown, MD 25678* |
| | Duties include writing and editing the company newsletter and marketing and public relation articles for a variety of business and trade publications. |
| *Senior Technical Writer* | Developed documentation, online help, and training materials for a variety of companies. |
| **June 1993–May 1996** *Technical Writer* | **First Bank of Maryland** *Middletown, MD 25678* |
| | Duties included developing documentation, online help, and training materials for teller software packages. |
| **June 1990–June 1993** *Work Study* | **The Graduate School** *Maryland State* |
| | Duties included preparing graduate student packages for prospective graduate students and editing master's theses. |

## Education

| | |
|---|---|
| *1993–1996* | Master of Science in Communication from the University of Maryland. GPA 4.0 |
| *1989–1993* | Bachelor of Arts in English from Maryland State. GPA 3.8 |

*References available upon request.*

Artistic Format

*She reread the job description and highlighted the phrases she wanted to focus on in her cover letter. She knew that if she could tie her experience to these highlighted phrases, she could get an interview with Bilin.com.*

| | |
|---|---|
| **Job Title:** | **Documentation and Training Team Leader** |
| **Description:** | Internet start-up located in Greensboro, NC, looking for enthusiastic individual to join our growing company. We are seeking a Documentation and Training team leader with 5–7 years of team leadership, and knowledge-based experience. The D&T team leader will be responsible for hiring, leading, and developing a team of 5–7 writers, curriculum developers, and trainers. Primary responsibilities will be to determine the documentation and training set and schedule for each release, schedule training for new clients, provide ongoing internal training for the organization, and manage the training facility. |
| **Contact:** | Send resumes to **applications@bilin.com**. Please put D&T leader in the subject line. |

**< back >**                                                    **< next >**

## Writing a Compelling Cover Letter

Recently, we did an Internet search on the phrase *résumé and cover letters*. The search returned 931,539 hits. That's almost a million websites with information about résumés and cover letters. Before you begin your résumé, look at the examples on some of these sites. Borrow the best formats, wording, and styles you find. You don't have to reinvent the wheel. Just make sure that whatever you borrow is appropriate for the type of job you are applying for.

Think of a cover letter as your first impression. A good cover letter introduces you to a prospective employer and highlights your credentials. A poorly written cover letter will get you eliminated from the running without a second glance. Excellent cover letters target a specific audience. Often, job announcements will contain the name and/or title of the person who placed the announcement and is responsible for the hiring process. If not, you will have to track it down. First, call the company and ask for the person's name and correct title. While you're on the phone, verify the address. Some companies use a dummy e-mail or title in their announcements. You might avoid having your résumé sit in a pile waiting to be sifted through, simply by asking if the person has a direct e-mail address or postal address you can use.

If a phone call doesn't work, don't be discouraged. It might be possible to find the information you need at the company's website. While you're there, learn as much about the company as possible. This information can be used in the cover letter and later at an interview.

Attend to the basics—if you are writing a standard cover letter, follow standard letter writing formats. Microsoft Word has a template for business letters. Be sure to include your name, your address, and additional contact information.

Keep it short. A cover letter should highlight your experience; it shouldn't duplicate your résumé. A cover letter shouldn't ever be longer than one page. Put your reason for submitting the résumé in the first or second line.

---

**SHANNON GREEN**

790 Snowgoose Cove
Middletown, MD 25678
210 555-5555
sgreen@middletown.com

May 10, 2006

Ling Cyan
Bilin.com
555 Frontage Road
Greensboro, NC 27485

Mr. Cyan,
After reading your posting on the Society for Technical Communication job board, I knew I had to submit my resume. I have been considering a change since receiving my master's degree a few months ago. The job you posted resonated closely with many of the goals I have established for myself.

I am a motivated and experienced technical writer with over ten years of experience. For the past four years, I have worked for a consulting company creating documentation and training materials for a variety of companies and industries, developing a broad range of technical and writing knowledge. I have led a number of project development teams and I know how to motivate writers and trainers. I have developed documentation and training sets for both internal and external training audiences, determined schedules, and managed training facilities for a number of clients.

I am looking for a position with a fast-growing company. I enjoy the change and challenge that are part of the Internet experience. I am looking forward to discussing my qualifications with you. You can contact me at the above number or e-mail address.

Sincerely,

Shannon Green

---

*After several drafts, Shannon had crafted her cover letter.*

If you are responding to a particular announcement, say so. If you are interested in a position with a particular company but aren't sure whether it has a specific opening, explain why you believe you would be a valuable addition to the organization.

Sell yourself—if you don't, no one will. The cover letter is an opportunity to tell your audience why you are the perfect person for the job. Refer to the job announcement and highlight places where your experience and the employer's needs dovetail. For example, if the job announcement is for someone to develop training materials for a bank, you might say, "I have extensive experience developing online help systems and training materials for the financial market."

Highlight your accomplishments. If you've led a team, exceeded sales goals, initiated a program, or developed a product, include that in your cover letter. Use action words that depict a positive, goal-oriented achievement.

Proofread carefully. You would be amazed at how many cover letters are sent out with glaring mistakes. Misspelling the company's name or, worse, the name of the person you are sending the cover letter to are sure ways to have your résumé placed in the "No!" file. Proofread your cover letter and résumé carefully and then ask someone else to check it over before you send it.

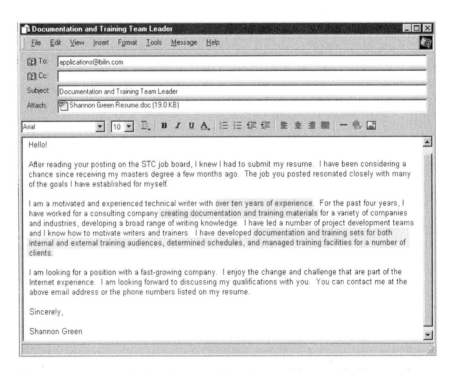

*Shannon was targeting a high-tech company that only provided an e-mail address, so she submitted her cover letter and résumé via e-mail.*

Look carefully at the phrases highlighted in Shannon's e-mail cover letter. Compare those to the phrases highlighted in the job description. Notice anything? Shannon worked the phrases from the job description into the letter. The phrases give her cover letter punch. The letter is written specifically for Bilin.com. Just as the résumé is customized, so is the cover letter, using the keywords and phrases from the job description.

## BEST PRACTICES

### Submitting Résumés and Cover Letters

In this age of Internet and high-tech job searches, you have some decisions to make about how you submit résumés and cover letters. This can be a delicate call for some positions and organizations, but how you submit your résumé and cover letter can determine whether or not you get an interview. To ensure that your résumé is seen, you need to match the method of submission to the type of organization and the job posting. Here are a few things to keep in mind.

- ✦ Conservative or traditional organizations (law; accounting; large, established organizations with a long history): Submit your résumé by mail, on good-quality cream-colored paper, using a traditional layout. Use a matching, legal-size envelope. Do not handwrite the envelope. Use a typewriter or printer to print the return address and mailing address on the envelope. If you are applying to a conservative organization that provides only an e-mail address, however, by all means, use e-mail.

- ✦ High-tech, Internet, and progressive organizations: Submit your résumé via e-mail. In most fast-paced organizations, managers are e-mail, not snail mail, oriented. Your résumé may sit unopened on the manager's desk while someone else's résumé is read immediately.

- ✦ Artistic and creative organizations: Submit your cover letter, résumé, and supporting materials by mail, unless your supporting materials are contained in files that can be sent over the Internet.

### Focus on Ethics

Shannon feels confident that she has a great résumé. There's only one small snag: a few years ago, she took a short assignment with an Internet startup. She was let go after six weeks because the company couldn't afford to pay her. She found her current position within a week of losing the job. Rather than get into a discussion about what Shannon sees as a brief, unfortunate experience, she has chosen to leave the six weeks with the startup off her résumé.

Is Shannon's omission unethical? Is she required to include *all* of her job experience on her résumé? Is an omission the same as lying?

# Coordinating: Preparing for the Interview

"Ling," Valerie said, "I have a résumé I want you to look at."

Ling groaned. "Do I have to? So far we've seen fifteen great résumés, but when we talk to these people, they aren't anything like they seemed."

"Why don't I give this one a call and do a screening?" Valerie offered. "If I think she's worth it, then we'll bring her in."

"Fine," Ling said. "If you like her, set something up for Monday and coordinate it with the interviewing team."

"No problem."

Valerie hoped Shannon would interview better than the last two candidates. When she returned to her office, she decided to call Shannon to schedule a phone interview. She could send an e-mail, but she had a good feeling about Shannon and wanted to speak to her as soon as possible.

"Shannon, this is Valerie Shaw with Bilin.com. We received your résumé, and I would like to set up a time to conduct a phone interview."

"That would be great," Shannon said. "I was hoping I would hear from you. When would you like to do the interview?"

"Well, I know I called your work number and this is probably not a good time. Is there a time either later today or tomorrow that we could talk for an hour or so?"

"Sure," said Shannon. "I picked up clients at the airport this morning at 6:30, so I planned to leave a bit early. Could I call you around 4:00 eastern time?"

"That would be great," Valerie replied. "I'm looking forward to talking to you. But let me call you. Will you be at your home number?"

"Yes," Shannon said. "Do you have that number?"

"Sure do," said Valerie. "I'll talk to you in a few hours."

"Thanks for calling," said Shannon. "I'm really eager to hear more about the job and the company. Bye."

"Bye," Valerie said, smiling. Even in that short exchange, she had heard an enthusiasm and ease that the other candidates lacked.

## Participating in a Phone Interview

As Shannon drove home, she made a mental list of the things she needed to have in front of her for the interview. She needed her cover letter and résumé, as well as the job description, and she thought she should have the company's website up so she could refer to it at some point. When she got home, she arranged all the things she needed on her desk and got comfortable. She turned off call waiting and put a "Do not disturb" note on her apartment door.

Meanwhile, Valerie was preparing for the interview, too. She also had copies of the cover letter, résumé, and job description in front of her. She had copies of the other interviewees' résumés, as well. She had underlined the areas on each résumé that had not rung true during the interviews. At exactly 4:00, she dialed Shannon's number.

Shannon answered after the second ring. She didn't want to appear too excited, even if she was. "Hello," she said.

"Hi, this is Valerie. I hope you didn't have to rush too much to get home."

"No, no problem. I've really been looking forward to this," Shannon said.

After an hour and fifteen minutes of one of the best phone interviews Valerie had ever participated in, she started wrapping things up.

"Shannon, I would like to bring you in for an interview. I know it's already Wednesday and this is short notice, but we need to fill this position quickly. Could you fly down on Sunday evening and interview on Monday?"

"Let me look at my PDA and see what I have next week. Can you hold for just a second?" Shannon asked.

"Sure," Valerie said. "Take your time."

A few seconds later, Shannon said, "I think I can make that work. I do have a meeting Monday afternoon, but I can reschedule it."

"Great. I'll have Keisha, our human resources manager, give you a call first thing in the morning. She will handle your travel arrangements and interview schedule. Do you have any questions for me?" Valerie asked.

"Yes, a few. Who will I be interviewing with? And what is your company dress code?"

"You will be interviewing with myself; Ling, the director of customer support; Carmen, the quality assurance manager; Tom, the implementation manager; and Keisha, the human resources manager. It will be a busy day. As far as the dress code, as long as you don't show up in a bathing suit, I think you'll be okay." Valerie laughed. "This is an Internet company, populated by programmers, so you're bound to see everything from shorts and flip-flops to the salespeople in business suits. I would suggest something in between and comfortable."

"Thanks, that helps," Shannon said, smiling.

"Anything else?" Valerie asked.

"No, I think that does it. I'm really looking forward to meeting you in person."

"Me, too," Valerie said. "This has been great! If you have any questions, please don't hesitate to call or e-mail me. I e-mailed my contact information to you while we were wrapping up."

"Thanks," Shannon said. "I'll see you Monday."

Valerie hung up and immediately sent Keisha an e-mail asking her to arrange Shannon's interview. Then she left Ling a voice mail:

"Ling, it's Valerie. I just got off the phone with Shannon Green, and she's great! I think you are going to be really pleased. I set up her interview for Monday, and I've already e-mailed Keisha to get the ball rolling. I have a strong feeling about this candidate, so I'm going to call the people she listed as references. We should meet on Monday at 7:30 to review her information before the interview. Bye."

## Arranging the In-Person Interview

The next morning, Shannon received a call from Keisha, the human resources manager for Bilin.com.

"Shannon, this is Keisha. Valerie asked me to give you a call and work out the details for your interview," Keisha said.

Shannon would fly out of Baltimore at 6:00 on Sunday and arrive in Greensboro at 7:42. She would be staying at the Greensboro Hilton. The Hilton had an airport shuttle, and it was only a couple of blocks from the office. A number of restaurants would be close by for dinner Sunday evening. At 8:30 Monday, Valerie and Ling would meet her in the lobby for breakfast. Keisha would send her the itinerary for the rest of the day via e-mail. Her flight home would leave at 5:30 that evening, and Valerie would take her to the airport.

"Any questions?" Keisha asked.

"Actually, I was hoping to be able to see a little of the city. I've done a good bit of research on the company, and I'm impressed. But the location will have a lot to do with my decision, should I be offered a job. Would it be possible for me to fly in on Saturday so I'll have a chance to look around?" Shannon was a little nervous about asking, but she didn't want to take a job without seeing the city, and Valerie had indicated they would need an answer quickly.

"Sure! If you fly on Saturday, we can save money on the airfare, so I can get you a rental car. Let me check the flights for Saturday and I'll call you right back."

An hour later, Shannon had received the final itinerary from Keisha by e-mail. Her flight would leave on Saturday at 9:00, and she would be in Greensboro before lunch. Keisha had arranged for a realtor to meet her for lunch and drive her around for the afternoon. Sunday, she was on her own. She immediately started surfing the net for information on Greensboro.

## BEST PRACTICES

### Arranging Interviews

+ Be flexible, but not foolish. Make sure you are comfortable with the schedule, accommodations, and travel arrangements. If you don't think the schedule allows you adequate travel time, say so. If you are uncomfortable with the accommodations, say so. You cannot be at your best for an interview if you didn't sleep the night before or if you haven't eaten because the schedule didn't leave time for lunch.

+ Be understanding, but not gullible. Occasionally, you will encounter a small company or a startup that will ask you to pay for your travel and they will reimburse you later. If you can afford to pay, you really want the job, and you can afford not to be paid back, say yes. If you can't, ask if other arrangements are possible. Explain that, although you are really interested in the position and the company, you are not in the position to finance the trip. In most cases, the company will work something out. Be sure that you keep all your receipts so that you will have a record of your expenses later.

+ Make reasonable, not ridiculous requests. If you are a vegetarian, ask the human resources person if there is a vegetarian restaurant near the hotel. Don't ask for a suite, a luxury car, or a first-class seat on the plane unless you are interviewing for a CEO position.

## Dressing for Success in the Internet Age

The rules used to be so easy: Wear a conservative blue or gray suit. If you are a man, wear a conservative tie. If you are a woman, wear hose and pumps. These days, however, you might be sitting across the table from someone in khakis and a golf shirt, or jeans and a Hawaiian shirt, so you might feel a bit uncomfortable in a stiff business suit. How do you know what to wear? Ask! Just as Shannon asked Valerie, you should either ask the person arranging the interview or call the human resources department. Say that you will be interviewing (and with which department), and ask about the dress code. Then use common sense. Can you wear jeans and a Hawaiian shirt if you know that's how the interviewer dresses? No! You should dress less conservatively but still look professional. Follow the same rules as with cover letters and résumés: conservative company, conservative dress; progressive company, lean toward business casual.

The chart below shows some of the basic do's and don'ts for creating a positive appearance at a job interview.

| Do | Don't |
|---|---|
| + match your level of dress to the type of company you are interviewing with. | + wear heavy cologne or perfume. |
| + wear conservative clothes for interviews with conservative companies; wear professional clothes for all other interviews. | + wear distracting jewelry. |
| + have your hair cut before the interview in an attractive, simple style. | + chew gum, smoke, or eat during the interview. |
| + make sure your nails are well groomed; people notice the small things. | + wear heavy makeup. |
| + carry a professional briefcase or portfolio. | + wear extremely high heels. |

# Delivering: Practicing and Being Interviewed

*On Saturday, Shannon flew to Greensboro. She met with the realtor and looked at a few apartments, condominiums, and townhouses. By the end of the day, she had found exactly the right loft apartment in the downtown area, should she be offered the job. Sunday, she ate brunch and drove around the city on her own. She liked what she saw. Now it was time to go back to the hotel and practice for her interview.*

*In her hotel room, Shannon set up her laptop and connected to the Internet. She had always done well in interviews, but she wanted to brush up so she would be prepared for tomorrow. She entered the word* interviewing *in the search field. The search retrieved 114,625 websites. Two looked promising: Strategic Interviewing Tips at* http://www.jobweb.com/Resumes_Interviews/default.htm *and interviewing tips at* http://www.joblink-usa.com/interview.htm. *She scrolled through the sites to pick up as many tips as she could. One of the things she came across was information on the different styles of interviewing:* informal *and* formal.

## Interview Styles

Interviews can be conducted in either an informal or formal style. To be on the safe side, you need to practice for both styles.

### Informal Interviews

In an **informal interview,** the questions will be unstructured and will cover a wide variety of topics. Informal interviews make use of **open questions**— questions that require more than yes or no responses and that allow you a good bit of room to discuss your experience or perspective.

The advantages of this type of interview are that you can showcase your experience, expound on your accomplishments, use your personality, and display your ability to speak clearly and confidently. The disadvantage is that people who are not confident speaking off the cuff may have a difficult time. The interviewee bears most of the responsibility in informal interviews, which means you have to have something to say. Otherwise the interview doesn't tend to be very fruitful.

### Formal Interviews

**Formal interviews** are structured and center on questions designed to gather specific information. These interviews tend to be tightly scripted in advance. They frequently make use of **closed questions**— questions that require specific, concrete answers and that provide little opportunity to elaborate.

The advantages of the formal interview are that it works well for interviewers who don't know a great deal about interviewing. It allows the interviewer to learn from the interviewee without giving away how little he or she knows about the interview area. The disadvantage is that a formal interview

Michelle D. Bridwell /PhotoEdit

doesn't allow the interviewer to get to know the interviewee. It provides a very flat, one-sided view of the person.

In a formal interview, you might be asked questions like these:

+ This position requires a good bit of travel. Is travel a problem for you?
+ How many days of work did you miss last year?
+ Do you have plans to return to school?
+ Will relocating be a problem?
+ We are a much smaller company than you have been working for. Have you thought about how that might affect your plans for promotions?

## Practicing the Interview

To ensure that you don't have problems knowing what to say during an interview, practice responding to the following questions and prompts. Most of them are the kinds of open questions you would be asked in an informal interview. Some of Shannon's practice answers are included.

+ *Tell me about yourself.* Plan an answer to this question in advance, and keep your answer focused on the job and the interview. The interviewer is not interested in your family, friends, hobbies, or dog unless these things somehow relate to the position you are applying for. Stick to the details of your résumé and focus on your college courses and work experience. Find a theme that unites the decisions you have made into a cohesive plan, ending with why you decided to apply for this position.

*Shannon thought about this question and came up with the following answer:*

*"I really enjoy my work. I have always believed it is important to do something you really enjoy, and I enjoy technical communication. I like working on a variety of projects with a lot of different people. I am best when I have a lot of irons in the fire, which this position seems to require. And I work really well in a team environment."*

+ *How did you decide to enter your current field of employment?* Few people grow up knowing what they want to be, and some never make a clear and conscious choice to major in something in college. However, you don't want a prospective employer to think that you just fell into your current job or that you selected your career only because you could make a lot of money or because your parents told you to become an accountant.

*"Okay," Shannon thought, "this one is easy":*

*"I took a communication class my freshman year and immediately knew I wanted to be in communications. When I was a junior, I interned at a software company and worked in the documentation and training department. By the end of my internship, I knew that was what I was going to do."*

+ *Where do you want to be in five years?* Refrain from saying, "I want your job." Do, however, map a future plan that includes realistic, achievable goals without outwardly threatening the interviewer.

*Shannon found this question difficult. After a good bit of deliberation, she decided on an answer:*

*"I've been giving this a lot of thought lately, and I know that my next position will greatly influence my plan. I know that I am ready for a leadership position. I am very eager to develop a department and watch it grow—which should keep me busy for at least five years. Beyond that, I have thought about consulting, but I expect I need at least five more years of corporate experience first."*

+ *Why do you want to leave your current job?* This is a big red-flag question. The interviewer is looking for problems you might have with coworkers, your boss, authority figures, or your ability to do the job. Focus on the opportunities associated with the position you are interviewing for, rather than the disappointments of your current position. Do not, under any circumstances, knock your current employer.

*"This one is a trick question," Shannon thought. "If I'm completely honest, I could come off looking like a disgruntled employee. I'll keep it short and sweet."*

*"Until six months ago, I was very happy in my current position. Then my manager, Lisa, went on maternity leave and I was charged with managing the department while she was gone. I found the new responsibilities challenging but extremely rewarding, and the department performed really well during that period. When Lisa returned, I realized that it was time for me to begin looking for a leadership position."*

+ *Describe your dream job.* Most of us have dreams of being paid to write the great American novel or an award-winning screenplay. Is that what your prospective employer is looking for? No! Nor should you say, "This is my dream job," if you are applying for a training or junior management position. Keep your answer focused on a logical career path for the position you are applying for.

+ *Why do you want to work for us?* Here is where your research pays off. Let the interviewer know you have researched the company.

*"Okay," Shannon thought, "this one I know."*

*"I am really impressed with the customers Bilin.com has attracted with the business-to-business product lines. I think I could learn a lot working with these types of clients. Also, the fact that Employment Inc. named Bilin.com as one of the top twenty-five companies to work for was very impressive."*

+ *Why should I hire you?* If you paint yourself as someone who can do anything and knows everything, you run the risk of being a big letdown if you get the job. That is, if the interviewer doesn't view your answer as a huge ego trip. When answering this question, be confident and keep your answer focused on your job and education.

*"I know why they should hire me. This is a piece of cake," Shannon thought.*

*"I am very motivated. I enjoy my work and work well with almost everyone. I have the project leadership skills you are looking for and the knowledge base the job requires. I'm ready for the work that is in front of whoever takes this position."*

+ *What are your greatest strengths and weaknesses?* The trick with this question is to be modest about your strengths and to turn a weakness into a plus.

*This one Shannon was ready for:*

*"I strive to accomplish all of my assignments on time and within budget. Doing this often requires that I go beyond what is expected, and I expect those around me to do the same. Occasionally, I will find myself overworked rather than confront a team member who isn't pitching in as they should."*

+ *What makes you a good leader?* Try to avoid clichés or trite phrases. Make your answer concrete, and focus on actual experiences.

*Shannon decided to focus on the certification program she had helped develop.*

"Recently, I was asked to lead a team tasked with developing a new certification program for our installation teams. After the first installation team received their certification, I got an e-mail from the company president thanking me for putting the program together so quickly and informing me that the last installation was the smoothest we have ever had."

+ *Do you have any questions?* Begin by focusing on the position and the fit within the organization. After a few questions about the organization, you can inquire about salary and benefits. However, don't delve too deeply into this area until you are offered the job.

## Being Interviewed

*Ling began the interview.*

*Ling: "What do you think about Greensboro?"*

*Shannon: "From what I've seen, I really like it. I was surprised at the number of parks and how green everything is. I was also really pleased by the variety of housing choices."*

*Ling: "Would leaving Maryland be difficult for you? I see from your résumé that you went to college in Maryland and then remained in the state. You must have deep ties to the area."*

*Shannon: "Actually, I'm an army brat. I've lived in Maryland longer than I've ever lived anywhere. Settling in a new place has always been something I do easily."*

*Valerie: "Tell Ling a little about your current position. I know we have already covered a good bit of this, but I would like him to hear it from you."*

*Shannon: "I am currently a senior technical writer. But that title doesn't really do my duties justice. We have a philosophy that everything flows from documentation. Which means that the documentation and online help should be the basis for the training. When a client goes through training, we refer back to the online help and documentation, so we are constantly reinforcing both. When the client returns to their office, they know where to get the answers to their questions in the documentation, online help, or training materials. Using this philosophy, we have reduced support calls by 82 percent.*

*"Because everything flows from the documentation, I am often in the position of team leader. I bring together the documentation writers, the curriculum developers, and the trainers for each project. I am responsible for the schedules, the resources, the deliveries, and the training classes."*

*Ling: "Sounds like you have your hands full. What are two things about your current job that you find challenging?"*

*Shannon: "The most challenging thing about my job is leading the project team. Often, people we hire come from very different environments from ours, and occasionally we have a case where a trainer or curriculum developer wants to run the show. It is my job to explain the department philosophy and keep that vision on track. At the same time, I strive to recognize each person's contribution to the project.*

"I also find the variety of clients we work with challenging. Each customer is a bit different, as is each delivery. That keeps me interested and learning."

Ling: "What are two things about your current job that you dislike?"

Shannon: "One of the reasons I am looking for a new position is the lack of room for growth. It is both a curse and a blessing having a great, competent boss. However, I don't see the department or the organization expanding any time soon.

"There is also a bit of resistance to new ideas and technology. I have introduced a number of ideas for distance training, upgrading our current computer-based training, and creating web-based online help, but most of these ideas have fallen flat. I feel that I keep growing and learning, but I can't seem to apply many of these skills in my current position."

Valerie: "What has been your biggest accomplishment at your current job?"

Shannon: "My biggest accomplishment was stepping in for my boss, Lisa, during her maternity leave. I kept the projects on track and developed new projects without our department missing a beat. I took a lot of pride in how seamlessly we operated while she was on leave. I attribute a good bit of this to how well she trained me and prepared me to assume a leadership role."

Ling: "What will you miss most about the company you work for?"

Shannon: "I will miss the people I work with. We have a great team and we work really well together. I helped hire a number of the people I work with, so I feel very connected to them."

Ling: "Interesting that you mentioned hiring people. This position requires hiring and developing a team of writers and trainers. How would you go about doing that?"

Shannon: "I think working with Valerie is a very smart move. She will help make this part of the job a lot easier. I would continue to tap the STC and training and development websites, and I would attend the local STC meetings to see if anyone within the organization is actively looking for a new position. This has been a great source of networking for us. I would have to investigate it further, but I imagine that the Raleigh-Durham Research Triangle area has a very strong STC organization, so I would attend one of their meetings, as well.

"When hiring trainers, it is important to do interviews and to have them do some stand-up training. We have avoided some potential mistakes this way. Some of the applicants with great résumés were not so great in front of the classroom.

"Finally, I would work the Internet job boards for both groups. A lot of people are putting out their résumés, and even though the job boards are time-consuming up front, they can save time in the long run."

Ling: "In this position, you'll be required to manage a team. What qualities do you think are important in a team environment?"

Shannon: "I think that even though you are working in a team environment, everyone needs to feel that their contributions matter. You have to maintain a balance between the needs of the team and the needs of the individuals on the team. Team members need to understand the goals and direction of the team and use their individual talents to help the team succeed. It's the team leader's job to give them the resources to ensure that happens."

Ling: "Okay, I'm a stickler for knowing what is going on. I like status reports, but right now I have two team leaders who hate doing them. As a team leader, you will be required to report the progress of your team. How do you feel about providing regular status reports?"

Shannon: "What I do with my current manager is to meet with her on Monday and Thursday. We go over what has been accomplished in the past week and what we will be working on in the next week. We work through any problems, issues, and snags. After the status meeting, I send her an e-mail recapping what we have discussed. How would that work?"

Ling: "That sounds good. I've been trying different things, and this mixes an informal reporting process with something formal I can use for my own status reports."

Valerie: "As the documentation and training team leader, you would be the liaison to other teams. What skills do you have that would facilitate this function?"

Shannon: "As a communication specialist, I understand the need for gathering and disseminating information. I am good at targeting the information people need and what I need to do my job. I have a real belief in sharing information. I think it makes everyone's life and job easier."

Ling: "How would this position further your career goals?"

Shannon: "Well, as I've said, I am looking for a position that will allow me to use the leadership skills I've developed in my current position. I am ready for this type of challenge and feel strongly that it is the next logical step in my career."

Ling: "What do you know about Bilin.com?"

Shannon: "I've done a good bit of research on the company through articles on the Internet, and I have spent time looking at your website. What I don't know is what it's like to work for Bilin.com and what challenges face the company. Can you tell me a bit about that?"

Ling: "I'm glad you asked. Our public image is that of a growing organization rocketing to the top of the Internet dotcoms, and to some extent, that is true. Organizationally, we are a group of mostly nice people who want to see this company succeed at the highest level. Overall we have a lot of fun, work really hard, and have our fingers crossed most of the time. In the next year, we have to grow up. Right now, we are still a small company. We need a formal training program, we need to deliver solid documentation and online help, we need to develop the support area, and we need to deliver what we promise to our customers. If you ask someone else, you will get a different answer, but to me, these are the important things."

Valerie: "How do you feel about working for an Internet startup, coming from such an established company?"

Shannon: "I'm excited about it. In some ways, I feel that I've missed out by staying with a more traditional company. I think it would be interesting and challenging."

Ling: "Bilin is a small, young company and we can't offer the benefits some organizations can. Is that a problem?"

Shannon: "To be honest, I would need to know more about what you do and don't offer. I need to have a medical plan, but dental isn't as important. I would like to participate in some form of retirement through a 401(k) or profit sharing, but being vested in a stock option plan would certainly offset the lack of a 401(k). Can you tell me more about the benefits?"

Ling: "I could, but I'm sure I would leave something out. Keisha has a presentation planned for you later today. Can we table this until then?"

Shannon: "Sure. I may have additional questions by then."

Valerie: "We have just signed three major contracts, which has tripled our deliverables overnight. To meet our schedules, we need to hire someone as quickly as possible. If offered the job, when could you start?"

Shannon: "I could start in a week. I would need at least a week to move and wrap things up in Maryland."

Ling: "Sounds great! Do you have any additional questions?"

Shannon: "Yes. Can you tell me a little about who I will be interviewing with the rest of the day?"

Throughout the day, everyone was impressed with Shannon. By the end of the day, Ling had gotten back in touch with everyone and was drafting an offer letter when Valerie brought Shannon by Ling's office to wrap up.

"Hi! How's it going?" Ling asked.

"Great! Everyone is so nice. Thanks for giving me the opportunity to come down and meet everyone," Shannon said.

"I'm so glad to hear it. I need to meet with Keisha and work out the details, but I would like to have a formal offer for you by tomorrow," Ling said, smiling. "If we can work out the details, could you start the first of next month? That gives you two and a half weeks to wrap things up in Maryland."

"Wow! I knew you were in a hurry, but I didn't expect you to make a decision this quickly. Yes, if everything works out, I'm sure I could start on the first. Thanks!"

Sitting on the plane a few hours later, Shannon couldn't believe how her life had changed in just a weekend. She couldn't wait to get home and see if Ling had e-mailed her the offer letter. She needed to send Ling and Valerie a thank-you note. She also had to plan her conversation with Lisa. She was glad she had spent so much time planning and preparing for her interview. It certainly had paid off.

## Summary

In this chapter, we followed Shannon through the process of conducting a conscious job search. We discussed the elements of a conscious search and applied the CCCD process to seeking a job. We began with choosing job goals. Without setting clear goals, chances are you will end up in a position that isn't right for you. We also emphasized how important research is in the job search process. We walked through the process of conducting research on the Internet, through company employees and tours, through friends and family, and through your campus recruitment office.

We then concentrated on the process of creating a résumé. We reviewed the formats you can use for a résumé and when to use each type. We talked about using the words from the job description when you are creating your résumé and cover letter.

In the section on coordinating, we provided tips for participating in a phone interview. We also talked about how to coordinate the travel arrangements for out-of-town interviews and how to decide what you will wear on your interview.

The delivery section explained the differences between informal and formal interviews. We emphasized how important it is to practice before you go for an interview. We also provided possible answers to standard interviewing questions. Finally, we walked through a typical interview, providing you with a script you can use to prepare for future interviews.

· · · · · · · · · · · · · · · · · · · · · · · · · · · · · · · · · · · · · · ·

## COMMUNICATING IN PROFESSIONAL CONTEXTS ONLINE

All of the following chapter review materials are available in electronic format on either the Communicating in Professional Contexts website or CD-ROM. In addition to the multimedia case studies, activities, and numerous other learning resources you'll find on the CD-ROM, the CD is your gateway to the book's premium web content, which is not accessible via the Internet. The book's basic web content is available both with the premium content and online at http://communication.wadsworth.com/goodall2 and includes the chapter learning objectives and activities, key-term digital glossaries, and quizzes. The CD is also your gateway to InfoTrac College Edition, our extensive online database of full-text articles that is fully keyword searchable and available twenty-four hours a day. Installation instructions for the CD appear on the inside of this book's back cover.

## What You Should Have Learned

The learning objectives below are available on the Communicating in Professional Contexts website, which is best accessed through the book's CD-ROM but is also available at http://communication.wadsworth.com/goodall2. Go to the Chapter 9 Resources and click on Learning Objectives.

Now that you have read Chapter 9, you should be able to do the following:

+ Establish goals for your next job.

+ Conduct research on possible jobs, potential companies, and career information.

+ Use a job description to create a résumé and cover letter.

+ Select the appropriate format for your résumé.

+ Select the appropriate format for submitting your résumé.

+ Participate in a phone interview.

+ Make arrangements for out-of-town interviews.

+ Select the appropriate clothing for an interview.

+ Use the practice interview questions to structure answers for an interview.

+ Do well during an in-person interview.

## Key Terms

The terms below are available in a digital glossary on the Communicating in Professional Contexts website, which is best accessed through this book's CD-ROM but is also available at http://communication.wadsworth.com/goodall2. Go to the Chapter 9 Resources and click on Glossary.

| | | |
|---|---|---|
| **closed questions** *(244)* | **informal interview** *(244)* | **open questions** *(244)* |
| **formal interview** *(244)* | **job goals** *(226)* | **résumé** *(231)* |

## Writing and Critical Thinking

The following activities can be completed online and, if requested, submitted to your instructor. You'll find them on the Communicating in Professional Contexts website, which is best accessed through this book's CD-ROM but is also available at http://communication.wadsworth.com/goodall2. Go to the Chapter 9 Resources and click on Writing and Critical Thinking Activities.

1. Find a job description for a job you might be interested in. Develop a résumé that is geared toward the job description.

2. Review the questions listed in the section "Practicing for the Interview." Prepare answers for five of the questions.

3. Go to the college recruitment office at your school. Ask about the services they offer. Look at the current list of corporate job openings. Select three job announcements that fit your career goals.

4. Below are three sets of interview situations. Working in groups of three, one person is designated the interviewer, the second person the interviewee, and the third the observer (or the class can act as observers). Using suggested questions from the chapter and other questions found in researching on the web, the interviewer develops a set of questions to be asked during the interview. After the interviewer and interviewee have completed the role-play, the observer provides feedback to both to the interviewer and the interviewee. Switch roles until all members of the group have played each role. If possible, videotape the interviews and write a short critique of your interview.

## Situation 1

You have had an public relations internship at XYZ Corporation for the past six months, and you are aware that a full-time entry-level position will be available in the PR department at the time of your graduation. During your internship, you have been responsible for filing and copying press releases. You want the challenge of the new position and feel you are qualified, but you worry that if you are hired, you will be perceived as the intern who does everyone's filing and copying. Based on the questions asked, you will have to convey confidence in your ability to take on a PR position.

## Situation 2

During a job fair at school, you and other classmates have been invited to interview for the same position in XYZ Technology Corporation. Although your technical skills are adequate, they are not as sharp as those of several of your classmates who will also be interviewed. You do, however, have excellent leadership and organizational skills learned from the community service work you have been doing as part of your curriculum. Based on questions asked, you will need to convince the interviewer you are a viable candidate and equally valuable to the company as someone with more technical skills.

## Situation 3

A job has recently become available at XYZ Corporation, and you have been invited to go in for an interview. Your qualifications match perfectly with the job description, and your friend who works for the company has assured you that you would be a perfect fit for the position. However, you are aware that the company has a long history of promoting from within, and at least two internal candidates have also applied for the position.

## Research and Explorations Online

The exercises below can be completed online and, if requested, submitted to your instructor. You'll find them on the Communicating in Professional Contexts website, which is best accessed through this book's CD-ROM but is also available at http://communication.wadsworth.com/goodall2. Go to the Chapter 9 Resources and click on Internet Exercises.

1. Select a company you may want to interview with at some point. Research the company on the Internet. Write about what you found.

2. In an Internet search engine, enter the professional title for a job you might want. Review the information you find. What are the professional requirements, starting salary, and career track for the position you selected?

3. Go to the Quintessential Careers website page http://www.quintcareers .com/dress_for_success.html. Read the article "When Job-Hunting: Dress for Success." Review your wardrobe. Are you ready for an interview? Make a list of the items you need to dress for success.

4. During the last five years, telecommuting has become a growing trend for company employees. To determine if you are well suited for this work style, enter *telecommuting self-assessment* in your search engine or in InfoTrac College Edition. Write a short report on the results of your assessment and the advantages and disadvantages of telecommuting in general.

5. Enter the terms *internet résumé* and *electronic résumé* in your search engine or in InfoTrac College Edition. Prepare for the class a short presentation in which you provide guidelines for preparing an electronic résumé and also compare the advantages and disadvantages of each type of résumé.

## Practicing Communication in Professional Contexts

A smooth interviewing style can come only with practice. This exercise is designed to give you control over the interviewing situation so that you can concentrate on developing a confident interview style.

1. Select a job description for a position you would like to interview for.
2. Using the job description, prepare a résumé and a cover letter.
3. Prepare an interview script (you may use the questions provided in Chapters 8 and 9).
4. Prepare the answers for your questions.
5. Select a group or class member to interview you.
6. Provide the group or class member with the interview script. (Do not include the answers you have prepared.)
7. Schedule the interview.
8. Have the group or class member conduct the interview.
9. Ask the group or class member to critique your performance using the following criteria:

Did I provide adequate answers to the questions?
Did I show knowledge of and enthusiasm for the position I selected?
Was I sincere?
Did my answers reflect the practice I have done?
Was I confident?
Would you hire me?

If possible, you should practice your answers at least three times before the interview, dress as you would for an actual interview, and have the interview videotaped so that you can review your performance.

## Communicating in Professional Contexts in Action!

Communicating in Professional Contexts in Action! is available on your CD-ROM and features model presentations and a dramatization of Shannon's interview, discussed on pages 248–251 of this chapter. Improve your own interview skills by watching, listening to, critiquing, and analyzing the scenario featured on this program. After completing an interview analysis and answering the questions provided, you can compare your work to our suggested responses. What did you think of the interview? Did Shannon's nonverbal communication play an important role in her interview? Watch the CD, and answer the other questions to test your understanding of the interviewing process.

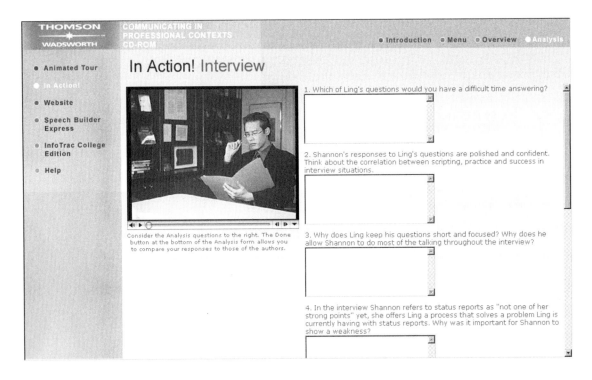

# Communicating in Groups and Teams

T he opportunity to lead a team excited Shannon. However, now that she was finally
a team leader, she was a bit overwhelmed. She knew she needed help getting things
off to a good start, so she called her mentor, Pam, who had been her first supervisor
and had always given her good advice. Pam had more than twenty years of experience in
documentation and training, and she had won numerous leadership awards.

"Shannon, it's about time!" Pam said after Shannon described her new position.

"Thanks, Pam. I'm really pleased, and I know I can do this job. But I have a few questions. What do I do first to make sure this team works together well and we accomplish
our goals?"

"I'll give you the process I use when I work with a new team," said Pam. "First, you
have to choose strategies for leadership, group participation, and selecting group members. Then you create a vision, goals, and objectives and develop a process for problem
solving that will guide your team. Next, you need strategies for coordinating the team's
activities with those of other teams in the organization. Finally, you have to deliver. If
you can do these things, you can create a successful team."

"That's all? Wow, I'll have that done by tomorrow," Shannon said jokingly. "It sounds
like I have a lot of work ahead of me."

"You do," said Pam, "but I know you'll do fine. And you can call me anytime you
need help."

"Thanks," said Shannon. "I'm sure I'll take you up on that!"

## Conscious Communication in Groups and Teams

In the workplace, a **team** is defined as a group of individuals who share a unifying goal. Organizations use teams to overcome communication problems in organizations and bring people together. Many of these teams were put in place
as organizations downsized and hierarchies were flattened. Teams allow organizations to eliminate middle managers who come between the goals and vision
of the organization and the people ultimately responsible for implementing the
goals and carrying out the organization's vision. However, many organizations
simply lumped people together, called those groups teams, and provided them
with little or no team training. The results, in many cases, were dismal. As you
can see from the continuum in Figure 10.1, simply applying the label *team* does
not a team make.

When people form groups and teams, misunderstanding and miscommunication become more likely—and so does conflict. Individuals may clash over
contradictory goals for the group, differ in preferred methods and strategies for
carrying out the group's work, and disagree about perceived individual realities.
The stress, boredom, and frustration that can result seldom provide the necessary environment for creative group communication. Add to these challenges

| Group of individuals | Group in name only | Collaborative group | Team | CONSCIOUS COMMUNICATION CHOICES |
|---|---|---|---|---|
| People who come together occasionally to pass information. Members have a laissez-faire attitude, individual orientation, lack of initiative, and no responsibility for group success. | Members are thrown together with little orientation or clear purpose. Main function of the group is meetings. After group work is done, members return to their individual jobs or departments. | Group members disagree over conflicting goals for the group, cite differences in preferred methods or strategies for carrying out the group's work, but use collaboration and conflict to move the group forward. | Members share a unifying goal. The team succeeds through shared knowledge, diversity of experiences, and collaborative energy. Members realize their individual success depends on the synergy of the team. | Give and take of information by participants who are informed and goal oriented. |

**Mindless Groups/Teams** ⟶ **Mindful Groups/Teams**

**Figure 10.1**
Conscious Communication and Group/Team Communication Continuum

the fact that one team's priorities often are at odds with those of another team within the organization and you have the potential for organizational chaos. Effective, conscious communication can help bring order to the chaotic environment in which many teams function.

Team communication, depicted toward the right of the continuum in Figure 10.1, occurs when a team achieves **synergy,** the stage at which people are truly working together. A synergized team recognizes that shared knowledge, diversity of experiences, and collaborative energy provide the team with powerful resources. When tackling a business or professional problem, what makes the difference between a group and a team are mindful communication processes and practices that improve the likelihood of success for everyone involved.

As you will see, the CCCD process offers an opportunity to develop the components of conscious communication necessary for a successful team experience. In this chapter, we will follow Shannon as she builds the documentation and training team at Bilin.com. After reading and studying the material in these sections, you should have a blueprint for communicating with others in groups and teams. However, for the purposes of this discussion, we will focus on teams as the most conscious form of group communication.

## Choosing: Strategies for Organizing Teams

Shannon needed to establish some strategies for organizing her new D&T team. She knew that many of the frustrations inherent in team participation could be avoided through conscious communication. Specifically, team experiences improve when the members choose productive strategies for organizing team activities. Successful teams do the following:

+ develop effective leadership strategies
+ outline strategies for team participation
+ develop criteria for the selection of team members
+ practice adaptive communication skills such as behavioral flexibility
+ create collaboratively stated goals and objectives for group work

In the remainder of this section, we will discuss the first four strategies listed above. In the next section, we will talk about creating goals and objectives.

## Developing Effective Leadership Strategies

At its most basic level, *leadership* in groups refers to a set of managerial functions (Barnard, 1938; Gouran, 1970; Hirokawa, 1992). For example, in most business and professional group meetings, the most senior member of the group—the person highest up in the organizational hierarchy—usually is thought of as the leader and is responsible for carrying out managerial tasks. Tasks might include scheduling meetings or sending weekly status reports to an executive team. As important as these management functions are to a group's success, leadership does not end with them. In fact, the real power of leadership emerges from the leader's ability to manage the communication of the group. In many ways, it is this attention to the communication among members that allows a group to develop the synergy needed to become a team.

How can a team leader manage the communication of the group? Let's take a look at the basic strategies and how each is used to create synergy within a team.

### Initiating Discussions

A team leader recognizes when the team needs to communicate and initiates the discussions needed to move the team forward. The team leader's role is to help team members make sense out of the organization's vision, objectives, and activities. The team leader knows that by sharing knowledge and information, the team will make decisions based on the experience and collaborative efforts of the team.

### Providing Information

A team leader must be a conduit for information. A team cannot function in isolation from other teams or other units of the organization. To be a conduit, the team leader has to learn to listen to the myriad conversations (verbal and electronic) that flow within an organization and transfer from them the information that the team needs to make good decisions.

## Seeking Information

An effective team leader recognizes when the team needs additional information to make decisions or move a project forward. The first component to seeking information is asking the right questions. A team leader must learn to ask team members what they need to succeed. An effective team leader helps team members identify the sources for additional information and, if necessary, arranges access to those sources.

## Consensus Building

Although a good team leader recognizes that teams are made up of individuals, he or she also knows that to move forward, the team must move forward together. It is the task of the team leader to build understanding among team members. Whether in meetings or through other means of communication, a team leader should ask the team members for points of agreement. The team leader then uses those points of consensus to develop a plan, which helps the team to progress.

## Giving Assignments

An important function of the team leader is to give the team members assignments. Too often, team leaders expect team members to know instinctively what they should do. Without direction, team members may step on one another's toes or go off in directions that may not help the team as a whole. Team leaders can ask for volunteers for assignments that don't require the skills of a specific team member, but ultimately, it is up to the team leader to ensure that the team stays on task and accomplishes its goals.

## Clarifying Goals

A **goal** is a concrete, achievable end. **Objectives** are the tasks required to reach a goal. Effective team leaders understand that often team members are working on a number of projects—and possibly on a number of teams—simultaneously. It is the team leader's responsibility to help team members prioritize their goals and tasks and keep projects on track. Team leaders should seek ways to move the team forward by having regular meetings with each individual team member and asking what that person requires to accomplish her or his goals.

## Summarizing and Evaluating

A team cannot succeed within an organization without someone who will report the progress of the team to outside members. A team leader keeps other teams and the executive team apprised of the team's progress. In their reports, team leaders should provide outside members with an evaluation of the team's

## Phrases Leaders Shouldn't Use

The phrases listed below kill participation and creativity. Team leaders should avoid pat negative phrases and say things that encourage participation and solutions.

1. That's not the way we do things here.
2. We tried that once before.
3. I don't think that will work.
4. We don't have the resources.
5. Don't you think that's more trouble than it's worth?
6. Please just stick to your job; I'll worry about everything else.
7. Let's just keep doing things the way we always have.
8. We've never gotten any cooperation, buy-in, or help from that department, so why try now?
9. Because I said so.
10. That will cause me way too much work, so forget it!

progress. They also should identify any additional resources that might be required and any dates associated with the team's project.

### Celebrating Success

An often overlooked but important function of a team leader is knowing when to celebrate success. Team leaders need to recognize both individual and team success and celebrate it. Celebration may come in the form of a congratulatory e-mail, an announcement at a team or organization meeting, or a party to celebrate completing a project. However the celebrations occur, it is important that they take place and that team members feel appreciated for their work.

## Participation

Choosing strategies for participation is another way to improve mindful team communication practices. *Participation* refers to what you contribute to the team effort and how you conduct yourself as a team member. One way to become a more mindful team participant is to learn from the mistakes your fellow team members make. Another way to improve your participation is by asking yourself the following questions:

+ What does the team expect from me?
+ How can I best serve the team?
+ Do I have any promises or commitments to the team I haven't fulfilled?

+ Is there any reason I cannot succeed?

+ What information do I need?

+ Is there any way that I can help other members of the team?

We want to underscore the importance of effective team participation. Toward that end, we stress a number of behaviors that contribute to effective participation:

+ Be fully committed to the team and its work, and remind yourself of this commitment regularly.

+ Prepare for dialogue on specific topics by thinking about the contributions you can make in meetings, informal team discussions, and e-mail conversations.

+ For any team meeting, prepare a list of personal goals that may serve as your guide to assessing your performance and the team's progress.

+ Listen carefully, and without interruptions, to the contributions of others.

+ Provide verbal and nonverbal feedback to members of the team.

+ Ask relevant questions publicly rather than keeping them to yourself or sharing them only in private with a coworker.

+ Be willing to adapt your behavior to the needs and expectations of *individualized* others; avoid stereotypical evaluations of others.

+ Avoid taking comments personally or engaging in personal attacks on other team members and thereby contributing to negative conflict.

+ In addition to offering sound evidence, be willing to share personal opinions and stories in order to support your arguments.

+ Be willing to participate fully in team traditions, rites, and rituals.

+ Help the team stay on task by avoiding commentary that leads them astray.

+ Trust the team process and the members of the team.

As you can see from the above-listed characteristics of effective leadership and participation, the coordination of personal goals and attitudes with communication strategies and behaviors increases the conscious effort you put into teamwork. Coordinating your communication with the team's vision and goals is essential to group success. Equally important is the selection of team members.

## Selection of Team Members

Choosing the most appropriate individuals for a team is associated with the team's success (Eisenberg, 1990; Bennis, 1999). Unless individuals understand why they were chosen for a team assignment and recognize that they have good reasons to participate in and contribute to a team, chances are they will feel that their time as team members is wasted.

In part, the success of a team is due to what researchers have come to label **jamming** (Eisenberg, 1990), a term borrowed from musicians. *Jamming* means engaging in a spontaneous, energetic group session. It refers to the positive energies (and fun) that emerge from total group coordination when every individual has a role to play in the team as well as a chance to demonstrate individual skills. The result is usually that the performance of the whole group improves, sometimes dramatically. However, as most musicians recognize, jamming requires that the group members have about the same skill levels. "Stars" detract from team play by intimidating those with less skill, and people who have little skill have a difficult time working at the team's level, which everyone notices. The selection of team members should be accomplished with regard to similar skill levels.

However, Warren Bennis (1999) argues that good leaders in organizations view teams as places where talented individuals can develop new understandings and skills. Part of the team process is a learning process. For this reason, you want to select individuals for team membership based not only on what you know they can contribute, but also for the synergistic power of the group to help further their organizational learning abilities and their ability to be flexible. In other words, select team members who will mix well with the other members of the team.

## Adaptive Skills

Team communication differs from group communication because of the level of collaboration and cooperation. This increase in cooperation occurs when team members develop what researchers call "adaptive skills" (Phillips, Pedersen, and Wood, 1990; Goodall, 1990). **Adaptive skill** refers to the ability of team members to adapt their behaviors to the needs and expectations of others. Adaptive communication skills involve behavioral flexibility, which consists of the following mindful processes (Goodall, 1990, pp. 133–34):

- developing a repertoire of self-presentations that can be used to formulate appropriate responses to situations and to others

- serving as an example of effective collaborative communication by actively demonstrating your desire to work well with others, by showing patience with emergent ideas, by actively listening and responding to the ideas and suggestions of others, and by complimenting the work and contributions of group members

- accepting the legitimacy and honesty of others' self-presentations by learning to expect and adapt to displays of diversity in meeting behavior, by not allowing personal conflicts or past performances to interfere with your ability to share information productively, and by staying on task

All of these knowledge and skill areas provide parameters for the sharing of task-oriented talk among team members. They provide a foundation for meeting management, because they demonstrate to team members the need to stay on task and on schedule, working together toward a common goal.

---

### Focus on Ethics

You are a member of Shannon's D&T team, and you've just gotten wind that she's planning a "visioning" meeting. You've been through the visioning thing numerous times and frankly, you think it is a complete waste of time. You can't believe this new manager is going to put you through this yet again. Before the meeting even begins, you've made up your mind not to participate.

What is your obligation as a team member? As an employee? Do you owe Shannon the chance to make her case, or is checking out a legitimate option?

---

## Creating: Defining the Goals and Strategies for a Team

Teams succeed when they have clearly stated goals and commonly perceived objectives. Team members feel more ownership of the team's goals and objectives when they participate in defining them.

> *Shannon had a clear idea of what Ling and the senior management team expected from her team; however, she believed it was important that the team develop a team vision and set of objectives together. She decided to have an off-site kickoff meeting to formally introduce the team members to one another and define the vision and objectives for the team.*

> *Shannon knew that, in organizations, the terms* shared vision *and* kickoff *meetings often elicit groans. She had delivered this response herself many times. In the past, team leaders, HR directors, and company owners, with the best intentions, had forced her to participate in visioning or kickoff meetings that fell short of everyone's expectations. The leader would stand in front of the group and deliver a speech about how this experience was going to be different. Then everyone would be asked to participate in "team-building exercises," many of which Shannon and the other participants had done before. Finally, they all would be served ice cream and sent back to their workstations. A week later, the participants would receive a memo that contained the vision statement. "Rarely," thought Shannon, "does the vision reflect the output from the visioning exercises or the input from the participants."*

> *"This time," she thought, "it is going to be different. I need this team to understand that their participation is key to our success. I need to organize the kickoff meeting to ensure we accomplish our goals. I need an agenda."*

## Agendas

Because so much of the business of a meeting is dedicated to sharing information, creating and managing an **agenda** is central to the success of any meeting. An agenda is a functional document that should include the date, time, and place of the meeting and a speaking assignment or role for any participant who is responsible for a specific area of the agenda. It should be organized chronologically, moving the talk from issues that remain to be resolved from previous meetings, to current topics, to assignments for the next briefing. Figure 10.2 provides an example of the agenda Shannon sent out announcing the kickoff meeting of the documentation and training team.

*The purpose of the kickoff meeting was to introduce the team members to one another and develop a vision and objectives for the D&T team based on the company vision and objectives. Shannon began to think about each of the agenda items and how she would accomplish each item during the meeting. Then she drafted a plan for each item on her agenda:*

*Opening remarks: Short, five-minute welcome and personal introduction. Use CCCD to organize this part.*

*Introduction of team members: Ask each team member to interview one other team member and then introduce the member to the team.*

*Discussion of management team vision and stated objectives: Read the Bilin.com vision and objectives statement. Ask Ling to attend this portion of the meeting so he can address any questions the team might have.*

*The D&T vision within the vision: Use the exercise from Peter Senge's* The Fifth Discipline *for creating a team vision.*

**Figure 10.2**
Sample Agenda

---

**Documentation and Training Team
   Kickoff Meeting**

*Date:*      14 December 2001

*Time:*      9:00 A.M.–1:00 P.M.

*Place:*     Inveress Conference Center—Pine Room

**Agenda**

Opening Remarks

Introduction of Team Members

Discussion of Management Team Vision and Stated Objectives

The D&T Vision within the Vision

Lunch

---

## Creating a Shared Vision

Within the context of an organization, a shared **vision** refers to the overall, far-reaching idea of what a team or organization should accomplish and the values that should inform those accomplishments. To help her team members develop their own vision for the team, Shannon adapted an exercise outlined in Peter Senge's book *The Fifth Discipline* (1994, p. 337). Her version is reproduced here:

## The D&T Vision

### Step 1: The Vision of the Future

It is five years from today's date and you have, marvelously enough, created the organization you most want to create. Now it is your job, as a team, to describe it—as if you were able to see it, realistically, around you. Consider these questions one by one, painting an ever-clearer shared vision of your future organization.

Make sure each member of the team has an opportunity to comment on each of the questions. Note the main points on a whiteboard that everyone in the group can see:

1. Who are the stakeholders associated with our team? (Remember, we are five years in the future.) How do we work with each stakeholder group? How do we produce value for them?

2. What are the most influential trends in our industry?

3. What is our image in the marketplace? How do we compete?

4. What is our unique contribution to the marketplace? What is the impact of our work on other teams, the organization, and our customers?

5. How do we make money?

6. What does our team look like? How does our team interact with other teams in the organization?

7. How do we handle good times? How do we handle hard times?

8. In what ways is our organization a great place to work?

9. What are our values? How do people treat each other? How are people recognized?

10. How do we know that the future of our team is secure? What have we done to ensure its future for ourselves?

11. What is our team's role in the organization?

After you answer each question above, ask the following question:

12. How will we measure our progress?

*(continued)*

## Step 2: Current Reality

Now come back to the current year and look at the organization as it is today.

13. What are the critical forces that allow us to succeed?

14. Who are the current stakeholders today—both inside and outside the organization? What changes do we perceive taking place among our stakeholders?

15. What are the most influential trends in our industry today?

16. What aspects of our team will empower people? What aspects of our team might disempower people?

17. How is the company's vision and objectives statement currently used by other teams?

18. What do we know that we need to know? What don't we know that we need to know?

## Step 3: Creating the Vision

Underline the key words in each answer. Did any words reoccur in the answers? Highlight these words. Make a list of the main themes that emerge from the answers. Draft a vision that incorporates the main themes and keywords that you identified from the answers.

*Shannon was pleased with how well things were going. The introductions went smoothly, and even though the process of introducing each other was a bit cheesy, it had helped break the ice and put everyone at ease. The discussion of the company's vision and objectives statement also went well. Ling did a great job of facilitating the questions without attempting to impose a vision on the group. So far, everyone seemed eager to participate.*

*After a short break, Shannon discussed the visioning exercise she had planned for the team. She provided each team member with a copy of the instructions and questions that would guide the process.*

*After two hours of work, the team agreed on the following vision statement:*

*The Documentation and Training Team will provide our stakeholders with task-oriented documentation and training materials that together solve problems, facilitate learning, and reduce customer uncertainty. Meeting this goal will increase customer confidence, reduce support needs, and add significant pre- and post-sales value to our products.*

*Shannon was thrilled! The clear agenda and organization plan allowed her team to create a shared vision that would unify the team. She praised the group for their hard work. She assigned each team member the task of creating one-year, six-month, and three-month objectives based on the team's vision. She asked that the team members submit their objectives to her by the following Wednesday.*

*"We'll discuss the objectives on Thursday at our status meeting," Shannon said. "We'll use your submissions to draft the objectives that will guide the group in the short and long terms. Thanks for your enthusiasm and creativity. I think we're off to a great start. Let's eat!"*

## Coordinating: Establishing a Creative Environment for Team Problem Solving

*A few weeks after the kickoff meeting, Shannon was faced with a dilemma. Two of the company's sales teams had promised training to two different customers for the same week. Neither sales team wanted to break its commitment. Shannon's team would have to come up with a solution. Frustrated, Shannon called her mentor, Pam.*

*"How are things?" Pam asked.*

*"Really good," said Shannon. "We had a kickoff meeting a few weeks ago that was very successful. We came up with a vision statement and objectives that we are using to frame our projects. But I have another question."*

*"Sure," Pam said. "What's up?"*

*"How do you go about solving problems or planning detailed projects?" Shannon asked.*

*"Good question," Pam said. "I found that in order to keep all of their projects moving forward, my team has to be creative. However, this means I had to create an environment that allows team members to offer creative ideas and solutions in a structured way. I also had to recognize that we were working under certain organizational constraints."*

*"Like what?" asked Shannon.*

*"Well, budgets for one. And time constraints. There never seems to be enough time to finish a project. Another big constraint is priorities, which of course are always changing. Oh, and let's not forget a lack of resources. Should I go on?" Pam laughed.*

*"No," said Shannon, "I get the picture."*

*"You have to balance the creative solutions of the team with the constraints of the organization," Pam said.*

*"How?" Shannon asked.*

*"Well," said Pam, "you have to establish an environment that can unleash the creative energy of your team members. But you have to be creative within the constraints that your company places on you. You also have to coordinate your team's activities with the activities of other teams."*

## Coordinating with Other Teams

In Chapter 7, Exploring Interpersonal Communication, we discussed how individuals within an organization should interact. We added to that foundation, at the beginning of this chapter, by listing the communication skills that

Mark Richards/PhotoEdit

should be developed by team leaders and participants. In this section, we will look at skills that can be used within and across teams to coordinate problem-solving efforts within an organization.

Often in organizations, a major communication breakdown occurs when teams must solve problems that affect more than one team. Team members may do a relatively good job of communicating within their team, but if needs, expectations, resource requirements, information, and deadlines are not being passed from one team to another, one or more teams may be set up for failure.

How do we make cross-team endeavors successful? One way is by encouraging teams to look for creative solutions to problems when they occur. **Creativity** results from giving people the freedom to explore alternatives to the traditional ways of doing things. However, too often, giving a team license for creativity is interpreted as freeing the team from the natural constraints inherent in any organization. **Constraints** are restrictions or limits, which in an organization may result from factors such as limited resources, time, or money. Charged with finding a creative solution to a problem, a team might feel free to suspend the need for a written agenda, abandon order in the discussions, or ignore the vision or objectives of the organization or team. Unfortunately, this type of creativity usually doesn't yield productive results.

Without a framework for sharing talk throughout the organization, creativity is unlikely. Organizational theorists such as David Bohm (1980) point out that creativity actually exists *because of* constraints, and that both forces, creativity and constraints, are necessary to produce innovation and change. Just as an artist works within the constraints of her or his materials, budget, and available time, so do problem-solving or planning teams work within the constraints of their own imaginations, budgets that have been given to them, and a projected deadline. Yet the artist still manages to produce great art, and problem-solving groups come up with interesting, if not unique, solutions. How does this happen?

## Coordinating the Problem-Solving Process

Successful planning and problem-solving begin with a shared understanding among team members about problem-solving processes. One of the oldest and most reliable methods for solving problems of any kind is the scientific method. For this reason, researchers and theorists of small-group and team behavior have long advocated adapting the scientific method to human problem solving (Dewey, 1912; Phillips, Pedersen, and Wood, 1979; Goodall, 1990). When applied in a business or professional setting, the problem-solving process consists of eight steps:

1. Understanding the charge
2. Phrasing the question
3. Fact-finding
4. Establishing criteria for a solution
5. Generating alternative solutions
6. Testing each alternative solution against the criteria
7. Formulating a solution
8. Presenting the solution

Each of these steps is more fully discussed below.

### Step 1: Understanding the Charge

What must the team accomplish? To understand their charge, the team must outline the problem to be solved. The team should answer the following questions:

+ What is the nature of the problem?
+ Who is involved?
+ What is each person's stake in the problem and solution?
+ What resources (financial, material, technological, and human) are currently available?
+ What are the deadlines?

*When Shannon's D&T team assembled in the conference room to discuss their scheduling problem, Shannon asked the team to answer the questions above. Their responses are shown below.*

| What is the nature of the problem? | The sales teams scheduled two clients for training in the same week. |
|---|---|
| Who is involved? | The sales teams, the D&T team, and both clients. |
| What is their stake in the problem and solution? | The sales teams' credibility.<br>Our reputation as being "team players."<br>The clients' trust that we, as an organization, will deliver what we say we will. |
| What resources (financial, material, technological, and human) are currently available? | We currently have the human resources to teach classes for both clients; however, we don't have the classroom facilities. If we have to secure off-site training facilities, we will have to ask for a budget increase to cover the rental costs. |
| What are the deadlines? | We need to have a solution by the end of the week. |

## Step 2: Phrasing the Question

Once the problem has been outlined, the team should determine the issues that will guide the remainder of the team's decision making. To accomplish this goal, the team must phrase the issue as a question, which will be used to guide all future interactions. Keep in mind the following points:

+ The wording should be clear.
+ The wording shapes the outcome and possible solutions.
+ The wording should reflect what is important or relevant for solving the problem.

*The D&T team wrote and rewrote their issue question and finally settled on their wording: "Can we, given our existing resources, provide quality training to both clients in the same week?"*

## Step 3: Fact-finding

To answer the question phrased in the second step of this process, the team must collect and organize as much relevant information about the issue as possible. In order to collect the necessary information, the team must be willing to share information among team members and with other members of the organization. There are three areas of fact and questions associated with each that the team should investigate:

+ *Background.* What decisions were made (and by whom) that led to the current situation? Has this problem arisen in the past? If so, how was it resolved? Was the resolution considered successful?

+ *Current state of the problem.* Who are the people involved who have information about the problem? What possible solutions do they have to offer? Is there anything we don't know that they might be able to tell us?

+ *Possible outcomes.* What are the customers' expectations? What are the organization's expectations? What are the team's expectations?

*The D&T team's responses are provided below.*

| | |
|---|---|
| **Background**<br>+ What decisions were made, and by whom, that led to the current situation?<br><br>+ Has this problem arisen in the past? If so, how was it resolved?<br><br>+ Was the resolution considered successful? | Two separate sales teams promised training to two separate customers for the same week.<br><br>This is the first time we have encountered this problem, so we don't have a historical solution. |
| **Current State of the Problem**<br>+ Who are the people involved who have information about the problem?<br><br>+ What possible solutions do they have to offer?<br><br>+ Is there anything we don't know that they might be able to tell us? | The sales teams, our group, and the clients.<br><br>Each sales team wants the other to renege on their promise.<br><br>We don't know if there are any other dates that might be acceptable for either client. |
| **Possible Outcomes**<br>+ What are the customers' expectations?<br><br>+ What are the organization's expectations?<br><br>+ What are the team's expectations? | The customers' expectations are that we will provide training when we promised.<br><br>The organization's expectations are that we find a solution for delivering training.<br><br>The team's expectations are that the sales teams learn a valuable lesson from this situation and no one promises training for specific dates without first consulting with the D&T team. |

## Step 4: Establishing Criteria for a Solution

Establishing criteria against which to measure possible solutions ensures that the team will settle on the solution that comes closest to meeting the needs of all the stakeholders. After the facts have been determined, and before a solution is articulated, the group needs to establish the standards that will be used to assess, evaluate, and test possible alternative solutions. To do this, the group should articulate an ideal solution that answers the following questions:

+ What would the ideal solution look like?

+ What might it include?

+ How would it impact the stakeholders?

+ What resources are necessary to implement the solution?

*The D&T team developed the following responses:*

| What would the ideal solution look like? | The ideal solution would be one that provides both clients with training without making it seem as if we cannot live up to our promises. |
|---|---|
| What might it include? | It might include incentives for either client to accept a flexible training solution. |
| How would it impact the stakeholders? | It would provide all the stakeholders involved a positive solution. |
| What resources are necessary to implement the solution? | A meeting with the sales teams, phone calls to the clients, and time for the D&T to work through possible solutions. |

### Step 5: Generating Alternative Solutions

The goal of this step is to create as many possible alternative solutions as the team can think of. Generally, the team will use a brainstorming technique to accomplish this purpose, and team members should articulate alternatives without interrupting the flow of talk with comments or criticism. A number of software packages are designed to facilitate the brainstorming process.

*The alternatives generated during the D&T team's brainstorming session are shown in Figure 10.3.*

## BEST PRACTICES

### Brainstorming

+ Write down everything. The beginning of a solution may lie within any thought or idea.

+ Don't criticize anyone's ideas. There are no bad ideas.

+ Keep going until the team is completely out of ideas.

+ Link or stream ideas to encourage creative, unique thinking. For example, one team member may say "classes," which leads to "new scheduling options," and the next may say "staggered classes," to which a third might add "joint membership."

+ After brainstorming, use clustering to group ideas together.

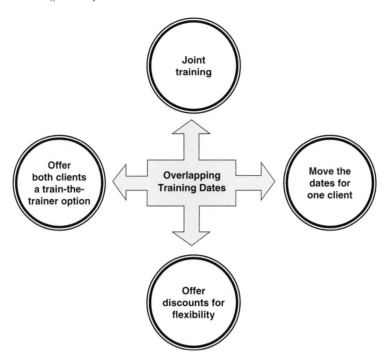

**Figure 10.3**
Brainstorming Results

## Step 6: Testing Each Alternative Solution against the Criteria

The team should expose each alternative to the criteria posed in the fourth step of the problem-solving process. When doing so, the team should fairly and accurately consider the merits and limitations of each proposed solution. Be sure to test all the alternatives, even if the first alternative seems to be a solution. The team may find a better solution in the third or fourth alternative.

If none of the alternative solutions clearly meets the criteria, combine two or more of them until you create a solution that does. Or you may need to go back to Step 5 and generate additional alternatives.

*The D&T team weighed each of the solutions generated in the meeting against the criteria they had established. Then they created the following chart to track each solution:*

| Solution Criteria | Allows us to live up to our agreement? | Allows for incentives if a flexible training solution is accepted? | Provides all the stakeholders a positive solution? | Can be implemented with minimal impact? |
|---|---|---|---|---|
| Move dates | No | Yes | Possibly, need more info. | ? |
| Train the trainer | Yes and No | Yes | Possibly, need more info. | Yes |
| Joint training | Yes | Yes | Yes | Yes |

### Step 7: Formulating a Solution

Once you have found a solution that meets the criteria, clearly state the solution so that all the team members understand the direction the team will take. This statement will be used to create your report or presentation.

*The D&T team developed the following proposal:*

*We propose that the sales team offer an incentive for both clients to participate in joint training at the corporate office and offer both clients a 20 percent discount for anyone attending the training. Alternatively, each client could designate a trainer who could attend the training for free and then train other members of his or her company.*

*If this solution is unacceptable, we suggest that the sales team approach each client to determine if other training dates are a possibility and offer a 20 percent reduction in the cost of training as an incentive for changing the dates.*

*Any reduction in course fees will be shifted back to the D&T budget from the sales budget.*

### Step 8: Presenting the Solution

The goal of the final step in the problem-solving process is to present a convincing argument to the charging authority or stakeholder in the organization. Presentation of the solution will be made in person, by written report, or via e-mail. Rarely does anyone have the time or patience to read a long report in business today. Frequently, solutions to a problem are offered in an e-mail response. To be certain your audience is familiar with all of the components of the problem, you should include the following information:

- a recap of the background
- who is affected by the problem and the solution
- the time frames involved (deadlines, how long the problem has been going on, and so forth)
- the relevant facts gathered during the fact-finding phase
- a brief summary of the alternative solutions and the criteria used to weigh the alternatives
- the recommended solution, including the cost, resources, and time frames required to implement the solution

## Delivering as a Team

*When the D&T team met with the sales team to present their solution, Shannon provided a brief history of the problem, the stakeholders affected, and the information that emerged during fact-finding. She then summarized the alternative solutions, after which she presented the team's recommended solution and the alternate, detailing the costs in-*

*volved and the revenue losses that would result from the discounts on class fees. The head of sales, Kurt, asked for a short break while he phoned each client and presented the team's proposal. In fifteen minutes, Kurt was back—and he was smiling.*

*"Thanks, guys, for a great effort. I spoke with both clients, and both agreed that joint training on-site here is a great solution," Kurt said. "The fact that they are getting a nice discount for cooperating didn't hurt," he added. "We definitely owe you guys!"*

*"Well," said Shannon, "you could start repaying us by putting some procedures in place that ensure this doesn't happen again."*

*"We've already thought about that," said Kurt. "In fact, I have a couple of people working on a program that allows our sales teams to record all the aspects of a sale as they are negotiating. The program will kick out any discrepancies like overlapping delivery dates or training. We really did learn a lesson from this. It won't happen again."*

*"Glad to hear it," Shannon said as they were leaving. "Let us know if there's anything else we can do to help your team."*

Most people think that teamwork is delivered primarily in formal meetings. However, organizations increasingly realize that meetings drain resources and time. Most informal team communication occurs in clusters of team members working around someone's computer or at a whiteboard. Formally, though, teamwork is delivered in five ways:

+ memos and reports
+ staff briefings and weekly sessions
+ planning and problem-solving meetings
+ virtual meetings
+ conferences, workshops, and seminars

Let's examine each of these delivery methods in more detail.

## Memos and Reports

With the rise in popularity of e-mail and its prevalence in organizations, most memos and reports are delivered online. In fact, we cannot remember the last time someone handed us a paper copy of a memo or report. One of the benefits of conveying reports and memos online is that it allows the reader to determine if the information needs to be printed, thus reducing the daily paper load. Another advantage is that information gets to the recipient quickly and responses generally are turned around quickly.

### Memos

**Memos** are quick snippets of information. They should focus on one concept, and the information in them should be direct and easy to follow. The format for memos is fairly standard, but memos should allow for style variations

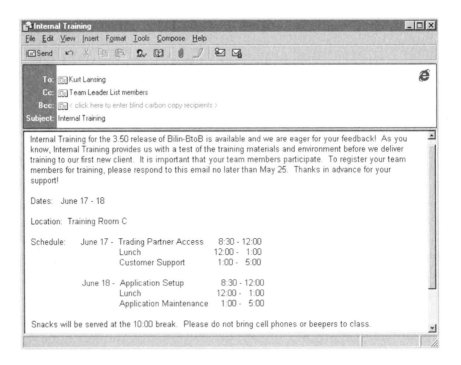

that reflect the information relayed. An example of an e-mail memo is shown above.

## Reports

**Reports** convey detailed information about a topic or a group of related topics. In today's busy organizations, few people have the time or the desire to read a long, detailed report. Before you begin drafting a detailed report, ask yourself the following questions:

+ Who is my audience?

+ What do they need to know?

+ How will they use the information I am providing?

+ When will the action need to occur?

+ Am I including information that is irrelevant to or unnecessary for my audience?

Depending on its length and intended audience, a business report may include the following elements:

+ cover page

+ executive summary

+ table of contents

+ list of illustrations (usually included in technical or scientific reports)

- abstract (usually included in technical or scientific reports)
- text (should be seven to twelve pages long)
- references
- appendixes

## Staff Briefings and Weekly Sessions

The most common type of meeting in a business or professional setting is the weekly staff briefing. Generally, these group meetings are organized for the purposes of sharing information and making plans for organizing work. They are typically held in a conference room, with each group member seated around a large table. Meeting leaders should do the following:

- provide an agenda for the meeting in advance
- call the meeting to order
- follow the agenda and not allow the meeting to get off course
- acknowledge the efforts of team members
- ask questions
- recap the main points
- recap points of consensus
- make assignments

The briefing or staff meeting ends when the leader, manager, or facilitator terminates it. In most cases, these meetings occur on an established schedule (for example, Mondays at 9:00 a.m. or Wednesdays at noon).

## Planning and Problem-Solving Meetings

Most organizations recognize planning and problem-solving meetings as an important part of their everyday operations. Planning sessions are held to create a shared vision and mission, to establish core business values, and to organize the development, manufacturing, marketing, and delivery of new services or products. Problem-solving meetings are used when gaps appear between the organization's vision or core values and the actual daily operation of the business, or when a particular issue arises that may negatively influence the development, marketing, manufacturing, or delivery of the service or product. (The elements of a problem-solving meeting were detailed in the section on Coordinating the Problem-Solving Process, page 271.)

## Virtual Meetings

**Virtual meetings** (for example, videoconferencing, networks, telephone conference calls, online chat) may occur across a wide geographical space. They use technology as the principal delivery system. They may include members of your team, members of cross-functional teams, vendors, suppliers, or customers. As the technology for virtual meetings has improved, the reasons and possibilities for conducting virtual meetings have increased.

Virtual meetings may not be defined by the standards applied to traditional face-to-face meetings. In virtual meetings you may find the following to be true:

- ✦ Members include people from inside and outside the organization.
- ✦ Teams using virtual meetings may form, break up, and reform as a need arises.
- ✦ Participants in virtual meetings have reporting responsibilities to different parts of the organization.
- ✦ Participants in virtual meetings may have goals and objectives that are different from or at odds with the goals and objectives of other participants.

In order to be successful, participants of virtual meetings and teams need to follow these guidelines:

- ✦ It isn't the technology that should influence the team, but rather the way the technology is used and for what purpose.
- ✦ Never substitute a virtual meeting for a face-to-face meeting if the face-to-face meeting is possible.
- ✦ If participants have multiple goals and objectives, the goals of a virtual meeting should be collaboration and communication rather than total agreement consensus.

## Conferences, Workshops, and Seminars

Conferences are large group meetings designed to facilitate talk about a specific topic or area of common interest. Workshops and seminars are smaller group meetings designed to improve knowledge and skills associated with task performance.

Conferences, workshops, and seminars often make use of panel presentations as a preferred format or agenda. Panels of three to six participants or experts are assembled, and each panel member presents a brief individual talk before opening up the session for general questions and remarks from others in attendance. Seminars and workshops also make use of specialized formats, such as problem-solving and brainstorming techniques. Many divide time between brief oral overviews (usually accompanied by computer-assisted slideshows) of a skill or idea delivered by the seminar or workshop leader, followed by actual practice in that skill or application of the idea by the participants.

## Summary

In this chapter, we discussed many of the communication skills needed to be both an effective team member and leader. We placed these skills in the context of CCCD. We examined the need to choose strategies that provide team leaders and members with ways to help the team accomplish its goals. We discussed creating a vision and objectives that allow team members to feel vested in the team and the organization. We looked at coordinating as a means for problem solving in teams and across teams. We talked about the importance of coordinating with all the teams within an organization. Finally, we discussed ways that teams deliver their information both within the team and to outside team members.

• • • • • • • • • • • • • • • • • • • • • • • • • • • • • • • • • • • • • •

## COMMUMICATING IN PROFESSIONAL CONTEXTS ONLINE

All of the following chapter review materials are available in electronic format on either the Communicating in Professional Contexts website or CD-ROM. In addition to the multimedia case studies, activities, and numerous other learning resources you'll find on the CD-ROM, the CD is your gateway to the book's premium web content, which is not accessible via the Internet. The book's basic web content is available both with the premium content and online at http://communication.wadsworth.com/goodall2 and includes the chapter learning objectives and activities, key-term digital glossaries, and quizzes. The CD is also your gateway to InfoTrac College Edition, our extensive online database of full-text articles that is fully keyword searchable and available twenty-four hours a day. Installation instructions for the CD appear on the inside of this book's back cover.

### What You Should Have Learned

The learning objectives below are available on the Communicating in Professional Contexts website, which is best accessed through the book's CD-ROM but is also available at http://communication.wadsworth.com/goodall2. Go to the Chapter 10 Resources and click on Learning Objectives.

Now that you have read Chapter 10, you should be able to do the following:

+ Understand the differences between groups and teams.

+ Apply the eight strategies for effective team leadership.

+ Apply strategies for effective participation in teams.

+ Develop criteria for selecting team members.

+ Discuss adaptive skills and behavioral flexibility as an adaptive communication skill.

+ Develop agendas for team meetings.

+ Discuss the concepts of vision, goals, and objectives and how they affect a team.

+ Discuss the concepts of creativity and constraint in problem solving.

+ Use the scientific method for team problem solving.

+ Use brainstorming as a team skill.

+ Determine the best method for delivering team communication.

## Key Terms

The terms below are available in a digital glossary on the Communicating in Professional Contexts website, which is best accessed through this book's CD-ROM but is also available at http://communication.wadsworth.com/goodall2. Go to the Chapter 10 Resources and click on Glossary.

| | | |
|---|---|---|
| **adaptive skill** *(264)* | **jamming** *(264)* | **team** *(258)* |
| **agenda** *(266)* | **memo** *(277)* | **virtual meeting** *(279)* |
| **constraint** *(270)* | **objective** *(261)* | **vision** *(267)* |
| **creativity** *(270)* | **report** *(278)* | |
| **goal** *(261)* | **synergy** *(259)* | |

## Writing and Critical Thinking

The following activities can be completed online and, if requested, submitted to your instructor. You'll find them on the Communicating in Professional Contexts website, which is best accessed through this book's CD-ROM but is also available at http://communication.wadsworth.com/goodall2. Go to the Chapter 10 Resources and click on Writing and Critical Thinking Activities.

1. Break into teams. Your assignment is to create a criteria list for team participation in a group presentation. Think about your experience in other groups and teams. What are your needs and expectations? How do they mesh with those of other members of your team? Generate criteria for your team that will balance the needs of the individual with the needs of the team.

2. Think about a leadership experience you have had. Write a paper discussing how you did or did not apply the eight strategies for becoming an effective leader. What would you have done differently, now that you have this information?

3. As a team, create a vision for your final presentations. Go through each of the stages of creating a vision. Share your vision with the class. How are your visions similar?

4. As a team, develop a list of communication challenges each of you has experienced in another team and how the team dealt with it. Each team member is then to interview a person who leads a team in a business environment and find out the most challenging communication problems he or she encounters and how he or she deals with them. Compare the two lists for similarities and differences and generate a master list of team challenges and criteria for dealing with problems. Next, your team is to draw up an agreement that specifies the criteria for interacting as team members for the team project.

5. Think of a supervisor you have worked for whom you view as a leader and one you do not view as a leader. Write an essay describing the traits you found in the leader but that the nonleader supervisor lacked. How did the leader approach decision making, delegation of tasks, and team communication? How many of the eight strategies identified in the chapter were evident or missing in each leader's communications? What are the most important lessons you have learned about team leadership as a result of working under the two supervisors?

6. Your team has been invited by the administration department to give a presentation of life on your campus to visiting student candidates. Brainstorm with your team to develop visual aids that would accurately portray academic and social life on your campus.

## Research and Explorations Online

The exercises below can be completed online and, if requested, submitted to your instructor. You'll find them on the Communicating in Professional Contexts website, which is best accessed through this book's CD-ROM but is also available at http://communication.wadsworth.com/goodall2. Go to the Chapter 10 Resources and click on Internet Exercises.

1. Do a keyword search for *brainstorming* on the Internet. Download a demo of a brainstorming application. Think of a problem that would benefit from brainstorming. Use the application you downloaded to conduct a brainstorming session. Write a brief paper or journal entry about your experience. Did the application help the process? Would you use it again?

2. Search the Internet for information on business writing. Develop a list of resources you can use to assist you with writing business reports, proposals, memos, and so forth. Print out your list and any useful samples you find. Share your samples and list with your team members. Develop a file of business writing information for future reference.

3. As a team, conduct one of your team meetings online. Have the team leader send out a question for the group ahead of time and have everyone respond to the question. Write about your experience. What techniques did you use to facilitate the process? How did the process succeed or break down? What could your team have done differently?

## Practicing Communication in Professional Contexts

### Handling Team Interviews

Break into teams and solve the following problem using the scientific method provided in this chapter for problem solving:

Student parking has been slashed 25 percent as a result of new buildings on campus. Although everyone agrees the new buildings are necessary, a solution to the limited student parking must be found.

## Communicating in Professional Contexts in Action!

Communicating in Professional Contexts in Action! is available on your Goodall Connection CD-ROM and features model group presentations that utilize the CCCD approach. Improve your own group presentation skills by watching, listening to, critiquing, and analyzing the group presentation on Billin.com featured on this program. After completing a presentation evaluation and answering the questions provided, you can compare your work to our suggested responses. Do the group members interact well? Do they deliver well as a team? Are they effective in their presentations? View the CD, and answer the questions in it.

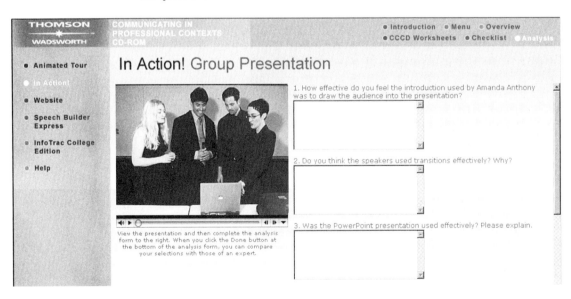

# Informative Presentations in the Workplace

A fter three years as an investment broker, Sam was finally asked to develop a presentation for his group. In the past, he had communicated his company's investment programs using presentations that others had developed. Now he was charged with developing a presentation for his company's newest investment vehicle—a modified 401(k) program. Sam had attended a number of seminars and training classes about the new program and was confident he could put together a good presentation. However, he wanted to go beyond good. This was a chance for him to really stand out.

*That night at dinner, Sam confided his concerns about the presentation to his girlfriend, Beth. She laughed. "Don't you remember a few months ago when I had to do that major presentation on a new advertising campaign for a client? I used a process from a workshop I'd been to, and everything went great! I'll give you all my notes. You'll do fine."*

*"Now that you mention it, I remember how excited you were when the presentation was over. You were gloating about how you had all your bases covered and everything went like clockwork," Sam said. "Your presentation went that well because of a process you learned at a workshop?" he asked.*

*"Yes, and it will work for you. After dinner, I'll show you how it works."*

## Revisiting the CCCD Process for Organizing a Presentation

This chapter focuses on the components of an informative presentation in a business setting. We explain the difference between an informative and a persuasive presentation. In addition, we show you how to design effective presentations using PowerPoint or other software.

As you may recall from Chapter 3, Beth used the CCCD process for organizing her *persuasive* presentation. The CCCD process, along with a series of worksheets, helped to organize her ideas, gather the information she needed, and manage the expectations of the audience. In this section, we will follow Sam as he uses the CCCD process and worksheets to organize an *informative* presentation. If you need additional background on any of the CCCD steps, please refer to Chapter 3.

For a brief review of how to use the CCCD process to organize a presentation, let's look at the outline Sam wrote for himself after going over Beth's notes and getting familiar with the worksheets.

+ *Choose: This is where I choose the goal for the presentation, but first I have to think about the people I will be speaking to, their expectations, and how they might interpret what I say.*

+ *Create: This is where I lay out a strategic and ethical plan for getting my message across. I also have to think about the verbal, nonverbal, and visual appeals I will include in my message.*

+ *Coordinate: This is where I coordinate the presentation with the other members of the company who might have an influence on how successful I am.*

+ *Deliver: This is a biggie. This is where I practice until I know the presentation backward and forward, and then I deliver my presentation.*

## Choosing a Goal for Your Presentation

*Sam realized that the first step in the CCCD process would be to establish a goal for his message. According to Beth's notes, he needed to determine the type of presentation he would give. Basically, there were two ways to go: informative, or persuasive.*

### Informative versus Persuasive Presentations

**Informative presentations** attempt to present facts and information in an objective, nonpersuasive manner. They can be short briefings, long reports, or detailed training presentations. Each type of informative presentation serves a specific purpose.

*Briefings* allow a speaker to disseminate a concise number of facts in a short amount of time. Briefings are best used when it is important to get information out quickly so that it can be acted upon. For example, when a sales manager has received changes to a sales program, she would brief her sales staff on the facts of the changes.

*Reports* allow a speaker to introduce and explain information over an expanded period. Reports are best used when information needs to be presented in greater detail. For example, when a sales manager is presenting a *new* sales program to her sales staff, she would do so using a report-style presentation that could be supplemented with a hard-copy report.

*Training presentations* are most often used when participants require examples, exercises, and practice to grasp the ideas presented. Training often occurs over a period of hours or days and can be accompanied by extensive online and hard-copy materials. For example, if a sales manager wants the sales staff to feel confident with a new process for financing office equipment, she can walk them through the new process in a training class that allows them to practice the process before meeting with clients.

**Persuasive presentations** are designed to bring the audience to a decision or to cause them to take some type of action. (Chapter 12 describes preparing a persuasive presentation.)

*Persuasion didn't seem right for Sam's presentation. Although the ultimate goal might be for clients to invest in the new program, the short-term goal was to educate investors. He knew from experience that knowledge was important to investors, and that when they sensed a sales pitch, most of them quickly lost interest in the conversation. So Sam decided he was going to do an informative presentation. With that decision made, he began thinking about what his audience was like and what their needs and expectations would be.*

## Establishing Credibility

Persuasive presentations require the speaker to identify the reasons the listener might agree or disagree with the speaker. Informative presentations don't require this step. Informative presentations are based on the presentation of **facts**—what is known to exist or has been proven to be true. In an informative presentation, the audience members are free to interpret the facts however they like.

*Because Sam would be doing an informative presentation, it was not his job to gain consensus or persuade. However, it was important for him to think about the types of facts, authorities, examples, and truths he would use to establish* **credibility**—*believability and trustworthiness—with the audience. The audience had to feel that they could believe the information he was presenting to them and that they could trust him to give them the facts.*

*Sam believed he had the credibility to speak about the new investment. He certainly had attended enough workshops and seminars on the topic. He had been with the firm for three years. He had a number of good clients with strong accounts who trusted him more and more with their investments. But was that adequate to establish his credibility with this audience? Beth's notes didn't provide him enough information, so he decided to browse the Internet. Within just a few clicks, he found a number of sites that had information on credibility.*

Sam learned that he could demonstrate credibility in several ways:

+ *Education.* List the workshops, seminars, courses, or training you have attended. List the degrees, honors, and awards you have received for research in a particular area.

+ *Expertise.* Talk about your length of time in a particular field or with a company. List any panels you have participated in, articles or books you have written, and professional associations you belong to that are relevant to the topic.

+ *Empathy.* Demonstrate to the audience that you have their best interests in mind. The information you are presenting is useful and important to them. Talk about the goals you have in common.

+ *Enthusiasm.* Show that you are interested in the topic and in providing your audience with information on it. Your enthusiasm will be contagious and help to engage your audience, which will increase your credibility. If you don't care about your topic, why should they?

✦ *Appearance:* Dress the part. If the majority of your audience consists of successful business leaders who are likely to show up at your talk in business attire, wear a suit. However, if you are hosting a seminar for a group of young, newly minted dotcom entrepreneurs, you might want to lean toward business casual. Wear what your audience wears.

*Sam knew that his opening statement would need to establish his credibility. How well he demonstrated his credibility would have a direct link to the success or failure of his presentation.*

| **Step 1:** CHOOSING A GOAL—Audience Needs and Expectations | |
| --- | --- |
| **Audience** | **Needs and Expectations** |
| Existing clients | ✦ Learn about a potential investment vehicle without a lot of pressure to make a decision right away.<br>✦ Gather as much information as possible, in the shortest amount of time, from an informed source. |
| Brokerage firm | ✦ Introduce a new product and provide the client with information without it sounding like a sales pitch.<br>✦ Convince the audience that providing information is a key component of the relationship between the firm and the client. |
| Sam | ✦ Make a professional-quality presentation that is well received by both the clients and the other brokers.<br>✦ Make a favorable impression on his boss and stand out a bit from the other brokers at his level. |

## Developing an Audience Profile

An early step in organizing a presentation is to determine the audience's characteristics, needs, and expectations. (Chapter 3 discusses how to assess your audience's needs and expectations; Chapter 12 describes how to prepare a needs assessment and explains an audience analysis.)

*As Sam thought about his audience, he made the following notes:*

✦ *savvy, experienced investors*

✦ *very busy people with little spare time for long presentations*

✦ *successful business leaders who would not respond well to being bored or talked down to*

*Given these points, Sam knew that the overall tone of his presentation would be crucial. He would need to emphasize knowledge distribution rather than try to sell his audience on the product or solve a problem.*

*Although Sam's main audience was this savvy group of investors, he knew that his colleagues and boss would also be an audience. After thinking about their needs and expectations, he wrote:*

+ *Brokers need a well-designed presentation they can give to other clients.*

+ *My boss needs to know that I can develop presentations that meet the needs of the firm's clients.*

*With his audience groups in mind, Sam worked through a couple of drafts before choosing the goals on the following page for each audience and himself.*

## Establishing Informative Outcomes

*According to the CCCD process, Sam had to develop a set of outcomes for his presentation. What did he want his listeners to know, believe, or do as a result of his presentation? As Sam knew from perusing Beth's notes, there were four possible communication outcomes: informing, persuading, entertaining, and improving the relationship with the listeners.*

*Sam already knew that the primary purpose of his presentation was to inform, but what about the other three? He immediately shelved persuading as an outcome, because it didn't fit with the goals he had established. He also ruled out entertaining as an outcome. As much as he would like to think he could entertain his audience, he was realistic about how entertaining investments could be. However, improving relationships was definitely a desirable outcome. Investments are all about relationships, and if he could improve his relationships and those of the firm as a result of his presentation, that would be a major benefit. Sam filled in the Personal Outcomes section of the worksheet, as shown on page 291.*

## Developing Criteria to Measure Success

*According to Beth's CCCD notes, the criteria used to measure the success of a persuasive presentation were the audience's adoption of the position, product, or decision put forth in the presentation. But how do you measure success for an informative presentation? What type of feedback would signal that Sam had successfully communicated his message?*

*Sam fell back on what every broker uses as criteria: numbers. If requests for information, phone calls, and movement from current investments to the new investment increased, he would know he had been successful. On the relationship side, if clients who attended his presentation sent more business to the firm or called for additional investment advice of any kind, he would know that the clients felt more vested in their relationship with the firm.*

*Within his firm, if his boss asked him to repeat the presentation or made it available to other brokers, Sam would know he had been successful. If the other brokers asked for his notes and additional information, he would have met their needs. He filled in the Criteria section of the worksheet, as shown on page 292.*

| Step 1: CHOOSING A GOAL—Personal Outcomes | | |
|---|---|---|
| **Audience** | **Needs and Expectations** | **Personal Outcomes** |
| Existing clients | ✦ Learn about a potential investment vehicle without a lot of pressure to make a decision right away.<br>✦ Gather as much information as possible, in the shortest amount of time, from an informed source. | ✦ Confirm that the firm has the investor's best interests in mind.<br>✦ Weigh the information gained to determine if changes need to be made in the investor's portfolio. |
| Brokerage firm | ✦ Introduce a new product and provide the client with information without it sounding like a sales pitch.<br>✦ Convince the audience that providing information is a key component of the relationship between the firm and the client. | ✦ Have a presentation that can be used for qualified clients.<br>✦ Feel they have met all of the clients' informational needs with the presentation. |
| Sam | ✦ Make a professional-quality presentation that is well received by both the clients and the other brokers.<br>✦ Make a favorable impression on his boss and stand out a bit from the other brokers at his level. | ✦ Be told that he has created a presentation that other brokers can and will want to present.<br>✦ Believe that he did the best job possible.<br>✦ Have his boss tell him that he approved of the presentation and the results. |

## Creating an Informative Presentation

*Sam was finished with Step 1 of the CCCD worksheet—Choosing a Goal. As he looked back over the ideas he had put on paper, he could feel his confidence growing. Looking at the CCCD worksheet for Step 2, Creating the Message, Sam saw that he needed to establish the purpose, main points, support, transitions, and introduction and conclusion for his talk. He didn't think he would have much trouble with purpose and main points; both seemed fairly straightforward. He reviewed the types of organizational patterns in Beth's notes and decided to follow a topical pattern, which would allow him to present the key pieces of information an investor would need to understand the new 401(k) product.*

*Sam made notes about the main points he wanted to cover. He wrote a few drafts of his purpose and thesis statement, focusing on the informative intent of his presentation. When he was satisfied, he filled out the first two columns on the Step 2 worksheet (as shown on page 293).*

*Sam reviewed his thesis statement. He felt it did a good job of setting audience expectations while also remaining neutral about the product. In his first draft he had said, "an exciting new investment opportunity," but he decided that "exciting" was a persuasive word he didn't want to use in his talk.*

| **Step 1:** CHOOSING A GOAL—Criteria | | | |
|---|---|---|---|
| **Audience** | **Needs and Expectations** | **Outcomes** | **Criteria** |
| Existing clients | • Learn about a potential investment vehicle without a lot of pressure to make a decision right away.<br>• Gather as much information as possible, in the shortest amount of time, from an informed source. | • Confirm that the firm has the investor's best interests in mind.<br>• Weigh the information gained to determine if changes need to be made in the investor's portfolio. | • Increased requests for information about the new investment vehicle.<br>• Movement from established investments to the new investment.<br>• New business moved to the firm, signaling a stronger relationship. |
| Brokerage firm | • Introduce a new product and provide the client with information without it sounding like a sales pitch.<br>• Convince the audience that providing information is a key component of the relationship between the firm and the client. | • Have a presentation that can be used for qualified clients.<br>• Feel they have met all of the clients' informational needs with the presentation. | • The other brokers nod and smile throughout the presentation.<br>• They ask for additional information and are ready to launch the presentation and product for their clients.<br>• Sam's boss asks that the other brokers begin using the presentation. |
| Sam | • Make a professional-quality presentation that is well received by both the clients and the other brokers.<br>• Make a favorable impression on his boss and stand out a bit from the other brokers at his level. | • Be told that he has created a presentation that other brokers can and will want to present.<br>• Believe that he did the best job possible.<br>• Have his boss tell him that he approved of the presentation and the results. | • Feels good about the presentation and walks away knowing he has passed on useful information.<br>• He doesn't second-guess his information, presentation, or ability.<br>• His boss thanks him for his hard work. |

## Conducting Research

To develop main points and subpoints in a presentation like Sam's, a speaker must do some research. Throughout high school and even into college, most students are taught to do research by finding articles in sources such as *Time*, *Newsweek*, and the *New York Times*. By now, you may have been encouraged by some of your professors to turn to the Internet to conduct research on a particular topic. However, for business presentations, you need to become even more specific. You should begin developing a list of resources for information in your chosen field.

| **Step 2:** CREATING THE MESSAGE—Purpose, Thesis, and Main Points | | | | |
|---|---|---|---|---|
| **Introduction** | | | | |
| **Purpose and Thesis Statement** | **Main Points** | **Support** | | **Transitions** |
| ◆ *To provide accurate and factual information about a new investment product to our existing clients.*<br><br>◆ *Today, I will present information on a new investment opportunity. After my talk, you will be equipped to make an informed decision about whether or not this investment is right for you.* | ◆ First, I will discuss who should consider investing in the product.<br><br>◆ Second, I will go over the investment rules and laws associated with the product.<br><br>◆ Third, I will examine the tax considerations associated with the product.<br><br>◆ Finally, I will cover the performance expectations for the product. | | | |
| **Conclusion** | | | | |

## Hint

When developing informative presentations, do not use words designed to entice your audience or motivate action. Words and phrases like those listed below are not appropriate for an informative talk.

| | |
|---|---|
| Apply now! | free |
| advantages | flexibility |
| easy | fun |
| simple | Available for a short time only! |
| new and improved | limited quantities |
| exciting | |

Using the right resource can be essential for establishing credibility in professional communication. For example, if you are giving a talk about investing to a group of investors, you might cite the *Wall Street Journal, The Economist, Barron's,* or *Forbes.* If you have conducted research online, you could cite

CNET *Investor* or the *Wallstreet Journal Interactive*. If your audience consists of younger, hipper investors, you might even mention *The Motley Fool* website.

One of the best methods for finding good information is to follow the paper trail. The majority of people in most industries consider a handful of top people to be the best sources for information in their field. Print out five to ten articles on your topic and flip to the references. Who has been referenced over and over in most of the articles you printed? Those are your most credible sources for information. Now go back to the Internet or the journal index and find articles by those sources. Use those articles as the main source of information for your presentation.

## BEST PRACTICES

### Conducting Research

+ Determine the most credible sources within your field by following the paper trail. Which experts are cited over and over again in articles published on your topic?

+ Read widely. Read the trade publications (magazines and newspapers), journals, and Internet publications associated with your field. Don't simply read the most popular publication.

+ Ask for help. If you aren't sure where to find the information you need, ask. You can ask a librarian, a coworker, or your boss or mentor.

+ Don't wait until the last minute. If you know your boss expects a presentation on Tuesday at 1:00 p.m., don't wait until Tuesday at 9:00 a.m. to do your research. Good, thorough research takes time. Give yourself plenty of time to gather information and to read and assimilate what you find.

*Sam conducted research on the Internet and reviewed all the research materials he had gathered on the product. As he went through his notes and the other information, he made a list of potential subpoints for each of his main points. After completely reviewing his materials, he added several subpoints to his worksheet (as shown on page 295).*

*Sam was beginning to see what Beth meant by support. After outlining the subpoints, he could clearly see where he needed charts, graphs, and figures to lend credibility to his information. In addition, there were places where showing the SEC rulings and the tax code would help clarify certain points. He also realized that examples would be extremely helpful when he was discussing who should invest. Sam completed the Support section of the worksheet (as shown on page 296).*

*After outlining the types of support he would use, Sam decided to make a slideshow presentation using PowerPoint, a software program he had used before.*

| Step 2: CREATING THE MESSAGE—Subpoints | | | |
|---|---|---|---|
| **Introduction** | | | |
| **Purpose and Thesis Statement** | **Main Points** | **Support** | **Transitions** |
| ✦ *To provide accurate and factual information about a new investment product to our existing clients.*<br><br>✦ *Today, I will present information on a new investment opportunity. After my talk, you will be equipped to make an informed decision about whether or not this investment is right for you.* | ✦ First, I will discuss who should consider investing in the product.<br>  ✧ Type of investor<br>  ✧ Type of portfolio<br>  ✧ Amount of investment<br>✦ Second, I will go over the investment rules and laws associated with the product.<br>  ✧ Percentage of portfolio rule<br>  ✧ Early withdrawals<br>  ✧ Penalties and charges<br>✦ Third, I will examine the tax considerations associated with the product.<br>  ✧ Estate planning<br>  ✧ Early retirement<br>✦ Finally, I will cover the performance expectations for the product.<br>  ✧ Conservative estimates<br>  ✧ Aggressive estimates | | |
| **Conclusion** | | | |

## Effective PowerPoint Presentations

Computer-assisted multimedia presentations have outstripped any other type of visual aid in the business environment. Although whiteboards abound in conference rooms across the country, flip charts and overhead projectors have

## Step 2: CREATING THE MESSAGE—Support

### Introduction

| Purpose and Thesis Statement | Main Points | Support | Transitions |
|---|---|---|---|
| ◆ To provide accurate and factual information about a new investment product to our existing clients.<br><br>◆ Today, I will present information on a new investment opportunity. After my talk, you will be equipped to make an informed decision about whether or not this investment is right for you. | ◆ First, I will discuss who should consider investing in the product.<br>  ◇ Type of investor<br>  ◇ Type of portfolio<br>  ◇ Amount of investment<br><br>◆ Second, I will go over the investment rules and laws associated with the product.<br>  ◇ Percentage of portfolio rule<br>  ◇ Early withdrawals<br>  ◇ Penalties and charges<br><br>◆ Third, I will examine the tax considerations associated with the product.<br>  ◇ Estate planning<br>  ◇ Early retirement<br><br>◆ Finally, I will cover the performance expectations for the product.<br>  ◇ Conservative estimates<br>  ◇ Aggressive estimates | ◆ Examples by investor type<br>◆ Examples by portfolio type<br>◆ Examples by investment amount<br><br>◆ Slide with SEC ruling<br>◆ Graph of percentages<br>◆ Graph showing early-withdrawal penalties<br>◆ Graph showing other penalties and charges<br><br>◆ Cite the tax code and examples<br><br><br><br>◆ Graph showing performance expectations for a conservative and aggressive investment approach. | |
| **Conclusion** | | | |

virtually disappeared. In fact, most companies don't even stock transparencies anymore. Walking into corporate America brandishing hand-lettered poster board sales charts just might get you fired. It is simply not done.

Throughout this section, we will refer to the PowerPoint software program. However, the information presented here can be applied to any of the presentation software on the market, including Autograph, Corel Presentations, Media Pro, and Presentation Pro. The main benefit of presentation software is that it allows a speaker to organize a variety of visual elements into one easy-to-use slideshow. The software lets you incorporate whatever type of information you need, including audio and video.

Using presentation software, you can create slides that show any of the following:

| | | |
|---|---|---|
| bulleted talking points | maps | photographs |
| tables | diagrams | schematics |
| product images | graphs and charts | flowcharts |

Many corporate employees are expected to know how to use presentation software. Knowing how to design and deliver these types of presentations could be critical to your presentation and career success. Just because everyone uses presentation software, however, doesn't mean everyone uses it effectively. But there's no reason you can't.

## BEST PRACTICES

## Using PowerPoint

### Use Slides as Support

The number-one rule when designing any type of visual aid, but especially Power-Point presentations, is to remember that the slides are a *supplement* to the talk, not the entire talk. The biggest mistake you can make is to cram the slides with every word you plan to say and then read from the slides. Not only will you bore your audience, but you will lose all credibility. This type of presentation is offensive to the audience and can cause your listeners to shut down before the presentation has gotten very far.

### Start with a Blank Slate

Many people begin their PowerPoint presentations with a fancy title page that states the title or subject of the talk and the speaker's name. A typical reaction from the audience is a long groan accompanied by, "Not another PowerPoint presentation!" Before you have even begun to talk, your audience is preparing to be bored.

You can change the audience's expectations by using the following strategies:

1. Begin your talk with a blank screen.
2. Introduce yourself and your topic, stating the main points and subpoints you outlined in the CCCD worksheets.
3. When you reach a point in the talk that requires a visual aid, bring up the first slide.

*(continued)*

4. When you have completely explained the slide, bring up another blank screen.

5. Continue to talk, using the slides where necessary to *enhance* your talk, and using blank screens between visuals.

Your audience will sit up and take notice of the screens you use and will marvel at your ability to integrate your talk with your visuals. That's how PowerPoint should be done!

## Limit the Number of Slides

One of the biggest mistakes a speaker can make in a PowerPoint presentation is having too many slides that contain too much information. Follow these basic rules:

+ No more than one slide per subpoint.

+ No more than four to six lines of text, or one sentence and three bullets, or one example or graphic per slide.

+ Remember: slides are used to enhance your talk, not replace it.

## Use Transitions

In PowerPoint, transitions are the methods used to switch to new slides. They range from simply replacing one slide with another, to over-the-top explosions that break one slide into a million pieces that come back together to form the next slide. Here are the basic rules for transitions:

+ Pick one transition technique and stick to it all the way through the slideshow. "Cover left," for example, moves the new slide onto the screen from right to left, covering the previous slide.

+ Keep whiz-bang transitions to a minimum.

+ Use blank slides while you are talking, so that the audience is not distracted by the slide for the previous point.

+ Transitions should not be distracting or interfere with the verbal message and the message on the slide. Most businesspeople have seen so many slideshows that fancy transitions don't stun and amaze us anymore; we simply find them an annoying waste of time.

## Use a Readable Font Size

**Font size** refers to the size of the lettering you are using for the text elements of your presentation. Choosing the right font size can make the difference between an effective presentation and a waste of time. Make the wording readable for the audience. The examples on page 299 show some basic font sizes and the distance from which they can be read.

## Use a Readable Font Type

**Font type** refers to the particular style of the text characters, such as Times Roman or Arial. Simply put, stick to basic sans-serif fonts such as Arial or Helvetica. Sans-serif

*(continued on page 300)*

| | |
|---|---|
| **36 point** | This size font can be read from 5 feet away.<br><br>Unless you are using a LCD panel, which actually magnifies your presentation, this point size is almost useless. |
| **72 point** | This size font can be read from 10 feet away.<br><br>You can get approximately 10 words of text on the slide using this size font. |
| **144 point** | This size font can be read from 20 feet away.<br><br>You can get approximately 3 words of text on the slide using this size font. |

fonts (those without curly ends) are the most readable fonts from a distance. On paper, other fonts might be more attractive, but trying to read these on a screen thirty feet away is very difficult. As you get more proficient, you can try other fonts, but for now, using Arial or Helvetica will ensure a clean, readable presentation.

## Use Colors Wisely

Developing your first presentation is not the time to discover the artist within. It is amazing how often people turn business presentations into truly hideous "works of art" that no one can read or bear to look at. As with many other areas within the world of business communication, apply the acronym "Kiss"—Keep it simple, stupid. Like transitions, color can be used incorrectly. It can be distracting and ruin your credibility. Perhaps the biggest thing to keep in mind when selecting color is that we all have our favorites; what I like best, you might hate. Neutral choices are best.

Color also introduces a readability issue. Although some colors work well together on paper, those relationships may not translate well to a light-based medium such as a computer screen. Listed below are a few basics for using color:

- Never use more than three colors per slide.
- Stick to the same three colors for the entire slideshow.
- White is a color.
- Ten percent of the population has red–green colorblindness, so unless it is Christmas or these are the colors in your company logo, you might want to avoid this combination.
- The greater the contrast between colors, the greater the readability. Using light colors such as white, pale gray, yellow, or cream on a dark background is more readable in a room where the lights will be dimmed.
- Use color to signal a key point or to highlight significant information.
- Use blocks of color to set off important information.

## Use Clip Art Wisely

**Clip art** consists of all the prepackaged, ready-to-use pictures, cartoons, and graphics that people add to their presentations. When it comes to clip art, less is more— or better yet, use none at all. However, if you feel you must use clip art, here are some things to keep in mind:

- Use one style of clip art on all your slides. Don't switch from animation to pictures to graphics.
- Use clip art only if it enhances a given slide.
- Be very selective about the clip art you use. If you can't find exactly the right image, don't use anything.

The bottom line is that PowerPoint is a very visual presentation aid that should be used to add emphasis, support a point, and add interest to your talk. Before using a PowerPoint presentation in front of an audience, practice your talk, using the slides, preferably in front of a colleague or friend.

## Verbal and Visual Support

*Sam expected to have between twenty and twenty-five people attend his presentation. He would be speaking in the firm's large conference room. The last row in the room was about thirty-five feet from the screen, but luckily the conference room was equipped with a "smart screen" projector that would magnify his presentation and allow him to simply touch the screen to move to the next slide. In addition to the technology available, Sam's firm already had in place a corporate standard that defined the graphics, colors, fonts, and other elements he would be required to use.*

*Sam looked back over each type of support he had indicated on the worksheet.*

Let's follow Sam as he decides whether to use verbal or visual support for each of the points he will make in his presentation.

### Examples

There is a difference between verbal and visual examples. *Verbal* examples are comparisons that help to make a point within your talk. Verbally, Sam might refer to other plans that have similar performance expectations or that allow a variety of investment options. *Visual* examples walk an audience through a complex concept.

*Sam decided that he could clarify at least three of his points using visual examples. He created the slide shown in Figure 11.1 for one of these points.*

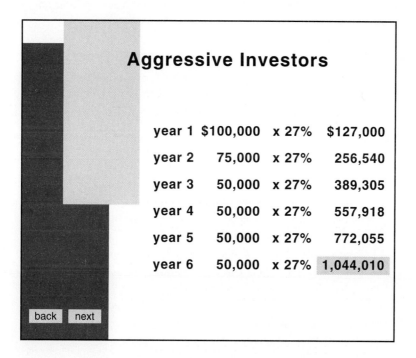

**Figure 11.1**

**Aggressive Investors**

| | | | |
|---|---|---|---|
| year 1 | $100,000 | x 27% | $127,000 |
| year 2 | 75,000 | x 27% | 256,540 |
| year 3 | 50,000 | x 27% | 389,305 |
| year 4 | 50,000 | x 27% | 557,918 |
| year 5 | 50,000 | x 27% | 772,055 |
| year 6 | 50,000 | x 27% | 1,044,010 |

back   next

## References

A **reference** is a citation of a noted authority. Including citations in your presentations lends authority and weight to your talk. They also can be used to clarify a point or to underscore the importance of a concept. However, unless there is a particular word or phrase in the reference that you can highlight using color, boldface type, or underlining, do not put a reference on a slide.

*Sam knew he needed to cite both the SEC and tax code rulings that applied to the new investment. It was important that his audience know about these rulings. He needed to demonstrate that he also was aware of them. Referencing these agencies would lend credibility to his talk.*

Here are some tips for using references effectively:

+ Use only references that are meaningful and appropriate to the audience. For example, a quote from a respected medical professional would be appropriate for an audience of health-care workers. Using a quote from a medical professional to an audience of autoworkers wouldn't work, unless you were discussing health care.

+ Keep references brief. If the passage you are quoting is long, paraphrase it. You might say, "Dr. Carver confirms these findings, adding that the percentages are growing every day."

+ Begin by citing the source of the reference if your audience will easily recognize the source.

+ Make sure your references and quotes accurately reflect the intentions of the original source.

## Statistics

**Statistics** refers to information presented in the form of numbers, such as percentages and averages. Don't use statistics unless they are needed to clarify or strengthen your talk. When you do use them, be sure that they meet the following guidelines:

+ Use statistics that are relevant for your point. For example, when Sam is talking about early-withdrawal penalties, he might say: "Thirty-five percent of investors lose a portion of their initial investment when they withdraw their investment early." However, referring to the percentage of early withdrawals when talking about types of portfolios wouldn't make sense and would confuse the listener.

+ Use statistics that can be easily absorbed. If you are working with large numbers, round off so that your listeners can easily assimilate the information. For example, instead of saying, "More than 78,918 people have invested in this vehicle to date," say, "Almost 80,000 people have invested to date." The second number is much easier to grasp.

**Figure 11.2**

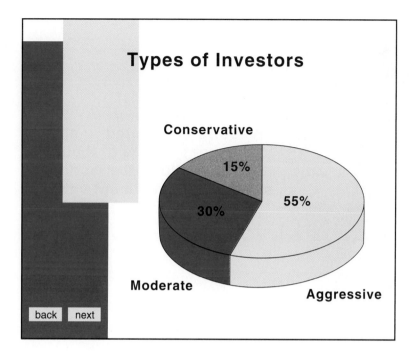

Graphs and charts are visual representations of numbers. To be effective, they must be clear and simple. They must also accurately reflect the type of information you need to present. Choose the right format for your statistics. For example, pie charts work well to present percentages, whereas bar graphs work well to compare data from year to year. Sam prepared the pie chart in Figure 11.2 for his presentation to illustrate different types of investors.

## Visual Cues

Visual cues can be statements, quotes, or other information placed on a slide to emphasize or strengthen a point. Often, seeing the words displayed as well as hearing them will make the point more strongly than just hearing them. Figure 11.3 shows a slide that Sam created to emphasize one of his statements during the presentation.

### Focus on Ethics

You and a coworker are asked to give a joint presentation. Your coworker wants to use inflated statistics. You know the statistics will mislead the audience and provide misinformation. What is your obligation to your audience? To your coworker? If the statistics are only a few points higher than they should be, is it really hurting anyone?

**Figure 11.3**

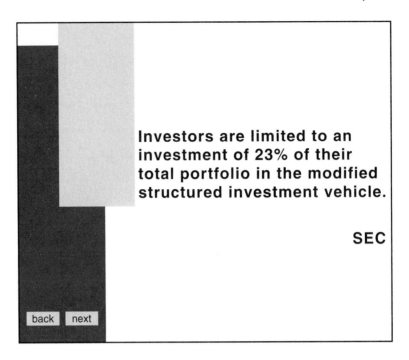

## Effective Transitions

As part of creating his message, Sam had to fill in the Transitions column on the CCCD worksheet (as shown on page 305). **Transitions** connect one topic or point to another. They help the audience listen more effectively. Some transitions signal a change in the point being made. Some transitions summarize what has been said and signal what is to come. (See Chapter 3 for more information on making transitions.)

*Sam thought about the types of transitions he might use. Then he put his ideas in the Transitions column on the CCCD worksheet. He included a transition statement for each of his main points.*

## Developing an Effective Introduction and Conclusion

*In her notes about presentations, Beth had drawn a big circle around the words "Introductions and conclusions are circular. The conclusion should always tie back to the introduction so the audience feels that your presentation has come full circle." Sam thought about the introduction to his presentation. According to Beth's notes, he should begin with an attention-getter. As he read about types of attention-getters, he considered how each would work for an informative presentation. He made notes about each type, as shown in Figure 11.4.*

## Step 2: CREATING THE MESSAGE—Transitions

### Introduction

| Purpose and Thesis Statement | Main Points | Support | Transitions |
|---|---|---|---|
| • *To provide accurate and factual information about a new investment product to our existing clients.*<br><br>• *Today, I will present information on a new investment opportunity. After my talk, you will be equipped to make an informed decision about whether or not this investment is right for you.* | • First, I will discuss who should consider investing in the product.<br>  ◇ Type of investor<br>  ◇ Type of portfolio<br>  ◇ Amount of investment<br><br>• Second, I will go over the investment rules and laws associated with the product.<br>  ◇ Percentage of portfolio rule<br>  ◇ Early withdrawals<br>  ◇ Penalties and charges<br><br>• Third, I will examine the tax considerations associated with the product.<br>  ◇ Estate planning<br>  ◇ Early retirement<br><br>• Finally, I will cover the performance expectations for the product.<br>  ◇ Conservative estimates<br>  ◇ Aggressive estimates | • Examples by investor type<br>• Examples by portfolio type<br>• Examples by investment amount<br><br>• Slide with SEC ruling<br>• Graph of percentages<br>• Graph showing early-withdrawal penalties<br>• Graph showing other penalties and charges<br>• Cite the tax code and examples<br><br>• Graph showing performance expectations for a conservative and aggressive investment approach. | • *Introduction*<br>  ◇ Preview the flow of the talk<br>• *Who should invest*<br>  ◇ Now that we have discussed who should invest and the amount of investment, I would like to review the rules and laws associated with the product.<br>• Tax considerations<br>  ◇ Another important factor you need to consider are the tax implications of investing in the product. Let's spend a few minutes discussing the tax implications.<br>• Performance expectations<br>  ◇ Examining the projected performance expectations of the product will provide you with additional information as you consider the product. Let's take a look at the performance expectations.<br>• Wrap up and call for questions<br>  ◇ Review main points |

| Attention-Getter | Informative Use |
|---|---|
| Interesting question | This might work if I were talking about a subject that is less conservative than investing. |
| Startling statement | I don't think I want to startle my audience. My goal is to educate not scare or sway. |
| Quotation | Too pushy. All the quotes I can think of would sound like a sales pitch. |
| Personal experience | This is a possibility. Maybe I could tie in my learning experience with the product and use this as a way to highlight my credibility. |
| Story | Can't think of one that would work with the subject. |
| Captivating image | Nothing comes to mind for investing. |

**Figure 11.4**

*His best option clearly was his personal experience in learning about the new investment vehicle. After writing a draft of his introduction, Sam made corresponding entries on his worksheet. Because he was giving an informative talk, he wanted to make sure he didn't begin to sell in his conclusion. So he decided a simple review and closing sentence would be the most effective way to conclude.*

| **Step 2:** CREATING THE MESSAGE—Introduction and Conclusion ||
|---|---|
| **Introduction** | ✦ As a broker, one of the most important aspects of my job is to learn as much about the products we offer as I possibly can. This ongoing commitment to learning ensures that I can pass on to our customers the information they need when they request it. Today, I will share the information I have gathered from the modified 401(k) seminars and workshops I have attended over the past six months. Statement of Thesis. |

| **Introduction**<br>(*continued*) | ✦ Preview of main points.<br>✦ After listening to my presentation, you will be able to de-termine if the modified 401(k) program should be incor-porated in your portfolio. |
|---|---|
| **Conclusion** | ✦ Today, we discussed the benefits, penalties, and tax con-siderations of the modified 401(k) investment program. I hope you have found the information valuable and will take from my talk the information you need to make an in-formed decision about our new product. If you have any additional questions, I will be happy to stay and speak to you individually. Thank you for your time. |

*Sam now had his presentation organized. When Beth telephoned to see how he was do-ing, he told her, "All I have to do is write about what I want to say for each main point, then practice, practice, practice."*

## Coordinating an Informative Presentation

*Sam went into the office with a full text of his presentation and his PowerPoint slides prepared. He sent copies of the text and slides to the other brokers in his group and to his boss. He asked that everyone review the presentation and the slides and give him any feedback they might have by Wednesday. He also asked that they provide him with a list of clients who should receive notice of the seminar.*

*By Wednesday afternoon, everyone in his group had responded to his request. Frank, the most senior member of the group, provided a number of good ideas that Sam decided to work into his presentation. Most of the remaining comments were "Good job!" or "You know way more about this than I do. I learned a lot."*

*The next Monday, Sam called the head of the marketing group, Ben, and asked for some of his time.*

*"Sure, Sam, what are you working on?" Ben asked.*

*"I've developed a seminar on the new modified 401(k) program. I need your help devel-oping a brochure that reflects the information we're providing. Do you have the time?"*

*"How about tomorrow at 4:00? In the meantime, if you could send me some informa-tion on the seminar, that would help me to prepare."*

*"I'll go one better," Sam said. "I'll send you a copy of the text and my PowerPoint slides."*

*"Great! If you can do that, I can have some ideas ready and we'll go from there. Any-thing else I should know that isn't in your text or slides?" Ben asked.*

Royalty-Free/Corbis

"Yes," said Sam. "The approach we are taking to the talk is informative. We don't want the brochure to be a sales pitch. I'll send you the client list, too. That should give you a solid idea about the target audience."

"You're making my job so easy," Ben said. "I'll see you tomorrow."

The next day, Sam went to Ben's office. Ben showed him a draft of the brochure he had designed. He had done a great job of presenting the seminar as an information-gathering opportunity. Ben had used one of Sam's PowerPoint slides on the front of the brochure and had inserted two sentences from his text on the inside as quotes.

"Thanks!" Sam said. "I'd like to run this by the rest of the group, but I think everyone will be as excited as I am." He was thrilled by how well Ben had interpreted his message. "How soon do you think we need to send the brochure out to our clients?"

"By the first of next week at the latest," Ben said. "Your audience books up pretty quickly. If you send me your changes by Thursday, I'll have it in Monday's mail."

Sam made copies of the brochure and circulated them to the members of his group, along with a memo requesting that any changes be submitted by the end of the business day on Wednesday. Then he called Sarah, the office supervisor, to ask her to reserve the seminar room for his presentation and order the standard seminar refreshments.

## Delivering an Informative Presentation

Sam was really pleased at how well his presentation had come together. He had followed CCCD, and so far, the feedback he had received from his coworkers and boss went beyond his expectations. Beth's notes emphasized how important practice was, so Sam

## SKILL BUILDER WORKSHOP

### INFORMATIVE PRESENTATION

Select your topic for your informative speech. Ask yourself the following questions:

+ Which format would work best for my topic—briefing, report, or training presentation?

+ Who is the audience for my presentation?

+ Will my topic allow me to demonstrate credibility (do I have experience with the topic), or does my credibility need to be developed from my research and knowledge of the subject?

+ What type of research should to conduct to ensure I have the best information for my presentation?

### SPEECH BUILDER EXPRESS WORKSHOP

Open Speech Builder Express. Select Informative Speech from the menu. Using Sam's example, complete the outline in Speech Builder Express. This process familiarizes you with the elements of a solid presentation and with the process of organizing a talk. In class, discuss the process with your group. How did the Speech Builder tool help you develop your presentation?

took out his planner and scheduled two practices a week for the next three weeks. He called Sarah and booked the seminar room for the afternoon before his presentation. He wanted to have one practice session in the room, using the equipment and his Power-Point slides.

The morning of the presentation, Sam put on one of his most conservative suits. He made sure that his shoes were polished and his tie was straight. He felt confident and ready. That afternoon, he went to the seminar room early to make sure everything was set up correctly. He distributed cards that clients could fill out and return to him if they wanted more information about the new investment. When the audience was in place, Sam delivered his presentation. Afterward, a number of people came up and asked him questions. Before leaving, twenty-seven people filled out cards asking for additional information. When Sam returned to his office, he discovered that his boss had sent him an e-mail telling him how pleased he was with the presentation. Sam called Beth to tell her all about it.

"Things went well?" Beth asked.

*"Unbelievable!" Sam said. "I felt so good about the whole thing. What I said was right on, my materials were really good, and the response was great. Thanks for your help, Beth."*

*"Hey, you did all the work. I just gave you the process to use," Beth told him.*

## Summary

In this chapter we discussed the basics of preparing an informative presentation. We contrasted some of the elements of an informative presentation with those for a persuasive presentation. We also explained how to use presentation software and provided tips for preparing an effective PowerPoint presentation, including choosing the number of slides, transitions, colors, and fonts. We provided examples of PowerPoint slides and discussed when each type of slide would be appropriate. We discussed verbal and visual supports, transitions, and introductions and conclusions for informative presentations. We also highlighted the importance of coordinating your efforts with others in your organization. Finally, we emphasized the importance of practicing for a smooth delivery of your presentation.

## COMMUNICATING IN PROFESSIONAL CONTEXTS ONLINE

All of the following chapter review materials are available in electronic format on either the Communicating in Professional Contexts website or CD-ROM. In addition to the multimedia case studies, activities, and numerous other learning resources you'll find on the CD-ROM, the CD is your gateway to the book's premium web content, which is not accessible via the Internet. The book's basic web content is available both with the premium content and online at http://communication.wadsworth.com/goodall2 and includes the chapter learning objectives and activities, key-term digital glossaries, and quizzes. The CD is also your gateway to InfoTrac College Edition, our extensive online database of full-text articles that is fully keyword searchable and available twenty-four hours a day. Installation instructions for the CD appear on the inside of this book's back cover.

### What You Should Have Learned

The learning objectives below are available on the Communicating in Professional Contexts website, which is best accessed through the book's CD-ROM but is also available at http://communication.wadsworth.com/goodall2. Go to the Chapter 11 Resources and click on Learning Objectives.

Now that you have read Chapter 11, you should be able to do the following:

+ Distinguish between an informative and a persuasive presentation.

+ Discuss the types of informative presentations.

+ Discuss issues of credibility and develop ways to lend credibility to your presentations.

+ Determine the best type of support to use for the points of an informative presentation.

+ Use PowerPoint or other presentation software effectively.

+ Understand the importance of coordinating your efforts with others in the organization to ensure a successful outcome.

+ Recognize the connection between preparation and practice and the success of a presentation.

## Key Terms

The terms below are available in a digital glossary on the Communicating in Professional Contexts website, which is best accessed through this book's CD-ROM but is also available at http://communication.wadsworth.com/goodall2. Go to the Chapter 11 Resources and click on Glossary.

| | | |
|---|---|---|
| **clip art** *(300)* | **font size** *(298)* | **persuasive presentation** *(287)* |
| **credibility** *(288)* | **font type** *(298)* | **reference** *(302)* |
| **fact** *(288)* | **informative presentation** *(287)* | **statistics** *(302)* |

## Writing and Critical Thinking

The following activities can be completed online and, if requested, submitted to your instructor. You'll find them on the Communicating in Professional Contexts website, which is best accessed through this book's CD-ROM but is also available at http://communication.wadsworth.com/goodall2. Go to the Chapter 11 Resources and click on Writing and Critical Thinking Activities.

For each of the activities listed below, you should pick a topic for an informative presentation. Be sure to choose a topic you already know something about and have an interest in developing further.

1. What makes you a credible speaker for this topic? Go through each of the types of credibility discussed in this chapter and describe how you can demonstrate your credibility. Make a list of your sources of credibility.

2. Brainstorm in your group the goals for a presentation on a particular topic. Remember that your job is to inform, not persuade. After twenty minutes, stop and discuss your results. Is your goal an informative one?

3. Pick an informative presentation you have heard recently. You can select a speech, a news story, or a class lecture. Were there elements that were more persuasive than informative? What were they? How did this affect you as a listener? How did these elements affect the speaker's credibility? What could the speaker have done differently?

4. Using the CCCD worksheet, develop a thesis statement and suggest visual aids you would use for the following speech topics:
   the magic of television ads
   how to become a smart consumer
   what is a liberal arts education?
   the difference between formal and informal business communication
   how to eat on a college student's budget

5. Collect and examine informative charts, graphs, and other visuals in a popular national newspaper (such as *USA Today*) or in your local paper and charts from a scientific or professional business journal. Prepare a short class presentation comparing the use of verbal and visual information presented in each publication. Is there a difference in how the publications address their reading audiences? Which rules for developing charts and graphs and statistical information are employed by the publications? If a chart or graph is unclear, what changes would you make to aid comprehension?

## Research and Explorations Online

The exercises below can be completed online and, if requested, submitted to your instructor. You'll find them on the Communicating in Professional Contexts website, which is best accessed through this book's CD-ROM but is also available at http://communication.wadsworth.com/goodall2. Go to the Chapter 11 Resources and click on Internet Exercises.

1. Use the Internet to research the topic for your informative presentation. Make a log of the sites you found and rate their helpfulness. Share your resources with other group members if you are developing a group presentation.

2. Go online and find examples of PowerPoint presentations. You can do this by typing "PowerPoint examples" in the search field on your browser and hitting Enter. Critique the example presentations you found. How effective were they? Did they meet the criteria for a good presentation established in this chapter? Explain why or why not.

3. Enter the term *Maslow's Hierarchy of Needs* in your search engine or Info-Trac College Edition. Write a short essay on how this model can be used in preparing an informative presentation on the traits of a good leader.

## Practicing Communication in Professional Contexts

### Developing an Informative Presentation Using the CCCD Worksheets

This is your opportunity to apply much of what you have learned throughout this course. In addition, you have the opportunity to create a well-planned and practiced presentation in a classroom setting, before your job or career depends on your success. Take full advantage of this opportunity by treating it as if you were speaking to a group of your professional peers. Think of your instructor as your boss. The grade you receive might reflect how well you would do in this type of situation in the workplace.

Select a topic within your chosen major and prepare a ten-minute informative presentation using the CCCD worksheets provided. Keep the topic focused on either a business or professional aspect of the field you are pursuing. For example, if you are a nursing student, you could make a presentation on giving injections or a new drug. If you are an accounting major, you could give a presentation on a new tax law.

Whatever topic you choose, remember that your goal is to inform, not to persuade. You should also use PowerPoint or other presentation software. If this technology is not available in your classroom, mount enlargements of your slides on foam board and provide handouts to your instructor.

Make sure that you think about ways to demonstrate your credibility to your audience. Dress for your presentation exactly as you might in the workplace. And practice, practice, practice.

## Communicating in Professional Contexts in Action!

Communicating in Professional Contexts in Action! is available on your Goodall Connection CD-ROM and features a model presentation that utilizes the CCCD approach. Improve your own presentation skills by watching, listening to, critiquing, and analyzing the individual presentations featured on this program. After completing a presentation evaluation and answering the questions provided, you can compare your work to our suggested responses.

Roger Persson

# Making the Persuasive Case at Work

G eorge sat musing over his cup of coffee as he waited for his best friend, Alex, to meet him for dinner. He had been a vice president for six months and hadn't seen Alex since his promotion. When George had called and invited him to dinner, Alex said, "I want to hear all about your new job and how it feels to be out of sales."

"Out of sales," George thought as he waited. "I spend more time selling as a VP than I ever did when I was in sales."

A few minutes later, Alex sat down. They spent the first hour or so catching up on family and friends. Eventually, the conversation turned to work, and George began to recount his week. "No, really, Alex, all I do is sell," George said. "Every day, I have to convince someone of something. This month alone, I had to persuade an employee to either accept demotion or be let go, convince the executive board to adopt our new marketing strategy, sell our new marketing strategy to our distributors, and close a contract that made the difference for launching the strategy. Instead of selling the product, I'm selling concepts, ideas, policy, and the organization. Almost everything I do requires some form of persuasion."

"Yeah, but you're good at it," Alex said. "I can tell by listening to you, you know exactly how to sell in any situation you encounter. It must be because you come from a sales background."

"My sales background helps, but that isn't why I've been successful," George told him. "I did some research about effective communication, and I learned a process called CCCD that really helps me organize what I need to say and how to say it to a particular audience. I use the CCCD process almost every day. It has really helped me through some tough situations. I also did some research on the Internet and got some books about persuasion."

"Really," said Alex, somewhat surprised. "You've never been a book guy."

"Well," George said, "maybe I'm evolving."

"That'll be the day!" Alex laughed. "Tell me about what you're reading."

"For one thing, there's the idea of concierge persuasion—persuading through personal connection."

## Concierge Persuasion

To succeed in business, we need to adopt an attitude of **concierge persuasion.** Concierge persuasion has been described as a persuasion "of discrete problem-solving and assiduous service" (Bennet, 2000). For example, a concierge in a hotel might provide one hotel guest with theater tickets, another a table in a good restaurant, and another the assurance that his dog will get walked at 2:00 every day. The purpose of having the concierge provide all these services is to convince guests that they have selected the best hotel and that they should stay there again.

| Brutal | Rational | Rational/ Emotional | Mindful | CONSCIOUS COMMUNICATION CHOICES |
|---|---|---|---|---|
| Characterized by one-sided persuasion. Uses the hammer method of persuasion. Provides the listener with no choice. | Characterized by two-sided exchanges. Uses the pro vs. con method of persuasion. Allows listener to test alternatives before coming to a conclusion. | Characterized by mass appeal to a large audience. Uses Monroe's Motivated Sequence to persuade. Presents listener with attention-getter, need, solution, and call to action. | Characterized by the connection between audience and speaker. Uses understanding of a need and a personal commitment to satisfy the need as persuasion. Emphasizes personal choice in decision-making. | A mindful approach to persuasion; appropriate in any context, but it takes more work by all parties. |
| Strong pathos | Logos | Pathos | Ethos | |

**Mindless Persuasion** ➡️ **Mindful Persuasion**

**Figure 12.1**
Persuasion by Personal Connection

This concierge concept applies at work. In each situation that arises, you have to persuade your audience that you have the best approach, contract, or product. You do this to retain existing employees and customers and to convince new ones to come on board.

Just as the hotel concierge adapts to each hotel guest's needs, we must adapt our persuasion strategies to each situation in business. To do so requires a personal connection between the participants and an understanding of the persuasive strategy that works best in each type of situation. Although some situations may require a subtle strategy, others may require a more direct, blunt approach. The persuasion continuum in Figure 12.1 illustrates when a particular persuasive strategy might be used.

As you can see in the continuum, the persuasive strategies range from brutal to mindful. As we move across the continuum, we also increase the range of choices available to the audience. In addition, the speaker becomes more focused on the needs of the audience and less focused on the simple goal of persuasion.

The goal is to be more mindful in most business situations, but sometimes one of the less mindful persuasive strategies is necessary. That is to say, not every business situation is about choice. Although situations offer choices, those choices may not always be good ones for the audience. When faced with a situation that requires you to provide your audience with little or no choice, you may find yourself using a brutal strategy.

In this chapter we will examine how each persuasive strategy in the continuum might be applied in a business context. We will also show how the CCCD process can be applied to each type of persuasive situation. We will use George's experiences to illustrate each step:

- ✦ choosing a persuasive strategy
- ✦ creating a persuasive message
- ✦ coordinating the strategy with the message
- ✦ delivering the message using a persuasive style

## Logos, Pathos, and Ethos

**Logos:** the ability of a speaker to sway an audience by using logic.

**Pathos:** The ability of a speaker to sway an audience by using emotion.

**Ethos:** The perceived credibility or expertise of a speaker.

## Conscious Persuasion in the Workplace

*One of the few things George disliked about being a vice president was dealing directly with other people's conflicts. For the past three months, Ivan, the head of implementation, and Mary, the head of product development, had been fighting like small children. Every meeting was the same. Ivan would accuse Mary of meddling in implementation, and Mary would accuse Ivan of being stubborn. George had repeatedly asked the two of them to work through their problems, but Ivan and Mary couldn't have a meeting without an argument.*

*Over time, George had come to the conclusion that this was not a business process conflict, but a personal conflict, and at the root of it was Ivan's resistance to change. Ivan, a longtime employee of the company, had been head of implementation for seven years and was stuck in a "This is how I have always done things" frame of mind. He resisted Mary's ideas, as well as any efforts to compromise. Ivan was a valuable employee, but his resistance to change was hurting his department, his relationships with other department heads, and the organization.*

*After much thought, George decided to place Ivan in charge of the new custom development area. This department was just getting started and would require a good bit of product and implementation knowledge, something Ivan certainly had. However, it was a much smaller department than implementation, so the move could be viewed as a demotion. How should he tell Ivan about the transfer? George needed to choose a persuasive strategy that was appropriate for the situation and for Ivan.*

## Choosing a Persuasive Strategy

*George decided to use a selection criteria strategy worksheet to help him choose the best strategy. His chart looked like the one shown on page 318.*

*After completing the chart, George realized that a brutal strategy was needed.*

| STRATEGY SELECTION CRITERIA WORKSHEET | | | | |
|---|---|---|---|---|
| **Strategy** | **Brutal** | **Rational** | **Rational/ Emotional** | **Mindful** |
| What type of presentation would work best? | ☑ One-on-one | ☐ Any audience | ☐ Any audience | ☐ Any audience |
| What are the needs of your audience? | ☑ Not considered | ☐ Clearly definable | ☐ Somewhat definable/ somewhat fluid | ☐ Clearly definable |
| What type of choices will your audience be presented with? | ☑ None or either/or | ☐ Multiple with best alternative presented | ☐ Call to action | ☐ Choice that reflects personal responsibility and organizational accountability |
| How open to your position, product, or idea has your audience been in the past? | ☑ Closed or resistant | ☐ Open | ☐ Unaware or open | ☐ Open |
| What method of persuasion would work best? | ☑ Strategic control— the use of authority to warrant compliance | ☐ Logos—an appeal that is based in evidence and logic | ☐ Logos/pathos— a logical appeal that induces the emotions of the audience | ☐ Ethos—an appeal that is based on the credibility of the speaker and his or her ability to follow through on commitments |
| What personal trait does your argument rely on: organizational authority, personal credibility, knowledge or expertise? | ☑ Authority | ☐ Knowledge or expertise | ☐ Credibility | ☐ All |
| What is your goal? | ☑ Compliance | ☐ Consensus | ☐ Action | ☐ Commitment |

A **brutal strategy** (Covino and Jolliffe, 1995; Woods, 1997) is appropriate when the following conditions apply:

+ You are not offering the audience a choice, yet you want to convince your audience that clearly this is the best approach.

+ Your audience has a history of being resistant or closed to your ideas or product.

+ The needs of your audience are less important than the outcome you are presenting.

+ You need to make the presentation in a one-on-one setting to avoid publicly embarrassing or undermining your audience.

+ Your ability to persuade your audience lies more with your position of organizational authority than with your personal credibility.

+ All other forms of negotiation and persuasion have failed.

+ Your main goal is compliance, in the form of agreement with your position or proposal.

*George wasn't offering Ivan a choice. Ivan could either take the new position or resign. In the past, George had considered Ivan's needs when he tried to negotiate with him and when he tried to resolve the conflict between Ivan and Mary, but now George had to think about what was best for the company, not about what was best for Ivan. He definitely wanted to present his proposal to Ivan one-on-one to avoid embarrassing him. George had the authority to move Ivan, and as much as he wished it hadn't come to this, George knew he had to use a brutal strategy.*

## Creating the Message

*George knew it would be difficult to script a conversation for his meeting with Ivan. There were just too many variables. He didn't know what Ivan would say or how emotional he might become. However, George believed he could keep the conversation focused if he clearly stated the problem, the evidence, and his proposal. To clarify these goals, George created a chart that he decided to keep in front of him on his desk during the meeting, to refer to as a visual cue:*

| Step | Your Message |
|---|---|
| + Clearly state the problem. | + Ivan's resistance and inability to change are hurting the company. |
| + Cite any supporting evidence for your case. | + Ivan refused to incorporate Mary's ideas, even when I asked him directly to do so. |
| + Clearly state the proposal. | + Ivan must take the position of department head for custom development or find a new job. |

## Coordinating the Message

*George's next step was to call his boss, Alita, the president of the company. He explained his decision to Alita, as well as his plan of action. She agreed with George that this was the best way to handle the situation and thanked him for keeping her informed.*

As a result, Alita would not be caught off guard if Ivan decided to come to her after his conversation with George. Next, George called Ivan and asked him to meet with him in his office the next day at 4:00.

## Delivering the Message

Before meeting with Ivan, George reviewed his strategy for delivering a brutal message. He had to be clear and straightforward. He also knew he had to remain neutral and nonemotional—he must not allow Ivan to make him angry or defensive. He thought he could do that, given that he knew what he wanted to say. He had mentally rehearsed some of his statements. He felt prepared to present his case to Ivan.

"Thanks for coming, Ivan," George said when they began their meeting. "Have a seat."

Ivan sat down and looked around the room. "Looks totally different from when Bob was in here," he said. "This office hadn't changed in almost nine years before you became VP."

"Really?" George said. "That amazes me. I've made so many changes in the past six months, I'm surprised anything can stay the same for very long in this business."

"Well, change for change's sake isn't always a good thing," Ivan said defensively.

"I agree," George replied. "And although I don't think processes or people should be changed without careful consideration, I don't think resisting change is good for business, either. I've been giving a lot of thought to Mary's ideas and to your resistance of them."

"It's not that I don't think there may be a few good points to what she has to say," Ivan told him. "I just don't think anything is wrong with the way we're doing things. We have been implementing systems successfully for years, and I don't see stirring up a bunch of change if things are working fine the way they are. We've been over this already, George."

"Yes, we have, Ivan, and the last time we spoke I explained to you that I agreed with Mary's ideas and wanted you to come up with a plan to incorporate them into your current processes. Have you done that?" George asked.

"No, I don't see the point. I told you then I didn't, and I still don't."

"Well," said George, "given that you have resisted all efforts to implement the changes that I asked for, I think it is time to take a different approach."

"Like what?" Ivan asked a bit apprehensively.

"As you know, we are putting together a custom development department, and we need someone to be in charge of it. This position requires someone with knowledge of both the product and the implementation process. Initially it will be a small department, but we expect it to grow during the next five years. Ivan, I would like you to become the head of that department."

"You want me to leave a position I've held in this company for seven years and start some lame department that may never come to anything?" Ivan lamented. "This is insulting!"

"The custom development department has a lot of growth potential for the right person," George replied. "And it will provide you and the implementation department with a change that is needed right now."

"What if I refuse?"

"The offer is not negotiable, Ivan," George said. "This company has to be open and willing to change. We change our products to keep them current in the marketplace, we change our clients as new lines of business open up, and we have to change the way we do business as new ideas are presented to us. We're offering you an opportunity to move to a new area and gain a fresh perspective. We value your contribution to the company. You're a valuable asset that we do not want to lose. However, you either accept the new position, or we will begin putting together a severance package for you. I would like you to take some time to think about it and give me a call tomorrow."

The next day, Ivan called and accepted the new position. "You didn't give me much choice," he said.

"No, I didn't," George said. "But I'm glad you've decided to stay. I'll help you any way I can to make your new position a successful move."

---

### Focus on Ethics

If you had been George, what strategy would you have chosen? Would you have tried to work with Ivan, or would you simply have fired him and moved on? What obligation does Ivan have to his coworkers? Is it is job to get along with others and work as part of the team? Is it ethical for Ivan to stay with the company if he doesn't intend to accept the changes graciously?

---

## Persuading through Reason

When George became vice president, one of the tasks assigned to him by the executive board was to come up with a new corporate marketing strategy. George formed a special marketing strategy team composed of stellar employees from a number of departments. For the past few months, he had been meeting with this team, the marketing department, advertising agencies, and the company's public relations firm, all in an effort to develop a new approach to marketing the company and its products. After much work, he and his team had developed a marketing plan around a new approach called "identity immersion." The idea was that they would market the company as something that their clients and vendors could identify with, and the products would then become identified with the company. It was similar to the approach Target, Coke, and Mercedes had been using, but it was a first for George's company.

Now George had to convince the executive board that all the time and money he had spent developing this concept was worth it. He needed their approval to begin work on the marketing campaigns that would take the concept to their customers. Because this

## BEST PRACTICES

### Using a Brutal Strategy

1. Be sure. Be absolutely certain before you walk into the room that a brutal strategy is the only choice you have to effect change or gain acceptance for your position. Use the brutal strategy only when all else fails. This should be the last method of persuasion you try.
2. Be kind. Just because you are using a brutal strategy doesn't mean you have license to embarrass, belittle, or humiliate someone. Use the brutal strategy only in one-on-one settings. If it is necessary to use this strategy with a team or a department, consider presenting your decision to the team leader or department head and allowing that person to present it to the rest of the group. Or present your decision in a closed-door session with only those who are directly affected.
3. Be considerate. Give your audience some time to absorb your idea or proposal. They will need time to think about what you have said. They will also need time to develop a way to agree without losing face or looking bad in the process.
4. Be prepared. Lay out your case before your meeting. Have your reasons firmly in hand and present a clear and reasoned proposal to your audience.
5. Be firm. You will lose all credibility and authority with your audience if you cave in or back-pedal once you have stated your case in a brutal manner.

*was the first big initiative he would bring to the board, he wanted it to go well. If he succeeded, the board would have more confidence in him, which would pave the way for any changes he might present in the future. If he failed, the board would second-guess any future ideas he presented.*

*A lot was riding on this presentation: his credibility with the board, his ability to rally the board for future change efforts, and his ability to move ideas forward from concept to reality. He needed to plan this presentation to the board carefully if he was going to convince them.*

*George knew a brutal strategy was out. "No way would the board put up with me just telling them what we're going to do," he thought. "I need a strategy that helps me to guide them to my point of view."*

## Choosing the Rational Persuasive Strategy

*George decided to use a selection criteria strategy worksheet to determine the best strategy to use with the executive board. When it was finished, his chart looked like the one shown on page 323.*

*After completing the worksheet, George decided that a rational strategy would work well. Although he could see elements of the rational/emotional style in the situation, he didn't think appealing to the board's emotions was appropriate in this case. As for the mindful style, he was all for communicating mindfully, but his goal was really consensus rather than commitment. Also, the board's decision would have to be based on more than his credibility and past performance.*

| STRATEGY SELECTION CRITERIA WORKSHEET | | | | |
|---|---|---|---|---|
| **Strategy** | **Brutal** | **Rational** | **Rational/ Emotional** | **Mindful** |
| What type of presentation would work best? | ☐ One-on-one | ☑ Any audience | ☑ Any audience | ☑ Any audience |
| What are the needs of your audience? | ☐ Not considered | ☑ Clearly definable | ☐ Somewhat definable/ somewhat fluid | ☑ Clearly definable |
| What type of choices will your audience be presented with? | ☐ None or either/or | ☑ Multiple with best alternative presented | ☑ Call to action | ☐ Choice that reflects personal responsibility and organiza- tional account- ability |
| How open to your position, product, or idea has your audience been in the past? | ☐ Closed or resistant | ☑ Open | ☐ Unaware or open | ☑ Open |
| What method of persuasion would work best? | ☐ Strategic control— the use of authority to warrant compliance | ☑ Logos—an appeal that is based in evidence and logic | ☐ Logos/pathos— a logical appeal that induces the emotions of the audience | ☐ Ethos—an appeal that is based on the credibility of the speaker and his or her ability to follow through on commitments |
| What personal trait does your argument rely on: organizational authority, personal credibility, knowledge or expertise? | ☐ Authority | ☑ Knowledge or expertise | ☐ Credibility | ☑ All |
| What is your goal? | ☐ Compliance | ☑ Consensus | ☐ Action | ☐ Commitment |

A **rational strategy** (Covino and Jolliffe, 1995) is appropriate when the following conditions apply:

+ You want to lead your audience to consensus after presenting alternatives and then the best alternative.

+ Your audience is open and receptive to your ideas.

+ The needs of your audience must be met within the presentation.

+ Your ability to persuade your audience lies more with your knowledge of the subject or product than with your position of organizational authority or your personal credibility.

+ Your main goal is consensus for your position or proposal.

*George wanted to build the presentation toward the idea of identity immersion by first presenting the alternatives the team had considered. He knew his audience was open to new ideas, because they had asked him to come up with a new approach. He believed the board would be swayed by his knowledge of the product, the market, and the clients rather than by his authority or his credibility, especially because this was the first time he had presented an initiative to them. But the most important factor was that he wanted to develop a consensus for his new approach. He wanted the board members to be in agreement with the approach and to feel they had a part in developing it. Given all of that, George decided he would use a rational strategy for his presentation to the board.*

## Creating the Rational Persuasive Message

*Now that he had selected his persuasive strategy, George was ready to create his message. He wanted to present the charge from the board, the criteria they developed, the alternatives generated, and finally the best alternative. To help him create his message, George prepared a presentation organization chart. He worked for a couple of hours, carefully thinking about each heading. When he was finished, his chart looked like the example shown on page 325.*

## Coordinating the Rational Persuasive Message

*One of the supports for George's meeting with the board was a digital slideshow presentation. George would have to coordinate this with the marketing department, so he called Cynth. She was the best marketing designer the company had, and she was also a member of his marketing strategy team. He could develop the slideshow presentation himself, but he knew that Cynth would do a much better job.*

*"Sure, I'd be happy to whip up your slides," Cynth told him after George explained the project. "When do you need them?"*

*"I want to do a dry run for the team on Friday. Could you have everything to me by Thursday so I can practice it a couple of times before Friday?"*

*"No problem," Cynth said. "Do you have all the information for each slide?"*

## PRESENTATION ORGANIZATION CHART

| Introduction | ✦ Attention-getter—Tell the story about the man and the elephant. |
|---|---|
| | ✦ Statement of thesis—Today I will show you that our new strategy meets the criteria we developed and gives us an edge over our competition. |
| | ✦ Preview of main points. |
| | ✦ Inducement |

| Purpose and Thesis Statement | Main Points | Support | Transitions |
|---|---|---|---|
| ✦ *To inform the board about the progress George's team has made in developing a new marketing strategy and to convince the board that identity immersion is the best strategy.*<br><br>✦ *I will show you that our new strategy meets the criteria we developed and gives us an edge over our competition.* | ✦ *First, I will introduce the members of the team and others who helped us with the process.*<br>◇ Team<br>◇ Outside consultants<br><br>✦ *Second, I will walk you through the process we followed as we developed our strategy.*<br>◇ Establishing criteria<br>◇ Generating alternatives<br>◇ Selecting the best strategy<br><br>✦ *Third, I present the strategy we selected.*<br>◇ Concept<br>◇ Goals<br>◇ What's next<br><br>✦ *Finally, I ask for your input and answer any questions you may have.*<br>◇ Questions<br>◇ Vote for consensus | ✦ None required<br><br><br><br><br><br>✦ PowerPoint<br>◇ List of the criteria<br>◇ List of alternatives<br><br><br><br><br><br><br><br>◇ Slide showing the statistics of sales increases for organizations using an identity-immersion marketing strategy<br>◇ Slide with goals | ✦ *Introduction*<br>◇ Preview the flow of the talk<br>✦ *Process*<br>◇ With the team in place, we began the process by generating the criteria our final strategy should include.<br>◇ Once we had the criteria in place, it was time to develop possible strategies.<br>◇ After reviewing all the possible strategies generated by the team and comparing each strategy to our criteria, it was clear that identity immersion was the best strategy.<br>✦ *Best Strategy*<br>◇ Now that we have discussed the general concept, I would like to explain the goals we have established for the strategy.<br>◇ The logical next step in the process is to develop a marketing plan and a budget. I would like to spend a few minutes discussing a timeline for that process.<br>◇ Return to introduction<br>◇ Of course, to be effective, a corporate strategy requires corporate buy-in. However, before we take a board vote, I would like to give you all an opportunity to ask any questions you might have. |

| Conclusion | ✦ Review of main points |
|---|---|
| | ✦ We have to approach a new marketing strategy the way a blind man perceives an elephant. Identity immersion allows us the opportunity to be perceived by the market in a new way, which is the goal of a great marketing strategy. |

"Yes," George said. "I'll e-mail it to you when we hang up."

"Good," said Cynth. "That will make things go very quickly."

George's next call was to Martin, another marketing strategy team member. He requested that Martin send out an e-mail asking the team to attend a dry run on Friday, reserve the conference room, and make sure that the equipment needed would be there and working. He also asked Martin to make arrangements for refreshments in the conference room.

After George's dry run on Friday, the team spent several hours fine-tuning the presentation until it was as close to perfect as possible. The team members provided excellent feedback that filled in the gaps in the presentation. George was ready for the board meeting the following week.

## Delivering the Rational Persuasive Message

The morning of the board meeting, George selected a conservative suit and tie. He made certain that his shoes were shined and his hair and nails were groomed. There was no way he was going to allow his personal presentation to take away from his professional presentation. An hour before the meeting, George went to the boardroom and checked the equipment. He made sure the refreshment table was set up. Then he went back to his office.

A few minutes before the meeting, George reviewed his preparations for delivering a rational message. He needed to follow his organizational chart and present his message in a straightforward and nonemotional manner. He also needed to be positive, upbeat, and ready for questions. He felt ready.

After the presentation, George was in his office, thinking about how things had gone with the board, when the phone rang. The call was from Alita, the company president.

"Congratulations, George," Alita said. "That was a great presentation. Very well organized and planned. Everyone was impressed."

"Thanks!" George said. "What was the outcome?"

"You got your consensus. Of course, a couple of people had some reservations, but the decision was made to go with your strategy and move to the planning and budgeting phase," Alita said. "I'm pleased for you, and I'm eager to start moving forward."

"I'm ready," said George. "I'll get the team together on Monday and we'll get started. Thanks for the support, Alita."

## Persuading through Emotion

Three months after George's successful presentation to the board, his team was ready to launch the first promotion based on the identity immersion marketing strategy. They had determined through research that their company had three advantages to promote: the price points of its products, a sound reputation for service, and a reputation for doing

## BEST PRACTICES

### Using a Rational Strategy

1. Select an organizational pattern that allows you to present your case in a logical and organized manner. Many of the patterns discussed in Chapter 3 are effective, including cause/effect, problem/solution, and criteria/alternatives/best solution.
2. Prepare your organizational chart, laying out all the elements required for a complete and planned presentation.
3. Practice your presentation in front of your team or group. Ask for feedback to fill in any gaps you may have left in your preparation or planning.
4. Develop visual support that enhances your presentation. (See Chapter 11 for tips for developing visual support.)
5. Dress in a way that enhances your credibility and doesn't distract from your message.
6. Deliver your presentation with confidence and enthusiasm.

*what they said they would do. The marketing strategy team decided to launch a campaign that promoted value, service, and credibility.*

*They had buy-in from the board, but now they needed to sell the concept to their distributors. The team had determined that for identity immersion to be successful, they needed customers to identify with the company, their products, and their distributors. Their goal was to enter into as many co-advertising agreements as possible with their distributors. Thus far, the company had not been very successful with co-advertising, which split advertising costs between the company and the distributors. In the past, distributors had regarded advertising as the company's responsibility. George had a major sales job ahead of him to change their minds. He wanted to present the identity immersion concept at the next quarterly distributors meeting, and he needed to develop a presentation that would get the distributors excited about the concept. He wanted at least 25 percent of his audience to sign co-advertising agreements by the end of the three-day meeting.*

## Choosing the Rational/Emotional Persuasive Strategy

*George knew from his sales experience that to get the distributors excited, he had to use a strong sales pitch. He prepared a strategy selection criteria worksheet to see if the rational/emotional strategy would work. When it was finished, his chart looked like the one shown on page 328.*

*After completing the chart, George decided that a rational/emotional strategy would work well. Although elements of the other strategies were present in the situation, the rational/emotional strategy seemed the best choice.*

| STRATEGY SELECTION CRITERIA WORKSHEET | | | | |
|---|---|---|---|---|
| **Strategy** | **Brutal** | **Rational** | **Rational/ Emotional** | **Mindful** |
| What type of presentation would work best? | ☐ One-on-one | ☑ Any audience | ☑ Any audience | ☑ Any audience |
| What are the needs of your audience? | ☐ Not considered | ☐ Clearly definable | ☑ Somewhat definable/ somewhat fluid | ☐ Clearly definable |
| What type of choices will your audience be presented with? | ☐ None or either/or | ☐ Multiple with best alternative presented | ☑ Call to action | ☐ Choice that reflects personal responsibility and organizational accountability |
| How open to your position, product, or idea has your audience been in the past? | ☐ Closed or resistant | ☑ Open | ☑ Unaware or open | ☑ Open |
| What method of persuasion would work best? | ☐ Strategic control— the use of authority to warrant compliance | ☐ Logos—an appeal that is based in evidence and logic | ☑ Logos/pathos— a logical appeal that induces the emotions of the audience | ☐ Ethos—an appeal that is based on the credibility of the speaker and his or her ability to follow through on commitments |
| What personal trait does your argument rely on: organizational authority, personal credibility, knowledge or expertise? | ☐ Authority | ☐ Knowledge or expertise | ☑ Credibility | ☐ All |
| What is your goal? | ☐ Compliance | ☐ Consensus | ☑ Action | ☐ Commitment |

A **rational/emotional strategy** is appropriate when the following conditions apply:

+ Your goal is a call to action.
+ Your audience is open and receptive to your ideas.

✦ You need to persuade your audience that you can meet their needs, especially when they might be unaware of what their needs are.

✦ Your ability to persuade your audience lies more with meeting the emotional needs of your audience and personal credibility.

*George's goal was to persuade at least 25 percent of the distributors to sign a co-advertiser agreement by the end of the meeting. He knew that his audience was open and receptive to his products, because they were already distributors. However, he needed to make them aware of the advantages of co-advertising within the identity immersion strategy. Most of all, he wanted to get them excited about the new marketing strategy. He knew if he could get them excited, he could persuade them to sign up.*

## Creating the Rational/Emotional Message

*George realized that a rational/emotional persuader is a facilitator. The rational/emotional speaker brings the audience to a particular action by showing them their needs, explaining how those needs can be satisfied, and helping them visualize how a product or service can meet those needs. In order to accomplish this at the distributors meeting, George had to determine the needs of his audience. He decided to conduct a needs assessment.*

## Needs Assessment versus Audience Analysis

In most cases, when you develop a presentation for a business situation, you know in advance who your audience is. For example, when George spoke to the board, he knew who each of the board members was, how long each had served on the board, what positions they held on other boards or in other organizations, how old each board member was, and each member's race and gender. These are the demographic traits that are commonly referred to as an **audience analysis.**

George's company had an online database that could help him analyze the following information:

✦ the geographic location of each distributor, sorted by the region, state, city, or zip code

✦ the products each distributor had purchased in the last ten years, sorted by product number, name, or price

✦ profiles of each distributor's top management, including name, title, age, birthday, education, length of service, and hobbies

✦ notes that sales personnel had entered after each visit, phone call, or e-mail to anyone at a particular distribution site

*All this information gave George a solid profile of the group of people he would be speaking to. Yet it didn't give him any information on what his audience needed from him and his company. His goal was to use his presentation on identity immersion to tap*

into a need of the distributors. But to do that, he had to determine what their needs were. George decided to conduct a **needs assessment**—a survey to find out what the audience needed or wanted, or what problems they might have. He called a meeting of the marketing strategy team for the next morning.

"To sell the identity immersion concept to the distributors, we have to tap into a need that the distributors have," George explained to the team. "To do that, we have to conduct a needs assessment. We have two weeks to develop the needs assessment and a cover letter, distribute it, and get it back. We have one week to assimilate the information and develop the presentation. Can we do it?" George asked.

"I was going to send out the invitations to the distributors dinner today," Cynth said. "I could hold off for two days and we could send the needs assessment with the invitations. If we make the assessment fit the RSVP envelope, I think we could expect a higher return than if we sent them out separately." Cynth turned to Nate, the director of marketing and sales. "Nate, what's the average RSVP rate for the dinner?" she asked.

"Normally, it's 75 to 78 percent," Nate said. "That sounds like a good plan to me, George. I don't mind holding the mailing two days if you think you can get the needs assessment to us by then. A needs assessment of the distributors is long overdue. The information you get back will be helpful to us, as well. What else do you need from us?"

"How about some examples of the assessments you've conducted in the past and some of Cynth's time to pull everything together?"

"Sure," Nate said. "Most of Cynth's time right now is dedicated to the distributors meeting anyway. And she helped develop the assessment we used for the sales force, so she's familiar with the process."

An hour later, Cynth and George sat at his conference table with her laptop and the printouts of the distributors database. "Let's start with the sales notes," Cynth suggested. "They usually have suggestions or complaints. Then we can create a list of what we find and develop the assessment from that."

"Good idea," George said. "Let's see what we have."

For two hours, they pored over the sales notes. When they were done, they had created the following list:

+ more equity in pricing from distributor to distributor

+ better communication about special discounts and sales

+ higher-profile product advertising

+ education for the customer on the service process

+ advertising that is connected, rather than spread out across too many sources

+ lower-end products that could induce customer to buy up

"I see two areas here that fit right into the direction we want to take," George said. "Let's design some questions around these topics and see what kind of response we get."

*Later that night, when they finished their draft of the needs assessment, George e-mailed copies to the marketing strategy team. He asked them to review the assessment and return it to him no later than 11:00 the next morning with any changes or concerns.*

The needs assessment that was sent to the distributors is shown below.

---

**Assessment review**     _ □ ✕

File   Edit   View   Insert   Format   Tools   Compose   Help

Send   ↶   ✂   ▣   ▤   Ω✓   ▦   🖉   ▨   ▩

**From:** George

**To:** Nate

**Cc:**

**Subject:** Review, urgent

---

As many of you know, we have been working to improve the services we offer you, the distributor.

You are a valued and indispensable member of our team.  As such, we believe it is important for us to stay on top of your needs and to develop ways we can help make you more successful. To help us in the endeavor, please take a few minutes to answer the following questions.  The completed assessment can be placed in your RSVP envelope.  Thank you!

1.  How important to you is pricing equity from distributor to distributor?
☐ Very important — we have to match other distributors' prices.
☐ Important — we try to match prices, but we don't have a policy that we will.
☐ Somewhat important — we'd like to keep prices low, but we don't have any competition.
☐ Not at all important

2.  Should there be a price break based on distributor size or number of locations?
☐ Yes — if we sell more product, we should have a lower price point.
☐ No — all the smaller distributors combined sell as much or more than a few large distributors and that should be taken into consideration.

3.  What would you like us to do to improve communication about special discounts and sales? Check all that apply.
☐ Use email bulletins for any sales notices.
☐ Send out notices by mail.
☐ Have my salesperson call me personally and let me know of upcoming sales.
☐ Announce sales or special discounts during the quarterly distributors meeting.
☐ Other _____

4.  What advertising venues would you like to see us use to advertise the product?
☐ Television commercials
☐ Monthly magazines aimed at a targeted audience
☐ Trade publications
☐ Local newspaper
☐ Internet
☐ Radio

---

*(continued)*

5. How important do you think it is to participate in an advertising campaign?

☐ Very important. Our customers can know all about a product, but if they don't know we have it, it doesn't do us any good.

☐ Important. However, we are a national chain and when our customers think about the product, they know we have it.

☐ Somewhat important. We are pretty much the only game in town, so customers come to us first anyway.

☐ Not important. We only have a budget for local advertising.

6. How open would you be to co-advertising if the pricing structure was equitably defined and the benefits were obvious?

☐ Very. We do already participate in co-advertising with other companies.

☐ Open. We don't do much co-advertising now, but if we could see a benefit, we would consider it.

☐ Not open. We've tried co-advertising in the past, but it wasn't worth the costs.

☐ Not sure. We've never used co-advertising so we aren't sure why we would want to.

7. One recommendation we have received is to develop a more cohesive approach to marketing. Which of the following do you think would be the most effective approach?

☐ A national campaign that includes the product, the company, and the distributor.

☐ A single message about either the product, the services, or the value that is used across advertising venues.

☐ A strategy that allows the customer to identify the product with the company, service process, and the distributor.

☐ I like the approach you are currently using.

☐ Other _____

8. Many of you would like to provide your customers with more information about our service process. What method of customer education do you believe would be most effective?

☐ Make it part of an advertising campaign.

☐ Provide more information along with the product.

☐ Develop a training video that can be shown to your sales team.

☐ Develop a brochure that can be sent to customers after they make a purchase or given to a customer considering a purchase.

☐ Other _____

*When the needs assessments were back, George and Cynth compiled the results. They developed the table shown on page 333 to organize the statistics drawn from the distributors' responses.*

*They zeroed in on the marketing questions and identified the following needs:*

1. *To develop an approach to advertising that would allow the distributor to participate. Seventy percent of the distributors who had returned the assessment considered this need very important or important.*

2. *To develop a new campaign strategy that was either national in scope or centered around identity immersion. This need was supported by more than 60 percent of the respondents.*

| Pricing equity | Very Important | Important | Somewhat Important | Not Important |
|---|---|---|---|---|
| | 38% | 42% | 18% | 2% |

| Price break by size or location | Yes | No | | |
|---|---|---|---|---|
| | 24% | 76% | | |

| Communication about special discounts | E-mail | Mail | Phone calls | Quarterly announcements |
|---|---|---|---|---|
| | 63% | 12% | 10% | 15% |

| Advertising venues | Television | Magazines | Trade publications | Local newspaper |
|---|---|---|---|---|
| | 21% | 14% | 12% | 12% |
| | Internet | Radio | | |
| | 27% | 14% | | |

| Participation in advertising | Very Important | Important | Somewhat Important | Not Important |
|---|---|---|---|---|
| | 57% | 23% | 22% | 8% |

| Co-advertising | Very Open | Open | Not Open | Not Sure |
|---|---|---|---|---|
| | 27% | 33% | 31% | 9% |

| Cohesive approach | National campaign | Single message | Identity immersion | Current approach |
|---|---|---|---|---|
| | 32% | 13% | 37% | 8% |
| | Other | | | |
| | 10% | | | |

| Customer education about the service process | Advertising | Information provided with the product | Training video for sales | Brochure |
|---|---|---|---|---|
| | 12% | 35% | 23% | 20% |
| | Other | | | |
| | 2% | | | |

*In addition to these findings, George concluded that only 8 percent of the respondents believed the current campaign was working. More importantly, he discovered that 60 percent of his audience would be very open or open to co-advertising. He began to think his goal of signing 25 percent of the distributors by the end of the meeting was achievable. George sent copies of the assessments, his table, and his findings to Nate for further analysis by the marketing department.*

## Monroe's Motivated Sequence

*George concentrated on developing the message he would deliver at the distributors meeting. He would use a process called Monroe's Motivated Sequence: get the audience's attention, present the need, show how he could satisfy it, help the audience visualize it, and then call the audience to action (McKerrow, Grombeck, Ehninger, and Monroe, 2000). George worked for a couple of hours on a chart to organize his ideas. When he was finished, his chart looked like the example shown on page 335.*

### Steps in Monroe's Motivated Sequence

**Attention-getter:** The story, joke, or first line of a message, designed to pull the audience into your message.

**Need:** The part of a message that details the audience's need or problem.

**Satisfaction:** The part of a message that conveys the solution to the audience's need or problem.

**Visualization:** The part of a message that helps the audience imagine the satisfaction of their need.

**Call to action:** The direct or indirect statement of action you want the audience to take after listening to your message.

## Coordinating the Rational/Emotional Message

*George, Cynth, Nate, and the rest of the team worked for two days to flesh out the presentation and develop the visual support it required. George practiced in front of the team a number of times to ensure that he was hitting each point of the presentation with just enough emotion. By the end of the week, he was satisfied. However, before he presented his message to the distributors, he wanted to share the presentation with the sales representatives and Alita, the CEO.*

*George sent out an e-mail asking that all the sales reps in town for the distributors meeting attend a preview of his talk before the first session. He wanted to be sure that they were on the same page with the marketing and sales teams. Even though he and Alita had had numerous discussions about the new marketing strategy, he wanted to be sure that she knew exactly what was in the presentation. The last thing he needed was for*

## MOTIVATED SEQUENCE ORGANIZATION CHART

| Introduction | ◆ Attention-getter—Most of us have heard the story of the blind men and the elephant. According to the story, each man describes the elephant differently. One describes the elephant as a strong tree, one as a mighty sword, and one as a strong rope. However, the real beauty of this story is that to learn about the elephant, the blind men must first learn that they need to learn. Second, the blind men need to listen to each other and set aside their previous notions of what an elephant is. Third, they need to understand that only together will they develop a true understanding of the whole elephant. |
| --- | --- |
| | In the past, our advertising efforts have been similar to the efforts of the blind men identifying the elephant. Our new approach identifies the bits and pieces that we have often overlooked. What we need is a new approach to marketing that gives our customers the whole picture. |

| Purpose and Thesis Statement | Main Points | Support |
| --- | --- | --- |
| ◆ *To convince the distributors that we need a new approach to marketing and that they are critical to the success of the new approach.* | ◆ *Need*—new approach is needed<br>  ◇ Past efforts<br>  ◇ Sales figures<br>  ◇ Customer survey conducted on the current approach to advertising | ◆ Slides showing examples of past advertising from a variety of media and different campaigns<br>◆ Slide showing sales figures before and after each campaign<br>◆ Slide showing results of customer survey |
| | ◆ *Satisfaction*—identity immersion<br>  ◇ Create identity with customer for the product, company, and the distributor<br>  ◇ Provides a cohesive advertising strategy<br>  ◇ Discuss the impact of co-advertising | ◆ Slide showing a diagram that links all the elements of the campaign together |
| | ◆ *Visualization*<br>  ◇ Show an example of a successful identity-immersion campaign<br>  ◇ Discuss the sales figures from before identity immersion campaign and after<br>  ◇ Show the distributor's logo on sample ads | ◆ Slides and video that show an example of the TV, magazine, and newspaper ads from an identity immersion campaign<br>◆ Slide showing before and after sales figures<br>◆ Slide showing a sample ad with a distributor's logo |
| | ◆ *Action*<br>  ◇ For this new approach to be successful, we need you the distributor to join us.<br>  ◇ Outline the points of the co-advertising agreement. | ◆ Slide that outlines the points of the agreement. |

| Conclusion | ◆ *Call to action*—When our customers see our products, we don't want them to see just a product. We want them to see our product, our excellent service policy, exceptional value, an established and innovative company, and a local distributor who is knowledgeable and dependable. We want them to see the whole elephant! Join us in this exciting new approach, sign up today as a co-advertiser, and together we will create a marketing strategy the customer can identify with in a new way, which is the goal of a great marketing strategy. |
| --- | --- |

*Alita to be caught off guard after his session. If she previewed the presentation, she would be able to address any questions the distributors might have.*

## Delivering the Rational/Emotional Message

*George knew there would be a fine line in his presentation between too much emotion and not quite enough. He wanted his audience to be excited about co-advertising and the new marketing strategy. However, he also wanted to maintain his credibility. He had to convince the distributors that they needed a new marketing strategy, and that the strategy he proposed would strengthen the customers' identification with the product, the company, and the distributor, which would result in increased sales. He needed to hit a note of excitement mixed with credibility. That was the balance he was looking for. After all of his practice sessions and the preview for Alita and the sales reps, he was confident he had it.*

*As he spoke, George kept an eye on his audience. He was looking for feedback: a nod, a smile, a bored look. As the speech progressed, the nods increased and the smiles widened. The distributors liked what they were hearing. George gauged their reaction and put a bit more excitement into his voice. He increased the strength of his voice and the audience went along, nodding and smiling more. A few times, George saw one distributor nudge another and nod as if to say, "See, I told you that's what we needed." By the end of his presentation, George was sure he had the 25 percent sign-up he had hoped for.*

---

## BEST PRACTICES

### Using a Rational/Emotional Strategy

1. Determine your purpose and your audience.
2. Identify the needs of your audience and ways that their needs can be served by your purpose.
3. Use Monroe's Motivated Sequence to organize your ideas. Clearly lay out the need, satisfaction, visualization, and call to action for the audience.
4. Practice your presentation, modulating the emotion of your appeal to ensure you have the right balance for your audience.
5. Develop visual support for your presentation that enhances the visualization portion of the presentation and draws your audience toward the call to action.
6. Deliver your presentation with strength, and use words that help generate the emotions you want to elicit from the audience.

---

## Persuading through Mindful Communication

*Charlotte Lansing represented one of the largest distributors on the East Coast. After George's presentation at the distributors meeting, she asked to meet with him the next morning to discuss the details of the co-advertising agreement. They set up a breakfast meeting for 8:00 in George's office. George realized that if he could convince Charlotte to sign the agreement, most of the other distributors would be easy to sign.*

*To help him decide the best approach to use with Charlotte, George prepared a strategy selection criteria worksheet. When he was done, his chart looked like the one shown on page 338. After completing the chart, he decided that a **mindful strategy** would work.*

A mindful strategy (Covino and Jolliffe, 1995) is appropriate when the following conditions apply:

+ Your goal is for the audience to make a commitment to your position, product, contract, or candidate.

+ Your audience has a history of being open to your concept, idea, or product.

+ The needs of your audience are vital to the outcome you are presenting.

+ Your ability to persuade your audience lies as much with your position of personal credibility as it does with your organizational authority and knowledge of the situation or product.

*George's main goal was for Charlotte to commit to being a co-advertiser and sign the co-advertising agreement. To get her to sign, he knew it was important that she trust him and believe he would honor his commitments, something he had demonstrated in the past. He also knew he would have to show Charlotte that he understood her company's*

*needs and concerns and that he would work hard to ensure that those needs were met.
Although he could see elements that fit the other strategies, overall he thought that a
mindful strategy would work best.*

| STRATEGY SELECTION CRITERIA WORKSHEET | | | | |
|---|---|---|---|---|
| **Strategy** | **Brutal** | **Rational** | **Rational/ Emotional** | **Mindful** |
| What type of presentation would work best? | ❑ One-on-one | ❑ Any audience | ❑ Any audience | ☑ Any audience |
| What are the needs of your audience? | ❑ Not considered | ☑ Clearly definable | ❑ Somewhat definable/ somewhat fluid | ☑ Clearly definable |
| What type of choices will your audience be presented with? | ❑ None or either/or | ❑ Multiple with best alternative presented | ☑ Call to action | ☑ Choice that reflects personal responsibility and organizational accountability |
| How open to your position, product, or idea has your audience been in the past? | ❑ Closed or resistant | ❑ Open | ☑ Unaware or open | ☑ Open |
| What method of persuasion would work best? | ❑ Strategic control— the use of authority to warrant compliance | ❑ Logos—an appeal that is based in evidence and logic | ❑ Logos/pathos— a logical appeal that induces the emotions of the audience | ☑ Ethos—an appeal that is based on the credibility of the speaker and his or her ability to follow through on commitments |
| What personal trait does your argument rely on: organizational authority, personal credibility, knowledge or expertise? | ❑ Authority | ❑ Knowledge or expertise | ☑ Credibility | ☑ All |
| What is your goal? | ❑ Compliance | ❑ Consensus | ❑ Action | ☑ Commitment |

## Creating a Mindful Persuasive Message

To communicate mindfully, George would need to do the following:

- ✦ analyze the situation
- ✦ adapt his message to the audience
- ✦ evaluate feedback as it occurred
- ✦ be willing to take risks that might lead to a better understanding
- ✦ listen consciously to what was said during the meeting
- ✦ provide feedback

*In the past, George had relied heavily on wit, charm, and a fast-paced conversational style to close deals. Thinking back, he marveled at how often he joked about "leaving so-and-so in the dust" and how "so-and-so didn't stand a chance once I walked into the office." Although George had lived up to his end of the contracts he signed and the promises he made, he was beginning to see that those promises were clearly tipped in his favor. He also began to view his meeting with Charlotte as a very different situation. The message he gave Charlotte not only would pave the way for future interactions with his company's largest distributor, but it could set the tone for negotiations with a number of the other distributors. He wanted to let Charlotte know that he and the company valued her business and their working relationship. He thought a mindful approach would help him do just that.*

*To help him organize his ideas, George prepared a persuasive message worksheet, shown below. George realized that he could not script his conversation with Charlotte.*

| PERSUASIVE MESSAGE WORKSHEET | |
|---|---|
| **Step** | **Your Message** |
| *Analysis of the situation* | ✦ Convince Charlotte that signing the co-advertising agreement is:<br>◇ Vital to the success of the new marketing strategy.<br>◇ In her company's best interest. |
| *Audience needs* | ✦ Charlotte needs to clearly see:<br>◇ How co-advertising will benefit her company.<br>◇ How co-advertising complements the new marketing strategy. |
| *Necessary risks* | ✦ May need to make disclosures that will assure Charlotte I am being honest. |

**Persuasive Message Worksheet**

| Step | Your message |
|---|---|
| *Analysis of the situation* | Convince Charlotte that signing the co-advertising agreement is:<br><br>1. Vital to the success of the new marketing strategy.<br><br>2. In her company's best interest. |
| *Audience needs* | Charlotte needs to clearly see:<br><br>1. How co-advertising will benefit her company.<br><br>2. How co-advertising complements the new marketing strategy. |
| *Necessary risks* | May need to make disclosures that will assure Charlotte that I am being honest. |

Stop Talking!

Listen! — for position, motivation, intention.

Recap.

Ask for confirmation.

Make Suggestions!

Listen to Feedback!

He printed out the worksheet and made some notes on the page. His annotated worksheet is shown above.

George would use this annotated sheet as his guide through the conversation. If he looked at the notes, he would remember to stop talking and listen. Hopefully, the notes would remind him not to fall into his pattern of talking, charming, and schmoozing his way into a deal. His goal was not just a signed agreement, but a true partnership with Charlotte's company that set a tone for the company–distributor relationship in the future.

## Coordinating the Mindful Persuasive Message

*Before leaving the office, George put his notes in a folder on his desk. He added a copy of the presentation he had delivered at the distributors meeting. He wanted to have that on hand in case Charlotte asked a question specifically about the presentation. He stopped by his administrative assistant's office and asked her to make arrangements to have breakfast set up in his office in the morning. There were no charts to prepare and no one else to coordinate with for his meeting tomorrow. The rest was up to him.*

## Delivering the Mindful Persuasive Message

*George arrived in the office at 7:30. He reviewed the notes he had made the previous day. He had spent most of the previous night turning the conversation over in his mind, playing out possible questions and objections.*

*When Charlotte arrived, they spent a few minutes chatting about the distributors meeting and eating breakfast before Charlotte opened the topic of the agreement.*

*"As I said yesterday, George, I was very impressed by your presentation. I've thought for a year or so that you needed a new approach to marketing."*

*"So have I," George agreed. "It was very frustrating for the sales reps to work as hard as they did to get the product to you and the other distributors and then have it languish on the shelves because of a lack of marketing focus."*

*"I'm a bit surprised to hear you admit that," Charlotte said.*

*"It isn't a big secret that our past approach to marketing has been a problem. We've known it, and the distributors have known it. However, I give the board credit for recognizing the problem and for giving me the resources to deal with it. We're confident our new strategy will address the problems we've had in the past." He started to continue but looked down at his sheet and realized that he needed to stop talking and listen.*

*"Which is why I wanted to meet with you today," Charlotte said. "It was clear to me that the company has made an investment in this new approach. I spoke with Tom, our CEO, last night, and he thinks we should give you a shot at making this work. However, we do have a few reservations."*

*"I'd be surprised if you didn't," George said. "This is a new direction for us. Why don't you tell me what your reservations are and we'll walk through each one and see if we can come to terms on them."*

*"Okay," said Charlotte. "First, we don't want to commit a year to the co-advertising program. We think six months is plenty of time to see if the ads are working. After six months, if the numbers haven't improved significantly, we want to terminate the agreement. Second, we think that in the first year of the agreement, a 60–40 split is too high. We would like to amend the agreement so that you pay 70 percent of the advertising costs for the first year. If the numbers come in the way we hope, we'll agree to a 60–40 future split. Finally, we need to have final approval over anything that has our*

*name on it. The agreement states that we'll have approval at the creative level, but we'd like to have approval at the editing stage. If we can agree to those points, I can sign the agreement today."*

*While Charlotte was talking, George was making notes and scanning his worksheet. When Charlotte finished, he said, "Let's take each point one at a time, so that we are both clear. First, I believe I understand your concerns about the length of the agreement. If the new strategy doesn't pan out, you don't want to be forced to continue with an ineffective program. Is that right?"*

*"Yes," Charlotte said.*

*"Okay, then I propose that we amend the agreement to read that you can terminate the agreement six months after the first ad runs. It's important to the success of the program that we have at least six months to run the numbers and evaluate the saturation of the message."*

*"I can live with that," Charlotte said. She made a few notes on her copy of the agreement.*

*Point by point, George restated his understanding of what Charlotte had said and they discussed any accommodations that could be made.*

*"That was actually pretty easy," Charlotte said when they finished their discussions. "I was expecting you to try to sell me or talk me out of each point. Instead, I feel as if we just had a really good negotiation that worked out for both of us."*

*George smiled. "To be honest, six months ago that's exactly what I would have done. But since becoming VP, I've realized that a hard sales approach doesn't always work. Sometimes, you have to be willing to give a little to get a little. I'll call Frank in legal and ask him to amend the agreement with our changes. He should be able to run it up in about fifteen minutes."*

## BEST PRACTICES

## Using a Mindful Persuasive Strategy

1. Analyze the situation before you begin. Develop a deep understanding of the positions of each party before you enter the conversation.
2. Listen. You cannot be mindful if you aren't listening to the other parties involved. Listen for intention, position, objections, and emotion.
3. Recap. Make sure that you understand the positions of the other parties by recapping what they have said. Then ask for confirmation before moving on.
4. Give feedback. Make sure that the other parties understand your position by giving them accurate and clear feedback.

## Summary

In this chapter, we explored the notion of concierge persuasion—persuasion through personal connection that is intended not only to meet the immediate needs of a situation, but to develop long-term relationships. We discussed four strategies of persuasion: brutal, rational, rational/emotional, and mindful. We laid out the reasons for using each type of strategy and provided worksheets to organize the messages for each strategy. We also showed how CCCD applies to a persuasive situation. We hope this discussion has helped you reframe your thinking of persuasion as a necessary part of communicating in a business and professional environment.

• • • • • • • • • • • • • • • • • • • • • • • • • • • • • • • • • • • • • • •

## COMMUNICATING IN PROFESSIONAL CONTEXTS ONLINE

All of the following chapter review materials are available in electronic format on either the Communicating in Professional Contexts website or CD-ROM. In addition to the multimedia case studies, activities, and numerous other learning resources you'll find on the CD-ROM, the CD is your gateway to the book's premium web content, which is not accessible via the Internet. The book's basic web content is available both with the premium content and on-line at http://communication.wadsworth.com/goodall2 and includes the chapter learning objectives and activities, key-term digital glossaries, and quizzes. The CD is also your gateway to InfoTrac College Edition, our extensive online database of full-text articles that is fully keyword searchable and available twenty-four hours a day. Installation instructions for the CD appear on the inside of this book's back cover.

### What You Should Have Learned

The learning objectives below are available on the Communicating in Professional Contexts website, which is best accessed through the book's CD-ROM but is also available at http://communication.wadsworth.com/goodall2. Go to the Chapter 12 Resources and click on Learning Objectives.

Now that you have read Chapter 12, you should be able to do the following:

+ Discuss the concept of concierge persuasion and how choosing the right persuasive strategy helps to build relationships.

+ List the four persuasive strategies and the uses for each strategy.

+ Discuss a situation for which a brutal strategy might be required.

+ Discuss the criteria for choosing a brutal strategy.

+ Give examples of situations for which a rational strategy might apply.

+ Discuss the criteria for choosing a rational strategy.

+ Discuss situations for which a rational/emotional strategy might be required.

+ Discuss the criteria for choosing a rational/emotional strategy.

+ Discuss situations for which mindful persuasion might be required.

+ Discuss the criteria for choosing a mindful persuasive strategy.

+ Use the worksheets provided in this chapter to create a persuasive message.

## Key Terms

The terms below are available in a digital glossary on the Communicating in Professional Contexts website, which is best accessed through this book's CD-ROM but is also available at http://communication.wadsworth.com/goodall2. Go to the Chapter 12 Resources and click on Glossary.

| | | |
|---|---|---|
| **attention-getter** *(334)* | **ethos** *(317)* | **pathos** *(317)* |
| **audience analysis** *(329)* | **logos** *(317)* | **rational strategy** *(324)* |
| **brutal strategy** *(318)* | **mindful strategy** *(337)* | **rational/emotional strategy** *(328)* |
| **call to action** *(334)* | **need** *(334)* | **satisfaction** *(334)* |
| **concierge persuasion** *(315)* | **needs assessment** *(330)* | |

## Writing and Critical Thinking

The following activities can be completed online and, if requested, submitted to your instructor. You'll find them on the Communicating in Professional Contexts website, which is best accessed through this book's CD-ROM but is also available at http://communication.wadsworth.com/goodall2. Go to the Chapter 12 Resources and click on Writing and Critical Thinking Activities.

1. Jon is required to pass a certification test before he can use a specific piece of machinery. He has failed the test three times and refuses to take the test again. You want to keep Jon as an employee, and eventually you would like to promote him to a team leader position, but you can't until he passes the test. What persuasive strategy would you use to persuade Jon to retake the test? Write a three-to-five-page paper discussing your choice of strategy and the possible outcome.

2. In your group, share a recent situation in which you used persuasion. Analyze the persuasive strategy you used. How successful were you? What would you do differently, having read this chapter?

3. Select a television, Internet, or print ad. Analyze the ad using Monroe's Motivated Sequence. Identify the attention-getter, need, satisfaction, visualization, and call to action used in the ad. Was the ad successful? Why or why not?

4. Working in groups of three, develop three short presentations, each with a different focus. The first appeal will focus on logic (*logos*), the second on emotion (*pathos*), and the third on expertise (*ethos*) to support or argue the statements listed below. Each member delivers one of your group's speeches to the class using the appeal. As an audience member, identify each speaker's appeal through the statements made, and evaluate how effective the appeal was.

Some lyrics in rap music should be banned because they incite violence.

Women are better suited to be caregivers than to be corporate executives.

The grading system at our school should be a simple pass/fail rather than letter grades.

In order to vote, citizens should be able to demonstrate knowledge of the issues.

## Research and Explorations Online

The exercises below can be completed online and, if requested, submitted to your instructor. You'll find them on the Communicating in Professional Contexts website, which is best accessed through this book's CD-ROM but is also available at http://communication.wadsworth.com/goodall2. Go to the Chapter 12 Resources and click on Internet Exercises.

1. Identify the position or professional field you plan to enter after you graduate. Enter the position name and *persuasion* as keywords in the search engine or InfoTrac College Edition (for example, enter *sales and persuasion*, or *education and persuasion*). Write a report on the influence of persuasion in your field and situations in which you would employ each of the strategies listed in the chapter.

2. Enter the words *logos*, *pathos*, and *ethos* in a keyword search. Select two or three articles to read. How did what you found improve your understanding of the strategies discussed in this chapter?

3. Enter the term *needs assessment* in a keyword search. Browse through the websites and articles provided by the search. Print out a few examples of assessments that you can use to create your own needs assessment.

## Practicing Communication in Professional Contexts

Throughout this book, we have emphasized CCCD (choose, create, coordinate, deliver) and conscious communication. In this exercise, you will be asked to use much of what you have learned in this book to create a successful presentation.

Review the main topics in the book and the CCCD process. Before you begin, make a list of the topics you might find helpful to complete the project.

*Situation: You have been asked to create a new handheld personal digital assistant specifically for a college market. The head of research and development would like to hear your ideas in two weeks. He has asked that you provide him with an overview of the market, a needs assessment, and a name for the product.*

To gather this information, you need to conduct interviews, surf the Internet, and develop a needs assessment. You will then need to prepare a presentation that persuades the head of research to produce the product you propose. Good luck!

## Communicating in Professional Contexts in Action!

Communicating in Professional Contexts in Action! is available on your Goodall Connection CD-ROM and features a group presentation that utilizes the CCCD approach. Improve your own group presentation skills by watching, listening to, critiquing, and analyzing the CCCD worksheet used in the group presentation and featured on this program. After completing a worksheet evaluation and answering the questions provided, you can compare your work to our suggested responses.

Roger Persson

# Appendix

| CCCD Worksheets for Persuasive or Informative Presentations | | | |
|---|---|---|---|
| **Step 1:** CHOOSING A GOAL | | | |
| **Audience** | **Needs and Expectations** | **Outcomes** | **Criteria** |
| Client | ◆ | ◆<br>◆ | ◆<br>◆<br>◆ |
| Firm | ◆ | ◆<br>◆ | ◆<br>◆<br>◆ |
| Self | ◆<br>◆ | ◆<br>◆ | ◆<br>◆ |

## CCCD Worksheets for Persuasive or Informative Presentations

**Step 2:** CREATING THE MESSAGE

| Introduction | ✦ Attention-getter<br>✦ Statement of thesis<br>✦ Preview of main points<br>✦ Inducement | | |
|---|---|---|---|
| **Purpose and Thesis Statement** | **Main Points** | **Support** | **Transitions** |
| ✦ *Purpose*<br>✦ *Thesis Statement* | ✦ *Main Point 1*<br>  ◇ Subpoint<br>  ◇ Subpoint<br>✦ *Main Point 2*<br>  ◇ Subpoint<br>  ◇ Subpoint<br>✦ *Main Point 3*<br>  ◇ Subpoint<br>  ◇ Subpoint | ✦ *Support for Main Point 1*<br>✦ *Support for Main Point 2*<br>✦ *Support for Main Point 3* | ✦ *Transition 1*<br>Transition between Main Point 1 and Main Point 2<br>✦ *Transition 2*<br>Transition between Main Point 2 and Main Point 3 |
| **Conclusion** | ✦ Review of main points<br>✦ Return to the attention-getter and wrap up | | |

| Motivated Sequence Organization Chart | | |
|---|---|---|
| **Introduction** | ✦ *Attention-Getter* | |
| **Purpose and Thesis Statement** | **Main Points** | **Support** |
| ✦ *Purpose*<br>✦ *Thesis Statement* | ✦ *Need*<br>   ◇<br>   ◇<br>   ◇<br>✦ *Satisfaction*<br>   ◇<br>   ◇<br>   ◇<br>✦ *Visualization*<br>   ◇<br>   ◇<br>   ◇<br>✦ *Action*<br>   ◇<br>   ◇ | ◇<br>◇<br>◇<br><br>◇<br>◇<br>◇<br><br>◇<br>◇<br>◇<br><br>◇<br>◇ |
| **Conclusion** | ✦ *Call to Action* | |

## Types of Visual Support and Audiences

| Type of Visual Support and Audiences | Should Be Used To: | Don't: | Things to Keep in Mind |
|---|---|---|---|
| **Slide presentations (see Chapter 11 for tips on using presentation software)** | | | |
| Appropriate for:<br><br>♦ Business and professional groups that are familiar with technology or operate in a technologically comfortable environment | ♦ Stay on agenda<br><br>♦ Provide transitions between multiple speakers<br><br>♦ Present statistical support in the form of graphs, or graphic charts, or pictures | ♦ Create elaborate complicated slideshows that distract from your message<br><br>♦ Get bogged down in moving the slides along and forget to speak to your audience<br><br>♦ Develop or use without practice, practice, practice | ♦ Make sure that the technology to support your slideshow is available at the talk site or plan to bring your own<br><br>♦ Develop a backup plan in case something goes wrong with the technology<br><br>♦ Be prepared to veer from your use of the slideshow if your audience shows signs of boredom or visual fatigue |
| **Internet-based presentations** | | | |
| Appropriate for:<br><br>♦ Audiences doing business on the Internet<br><br>♦ Audiences that will access your Internet site<br><br>♦ Internal customers that will access the company Intranet site | ♦ Demonstrate the capabilities of your site<br><br>♦ Demonstrate the type of information available on your site<br><br>♦ Highlight the advantages of your site vs. other sites | ♦ Get bogged down in the features of a site and forget the important points of your presentation<br><br>♦ Get bogged down in the technical aspects of the site, especially if your audience is not technical<br><br>♦ Deliver a presentation based on Internet technology without practice, practice, practice | ♦ Make sure that the technology to support your Internet-based presentation is available at the talk site<br><br>♦ Develop a backup plan in case something goes wrong with the technology<br><br>♦ Be prepared to veer from your use of the Internet if your audience shows signs of boredom or visual fatigue |

| Types of Visual Support and Audiences | | |
|---|---|---|
| **Type of Visual Support and Audiences** | **Should Be Used To:** | **Don't:** | **Things to Keep in Mind** |

**Slide presentations (see Chapter 11 for tips on using presentation software)**

| Type of Visual Support and Audiences | Should Be Used To: | Don't: | Things to Keep in Mind |
|---|---|---|---|
| **Videotape**<br><br>Appropriate for:<br>♦ Audiences that require visual demonstration of a sales technique, product, or competitor's product or service<br>♦ Audiences that are geographically dispersed<br>♦ Cases where the featured speaker (CEO, president, or motivational speaker) is unavailable for an appearance | ♦ Demonstrate the capabilities of your product or service<br>♦ Demonstrate a technique or process<br>♦ Deliver personal message from a CEO, motivational speaker, or other source not available for a personal appearance | ♦ Simply turn on the videotape and walk away. Videotape should be used to enhance a presentation, not substitute for one<br>♦ Use poor-quality video. If you can't find or develop a video that has high audio and video quality, find another type of support<br>♦ Deliver a presentation based on video technology without practice, practice, practice | ♦ Make sure that the technology to support the portion of your videotape presentation is available at the talk site<br>♦ Develop a backup plan in case something goes wrong with the technology |
| **Models**<br><br>Appropriate for:<br>♦ Presentations that require a 3D or visual demonstration of a product or idea<br>♦ Cases where a visual representation is important or will improve understanding. For example, architects often use models to present building concepts | ♦ Illustrate or clarify points that are confusing. For example, crime scene models are often used in court cases to help with a witness's testimony<br>♦ Create excitement about a product or idea that is in the development stage | ♦ Use models that have not been professionally prepared<br>♦ Rely on the model to make your case or sell your idea. The model is a support for the presentation, not the presentation | ♦ Should be professionally prepared.<br>♦ If model is a large visual model, be sure that it is backed on foam board. Foam board is more stable than poster board and doesn't buckle when placed on an easel |

## Types of Visual Support and Audiences

| Type of Visual Support and Audiences | Should Be Used To: | Don't: | Things to Keep in Mind |
|---|---|---|---|
| **Flip charts** | | | |
| Appropriate for:<br><br>♦ Audiences that will be brainstorming or generating ideas on the fly<br><br>♦ Audiences that are less formal in nature, like teams or groups, or for meetings<br><br>♦ Audiences meeting in places where technology is not available<br><br>♦ Training classes | ♦ Brainstorm or draw<br><br>♦ Collate the ideas or views of a group or meeting | ♦ Allow flip charts prepared in advance to become dated or soiled<br><br>♦ Use poor-quality flip charts in professional situations. With the availability of technology, few audiences have any tolerance for hand-drawn charts or hand-labeled graphics<br><br>♦ Use flip charts in a technological environment. Learn the technology that is appropriate for the audience you are speaking to | ♦ Make sure you have an easel or other way to display the charts<br><br>♦ Use charts big enough for the space you are speaking in. If you are speaking to more than 20 people, chances are someone in your audience will not be able to see your flip chart |
| **Whiteboards** | | | |
| Appropriate for:<br><br>♦ Audiences that will be brainstorming or generating ideas on the fly<br><br>♦ Audiences that are less formal in nature, like teams or groups, or for meetings<br><br>♦ Audiences meeting in places where technology is not available<br><br>♦ Training classes | ♦ Brainstorm or draw<br><br>♦ Collate the ideas or views of a group or meeting | ♦ Use whiteboards as your primary visual aid for a formal presentation | ♦ Write legibly and large enough for everyone to read what you put on the board<br><br>♦ Erase completely<br><br>♦ Bring markers and erasers with you if you aren't sure they will be available |

## Types of Visual Support and Audiences

| Type of Visual Support and Audiences | Should Be Used To: | Don't: | Things to Keep in Mind |
|---|---|---|---|
| **Transparencies**<br><br>Appropriate for:<br>♦ Audiences meeting in places where higher levels of technology are not available<br>♦ Training classes | ♦ Collate the ideas or views of a group or meeting<br>♦ Present training points<br>♦ Back up higher technology options when technology fails or is unavailable | ♦ Keep using transparencies that have become dated or faded<br>♦ Use transparencies simply because you don't want to learn new technology | ♦ Make sure an overhead projector is available at your site. These have become rare in most business environments<br>♦ Use overheads big enough for the space you are speaking in. If you are speaking to more than 30 people, chances are someone in your audience will not be able to see your transparancy |
| **Handouts**<br><br>Appropriate for:<br>♦ Audiences meeting in places where higher levels of technology are not available<br>♦ Cases where supplemental materials are necessary<br>♦ Training classes or where hard-copy supporting materials are needed | ♦ Provide hard-copy supporting materials<br>♦ Provide graphics to large groups where technology is not available or would not be clearly viewed by the entire audience<br>♦ Back up higher technology options when technology fails or is unavailable | ♦ Distribute unless what is on the paper is highly valuable. We all have too much paper to deal with<br>♦ Dump your entire presentation to a handout that you then read from | |
| **Chalkboards—Seen one lately?** | | | |

## Tips for Successful Interpersonal Communication

| Type | Definition | Tips for Success |
|------|-----------|------------------|
| Downward Communication | Communication flows from the top of the organizational chart down. Some examples are:<br>+ Goals, values, and vision<br>+ Tasks<br>+ Schedules<br>+ Policies and procedures<br>+ Performance appraisals and raise information | 1. When communicating tasks to subordinates, tell them how to do a task and why the task is important or fits into the overall scheme of the business.<br>2. When discussing a problem or conflict, stay on the topic and deal with the employee's behavior, rather than the person.<br>3. Use written messages only when appropriate and with follow-up and feedback. |
| Upward Communication | Communication flows from the bottom of the organizational chart up. Some examples are:<br>+ Task reports, monthly memos, and status reports<br>+ Suggestions for improvement<br>+ Complaints about working conditions or co-workers<br>+ Problems to be resolved<br>+ Feedback about messages from a supervisor | 1. Don't conceal or sugarcoat bad news or problems. Eventually, your supervisor will discover the problem and you will lose credibility.<br>2. Do not distort the facts about a situation that occurs with a co-worker. State the facts and give your manager time to respond to the situation.<br>3. Keep you supervisor aware of your and your team members' significant achievements. |
| Peer Communication | Communication flows from side to side, between team members, work groups, or department members. Some examples are:<br>+ Task coordination<br>+ Job sharing scheduling<br>+ Invitations to lunch | 1. Keep gossip out of the workplace. Gossip is not only detrimental, it is unethical professional behavior.<br>2. Be helpful, be kind, and be smart. Never say or write anything you don't want repeated. |

| Tips for Successful Written Communication | | |
|---|---|---|
| **Type** | **Definition** | **Tips for Success** |
| E-mail | Short, brief written conversations that call for a quick decision, impart specific or general knowledge, or provide opportunities for networking. Some examples are:<br>+ Request for a decision<br>+ Directions to a customer's site<br>+ Appointment confirmations<br>+ Invitation to a group lunch<br>+ Follow-up on a memo or report | 1. Don't send memos in e-mail form. Studies show that people have limited time in the day to respond to e-mail messages. E-mails that contain detailed information or complex instruction sets may not be given the attention they deserve. Write a brief e-mail describing the memo and requesting the reader print and read the attached memo.<br>2. Don't abuse e-mail. You will lose credibility if you send out e-mails without purpose or substance.<br>3. Purge and archive e-mails regularly to avoid becoming overwhelmed by your inbox. |
| Memos | Official company messages that impart *specific* information or a *specific* request. Examples are:<br>+ Changes in policies or procedures<br>+ Changes to schedules<br>+ Sales reports<br>+ Status reports<br>+ Requests for equipment or staff | 1. Memos should be 1–5 pages. Beyond 5 pages, the memo becomes a report.<br>2. Memos should cover 1–3 specific *and* related topics.<br>3. Memos should contain a request for feedback where necessary.<br>4. Use subheads for memos that are longer than 2 pages to orient your audience. |
| Reports | Informational messages that contain large amounts of complex or detailed knowledge. Examples are:<br>+ Corporate prospectus<br>+ White papers<br>+ Quarterly and annual sales reports<br>+ Needs assessments<br>+ Requests for equipment or staff | 1. Begin by outlining the purpose, scope, and major headings for the report.<br>2. Analyze the audience for the report.<br>3. If you are preparing a report for the first time, request copies of previous reports to use as an example.<br>4. If you are stating a problem, end with recommendations for improvement.<br>5. Provide only the information that is necessary to inform, educate, and lead your audience to an appropriate decision or conclusion. |

| Tips for Successful Group and Team Communication | | |
|---|---|---|
| **Type** | **Definition** | **Tips for Success** |
| Groups | Work groups, departments, or units formed for specific projects. In groups the operation is more informal, jobs are less connected, and the charge of the group is less specific than in teams. Some examples are:<br>✦ Committee formed to plan the 25th anniversary celebration of a school<br>✦ Managers that meet once a month to discuss customer complaints<br>✦ Committee formed to review a faculty member for tenure | 1. Help your group define the purpose of the group and stay on track.<br>2. Don't belittle other group members' ideas or contributions.<br>3. Complete group assignments on time and with a high level of quality.<br>4. Keep information about the group in the group unless all group members agree to make the information public. |
| Teams | Formally appointed groups of employees whose jobs cut across departments, function, or capability. Teams are given a specific charge to solve a problem, design a product, or change a procedure. Examples are:<br>✦ Reengineering group charged with redesigning the accounting department<br>✦ Y2K team charged with bringing your organization into compliance<br>✦ Product design team charged with creating a car for the 2010 auto show | 1. Don't allow conflict or disagreements to interfere with the effectiveness of the team.<br>2. Ask team members for feedback to ideas you offer and be open to the feedback received.<br>3. Keep team meetings short and to a minimum.<br>4. Recognize when your team has accomplished its goal and is no longer needed. |

| STRATEGY SELECTION CRITERIA WORKSHEET | | | | |
|---|---|---|---|---|
| **Strategy** | **Brutal** | **Rational** | **Rational/ Emotional** | **Mindful** |
| What type of presentation would work best? | ❏ One-on-one | ❏ Any audience | ❏ Any audience | ❏ Any audience |
| What are the needs of your audience? | ❏ Not considered | ❏ Clearly definable | ❏ Somewhat definable/ somewhat fluid | ❏ Clearly definable |
| What type of choices will your audience be presented with? | ❏ None or either/or | ❏ Multiple with best alternative presented | ❏ Call to action | ❏ Choice that reflects personal responsibility and organizational accountability |
| How open to your position, product, or idea has your audience been in the past? | ❏ Closed or resistant | ❏ Open | ❏ Unaware or open | ❏ Open |
| What method of persuasion would work best? | ❏ Strategic control— the use of authority to warrant compliance | ❏ Logos—an appeal that is based in evidence and logic | ❏ Logos/pathos— a logical appeal that induces the emotions of the audience | ❏ Ethos—an appeal that is based on the credibility of the speaker and his or her ability to follow through on commitments |
| What personal trait does your argument rely on: organizational authority, personal credibility, knowledge or expertise? | ❏ Authority | ❏ Knowledge or expertise | ❏ Credibility | ❏ All |
| What is your goal? | ❏ Compliance | ❏ Consensus | ❏ Action | ❏ Commitment |

| Example Interview Script | |
|---|---|
| Establish rapport | These questions should put the interviewee at ease and break the ice. Examples are:<br>◆ How was your flight?<br>◆ Did you have trouble finding us? |
| Define the interviewee's experience | These questions arise from the cover letter, resume, and references. Examples are:<br>◆ I see that you majored in communication. How has your major prepared you for this job?<br>◆ Tell us a little about your current position.<br>◆ What are two things about your current job that you find challenging?<br>◆ What are two things about your current job that you dislike?<br>◆ What has been your biggest accomplishment at your current position?<br>◆ What will you miss most about the company you work for?<br>◆ Of all the jobs you have had, which has been the best fit and why? |
| Clarify the requirements for the position | These questions zero in on the requirements for the position. Examples are:<br>◆ This position requires hiring and developing a team of writers and trainers. How would you go about doing that?<br>◆ In this position, you will be required to manage a team. What qualities do you think are important in a team environment?<br>◆ As a manager, you will be required to report the progress of your team. How do you feel about providing regular status reports?<br>◆ An important function of this position is liaison to other teams. What skills do you have that will facilitate this function?<br>◆ How would this position further your career goals? |
| Present the organization | These questions open a discussion of the organization. Examples are:<br>◆ What do you know about Bilin.com?<br>◆ How do you feel about working for an Internet start-up, coming from such an established company?<br>◆ Bilin is a small, young company and we can't offer the benefits some organizations can. Is that a problem?<br>◆ We have just signed three major contracts, which has tripled our deliverables overnight. To meet our schedules, we know that we have to work extremely long hours. Is there anything to prevent you from working long weeks when necessary? |
| Provide closure | These questions signal the interview is ending and allow for a final opportunity to clarify information. Examples are:<br>◆ Do you have any additional questions?<br>◆ If offered the position, when could you start? |

| **Employer Performance or Grievance Review Checklist** | |
|---|---|
| Before the Review | ◆ Ask for a written evaluation from the employee of his or her performance. |
| | ◆ Carefully read the employee evaluation *before* you complete your evaluation. |
| | ◆ Review (if a record exists) the employee's past two performance appraisals. |
| | ◆ Outline the areas of the employee's performance that exceeded expectations, met expectations, and fell short of expectations for the appraisal period. |
| | ◆ Indicate areas that over the past two review periods have fallen below expectations. |
| | ◆ Outline a course of action for the employee to follow that will meet expectations. |
| | ◆ Document the course of action in a memo for both you and the employee to sign. |
| During the Review | ◆ Present the evaluation to the employee beginning with areas that exceeded expectations, followed by those that met expectations, and ending with those that were below expectations. |
| | ◆ Keep the focus on the employee's job performance and team and group interactions. |
| | ◆ Avoid making vague references to the employee's "attitude" or other subjective references. |
| | ◆ Present the course of action for improvement. |
| | ◆ Ask the employee if he or she has have questions. |
| | ◆ Offer the employee a brief period to think about the evaluation and respond either in writing or in person. |
| | ◆ Indicate that you expect the memo to be signed by the employee by a specific date and that a nonresponse on the part of the employee indicates agreement with the memo as is. |
| After the Review | ◆ Follow up on the memo if the employee has not signed it by the date specified. |
| | ◆ Continue to document problems as they arise, but don't harp on problems that have been discussed and solved. |
| | ◆ Praise the employee for changes and progress made. |
| | ◆ Follow up with additional reviews as needed at 3-month periods. |

| **Employee Performance and Grievance Review Checklist** | |
|---|---|
| Before the Review | ✦ Prepare a written evaluation of your work prior to the manager's evaluation.<br><br>✦ If you are not asked for a self-evaluation, check with your manager two weeks before your review date and request the opportunity to provide a self-evaluation.<br><br>✦ In your evaluation, give an honest assessment of your performance. Include the areas where you believe you went above and beyond the requirements of the job and the areas where you need improvement.<br><br>✦ Outline goals for the next review cycle. The goals you outline should reflect your individual and team goals.<br><br>✦ Submit a well-thought-out, well-reasoned, organized appraisal of your work. |
| During the Review | ✦ Listen, listen, listen. By now, your manager knows what you think. Now, it is his or her turn. Listen carefully to everything your manager has to say.<br><br>✦ Take notes.<br><br>✦ Be gracious when given praise or high marks for doing well.<br><br>✦ Acknowledge areas you know need improvement.<br><br>✦ Ask for a period to reflect on and respond to areas that may be in dispute.<br><br>✦ Walk away from the appraisal without being defensive, negative, or closed to suggestions offered by your manager. |
| After the Review | ✦ Spend some time honestly thinking about your appraisal.<br><br>✦ Don't talk about it with co-workers or vent only your side to friends and family.<br><br>✦ Submit a well-thought-out, well-reasoned, organized assessment of your appraisal, if you believe any areas were unfair.<br><br>✦ Indicate areas of agreement and areas that you think were unfair or too harsh. Suggest ways to remedy the disagreement. Indicate that you are willing to work on your performance and toward an amicable conclusion.<br><br>✦ Give your employer an opportunity to respond. |

# Glossary

**adaptive skill** *The ability to adapt behaviors to the needs and expectations of others.*

**agenda** *A functional document used to organize a meeting.*

**attention-getter** *The story, joke, or first line of a message, designed to pull the audience into your presentation.*

**audience analysis** *A demographic reading of an audience based on findings such as age, race, gender, years of service, and position.*

**audience needs and expectations** *What the listener should gain and expects to gain from a presentation.*

**brutal strategy** *A one-sided strategy of persuasion that offers the listener little or no choice.*

**bureaucracy** *A system of organization marked by hierarchy, set rules, and fixed divisions of labor.*

**call to action** *The direct or indirect statement of action you want the audience to take after listening to your message.*

**causal pattern** *A cause-and-effect organizational structure for a presentation.*

**CCCD** *A four-step process of choosing, creating, coordinating, and delivering a conscious communication message.*

**channel** *The thoroughfare a message takes from sender to receiver, including electronically mediated methods of message delivery such as radio, television, computers, and satellites, as well as the full range of print media, including office memos and letters, newspapers, magazines, advertising flyers, brochures, and books.*

**choosing** *Analyzing the possible outcomes of a communication situation to select the best strategy for a given communication goal.*

**chronological** *An organizational structure for a presentation that relies on past, present, and future or a series of dates to frame a talk.*

**clip art** *Prepackaged, ready-to-use art and graphics that can be dropped into a document to add impact or interest.*

**closed questions** *Questions that require specific, concrete responses and provide little opportunity for elaboration.*

**communication** *All forms of speaking, listening, relating, writing, and responding, both human and electronically mediated.*

**communication history** *The cumulative record of communication events between participants.*

**concierge persuasion** *Persuasion that is adapted to fit a particular person and situation.*

**conflict** *Feelings or perceptions of imbalance that arise in a relational setting.*

**conscious communication** *Communication that has been carefully chosen, created, coordinated, and delivered.*

**conscious listening** *Listening openly to a speaker's point of view and reflecting on how talk affects the whole.*

**constraint** *A restriction or limit.*

**context** *The physical, historical, and cultural environment that informs a communication situation or episode.*

**coordinating** *The act of bringing together everyone required to successfully deliver the message.*

**creating** *The process of developing a presentation plan designed to carry out a chosen strategy.*

**creativity** *What results from giving people the freedom to explore alternatives beyond the traditional ways of doing things.*

**credibility** *A demonstration of believability and trustworthiness.*

**criteria** *The parameters against which you measure the success of a presentation.*

**critical listening** *The ability of a listener to deliberate on what is said by exploring the logic, reason, and point of view of the speaker.*

**cultures** *The evolved standards of communication practice, acquired through observation and experience, that may be unique to an organization.*

**delivery** *The process of practicing and articulating your message for an audience.*

**dialectic** *The interaction of two arguments that by nature are oppositional.*

**dialogue** *Communication that focuses on mutuality and relational growth, rather than on self-interest.*

**diversity** *The cultural, gender, racial, religious, and socioeconomic differences that inform communication in the workplace.*

**downward communication** *Communication that occurs between you and anyone lower than you within the organizational hierarchy.*

**electronically mediated communication** *Includes radio, television, computers, and satellites, as well as the full range of print media, such as office memos and letters, newspapers, magazines, advertising flyers, brochures, and books.*

**e-mail** *Electronic mail transmitted to or from your computer almost instantaneously anywhere in the world.*

**employment interview** *An interview designed to bring together potential employees and employers to test the fit of someone for a position.*

**empowerment** *The process of enabling and motivating employees, mainly by removing roadblocks, which builds feelings of personal effectiveness and control.*

**environment** *The integral parts of an organization that overlap to create a space for communication and understanding.*

**equity** *The principle that we should be treated fairly by others and in turn should treat them fairly.*

**ethos** *The perceived credibility or expertise of a speaker.*

**exclusive message strategies** *Autocratic communication that reveals a me-oriented pattern of behavior.*

**fact** *Something that is known to exist or has been proven to be true; basic, empirically verifiable information that has credibility for a given audience.*

**feedback** *The responses provided to the communication, ideas, and identities received in a message; an evaluation of the effectiveness of the actions of others.*

**fluency** *Smooth or effortless articulation of a speech or presentation.*

**focus group** *A group assembled to help explore an idea or test a product or a concept.*

**font size** *The size of the lettering in a text.*

**font type** *A particular style of text characters, such as Times Roman or Arial.*

**formal interview** *A structured, tightly scripted interview that centers on questions designed to gather specific information.*

**gendered talk** *Conversation marked by the differences between the way men and women tend to communicate.*

**goal** *A concrete, achievable end.*

**goals** *The set and planned accomplishments of an organization.*

**haptics** *The study of touching as nonverbal communication.*

**hearing** *The passive and physical process of listening.*

**hierarchical noise** *The shadings in meaning attributed to rank or status within an organization.*

**hierarchy** *The system of authority, rank, and status within an organization.*

**hostile work environment** *An environment in which intimidating or offensive verbal or nonverbal communication interferes with someone's work.*

**human relations movement** *A theoretical movement that viewed employees as sources of group information and skill that could be developed through training and education.*

**identity** *The way people see and respond to you in the workplace, including your organizational persona, credibility, and savvy.*

**inclusive message strategies** *A democratic form of communication taking into account the group or culture, thoughts and feelings of others, and others' contributions and differences.*

**informal interview** *An unstructured interview that covers a wide variety of topics and uses open questions.*

**information interview** *An interview designed to gather specific information, further understanding, or test a concept.*

**information overload** *What occurs when too many forms of communication intersect at one time, rendering decision making and response difficult.*

**information transfer model** *A model that posited information was passed directly from sender to receiver.*

**informational listening** *The stage in the listening process where meaning is assigned to the words we hear.*

**informative presentation** *A presentation that attempts to present facts and information in an objective, nonpersuasive manner.*

**interdependence** *The pattern of contingent decision making that understands the need to revise decision making based on new information and the effects of past decisions.*

**interpretation** *The meanings we assign to messages.*

**interrogation** *A one-sided form of interviewing that concentrates on the negative aspects of a problem.*

**interview script** *A plan of questions used for an interview.*

**jamming** *Engaging in a spontaneous, energetic group session in which the members are totally coordinated.*

**job description** *A description of an open position that usually includes experience, salary, and education requirements.*

**job goals** *The type of position you want and the outcomes you want from your employment.*

**kinesics** *The study of body movement, including facial expressions, eye contact, and gestures.*

**learning organization** *An organization marked by conscious systems-based thinking and an ability to continually adapt communication to organizational, cultural, and individual changes.*

**listening** *The process of hearing and interpreting messages.*

**logos** *The ability of a speaker to sway an audience using logic.*

**Luddite** *A person who refuses to adapt to new forms of technology.*

**memo** *A short document containing information about a specific topic.*

**mental models** *The images, assumptions, and stories that permeate the minds of the people working in organizations.*

**message** *What is said and done during a communication interaction, both verbally and nonverbally.*

**mindful communication** *An approach to communication that is both purposeful and strategic and emphasizes the audience and expected outcomes.*

**mindful strategy** *A persuasive appeal that emphasizes a deep connection between the speaker and the audience.*

**mindless communication** *Episodes of small talk or automatic talk that occur in familiar situations.*

**monitoring** *Checking the accuracy of your perceptions and questioning the factors that lead to those perceptions.*

**motivation** *The force or reason that drives us to do something.*

**narrative** *The representation of experience in the form of a story.*

**naturalness** *An easy, genuine manner of speaking.*

**need** *The part of a message that details the audience's problem or need.*

**needs assessment** *A survey or questionnaire developed to find out what an audience needs or wants or what problems they might have.*

**netiquette** *The rules of etiquette that govern online interaction on the Internet.*

**network** *Two or more computers that are connected either locally (within a company or building) or widely (across different geographic locations) by cable, phone lines, or satellite.*

**noise** *The physical, semantic, and hierarchical influences that either disrupt or shape the interpretation of messages; any sound that disrupts or interferes with the delivery of a message.*

**nonsupportive messages** *Messages that communicate superiority, disrespect of others, and lack of cooperation in the workplace.*

**nonverbal competence** *The ability of a speaker to maintain eye contact, use gestures and body movement to enhance speech, and incorporate visual aids in the presentation.*

**objective** *A task required to reach a goal.*

**oculesics** *The study of the eyes as a source of communication information.*

**open questions** *Questions that require more than yes or no responses and that allow you to discuss your experience or perspective.*

**organizational credibility** *The values associated with being a trustworthy, honest, responsible, fair, and ethical person in the organization.*

**organizational culture** *The histories, habits, values, and rules*

for conduct that make working in an organization feel unique.

**organizational persona** *The position, status, rank, years of service, and role in a company that determine who we are perceived as within an organization.*

**organizational savvy** *The ability a person has to successfully negotiate political and social boundaries in an organization.*

**outcome** *What you achieve as a result of a presentation.*

**pathos** *The ability to sway an audience using emotion.*

**perception** *The way we process and interpret cues from a person's outward appearance, voice, and language usage.*

**performance review** *A review or critique of an employee's work and job performance.*

**person prototypes** *The stereotypes we assign to people when we first meet them.*

**personal constructs** *The specific evaluations we make of people based on our assessment of their habits and behaviors.*

**personal mastery** *A form of empowerment that emphasizes the need for continuous growth and renewal as vital to the individual and the organization.*

**personal space** *The spatial distance we keep between ourselves and others.*

**persuasive interview** *A sales-oriented form of interviewing intended to convince a client or customer to buy into an idea or make a purchase.*

**persuasive presentation** *A presentation designed to bring the audience to a decision or action.*

**phatic communication** *The patterned sequences of talk or scripts we use every day.*

**physical diversion** *Any physical element that disrupts or interferes with the delivery of a message.*

**policies** *The guidelines that oversee conduct in the workplace.*

**power** *The sources of influence derived by an individual within an organization; our ability to influence others and outcomes.*

**problem-solution pattern** *An organizational structure that begins with a problem and offers a solution or potential solutions.*

**proxemics** *The study of interpersonal space and distance.*

**quid pro quo** *"This for that" an exchange of favors or actions.*

**rational strategy** *A two-sided persuasive exchange that presents alternatives and a best solution.*

**rational/emotional strategy** *Persuasion that appeals to logic and emotion and makes use of need, satisfaction, visualization, and a call to action.*

**receiver** *The person to whom a message is directed.*

**reference** *A citation of a noted authority, which lends credibility to a presentation.*

**report**  A document containing detailed coverage of one or more related topics.

**résumé**  The formal statement of who you are; it combines autobiography, work history, and sales presentation.

**reward**  The benefit received from an activity (e.g., money, identity, power, support, companionship, a skill set) in relation to what it costs (physical labor, mental and emotional stress, free time, time away from families, subordinating personal goals, dealing with difficult people, harassment).

**rules**  The assumptions and formal pronouncements about communication among employees.

**satisfaction**  The part of a message that conveys the solution to the audience's need or problem.

**schemata**  The mental pattern recognition plans that help us identify and organize incoming information.

**scientific management**  The theory that posited organization should be operated as efficient machines governed by scientific principles, rules, and laws.

**scripts**  The patterned sequences of talk we use every day.

**self-disclosure**  Providing personal information within a conversation.

**self-reflexive listening**  Listening for the way in which a message applies to the listener's life.

**semantic noise**  Differences in how people interpret the meanings of words, including the gender, racial, and cultural biases of the receiver, as well as jargon and misunderstandings.

**sender**  The originator of a message.

**sense-making**  Our attempt to construct the versions of reality we perceive and respond to based on our own experiences, knowledge, feeling, needs, and expectations.

**sensitivity**  Taking into consideration the speaking differences of a communication partner.

**sexual harassment**  In the workplace, any form of sexually explicit verbal or nonverbal communication that interferes with someone's work.

**shared vision**  An organizational vision and mission that is built upon a foundation of trust, openness, empowerment, and honesty.

**statistics**  Any basic, empirically verifiable numerical representation of information; information presented in the form of numbers, such as percentages or averages.

**strategic communication**  Communication that is planned with specific audiences and intentions in mind.

**supportive messages**  Messages that communicate concern and respect for others, as well as cooperation.

**synergy**  The shared knowledge, diversity of experience, and collaborative energy that result from mindful team communication.

**systems thinking**  A perception of an organization as a system of interconnected individuals and teams.

**team**  A group that shares a unifying goal and recognizes the synergy of shared knowledge, diversity of experience, and collaborative energy.

**team learning**  The conscious, coordinated action that translates shared vision, mental models, and personal mastery into thinking and acting as a team.

**technological diversion**  Any technological element that disrupts or interferes with the delivery of a message.

**telecommuting**  Working from your home or away from your company's primary location, but connected by telephone, fax, and computer.

**thesis statement**  A simple declarative sentence that introduces your message and announces your intentions.

**topical pattern**  An organizational structure that allows development of a talk based on a theme and the logical topics associated with the theme.

**transactional process model**  A model that posits all persons are continually sending and receiving messages and constantly affecting each other.

**transition**  A connection of one point or topic to another; a movement from one item to another.

**upward communication**  Communication that occurs between you and anyone higher than you within the organizational hierarchy.

**videoconferencing**  Conducting a conference between two or more participants at different sites by using computer networks or audio and video equipment.

**virtual communities**  Communities that exist primarily on the Internet.

**virtual meeting**  A meeting that may occur over wide geographical space and that uses technology as the principal delivery system.

**vision**  The overall, far-reaching idea of what a team or organization should accomplish and the values that should inform those accomplishments.

**visualization**  The part of a message that helps the audience imagine the satisfaction of their need.

**vivacity**  Energy and enthusiasm used in a speech or presentation.

**voice mail**  Messages left on a telephone answering system.

# References

Abernathy, D. J. (1999, May). A chat with Chris Argyris. *Training and Development, 53,* 80–85.

Albrecht, K. (1992). *The only thing that matters: Bringing the power of the customer into the center of your business.* New York: HarperBusiness.

Allen, M., & Caillouet, R. (1994). Legitimation endeavors: Impression management strategies used by an organization in crisis. *Communication Monographs, 61,* 44–62.

Alvesson, M. (1993). *Cultural perspectives on organizations.* New York: Cambridge University Press.

Alvesson, M. (2002). Indentity regulations as organizational control: Producing the appropriate individual. *Journal of Management Studies, 39*(5), 619–644.

Andersen, P. A. (1993). Cognitive schemata in personal relationships. In S. Duck (Ed.), *Individuals and relationships* (pp. 207–230). Newbury Park, CA: Sage.

Andersen, P. A. (1999). *Nonverbal communication.* Mountain View, CA: Mayfield.

Andersen, P. A., Andersen, J. F., & Landgraf, J. (1985). *The development of nonverbal communication competence in childhood.* Paper presented at the annual convention of the International Communication Association, Honolulu.

Andersen, P. A., Todd-Mancillas, W. R., & DiClemente, L. (1980). The effects of pupil dilation in physical, social, and task attraction. *Australian Scan: A Journal of Communication, 7 & 8,* 89–95.

Anderson, J. (1987). *Communication research: Issues and methods.* New York: McGraw-Hill.

Anderson, J. (2003). Forum response: Ethics in business and teaching. *Management Communication Quarterly, 17,* 155–164.

Anderson, R., Cissna, K., & Arnett, R. (1994). *The reach of dialogue.* Cresskill, NJ: Hampton Press.

Anderson, W. T. (1995). *The truth about the truth.* New York: Tarcher/Putnam.

Argyris, C. (1994, July–August). Good communication that blocks learning. *Harvard Business Review,* 77–85.

Argyris, C., & Schon, D. (1978). *Organizational learning: A theory of action perspective.* Reading, MA: Addison-Wesley.

Arnett, R., & Cissna, K. (1996). *The reach of dialogue: Confirmation, voice, and community.* Cresskill, NJ: Hampton Press.

Ashford, S., & Cummings, L. (1983). Feedback as an individual resource: Personal strategies of creating information. *Organizational Behavior and Human Performance, 32,* 370–398.

Atkouf, O. (1992). Management and theories of organizations in the 1990s: Toward a critical radical humanism? *Academy of Management Review, 17,* 407–431.

Axley, S. (1984). Managerial and organizational communication in terms of the conduit metaphor. *Academy of Management Review, 9,* 428–437.

Bales, R., & Strodtbeck, F. (1960). Phases in group problem solving. In D. Cartwright & A. Zander (Eds.), *Group dynamics: Research and theory* (pp. 624–638). New York: Harper & Row.

Banta, M. (1993). *Taylored lives: Narrative productions in the age of Taylor, Veblen, and Ford.* Chicago: University of Chicago Press.

Bantz, C. (1993). *Understanding organizations: Interpreting organizational communication cultures.* Columbia: University of South Carolina Press.

Barker, R. T., & Camarata, M. R. (1998). The role of communication in a learning organization. *Journal of Business Communication, 35*(4), 443–467.

Barley, S. (1983). Semiotics and the study of occupational and organizational culture. *Administrative Science Quarterly, 23,* 393–413.

Barnard, C. (1938/1968). *The functions of the executive.* Cambridge, MA: Harvard University Press.

Barnet, R., & Cavanagh, J. (1994). *Global dreams.* New York: Simon & Schuster.

Barnlund, D. (1994). *Communicative styles of Japanese and Americans.* Belmont, CA: Wadsworth.

Bateson, G. (1992). *Sacred unity: Further steps toward an ecology of mind.* San Francisco: HarperSanFrancisco.

Bavelas, A. (1951). Communication patterns in task oriented groups. In D. Lerner & H. Laswell (Eds.), *The policy sciences* (pp. 193–202). Stanford, CA: Stanford University Press.

Baxter, L. A. (1988). A dialectical perspective on communication strategies in relational development. In

S. Duck (Ed.), *Handbook of personal relationships* (pp. 257–273). Chicester, UK: Wiley.

Baxter, L. A., & Montgomery, B. M. (1996). *Relating: Dialogues and dialectics*. New York: Guilford Press.

Bellah, R., Madsen, R., Sullivan, W., Swidler, A., & Tipton, S. (1985). *Habits of the heart*. Berkeley: University of California Press.

Bellah, R., Madsen, R., Sullivan, W., Swidler, A., & Tipton, S. (1991). *The good society*. New York: Knopf.

Benne, K., & Sheats, P. (1948). Functional roles of group members. *Journal of Social Issues, 4*, 41–49.

Bennis, W. (1999). *Managing people is like herding cats: Warren Bennis on leadership*. Provo, UT: Executive Excellence.

Berger, C. R., & Calabrese, R. J. (1975). Some explorations in initial interaction and beyond: Toward a theory of interpersonal communication. *Human Communication Research, 1*, 99–112.

Berger, P., & Luckmann, T. (1967). *The social construction of reality*. Garden City, NY: Anchor.

Berlo, D. (1960). *The process of communication*. New York: Holt, Rinehart & Winston.

Beyer, J., & Trice, H. (1987). How an organization's rites reveal its culture. *Organizational Dynamics, 15,* 4–35.

Bingham, S. (1991). Communication strategies for managing sexual harassment in organizations: Understanding message options and their effects. *Journal of Applied Communication Research, 19*, 88–115.

Birdwhistell, R. L. (1970). *Kinesics and context*. Philadelphia: University of Pennsylvania Press.

Blumer, H. (1969). *Symbolic interactionism: Perspective and method*. Englewood Cliffs, NJ: Prentice-Hall.

Bochner, A. (1982). The functions of human communication in interpersonal bonding. In C. Arnold & J. Waite-Bowers (Eds.), *Handbook of rhetorical and communication theory* (pp. 544–621). Boston: Allyn & Bacon.

Bochner, A. P. (1994). Perspectives on inquiry II: Theories and stories. In M. L. Knapp & G. R. Miller (Eds.), *Handbook of interpersonal communication* (pp. 21–41). Newbury Park, CA: Sage.

Bochner, A. P. (1997). It's about time: Narrative and the divided self. *Qualitative Inquiry, 3*, 418–439.

Boje, D. (1991). The storytelling organization: A study of story performance in an office-supply firm. *Administrative Science Quarterly, 36*, 106–126.

Boje, D. (1995). Stories of the storytelling organization: A postmodern analysis of Disney in "Tamara-Land." *Academy of Management Journal, 38*, 997–1035.

Bracci, S. (1999, November). *Visions of community: Ethical issues in public relations and community building*. A highlighted panel, National Communication Association annual meeting, Chicago.

Brown, M., & McMillan, J. (1991). Culture as text: The development of an organizational narrative. *Southern Communication Journal, 57*, 49–60.

Brownell, J. (2002). *Listening: Attitudes, principles, and skills*. Boston: Allyn & Bacon.

Browning, L. (1992). Lists and stories as organizational communication. *Communication Theory 2*, 281–302.

Browning, L., & Hawes, L. (1991). Style, process, surface, context: Consulting as postmodern art. *Journal of Applied Communication Research, 19*, 32–54.

Buber, M. (1985). *Between man and man* (2nd ed.). New York: Macmillan.

Buck, R. (1979). Individual differences in nonverbal sending accuracy and electrodermal responding: The externalizing-internalizing dimension. In R. Rosenthal (Ed.), *Skill in nonverbal communication: Individual differences* (pp. 111–139). Cambridge, MA: Oelgeschlager, Gunn & Hain.

Buckman, R. H. (1997). [Interview, vice chairman of Buckman Laboratories International].

Bullis, C., & Bach, B. (1989). Socialization turning points: An examination of change in organizational identification. *Western Journal of Speech Communication, 53*, 273–293.

Bullis, C., & Glaser, H. (1992). Bureaucratic discourse and the goddess: Towards an ecofeminist critique and rearticulation. *Journal of Organizational Change Management, 5*, 50–60.

Burke, K. (1989). *On symbols and society*. Chicago: University of Chicago Press.

Burke, W. (1986). Leadership as empowering others. In S. Srivasta (Ed.), *Executive power* (pp. 51–77). San Francisco: Jossey-Bass.

Buzzanell, P. (1994). Gaining a voice: Feminist organizational communication theorizing. *Management Communication Quarterly 7*, 339–383.

Calas, M., & Smircich, L. (1993). Dangerous liaisons: The "feminine in management" meets "globalization." *Business Horizons, 36*, 71–81.

Canadian Manager Office Team. (1999). *Canadian Manager, 24*(2), 20.

Cheney, G., & Mumby, D. (1997). Communication and organizational democracy: Introduction. *Communication Studies, 48*, 277–279.

Chiles, A., & Zorn, T. (1995). Empowerment in organizations: Employees' perceptions of the influences on empowerment. *Journal of Applied Communication Research, 23*, 1–25.

Clair, R. (1993). The use of framing devices to sequester organizational narratives: Hegemony and harassment. *Communication Monographs, 60*, 113–136.

Clair, R. (1998). *Organizing silence*. Albany: State University of New York Press.

Clegg, S. (1989). *Frameworks of power*. Newbury Park, CA: Sage.

Coles, R. (1989). *The call of stories: Teaching and moral imagination*. Boston: Houghton Mifflin.

Conger, J., & Kanungo, R. (1988). The empowerment process: Integrating theory and practice. *Academy of Management Review, 13*, 471–482.

Conquergood, D. (1991). Rethinking ethnography: Towards a critical cultural politics. *Communication Monographs, 58*, 179–194.

Conrad, C. (1983). Organizational power: Faces and symbolic forms. In L. Putnam & M. Pacanowsky (Eds.), *Communication and organizations* (pp. 173–194). Beverly Hills, CA: Sage.

Conrad, C. (1991). Communication in conflict: Style-strategy relationships. *Communication Monographs, 58*, 135–155.

Contractor, N. (1992). Self-organizing systems perspective in the study of organizational communication. In B. Kovacic (Ed.), *Organizational communication: New perspectives* (pp. 39-65). Albany: State University of New York Press.

Covey, S. (1990). *Seven habits of highly effective people*. New York: Simon & Schuster.

Covino, W. A., & Jolliffe, D. A. (1995). *Rhetoric: Concepts, definitions, boundaries*. New York: Longman.

Csikszentmihalyi, M. (1990). *Flow: The psychology of optimal experience*. New York: Harper & Row.

Csikszentmihalyi, M. (1997). *Finding flow: The psychology of engagement with everyday life*. New York: Basic Books.

Cusella, L. (1987). Feedback, motivation, and performance. In F. Jablin et al. (Eds.), *Handbook of organizational communication* (pp. 624–678). Beverly Hills, CA: Sage.

Czarniawska-Joerges, B. (1988). Dynamics of organizational control: The case of Berol Kemi Ab. *Accounting, Organizations, and Society, 11*, 471–482.

Damasio, A. R. (1999). *The feeling of what happens: Body and emotion in the making of consciousness*. New York: Harcourt Brace.

Dansereau, F., & Markham, S. (1987). Superior–subordinate communication: Multiple levels of analysis. In F. Jablin et al. (Eds.), *Handbook of organizational communication* (pp. 343–388). Beverly Hills, CA: Sage.

Davis, K. (1953). Management communication and the grapevine. *Harvard Business Review, 31*, 43–49.

Deal, T., & Kennedy, A. (1982). *Corporate cultures*. Reading, MA: Addison-Wesley.

Deetz, S. (1991). *Democracy in an age of corporate colonization*. Albany: State University of New York Press.

Deetz, S. (1995). *Transforming communication, transforming business*. Albany: State University of New York Press.

Deetz, S., & Mumby, D. (1990). Power, discourse, and the workplace: Reclaiming the critical tradition. In J. Anderson (Ed.), *Communication Yearbook, 13*, 18–47.

Dillard, J., & Miller, K. (1988). Intimate relationships in task environments. In S. Duck (Ed.), *Handbook of personal relationships* (pp. 449–465). New York: Wiley.

Dillard, J., & Segrin, C. (1987). *Intimate relationships in organizations: Relational types, illicitness, and power*. Paper presented at the Annual Conference of the International Communication Association, Montreal, Canada.

Donnellon, A. (1992). Team work: Linguistic models of negotiating difference. In B. Shepard et al. (Eds.), *Research and negotiations in organizations* (Vol. 4, pp. 71–123). Greenwich, CT: JAI Press.

Dove, L. (1998). CPA standards elevated for complex profession. *Wichita Business Journal 13*(22), 16.

Dutton, J., & Dukerich, J. (1991). Keeping an eye on the mirror: Image and identity in organizational adaptation. *Academy of Management Journal, 34*, 517–554.

Ehninger, D. (1974). *Influence, belief, and argument: An introduction to responsible persuasion*. Glenview, IL: Scott, Foresman.

Eisenberg, E. (1984). Ambiguity as strategy in organizational communication. *Communication Monographs, 51*, 227–242.

Eisenberg, E. (1986). Meaning and interpretation in organizations. *Quarterly Journal of Speech, 72*, 88–98.

Eisenberg, E. (1990). Jamming: Transcendence through organizing. *Communication Research, 17*, 139–164.

Eisenberg, E., & Goodall, H. L. (2004). *Organizational communication: Balancing creativity and constraint*. New York: St. Martin's.

Eisenberg, E., Monge, P., & Miller, K. (1983). Involvement in communication networks as a predictor of organizational commitment. *Human Communication Research, 10*, 179–201.

Eisenberg, E., & Phillips, S. (1991). Miscommunication in organizations. In N. Coupland, H. Giles, & J. Weimann (Eds.), *"Miscommunication" and problematic talk* (pp. 244–258). Newbury Park, CA: Sage.

Eisenberg, E., & Witten, M. (1987). Reconsidering openness in organizational communication. *Academy of Management Review, 12*, 418–426.

Ekman, P. (1978). Facial expression. In A. W. Siegman & S. Feldstein (Eds.), *Nonverbal behavior and communication* (pp. 79–101). Hillsdale, NJ: Erlbaum.

Ellingson, L. L. (2003). Interdisciplinary health care teamwork in the clinic backstage. *Journal of Applied Communication Research, 31*, 93–117.

Etzioni, A. (1988). *The moral dimension: Toward a new economics*. New York: Free Press.

Evered, R., & Tannenbaum, R. (1992). A dialog on dialog. *Journal of Management Inquiry, 1*, 43–55.

Fairhurst, G., & Chandler, T. (1989). Social structure in leader–member interaction. *Communication Monographs, 56,* 215–239.

Fairhurst, G., Green, S., & Snavely, B. (1984). Face support in controlling poor performance. *Human Communication Research, 11,* 272–295.

Fairhurst, G., Rogers, E., & Sarr, R. (1987). Manager–subordinate control patterns and judgments about the relationship. *Communication Yearbook, 10,* 395–415.

Fairhurst, G., & Sarr, R. (1996). *The art of framing.* San Francisco, CA: Jossey-Bass.

Farace, R., Monge, P., & Russell, H. (1977). *Communicating and organizing.* Reading, MA: Addison-Wesley.

Farley, L. (1978). *Sexual shakedown: The sexual harassment of women on the job.* New York: McGraw-Hill.

Fayol, H. (1949). *General and industrial management.* London: Pitman.

Feldman, S. (1991). The meaning of ambiguity: Learning from stories and metaphors. In P. Frost et al. (Eds.), *Reframing organizational culture* (pp. 145–156). Newbury Park, CA: Sage.

Fisher, A. (1980). *Small group decision making* (2nd ed.). New York: McGraw-Hill.

Fisher, W. (1984). Narration as a human communication paradigm: The case of public moral argument. *Communication Monographs, 51,* 1–22.

Fisher, W. (1987). *Human communication as narration: Toward a philosophy of reason, value, and action.* Columbia: University of South Carolina Press.

Ford, J. D., & Ford, L. W. (1995). The role of conversations in producing intentional change in organizations. *Academy of Management Review, 20,* 541–570.

Ford, R., & Fottler, M. (1995). Empowerment: A matter of degree. *Academy of Management Executive, 9,* 21–31.

Fox, M. (1994). *The reinvention of work.* San Francisco: HarperCollins.

Franz, C., & Jin, K. (1995). The structure of group conflict in a collaborative work group during information systems development. *Journal of Applied Communication Research, 23,* 108–122.

French, R., & Raven, B. (1968). The bases of social power. In D. Cartwright & A. Zander (Eds.), *Group dynamics* (pp. 601–623). New York: Harper & Row.

Fritz, J. (1997). Men's and women's organizational peer relationships: A comparison. *Journal of Business Communication, 34*(1), 27.

Fulk, J., & Mani, S. (1986). Distortion of communication in hierarchical relationships. *Communication Yearbook, 9,* 483–510.

Fulk, J., Schmitz, J., & Steinfeld, C. (1990). A social influence model of technology use. In J. Fulk & C. Steinfeld (Eds.), *Organizations and communication technology* (pp. 143–172). Newbury Park, CA: Sage.

Furnham, A. (1999). Gesture politics. *People Management, 6,* 52.

Geertz, C. (1973). *The interpretation of cultures.* New York: Basic Books.

Geffen, D., & Straub, D. W. (1997). Gender differences in the perception and use of e-mail: An extension to the technology acceptance model. *MIS Quarterly, 21,* 389–401.

Geist, P., & Dreyer, J. (1992). *A dialogical critique of the medical encounter: Understanding, marginalization, and the social context.* Paper presented at the Annual Meeting of the Speech Communication Association, Chicago.

Geist, P., & Dreyer, J. (1993). The demise of dialogue: A critique of medical encounter ideology. *Western Journal of Communication, 57,* 233–246.

Gersick, C. (1988). Time and transition in work teams: Toward a new model of group development. *Academy of Management Journal, 31,* 9–41.

Gersick, C. (1991). Revolutionary change theories: A multi-level explanation of the punctuated equilibrium paradigm. *Academy of Management Review, 16,* 10–36.

Gilsdorf, J. (1998). Organizational rules on communicating: How employees are—and are not—learning the ropes. *Journal of Business Communication, 35*(2), 173.

Goodall, H. L. (1983). *Human communication: Creating reality.* Dubuque, IA: Brown.

Goodall, H. L. (1989). *Casing a promised land.* Carbondale: Southern Illinois University Press.

Goodall, H. L. (1990a). Interpretive contexts for decision-making: Toward an understanding of the physical, economic, dramatic, and hierarchical interplays of language in groups. In G. M. Phillips (Ed.), *Teaching how to work in groups* (pp. 197–224). Norwood, NJ: Ablex.

Goodall, H. L. (1990b). Theatre of motives. In J. Anderson (Ed.), *Communication Yearbook, 13,* 69–97.

Goodall, H. L. (1993). Empowerment, culture, and postmodern organizing: Deconstructing the Nordstrom's employee handbook. *Journal of Organizational Change Management, 5,* 25–30.

Goodall, H. L., Jr. (1995). Work-hate narratives. In R. Whillock & D. Slayden (Eds.), *Hate speech* (pp. 80–121). Thousand Oaks, CA: Sage.

Goodall, H. L., Jr. (1996). *Divine signs: Connecting spirit to community.* Carbondale: Southern Illinois University Press.

Goodall, H. L., Jr. (2000). *Writing the new ethnography.* Walnut Creek, CA: AltaMira.

Goodall, H. L., & Phillips, G. M. (1985). *Making it in any organization.* Englewood Cliffs, NJ: Prentice-Hall.

Goodall, H. L., Wilson, G., & Waagen, C. (1986). The performance appraisal interview: An interpretive re-assessment. *Quarterly Journal of Speech, 72,* 74–87.

Gouran, D. S. (1970). A response to the paradox and promise of small group communication research. *Speech Monographs, 37,* 217–218.

Grantham, C. (1995, September–October). The virtual office. *At work: Stories of tomorrow's workplace, 4(5),* 1, 12–14.

Gray, B., Bougon, M., & Donnellon, A. (1985). Organizations as constructions and destructions of meaning. *Journal of Management, 11,* 83–98.

Gray, J. (1992). *Men are from Mars, women are from Venus.* New York: HarperCollins.

Greene, J. O., & Sassi, M. S. (1997). Adult acquisition of message-production skill. *Communication Monographs, 64,* 181–201.

Gronn, P. (1983). Talk as the work: The accomplishment of school administration. *Administrative Science Quarterly, 28,* 1–21.

Hackman, R., & Associates. (1990). *Groups that work (and those that don't): Creating conditions for effective teamwork.* San Francisco: Jossey-Bass.

Hall, E. T. (1968). Proxemics. *Current Anthropology, 9,* 83–109.

Hall, E. T. (1973). *The silent language.* New York: Anchor Books.

Hall, S. (1997). *Representation in media.* Amherst, MA: Media Education Foundation.

Hammer, M., & Champy, J. (1993). *Reengineering the corporation.* New York: HarperCollins.

Harshman, E., & Harshman, C. (1999). Communicating with employees: Building on an ethical foundation. *Journal of Business Ethics, 19(1),* 3.

Hawes, L. (1974). Social collectivities as communication: Perspective on organizational behavior. *Quarterly Journal of Speech, 60,* 497–502.

Hawken, P. (1992). *The ecology of commerce.* New York: HarperCollins.

Hearn, G, & Ninan, A. (2003). Managing change is managing meaning. *Management Communication Quarterly, 16,* 440-445.

Hellweg, S. (1987). Organizational grapevines: A state of the art review. In B. Dervin & M. Voight (Eds.), *Progress in the communication sciences* (Vol. 8, pp. 213–230). Norwood, NJ: Ablex.

Heslin, R. (1974). *Steps toward a taxonomy of touching.* Paper presented at the annual convention of the Midwestern Psychological Association, Chicago.

Hirokawa, R., & Rost, K. (1992). Effective group decision making in organizations. *Management Communication Quarterly, 5,* 267–388.

Hodson, R. (2004). A meta-analysis of workplace ethnographies: Race, gender, and employee attitudes and behaviors. *Journal of Contemporary Ethnograhpy, 33,* 4–38.

Hofstede, G. (1983). National cultures in four dimensions. *International Studies of Management and Organization, 13,* 46–74.

Hofstede, G. (1991). *Culture and organizations: Software of the mind.* New York: McGraw-Hill.

Holt, G. (1989). Talk about acting and constraint in stories about organizations. *Western Journal of Speech Communication, 53,* 374–397.

Homans, G. (1961). *Social behavior: Its elementary forms.* New York: Harcourt Brace & World.

Huber, G. (1990). A theory of the effects of advanced information technologies on organizational design, intelligence, and decision-making. In J. Fulk & C. Steinfeld (Eds.), *Organizations and communication technology* (pp. 237–274). Newbury Park, CA: Sage.

Isaacs, W. (1993). *Dialogue.* New York: Currency Doubleday.

Jablin, F. (1979). Superior–subordinate communication: The state of the art. *Psychological Bulletin, 86,* 1201–1222.

Jablin, F. (1985). Task/work relationships: A life-span perspective. In M. Knapp & G. Miller (Eds.), *Handbook of interpersonal communication* (pp. 615–654). Newbury Park, CA: Sage.

Jablin, F. (1987). Organizational entry, assimilation, and exit. In F. Jablin, L. Putnam, K. Roberts, & L. Porter (Eds.), *Handbook of organizational communication* (pp. 679–740). Newbury Park, CA: Sage.

Jackson, S. (1983). Participation in decision-making as a strategy for reducing job-related strain. *Journal of Applied Psychology, 68,* 3–19.

James, J. (1996). *Thinking in the future tense: Leadership skills for a new age.* New York: Simon & Schuster.

Janis, I. (1971). *Victims of groupthink* (2nd rev. ed.). Boston: Houghton Mifflin.

Jhally, S. (1997). *Advertising and the end of the world* [Videotape]. Amherst, MA: Media Education Foundation.

Johnson, D., et al. (1993). *Circles of learning.* Edina, MN: Interaction Books.

Kassing, J. W. (2002). Speaking up: Identifying employees' upward dissent strategies. *Management Communication Quarerly, 16,* 193–207.

Kellett, P. (1999). Dialogue and dialectics in managing organizational change: The case of a mission-based transformation. *Southern Communication Journal, 64,* 211–231.

Kellett, P., & Dalton, D. (2001). *Managing conflict in a negotiated world: A narrative approach to achieving dialogue and change.* Walnut Creek, CA: Sage.

Kellett, P., & Goodall, H. L. (1999). The death of discourse in our own (chat) room: "Sextext," skillful discussion, and virtual communities. In D. Slayden & R. K. Whillock (Eds.), *Soundbite culture: The death of discourse in a wired world* (pp. 155–190). Thousand Oaks, CA: Sage.

Kendon, A. (1967). Some functions of gaze direction in social interaction. *ACTA Psychologica, 26,* 22–63.

Keyton, J. (2003). Teaching a pig to sing? *Management Communication Quarterly, 16,* 453–458.

King, P., & Sawyer, C. (1998). Mindfulness, mindlessness, and communication instruction. *Communication Education, 47,* 326.

Kotter, J., & Heskett, J. (1992). *Corporate culture and performance.* New York: Free Press.

Kramer, M. (1993). Communication and uncertainty reduction during job transfers: Leaving and joining processes. *Communication Monographs, 60,* 178–198.

Kramer, M. (1995). A longitudinal study of superior–subordinate communication during job transfers. *Human Communication Research, 22,* 39–64.

Kraut, R. E., & Johnson, R. E. (1979). Social and emotional messages of smiling: An ethological approach. *Journal of Personality and Social Psychology, 37,* 1539–1553.

Krippendorff, K. (1985). *On the ethics of constructing communication.* International Communication Association presidential address, Honolulu, Hawaii.

Krivonos, P. (1982). Distortion of subordinate to superior communication in organizational settings. *Central States Speech Journal, 33,* 345–352.

Kuhn, T., & Ashcraft, K. L. (2003). Corporate scandal and the theory of the firm: Formulating the contributions of organizational communication studies. *Management Communication Quarterly, 17,* 20–57.

Kunda, G. (1993). *Engineering culture: Control and commitment in a high-tech corporation.* Philadelphia: Temple University Press.

Lacy, D. (1995). *From grunts to gigabytes: Communication and society.* Urbana: University of Illinois Press.

Langer, E. (1989). *Mindfulness.* Reading, MA: Addison-Wesley.

Langer, E. (1992). Interpersonal mindlessness and language. *Communication Monographs, 59,* 324.

Langer, E. (1997). *The power of mindful learning.* Reading, MA: Addison-Wesley.

Lizzio, A., Wilson, K. L., Gilchrist, J., & Gallois, C. (2003). The role of gender in the construction and evaluation of feedback effectiveness. *Management Communication Quarterly, 16,* 341–379.

Lodge, D. (1997). *The practice of writing.* New York: Penguin.

Louis, M. (1979). Surprise and sense-making: What newcomers experience in entering unfamiliar organizational settings. *Administrative Science Quarterly, 23,* 225–251.

Lovitt, C. R., & Goswami, D. (1999). *Exploring the rhetoric of international professional communication: An agenda for teachers and researchers.* Amityville, NY: Baywood.

Luhmann, A. D., & Albrecht, T. L. (1990). *The impact of supportive communication and personal control on job stress and performance.* Paper presented at the International Communication Association, Chicago.

Lutgen-Sandvik, P. (2003). The communicative cycle of employee emotional abuse. *Management Communication Quarterly, 16,* 471–501.

Marshall, A., & Stohl, C. (1993). Participating as participation: A network approach. *Communication Monographs, 60,* 137–157.

Marshall, J. (1993). Viewing organizational communication from a feminist perspective: A critique and some offerings. In S. Deetz (Ed.), *Communication Yearbook, 16,* 122–143.

Martin, J. (1992). *Cultures in organizations: Three perspectives.* New York: Oxford University Press.

Maslow, A. (1965). *Eupsychian management.* Homewood, IL: Irwin.

Maslow, A. (1970). *Motivation and personality* (2nd ed.). New York: Harper & Row.

May, S. (1993). *Employee assistance program and the troubled workers: A discursive study of knowledge, power, and subjectivity.* Unpublished doctoral dissertation, University of Utah.

May, S. (2003). Case Study: Challenging change. *Management Communication Quarterly, 16,* 419–433.

Mayo, E. (1945). *The social problems of industrial civilization.* Cambridge, MA: Graduate School of Business Administration, Harvard University.

McGregor, D. (1960). *The human side of enterprise.* New York: McGraw-Hill.

McKerrow, R., Gronbeck, B. E., Ehninger, D., & Monroe, A. H. (2000). *Principles and types of speech communication.* New York: Longman.

McPhee, R., & Corman, S. (1995). An activity based theory of communication networks in organizations, applied to the case of a local church. *Communication Monographs, 62,* 132–151.

Mead, G. (1934). *Mind, self, and society.* Chicago: University of Chicago Press.

Meyer, G. J. (1995). *Executive blues.* San Francisco: Franklin Square Press.

Miller, J. G. (1978). *Living systems.* New York: McGraw-Hill.

Miller, K. (1995). *Organizational communication: Approaches and processes*. Belmont, CA: Wadsworth.

Miller, K., Ellis, B., Zook, E., & Lyles, J. (1990). An integrated model of communication, stress, and burnout in the workplace. *Communication Research 17*, 300–326.

Miller, K., & Monge, P. (1985). Social information and employee anxiety about organizational change. *Human Communication Research, 11*, 365–386.

Miller, K., & Monge, P. (1986). Participation, satisfaction, and productivity: A meta-analytic review. *Academy of Management Journal, 29*, 727–753.

Miller, K., Stiff, J., & Ellis, B. (1988). Communication and empathy as precursors to burnout among human service workers. *Communication Monographs, 55*, 250–265.

Miller, V., & Jablin, F. (1991). Information seeking during organizational entry: Influences, tactics, and a model of the process. *Academy of Management Review, 16*, 92–120.

Mintzberg, H. (1973). *The nature of managerial work*. New York: Harper & Row.

Mitroff, I., & Kilmann, R. (1975). Stories managers tell: A new tool for organizational problem-solving. *Management Review, 64*, 18–28.

Monge, P., Bachman, S., Dillard, J., & Eisenberg, E. (1982). Communicator competence in the workplace: Model testing and scale development. *Communication Yearbook, 5*, 505–528.

Monge, P., Cozzens, M., & Contractor, N. (1992). Communication and motivational predictors of the dynamics of organizational innovation. *Organizational Science, 3*, 250–274.

Monge, P., & Eisenberg, E. (1987). Emergent communication networks. In F. Jablin et al. (Eds.), *Handbook of organizational communication* (pp. 204–342). Beverly Hills, CA: Sage.

Monge, P., Farace, R., Eisenberg, E., Miller, K., & Rothman, L. (1984). The process of studying process in organizational communication. *Journal of Communication, 34*, 22–43.

Morgan, G. (1986). *Images of organization*. Newbury Park, CA: Sage.

Morrison, E., & Bies, R. (1991). Impression management in the feedback-seeking process: A literature review and research agenda. *Academy of Management Review, 16*, 522–541.

Motley, M. (1992). Mindfulness in solving communicators' dilemmas. *Communication Monographs, 59*, 306.

Moxley, R. (1994). *Foundations of leadership*. Greensboro, NC: Center for Creative Leadership.

Mumby, D. (1987). The political function of narratives in organizations. *Communication Monographs, 54*, 113–127.

Mumby, D. (1993). *Narrative and social control*. Newbury Park, CA: Sage.

Mumby, D., & Putnam, L. (1993). The politics of emotion: A feminist reading of bounded rationality. *Academy of Management Review, 17*, 465–486.

Noer, D. (1993). *Healing the wounds: Overcoming the trauma of layoffs and revitalizing downsized organizations*. San Francisco: Jossey-Bass.

Ochs, E., Smith, R., & Taylor, C. (1989). Detective stories at dinnertime: Problem solving through co-narration. *Cultural Dynamics, 2*, 238–257.

Okabe, R. (1983). Cultural assumptions of East and West: Japan and the United States. In B. Gudykunst (Ed.), *Intercultural communication theory* (pp. 212–244). Newbury Park, CA: Sage.

Oldham, G., & Rotchford, N. (1983). Relationships between office characteristics and employee reactions: A study of the physical environment. *Administrative Science Quarterly, 28*, 542–556.

O'Reilly, B. (1994, June 13). The new deal: What companies and employees owe each other. *Fortune, 44*.

Osborn, J., Moran, L., Musselwhite, E., & Zenger, J. (1990). *Self-directed work teams*. Homewood, IL: Business One Irwin.

Ouchi, W., & Wilkins, A. (1985). Organizational culture. *Annual Review of Sociology, 11*, 457–483.

Pacanowsky, M. (1988). Communication in the empowering organization. In J. Anderson (Ed.), *Communication Yearbook, 11*, 356–379.

Pacanowsky, M., & O'Donnell-Trujillo, N. (1983). Organizational communication as cultural performance. *Communication Monographs, 50*, 126–147.

Papa, M. (1989). Communicator competence and employee performance with new technology: A case study. *Southern Communication Journal, 55*, 87–101.

Papa, M. (1990). Communication network patterns and employee performance with new technology. *Communication Research, 17*, 344–368.

Perrow, C. (1986). *Complex organizations: A critical essay* (3rd ed.). New York: Random House.

Peters, T., & Waterman, R. (1982). *In search of excellence*. New York: Harper & Row.

Pettigrew, A. (1979). On studying organizational cultures. *Administrative Science Quarterly, 24*, 570–581.

Phillips, G. (1991). *Communication incompetencies: A theory of training oral performance behavior*. Carbondale: Southern Illinois University Press.

Philpott, J. S. (1983). *The relative contribution to meaning of verbal and nonverbal channels of communication: A meta-analysis*. Unpublished master's thesis, University of Nebraska.

Pinchot, G., & Pinchot, E. (1993). *The end of bureau-*

*cracy and the rise of the intelligent organization.* San Francisco: Berrett-Koehler.

Poole, M. S. (1981). Decision development in small groups I: A comparison of two models. *Communication Monographs, 48,* 1–24.

Poole, M. S. (1983). Decision development in small groups II: A study of multiple sequences in decision making. *Communication Monographs, 50,* 321–341.

Poole, M. S. (1992). Structuration and the group communication process. In L. Samovar & R. Cathcart (Eds.), *Small group communication: A reader* (6th ed., pp. 147–157). Dubuque, IA: Brown.

Poole, M. S. (1996, February). *A turn of the wheel: The case for a renewal of systems inquiry in organizational communication research.* Conference on Organizational Communication and Change, Austin, Texas.

Poole, M. S., & Desanctis, G. (1990). Understanding the use of group decision support systems: The theory of adaptive structuration. In J. Fulk & C. Steinfeld (Eds.), *Organizations and communication technology* (pp. 173–193). Newbury Park, CA: Sage.

Poole, M. S., & Holmes, M. (1995). Decision development in computer-assisted group decision making. *Human Communication Research, 22,* 90–127.

Poole, M. S., & Roth, J. (1989). Decision development in small groups V: Test of a contingency model. *Human Communication Research, 15,* 549–589.

Powell, G. N., & Graves, L. M. (2004). *Gender and leadership: Perceptions and realities: Sex differences and similiariaties in communication* (2nd ed.). Mahwah, NJ: Erlbaum.

Putnam, L., & Pacanowsky, M. (1983). *Communication and organizations: An interpretive approach.* Beverly Hills, CA: Sage.

Quinn, R. (1977). Coping with Cupid: The formation, impact, and management of romantic relationships in organizations. *Administrative Science Quarterly, 22,* 30–45.

Rafaeli, A., & Sutton, R. (1987). The expression of emotion as part of the work role. *Academy of Management Review, 12,* 23–37.

Rafaeli, A., & Sutton, R. (1991). Emotional contrast strategies as means of social influence: Lessons from criminal interrogators and bill collectors. *Academy of Management Journal, 34,* 749–775.

Ralston, S., & Kirkwood, W. (1995). Overcoming managerial bias in employment interviewing. *Journal of Applied Communication Research, 23,* 75–92.

Ray, E. (1987). Supportive relationships and occupational stress in the workplace. In T. Albrecht & M. Adelman (Eds.), *Communicating social support* (pp. 172–191). Newbury Park, CA: Sage.

Redding, W. C. (1991). *Unethical messages in the organiza-*

*tional context.* Paper presented at the annual convention of the International Communication Association, Chicago.

Redding, W. C. (1985a). Rocking boats, blowing whistles, teaching speech communication. *Communication Education, 34,* 245–258.

Redding, W. C. (1985b). Stumbling toward identity: The emergence of organizational communication as a field of study. In R. McPhee & P. Tompkins (Eds.), *Organizational communication: Traditional themes and new directions* (pp. 15–54). Beverly Hills, CA: Sage.

Rehfield, J. (1994). Cited in D. C. Barnlund, *Communicative styles of Japanese and Americans.* Belmont, CA: Wadsworth.

Richmond, V., & McCroskey, J. (1995). *Nonverbal behavior in interpersonal relations.* Englewood Cliffs, NJ: Prentice-Hall.

Roberts, K., & O'Reilly, C. (1974). Failures in upward communication: Three possible culprits. *Academy of Management Journal, 17,* 205–215.

Roy, D. (1960). Banana time: Job satisfaction and informal interaction. *Human Organization, 18,* 156–180.

Sahlins, M. (1976). *Culture and practical reason.* Chicago: University of Chicago Press.

Sailer, H., Schlachter, J., & Edwards, M. (1982, July–August). Stress: Causes, consequences, and coping strategies. *Personnel, 59,* 35–48.

Salopek, J. (1999, September). Is anyone listening? *Training and Development, 53,* 58.

Salopek, J. (1999, November). Liar, liar, pants on fire. *Training and Development, 53,* 16.

Samovar, L., Porter, R. E., & Jain, N. C. (1991). *Understanding intercultural communication.* Belmont, CA: Wadsworth.

Scheidel, T., & Crowell, L. (1964). Idea development in small discussion groups. *Quarterly Journal of Speech, 50,* 140–145.

Schein, E. (1991). The role of the founder in the creation of organizational culture. In P. Frost et al. (Eds.), *Reframing organizational culture* (pp. 14–25). Newbury Park, CA: Sage.

Scollon, R., & Scollon, S. (1995). *Intercultural communication.* Cambridge, MA: Blackwell.

Scott, J. (1990). *Domination and the arts of resistance: Hidden transcripts.* New Haven, CT: Yale University Press.

Senge, P. (1991). *The fifth discipline: The art and practice of the learning organization.* New York: Doubleday/Currency.

Senge, P., Roberts, C., Ross, R., Smith, B., & Kleiner, A. (1994). *The fifth discipline fieldbook.* New York: Doubleday/Currency.

Shockley-Zalabak, P., & Morley, D. (1994). Creating a culture. *Human Communication Research, 20,* 334–355.

Shorris, E. (1984). *Scenes from corporate life*. Hammonds-worth, UK: Penguin.

Sias, P., & Jablin, F. (1995). Differential superior–subordinate relations, perceptions of fairness, and coworker communication. *Human Communication Research, 22*, 5–38.

Simon, H. (1957/1976). *Administrative behavior* (3rd ed.). New York: Free Press.

Smith, D. (1972). Communication research and the idea of process. *Speech Monographs, 39*, 174–182.

Smith, H. (1995, May 14). *The three faces of capitalism*. Public Broadcasting System.

Smith, R., & Eisenberg, E. (1987). Conflict at Disneyland: A root metaphor analysis. *Communication Monographs, 54*, 367–380.

Sommer, R. (1969). *Personal space*. Englewood Cliffs, NJ: Prentice-Hall.

Sundstrom, E., DeMeuse, K., & Futrell, D. (1990). Work teams: Applications and effectiveness. *American Psychologist, 45*, 120–133.

Tannen, D. (1990). *You just don't understand: Women and men in conversation*. New York: Morrow.

Tannen, D. (1994a). *Gender and discourse*. New York: Oxford University Press.

Tannen, D. (1994b). *Talking from 9 to 5: Women and men in the workplace, language, sex, and power*. New York: Simon & Schuster.

Taylor, F. (1913). *The principles of scientific management*. New York: Harper.

Taylor, F. (1947). *Scientific management*. New York: Harper.

Tjosvold, D., & Tjosvold, M. (1991). *Leading the team organization*. New York: Lexington Books.

Trenholm, S. (2000). *Thinking through communication: An introduction to the study of human communication*. Boston: Allyn & Bacon.

Trenholm, S., & Jensen, A. (1992). *Interpersonal communication*. Belmont, CA: Wadsworth.

Triandis, H., et al. (1988). *Handbook of industrial and organizational psychology*. Palo Alto, CA: Consulting Psychology Press.

Trujillo, N. (1985). Organizational communication as cultural performance: Some managerial considerations. *Southern Speech Communication Journal, 50*, 201–224.

Turner, P. K. (2003). Paradox of ordering change: I insist that we work as a team. *Management Communication Quarterly, 16*, 434–439.

Van Maanen, J. (1991). The smile factory: Work at Disneyland. In P. Frost et al. (Eds.), *Reframing organizational culture* (pp. 58–76). Newbury Park, CA: Sage.

Van Maanen, J., & Barley, S. (1984). Occupational communities: Cultural control in organizations. In B. Staw & L. Cummings (Eds.), *Research in organizational behavior* (Vol. 6, pp. 265–287). Greenwich, CT: JAI Press.

Varner, I., & Beamer, L. (1995). *Intercultural communication in the global workplace*. Chicago: Irwin.

Victor, D. A. (1994). *International business communication*. New York: HarperCollins.

Von Bertalanffy, L. (1968). *General systems theory*. New York: George Braziller.

Vroom, V. (1964). *Work and motivation*. New York: Wiley.

Waldron, V. (1991). Achieving communication goals in superior–subordinate relationships: The multi-functionality of upward maintenance tactics. *Communication Monographs, 58*, 289–306.

Walster, E., Walster, G. W., & Bersheid, E. (1978). *Equity theory*. Boston: Allyn & Bacon.

Watzlawick, P., Beavin, J., & Jackson, D. (1967). *The pragmatics of human communication: A study of interactional patterns, pathologies, and paradoxes*. New York: Norton.

Weber, M. (1946). *From Max Weber: Essays in sociology*. In H. Gerth & C. Wright Mills (Eds.), New York: Oxford University Press.

Weick, K. (1979). *The social psychology of organizing* (2nd ed.). Reading, MA: Addison-Wesley.

Weick, K. (1980). The management of eloquence. *Executive, 6*, 18–21.

Weick, K. (1995). *Sensemaking in organizations*. Newbury Park, CA: Sage.

Wellins, R., Byham, W., & Wilson, J. (1991). *Empowered teams*. San Francisco: Jossey-Bass.

Wenberg, J., & Wilmot, W. (1973). *The personal communication process*. New York: Wiley.

Wheatley, M. (1992). *Leadership and the new science*. San Francisco, CA: Berrett-Koehler.

Wilkins, A. (1984). The creation of company cultures: The role of stories and human resource systems. *Human Resource Management, 23*, 41–60.

Wilson, G., & Goodall, H. L. (1991). *Interviewing in context*. New York: McGraw-Hill.

Witmer, D., & Katzman, S. L. (1997). On-line smiles: Does gender make a difference in the use of graphic accents? *Journal of Computer-Mediated Communication 2*(4). http://www.ascusc.org/jcmc/vol2/issue4/.

Wood, J. (1977). Leading in purposive discussions: A study of adaptive behavior. *Communication Monographs, 44*, 152–165.

Wood, J. (1996). *Gendered relationships*. Mountain View, CA: Mayfield.

Wood, J. (1997). *Communication as a field of study*. Belmont, CA: Wadsworth.

# Index

Page numbers followed by *f* or *t* indicate figures or tables, respectively.